Contested States in World Politics

Also by Deon Geldenhuys

DEVIANT CONDUCT IN WORLD POLITICS

FOREIGN POLITICAL ENGAGEMENT
Remaking States in the Post-Cold War World

ISOLATED STATES: A Comparative Analysis

THE DIPLOMACY OF ISOLATION
South African Foreign Policy Making

(WRITING AS TOM BARNARD) SOUTH AFRICA 1994–2004
A Popular History

Contested States in World Politics

Deon Geldenhuys
Professor of Politics, University of Johannesburg, South Africa

palgrave
macmillan

First published 2009 by
PALGRAVE MACMILLAN

Palgrave Macmillan in the UK is an imprint of Macmillan Publishers Limited, registered in England, company number 785998, of Houndmills, Basingstoke, Hampshire RG21 6XS.

Palgrave Macmillan in the US is a division of St Martin's Press LLC, 175 Fifth Avenue, New York, NY 10010.

Palgrave Macmillan is the global academic imprint of the above companies and has companies and representatives throughout the world.

Palgrave® and Macmillan® are registered trademarks in the United States, the United Kingdom, Europe and other countries

ISBN-13: 978-0-230-57552-3 hardback
ISBN-10: 0-230-57552-8 hardback

This book is printed on paper suitable for recycling and made from fully managed and sustained forest sources. Logging, pulping and manufacturing processes are expected to conform to the environmental regulations of the country of origin.

A catalogue record for this book is available from the British Library.

A catalogue record for this book is available from the Library of Congress.

10 9 8 7 6 5 4 3 2 1
18 17 16 15 14 13 12 11 10 09

Printed and bound in Great Britain by
CPI Antony Rowe, Chippenham and Eastbourne

To the memory
of the
Rand Afrikaans University

Contents

Acknowledgements

As before, I have been fortunate enough to receive generous support from two German institutions in preparing this book. Stipends from the Alexander von Humboldt Foundation in Bonn allowed me to pay several visits to the Arnold Bergstraesser Institute at Freiburg University. There, in a peaceful but stimulating environment, I was able to write the bulk of the manuscript.

On the home front there are major debts I gladly acknowledge. My wife Zelda, a university information librarian, went far beyond the call of professional (and marital) duty in guiding me through the arcane world of electronic data bases. She also had to carry extra domestic burdens during my annual absences abroad. Auriel Niemack, my live-wire research assistant, was an extraordinary information sleuth on whose skills and dedication I could always count. Her appointment was funded by the Faculty of Humanities at the University of Johannesburg.

Deon Geldenhuys

Introduction

Alluding to his involvement in the developing world, former President Bill Clinton quipped: 'I like working on it because it's not a particularly sexy topic'.[1] Among scholars in international relations, the phenomenon of what can loosely be called non-recognized states would no doubt qualify as an unsexy subject. Of the various types of wayward actors in world politics – including pariah or rogue countries – that of purported states lacking conventional international recognition is probably the least appealing to researchers. Sceptics in the fraternity would even question whether the topic merits academic inquiry. Yet because they are square pegs in a world of round holes, these presumptive states hold an attraction for a small band of students in international relations.

My own academic engagement with the misfits in the world of states began in the 1980s with a study of South African foreign policy making, published under the title *The Diplomacy of Isolation*.[2] This inquiry prompted me to compare the outcast status of South Africa with that of other countries, leading to the publication of *Isolated States: A Comparative Analysis*.[3] The collective efforts of the world community to rehabilitate states that failed to meet Western standards of governance after the Cold War were investigated in *Foreign Political Engagement: Remaking States in the Post-Cold War World*.[4] The prevailing international norms violated by rogue states and other non-conformist countries (and also non-state actors) featured in *Deviant Conduct in World Politics*.[5] The present volume is a logical continuation of a long-standing academic interest in the fate of states that do not fit the prevailing mould. For some charitable colleagues it might seem like a curious solidarity with the underdogs in world politics; others might simply dismiss my preoccupation as a perverse fascination with the world's lowlifes. Either way, I like working in this area because it is way off the beaten academic track.

Besides being an unorthodox topic, are there more substantive reasons for studying non-recognized states? Do these entities really matter in the larger scheme of global politics? One must concede that their number pales into insignificance when compared with the total of 192 internationally recognized states seated in the United Nations General Assembly and representing 6.7 billion people. There are presently only ten self-declared independent entities, comprising about 33 million people, which have been functioning like states for several years. Yet we should note that only one of these non-recognized states – South Ossetia with roughly 65,000 inhabitants – has less than 100,000 people. Among UN member countries 13 have populations smaller than 100,000; eight of them have fewer people than South Ossetia. Apart from South Ossetia, the wannabe states serving as our case studies are Abkhazia, Transdniestria, Nagorno Karabagh, Kosovo, Somaliland, Palestine, Northern Cyprus, Western Sahara and Taiwan.

The mere number of non-recognized states today does not tell the full story of failed quests for internationally recognized statehood. Unilateral attempts at state formation – a sure recipe for non-recognition – typically cause armed conflict between the central authorities and the break-away region. The climate of hostility between the two sides persists long after a secessionist entity has declared independent statehood, and may culminate in recurring wars. The five-day war that Georgia and Russia fought over South Ossetia in August 2008 highlights the destabilizing effects that self-proclaimed states can have on their surrounding areas. Today's affected neighbourhoods are spread across the world: our case studies are drawn from Europe, Eurasia, the Middle East and Africa. It is instructive that most if not all of the ten entities have featured in reports of the International Crisis Group.

We should also be reminded that non-recognized states are not merely a contemporary aberration. The 20th century witnessed several earlier abortive efforts at establishing internationally recognized states: Manchukuo (proclaimed in 1932), Croatia (in the early 1940s), Katanga (1960–3), Rhodesia (1965–80), Biafra (1967–70) and South Africa's four homeland states or Bantustans (Transkei, Bophuthatswana, Ciskei and Venda, which existed from the 1970s until 1994). East Timor experienced a brief period of self-declared independence in 1975 (and was recognized by some 15 states) before being forcibly incorporated into Indonesia. It was only 27 years later that East Timor eventually became independent with full international recognition. Bangladesh also began life as a state with a unilateral declaration of independence from (West) Pakistan in March 1971. This move triggered a civil war in which India came to rescue of the break-away state, thus helping to secure Bangladesh's survival and ensure its international recognition.

Turning to the future, further drives for statehood cannot be ruled out when one observes what the UN's *Human Development Report 2004* called 'the rise of identity politics'. Confrontations over culture and identity are set to increase in a world witnessing the spread of democracy, human rights and new global networks. With about 5,000 ethnic groups inhabiting the nearly 200 states – two-thirds of them having at least one 'substantial minority', defined as an ethnic or religious group constituting at least 10 per cent of the total population – identity causes are rife in today's world.[6] This prognosis is supported by the authoritative Center for International Development and Conflict Management at the University of Maryland. In *Peace and Conflict 2008* the Center reported an encouraging downward trend in the number of new and ongoing self-determination conflicts since the end of the Cold War, but added the sobering warning that 'relatively few post-World War II self-determination conflicts can be confidently considered ended'. Towards the end of 2006, the report recorded, 26 armed self-determination conflicts were still raging in countries ranging from India to Ethiopia and Myanmar to Russia.[7] Several of the disaffected groups campaigning for greater self-determination may yet secede from their existing states – but find their claims to sovereign statehood rejected by both their original states and the world community at large.

Despite the past, current and possibly future presence of non-recognized states, there is a scarcity of scholarly studies of the phenomenon. The major exceptions are three books: Pegg's *International Society and the De Facto State* (1998);[8] an edited volume entitled *De Facto States* (2004),[9] and *Engaging Eurasia's Separatist States* authored by Lynch (2004).[10] Pegg's work has much greater theoretical depth than the other two, but there is still scope for conceptual development. At the empirical level there is room for a wider range of case studies than offered in any the three existing inquiries. While fully acknowledging these worthy contributions, the present endeavour tries to cast a wider theoretical and empirical net.

The term 'contested states' is introduced to highlight a key feature of the existence of these peripheral entities: the internationally contested nature of their purported statehood. It is for this reason that they suffer a serious deficit in international recognition. Most contested states find their very right of statehood being challenged by their original (or central) states and the broader international community. Even if a prospective state's right of statehood is widely or universally recognized by established states, the translation of this conceded right into political reality can still be vigorously contested by a sizeable number of countries. For all contested states their interaction with the outside world is highly contentious, with attempts to keep them outside the international mainstream. Great controversy also surrounds contested states' ultimate political destination, given that their current unusual situation is only temporary. That transitory status amounts to life in international limbo. The aspirants lack the baptism of conventional recognition, by which is meant collective recognition of both their right to exist as separate sovereign states and of their actual existence as such, a process in which the UN plays a key role. The pretender states are consequently barred from normal international interaction and forced to languish at the fringes of the community of the duly initiated, which we will call 'confirmed states'.

To qualify for the designation 'contested state' – and hence inclusion in this study – the entity concerned must have been existing as a purportedly independent state for at least three years, desiring to be treated as a peer by confirmed states. This excludes from our inquiry such restive regions or communities as the Kurds in Iraq and Turkey, Islamic militants in the Philippines, the Aceh region in Indonesia, turbulent tribal territories in Pakistan, the Ogoni area in Nigeria, the Ogaden in Ethiopia, Republika Srpska in Bosnia and Herzegovina, and Anjouan in the Comoros. Chechnya (the self-styled independent Republic of Ichkeria) is also omitted because its contested statehood ended in 2000 when the break-away region was forcibly reincorporated into the Russian Federation.

The book is divided into two sections. Part I, 'Theoretical perspectives', sets out the broad analytical framework in three chapters. The first defines contested statehood and contrasts it with confirmed statehood as enshrined in international law and embodied in the practices of states. The next two chapters explore the origins of contested states and alternatives to contested statehood, respectively. Part II consists of ten case studies presented in more or less chronological order, from the youngest to the oldest contested states. Guided by the theoretical insights recorded in Part I, the case studies will explore the life cycles of these entities. Three broad phases of life in international limbo will be considered: getting in, getting on, and getting out. More concretely, we need to establish how entities become contested states, how they conduct themselves in a hostile external environment and undertake the domestic tasks of state- and nation-building, and finally how they could conceivably exit their unnatural and undesired international status.

Although the mode of inquiry falls broadly within mainline international relations, the topic compels us to draw also on studies in international law, political science, political philosophy, ethno-politics and conflict resolution. Elements of the comparative method will also be evident in the case studies. What ultimately matters, though, is whether the means of analysis serve the end of explanation.

Part I

Theoretical Perspectives

1
Confirmed *versus* Contested States

The defining feature of contested states is the internationally disputed nature of their purported statehood, manifested in their lack of *de jure* recognition. Although serious, the deficit in recognition is not the same for all contested states. In most cases their very right of statehood is challenged by the international community, resulting in no formal recognition at all or recognition by only a small number of established states. In a few instances contested states' right of statehood finds wide acceptance and may even be endorsed by the UN, but the realization of the right is internationally contested. But whatever differences among them, all contested states are denied conventional international recognition; this means they do not have collective recognition (typically through the UN) of both their right to exist as sovereign states and their actual existence as such. Conversely, they all experience collective non-recognition in the sense of being deliberately excluded from UN membership. This leaves contested states in a rather abnormal situation because the vast majority of contemporary states were accorded *de jure* recognition on gaining independence and accepted into the ranks of confirmed states without difficulty. The small group of aspirant states that has been turned away by those on the inside find themselves condemned to a twilight existence at the margins of the international community.

In trying to explain this lack of recognition and its repercussions, we need to look into the familiar criteria for statehood in international law. These represent the minimum formal preconditions for an entity's acceptance into the community of sovereign states. Were contested states refused recognition because they failed to meet the basic requirements of statehood? Or were they denied recognition on grounds unrelated to these standards? Conversely, have all confirmed states complied with the formal criteria of statehood or have different standards been applied to different candidates?

Requirements of confirmed statehood

A consideration of the formal requirements of statehood has to begin with the Montevideo Convention on Rights and Duties of States. Adopted at the 1933 International Conference of American States held in the Uruguayan capital, the Declaration reflected customary international law on what constituted a state. As a subject of international law (meaning an entity recognized as being capable of exercising international rights and duties), a state has to meet four qualifications: a permanent population, a defined territory, a government, and a capacity to enter into relations with other states.[1] Although the most widely accepted formulation of the minimum requirements of statehood found in international law,[2] this set of criteria is very broad indeed. What content has state practice since given to each of the four components, and have others been added? We should be particularly interested in the role of international recognition in constituting statehood.

Population

To meet the first formal requirement, an entity must have 'some population linked to a specific piece of territory on a more or less permanent basis and who can be regarded in general parlance as its inhabitants'.[3] A 'permanent' population does not imply that people cannot migrate across state boundaries, although the requirement may be problematic for some nomadic populations like the Roma of Central and Eastern Europe. Peoples who have traditionally been non-sedentary may find themselves in a stateless limbo. A nomadic population can nonetheless strive for statehood, as the Sahrawis – one of our case studies – have shown. Their link with the territory of Western Sahara is generally regarded as sufficiently strong to treat them as its permanent population.[4]

There is no requirement in international law that the population of a state should share significant commonalities other than finding themselves living on a particular national territory. They need not constitute a distinctive 'people' or 'nation' in terms of language, culture, religion or descent that would give them 'an intense, emotionally charged sense of belonging'.[5] This is not to deny that such bonds may be desirable and advantageous. As the German jurist and philosopher Von Wolff wrote in a seminal work on international law, '[i]t is not the number of men coming together into a state that makes a nation, but the bond by which the individuals are united'.[6]

In many cases the existence of a nation thus defined preceded the creation of the state. Where the territorial boundaries of the state by and large correspond with the location of a pre-existing nation – or where state and nation (the latter conceived in Weberian terms as a 'community of sentiment') coincide – we can speak of a nation-state in a very literal sense.[7]

Examples include Bangladesh, Swaziland and Eritrea. It is more common that states contain a diversity of nations. And because there are far more nations than territories that could be organized as independent states, the borders of nations and states will never be wholly congruent.[8] This lack of conformance is, as we will see, a major factor in the emergence of contested states.

International law does not prescribe that a population should have attained any particular level of readiness to qualify for independence. The UN's celebrated Declaration on the Granting of Independence to Colonial Countries and Peoples of 1960 expressly stated that '[i]nadequacy of political, economic, social or educational preparedness should never serve as a pretext for delaying independence' for dependent territories.

State practice over the 75 years since the adoption of the Montevideo Convention has steered clear of setting any minimum (or, for that matter, maximum) standard for population size. On the contrary, the world community takes the view that the smallness of its population may not deny an entity the right of independent statehood. This rule is fundamentally at odds with the mentality expressed by Adolf Hitler at the time of Nazi Germany's annexation of Austria in 1938: 'What can words like "independence" or "sovereignty" mean for a state of only six million?'[9]

The predictable result of the absence of any fixed limits is that population sizes among contemporary states vary enormously. The world's most populous country by far is China, currently with an estimated 1,328,629,000 inhabitants. The others making up the top five are India (1,169,015,000), the US (305,826,000), Indonesia (231,627,000) and Brazil (191,790,000). At the opposite extreme we find the tiniest among the bantam-sized states (or, less charitably, toy states):[10] Monaco (32,000 people), San Marino (30,000), Palau (19,000), Nauru (10,000) and Tuvalu (9,000). There are presently 13 states with fewer than 100,000 inhabitants each. Another eight are also under the 250,000 mark.[11]

Territory

A defined territory simply means that a state 'must have some definite physical existence that marks it out clearly from its neighbours'.[12] Borders serve as the confines of the area within which government powers are exercised.[13] There need not be complete certainty over the extent of a state's territory, though. Its frontiers may not be precisely demarcated and other states may even have claims to its territory.[14] And since the boundaries of states may change, their territorial composition must be treated as a variable rather than an *a priori* 'given'.[15] Even the requirement that there should be 'a consistent band of territory which is undeniably controlled by the government of the alleged state' has on occasion been overlooked. When Bosnia and Croatia were first recognized as independent states in 1991, both lacked firm, territorial control in the civil war conditions then prevailing.[16] The

'State of Palestine', unilaterally declared independent in 1988, did not control any segment of the territory its founders claimed but was nonetheless soon recognized by over 100 states (see Chapter 7).[17] As already suggested, international law does not require that state frontiers should correspond with demographic divisions.[18] In Africa, for instance, colonial and subsequent state boundaries were drawn without regard to ethno-political realities. In Europe and Asia state borders likewise cut through ethnic communities, in many cases causing endless conflicts between and within states.

As with population, there is no rule in international law prescribing the minimum (or maximum) size of a state's territory.[19] In the anti-colonial fervour of the previous century, the UN General Assembly specifically resolved that a dependent territory's modest geophysical endowment had no bearing on its entitlement to sovereign statehood. In resolution 2709 of December 1970, for instance, the Assembly '[e]xpresses its conviction that the questions of territorial size, geographical isolation and limited resources should in no way delay the implementation of the Declaration on the Granting of Independence to Colonial Countries and Peoples'. (The General Assembly evidently chose to disregard the concerns expressed by the UN Secretary-General in his 1968 annual report about the fate of sovereign entities that were exceptionally small in area, population and human and economic resources.)[20]

UN member states vary greatly in terms of land area. Russia is at the top of the league, extending over a gigantic 17,075,400 km^2 (as against 22,402,200 of the former Soviet Union). The next five largest states by geographic size are much smaller than Russia but far outclass the rest: Canada, the US and China each exceeds 9,500,000 km^2, followed by Brazil with 8,514,215 km^2 and Australia with 7,741,220 km^2. Then follow 23 states with sizes varying between three million and one million km^2. The contrast with states at the other end of the scale is again stark, with no fewer than 31 countries covering land areas under 10,000 km^2 each. The four smallest among them are San Marino (at 61 km^2 exactly half the size of Disney World in Florida), Tuvalu (26), Nauru (21) and Monaco occupying a single square kilometer.[21]

The size of a state's territory does not affect its sanctity under international law. This is clearly enshrined in the principle of the territorial integrity of the state and the accompanying obligation that article 2(4) of the UN Charter places on all members to refrain from the threat or use of force against the territorial integrity or political independence of any state.[22]

The formal acceptance of micro-states – in which a minute territory coincides with a miniscule population – into the international fold is a manifestation of the devaluation of the importance of territory in the 20th century. In the late 19th and early 20th centuries, the heyday of geopolitics, states were obsessed with the possession of physical territory based on commonly accepted notions of the material and political benefits flowing from such control. Boundaries between states were as a consequence sharply drawn. Towards the end of the previous century, as interdependence between states expanded, the salience of territory and borders declined. In the era of globalization, control of networks that reach across increasingly porous borders (involving finance, information, natural resources and so on) may be more important than control of physical space.[23]

International law does not provide guidelines on the economic viability of putative states either. It is, however, a matter that can have a material bearing on a state's economic, social and political fortunes and could influence existing states' response to an aspirant's claims to statehood. In a sensible approach to the question of economic viability, Schroeder defined it as 'the capability to exist and develop as a separate state in a world of highly economically interdependent states'. Viewed thus, economic viability focuses less on self-sufficiency (which cannot be complete for any modern state) than on the ability of the prospective state to function within the global economy. Among the factors that should then be considered are the entity's ability to produce goods and services for the competitive global market; its geographic proximity to potential markets; the level of literacy and skills in the population; the extent of infrastructural development; and the ability to pursue policies aimed at sustainable economic growth.[24] With states competing for market share in the global economy, territory is no longer the foundation for wealth creation; modern states do not have all the elements of a technologically advanced economy within their own borders.[25] For small countries in particular, prosperity requires international free trade and liberal economic policies at home – the very antithesis of the protectionist and isolationist world of the 1930s.[26]

Government

There is 'a strong case for regarding government as the most important single criterion of statehood', Crawford argued, 'since all the others depend upon it'. Thus international law defines 'territory' in terms of the extent of government power exercised, or capable of being exercised, over some area. Government, or 'effective government', is furthermore a basis for the capacity to enter into relations with other states.[27]

What, then, is meant by 'effective government' in contemporary international law? A functional as opposed to a moral approach to the question of government effectiveness has traditionally been followed in international law. First, an entity can only be regarded as a state if it possesses a government 'in general control of its territory, to the exclusion of other entities'. Second, there are no specific requirements in international law with respect to the nature and extent of such control, except that it should include 'some degree of maintenance of law and order', according to Crawford.[28] The external dimension of government effectiveness refers to its capability 'of controlling the affairs of the "state" in the international community'.[29]

For supporters of the declaratory theory of recognition, the key component of statehood is a government capable of maintaining control over its population and territory. If effective rule is present, the legitimacy of a government is said to be proven.[30] This is a view long held by practitioners and observers of politics too. As British poet Alexander Pope wrote centuries ago: 'For forms of government let fools contest; whate'er is best administered is best'. A contemporary endorsement comes from Huntington, who in a seminal study of 1968 argued that '[t]he most important political distinction among countries concerns not their form of government but their degree of government'.[31]

However, the latter half of the 20th century witnessed a tendency 'to regard sovereignty for non-independent peoples as the paramount consideration, irrespective of administrative conditions'.[32] The so-called Anti-Colonialists' Charter of 1960, alluded to earlier, played a major role in devaluing traditional criteria of statehood.[33] The wholesale decolonization of Africa in the 1960s proceeded under what Jackson called 'a novel doctrine of negative sovereignty'. It allowed for the granting of 'juridical statehood' to scores of entities displaying scant evidence of 'empirical statehood'.[34]

Seriously defective government capacity did not prevent the international recognition of Croatia and Bosnia and Herzegovina as they emerged from the turmoil that tore Yugoslavia apart. The patent collapse of government authority in Lebanon, Liberia and Sierra Leone in recent years did not jeopardize their status as juridical states either. Even anarchic Somalia, which has been without a central government for over 15 years, is still legally a state with a seat in the UN General Assembly. By contrast secessionist Somaliland, whose government maintains effective control and order in its territory, has its claims to statehood rejected by the world community. Likewise, effective government control has not managed to secure the Turkish Republic of Northern Cyprus or Taiwan the international recognition they seek.[35] Clearly Bodin's injunction that others 'should have neither intercourse, commerce, nor alliance' with 'sovereigns' that failed to provide order for their citizens – and the reverse of this rule – do not guide modern state practice.[36]

A new normative dimension to the question of government has gained considerable currency in recent years. The exercise of effective control over territory and people is no longer regarded as a sufficient test of a government's legitimacy; what also matters is the form of authority and the treatment of the population.[37] The development of the international human rights regime – already formalized in over two dozen international conventions and declarations – has given rise to the notion that the only internationally acceptable form of government in this day and age is

Western-style liberal democracy. In 1992 Franck wrote hopefully of an 'emerging right to democratic governance'.[38] In a resolution adopted in 1999, the UN Human Rights Commission for the first time referred to a universal 'right' to democracy for all peoples. The European Community took a major step in this direction when laying down criteria for the recognition of successor states of the disintegrating Yugoslav Federation in the early 1990s. Democratic governance was one of them.[39] Though radical, such notions are hardly novel: Rousseau had already advanced the ideal that a recognized state should be one expressing the general will.[40]

Although one could safely say that human rights and democracy have been universalized and institutionalized to the extent that they erode some state prerogatives traditionally associated with sovereignty,[41] it may still be premature to claim a right to democracy under international law. As Horowitz pointed out, international law's commitment to democracy has not been particularly deep or longstanding. This is because 'valorizing a right to democratic governance would imperil the universality of international law'. The governing arrangements of dozens of states would be undercut by such a right, undermining international law's ability to influence state behaviour.[42] The aspiration among scholars and others to make democratic governance a global legal entitlement is thus some way from becoming a right enshrined in international law. If, however, we accept the view that all governments have an obligation to observe at least the core of basic human rights – regardless of whether they have ratified international human rights instruments[43] – it becomes difficult to rule democratic governance out of the determination of statehood in the post-Cold War era.

Inter-state relations

Following Crawford, we will treat the capacity to enter into relations with other states as a consequence rather than a criterion of statehood. This capacity is a conflation of the requirements of government and independence. Although independence is a generally accepted prerequisite of statehood, it is not mentioned by name in the Montevideo Convention.[44]

To participate as fully as it chooses in international relations, an aspirant state should first be admitted to the international community of confirmed states. James maintained that the entrance requirement was simply one of constitutional independence, which he equated with sovereignty. For James constitutional independence meant that 'a state's constitution is not part of a larger constitutional arrangement'; it is a case of 'not being contained, however loosely, within a wider constitutional scheme'. Only after an entity's constitutional separateness has been established, can it become sovereign 'and thus ready, if it and others wish it, to join in the usual kind of international activity'.[45] But what if an entity enjoys constitutional independence yet fails to attract international recognition of its purported statehood? Some international lawyers argue that an aspirant state utterly lacking in formal international recognition 'cannot demonstrate its capacity to enter into relations with other states and, from a functional point of view, cannot be described as a state'. A contrary view holds that while a totally unrecognized entity would find it difficult to exercise state-like rights and duties internationally, this would not in international law constitute a decisive argument against its statehood.[46] As we will see, contested states' lack of formal recognition severely circumscribes their participation in international relations.

Finally, although states 'preeminently possess' the capacity to enter into relations with each other, scores of non-state actors have long since engaged in relations with states, in many instances under the rules of international law.[47] These include multilateral institutions like the UN and European Union (EU), international non-governmental organizations such as the Red Cross, multinational corporations and a motley band of less savoury actors including terrorist groups, crime syndicates and mercenaries.

Sovereignty

Like independence, sovereignty does not feature in the Montevideo Convention as a formal requirement of statehood. It is unthinkable, though, to discuss statehood without regard to the notion of sovereignty. Consider the representative definition of a state formulated by the (Badinter) Arbitration Commission of the European Conference on Yugoslavia in 1991: 'a community which consists of a territory and a population subject to an organised political authority...[and] is characterised by sovereignty'.[48] Leaders of contemporary states may also concur with De Vattel's assertion: 'Of all the rights that can belong to a nation, sovereignty is doubtless the most precious'.[49]

Although there is no single, universally accepted meaning of the term 'sovereignty', international lawyers and political scientists commonly break the concept down into internal and external components.[50]

The crux of internal sovereignty was already stated in the Treaty of Westphalia of 1648. In articles 64 and 65 the signatories declared that

> to prevent for the future any Differences...all and every one of the Electors, Princes and States of the Roman Empire, are so establish'd and confirm'd in their...free exercise of Territorial Right...that they never can or ought to be molested therein by any whomsoever upon any manner of pretence.[51]

In modern parlance internal sovereignty refers to 'the state's exclusive right or competence to determine the character of its own institutions, to ensure and provide for their operation, to enact laws of its own choice and ensure their respect'.[52] No other national or international entity can therefore legitimately dictate the activities of a state that enjoys supreme legal authority.[53] This, however, should not be interpreted as unqualified and exclusive power – a status no modern state has enjoyed in practice.[54] What internal sovereignty does require is constitutional separateness or independence. To repeat James, a state can only be sovereign if it is not contained, however loosely, within a wider constitutional arrangement.[55] These features are also expressed in Krasner's notion of 'Westphalian sovereignty': external authority structures are excluded from the territory of a (sovereign) state, thus according the state both *de jure* independence and *de facto* autonomy.[56]

Independence is at the heart of external sovereignty too, construed as 'the right of the state freely to determine its relations with other states or other entities without the restraint or control of another state'.[57] This Grotian notion that the state is sovereign in relation to others when it is free from external control, is a foundation of modern international law.[58]

Crawford distinguished between 'formal' and 'actual' independence. Formal (or legal) independence exists where the powers of government in internal and external affairs are vested in the separate authorities of the state. Such independence is not compromised by constitutionally enforceable restrictions on a government's freedom of action, treaty obligations, the presence of foreign military bases or other territorial concessions, membership of international organizations, or the exercise of certain governmental functions by bodies such as the EU.[59] The critical consideration is whether these arrangements are based on the consent of the state involved.

Only two situations derogate from formal independence. The first is the existence, as a matter of international law, of 'a special claim of right' – regardless of consent – to the exercise of governmental powers. If a state claims the right to exercise such powers over another territory, the formal independence of that polity is called into question. A case in point is China's claim of the right to rule Taiwan, which casts a shadow over the latter's statehood. Not all claims of a right to exercise power seem to detract from formal independence, though. For years most of Israel's neighbours denied its very right of existence, insisting that the right to rule that territory lay not with the Jews but the Palestinians. Despite this, Israel joined the UN and entered into diplomatic relations with scores of states. Another example is the Sahrawi Arab Democratic Republic, which has been given membership of the African Union (AU) even though Morocco not only claims the right to govern Western Sahara but is actually in control of most of the territory.

The second situation derogating from formal independence is discretionary power to intervene in the internal affairs of a putative state. France's undefined powers of intervention in respect of Monaco, for instance, create doubts about the latter's formal independence.[60]

When treated as a distinct legal or juridical status, sovereignty is an absolute category – not a relative condition or a variable. It does not fluctuate with the fortunes of political leaders, global trends or the ebb and flow of state power. 'A state either is sovereign or it is not', Holsti insisted. 'It cannot be partly sovereign or have "eroded" sovereignty no matter how weak or ineffective it may be'. Sovereignty exists as long as there is exclusive legal authority, i.e. 'the *right* to make and apply laws for the community'.[61]

Actual (or effective) independence was defined by Crawford as 'the minimum degree of real governmental power at the disposal of the authorities of the putative State, necessary for it to qualify as "independent"'.[62] This is what some political scientists refer to as *de facto* internal supremacy[63] but is more commonly called autonomy. A relative and informal category, autonomy involves the freedom of states to make policy choices or set their own rules. Autonomy is increasingly constrained by such trends as the mounting inability of governments to control the flows of capital, people, ideas, crime, disease, etc. in a 'borderless' world. The declining ability of public authorities to regulate such cross-border interactions in the age of globalization restricts what Krasner termed the interdependence sovereignty of states.[64] In addition the governmental power (autonomy) that states possess in international law has contracted over time. There are various *jus cogens* norms that bind all states, such as those restricting the use of force and outlawing genocide, slavery and servitude. The growth of an international human rights regime and increasing ecological awareness have the same effect.[65] When a state's autonomy is reduced, it does not mean that its legal authority is being eroded.[66]

Four situations do not derogate from actual (not to mention formal) independence, namely the diminutive size and resources of an aspirant state; its political and ideological links with other states; belligerent occupation by another state (for instance, Iraq's occupation of Kuwait in the early 1990s did not affect the continuity of the latter's statehood); and illegal intervention (as witnessed in the Soviet invasions of Hungary and Czechoslovakia).[67]

Of more immediate relevance for our purposes are the three situations that do undermine actual independence. The first of these, substantial illegality of origin, arises when an entity comes into existence in violation of basic rules of international law. This could constitute grounds for the non-recognition of such an entity's claims to statehood.[68] One of the most fundamental rules of international law – indeed a *jus cogens* norm – concerns the illegal use of force. The prohibition of the threat or use of force against the political independence or territorial integrity of any state is enshrined in, among other international instruments, the UN Charter under article 2(4). The world community has repeatedly refused to accept the legal validity of situations created by the illegal use of force. It is thus firmly established in international law that territory may not be validly acquired by the illegal resort to force. Where such an entity claims statehood, there is a presumption against its independence;[69] this applied to the state of

Manchukuo established by Japan on Chinese soil. South Africa's four homeland states point to another illegal origin, namely racial discrimination. The entities were given independence by Pretoria in pursuance of the policy of apartheid. International law expressly forbids the practice of racial discrimination. The self-proclaimed state of Rhodesia, also governed by a white minority, fell foul of the same rule as well as the broader principle of self-determination.[70]

Entities created under belligerent occupation, the second situation derogating from effective independence, is closely related to the first. Here too is a strong presumption in international law against the actual independence of a state thus established. It is regarded as 'no more than the agent of the belligerent occupant'. The classic interwar example of an entity created under belligerent occupation is again Manchukuo. Other examples that resemble Manchukuo were Japan's granting of independence to Burma in 1942 when the latter was occupied by the imperial power, and the creation of the Azerbaijan independence movement in northern Iran under Soviet occupation in 1945–6.[71]

There is considerable overlap between the latter category and the third, which deals with substantial external control of a putative state. The general rule is that an entity which, although displaying the formal features of independence, 'is in substance subject to foreign domination and control', is not regarded as 'independent' for the purposes of statehood under international law.[72] Let us briefly consider types of non-independent 'states'.

In the case of protected states or protectorates the very designation already tells us that the entities concerned fall under substantial external control. Examples are the British protectorate of Kelantan (1909–57) in what is now Malaysia, and the Bechuanaland protectorate which in 1966 became independent as Botswana.[73]

Puppet states refer to 'nominal sovereigns under effective foreign control, especially in cases where the establishment of the puppet State is intended as a cloak for manifest illegality'. Apart from being established illegally, by the threat or use of armed force, a puppet regime lacks the support of the vast majority of the population it claims to govern; it is subject to foreign direction or control in important matters; and key positions are occupied by nationals of the dominant state. For the entire duration of its putative statehood (1932–45) Manchukuo was regarded by the international community as acting at the behest of its creator and patron, Japan, and was hence denied formal recognition.[74] Imperial Japan fared no better with 'independent' Burma, mentioned above.[75] Much the same situation obtained in two wartime 'states' established by Nazi Germany in occupied Europe. Slovakia became a nominally independent part of Czechoslovakia, under German protection, from 1939 to 1945. The puppet state of Croatia was created on occupied Yugoslav territory in 1941, returning to the fold in 1944.[76]

The Turkish Republic of Northern Cyprus, created in the wake of Turkey's invasion of the island in 1974, is the product of an illegal use of force. The Turkish entity in Cyprus is regarded as a puppet state by the international community and its statehood has not been recognized by any country other than Turkey.[77]

The final, less familiar type of non-independent state involves a purported grant of colonial independence. This unusual situation obtains where a metropolitan power awards its colony only partial independence or where real control has evidently not been transferred. The status of Syria and Lebanon between 1942 and 1946, following their being granted 'independence' by the Free French administration, falls in this category.[78]

Jackson's concise definition of a sovereign state provides a neat summary of our discussion thus far: 'an authority that is supreme in relation to all other authorities in the same territorial jurisdiction, and that is independent of all foreign authorities'. The preceding inquiry has highlighted what Jackson portrayed as the Janus-faced character of sovereign statehood: facing inward, the sovereign is the supreme authority in the state; facing outward, the sovereign is in a position of independence *vis-à-vis* other states.[79]

Important legal implications flow from states' sovereignty in international law. They enjoy legal equality, which means equality of legal rights and duties. Among their duties are to respect the legal personality, independence and territorial integrity of other states, live in peace with them, and refrain from interfering in their domestic affairs.[80] Although sovereignty is supposed to serve as a 'no trespassing' sign,[81] foreign interference has all along been a feature of international relations. Given the contradiction between this formal rule (derived from sovereignty) and the practice of states, sovereignty has not surprisingly been portrayed as 'organized hypocrisy'.[82]

International law's recognition of the sovereign equality of states recalls De Vattel's celebrated 18th century dictum: 'A dwarf is as much a man as a giant; a small republic is no less a sovereign state than the most powerful kingdom'.[83] However, factual inequality between states – some being more substantial and capable than others – has always characterized international relations. So great are the variations today that a 'new type of sovereign state' has emerged out of European colonial empires, especially in Africa: one that is 'independent in law but insubstantial in reality and materially dependent on other states for its welfare'. Jackson termed them 'quasi-states', possessing juridical statehood but being sorely deficient in empirical statehood.[84] The former refers to the rights and responsibilities accorded to states by international law, whereas empirical statehood deals with the capacity of the state to ensure internal well-being and stability and enforce its external independence.[85] Expressed in terms of Krasner's categories of sovereignty, we are contrasting international legal sovereignty (the status of an entity in the international system flowing from the formal recognition of its statehood) with domestic sovereignty (the organization and effectiveness of public authority in a state).[86]

Quasi-states and their foreign support infrastructure displayed what Jackson termed 'a novel doctrine of negative sovereignty' designed specifically for the decolonization of Third World entities. Every colony had a categorical right to self-determination *à la* independence (juridical statehood) solely by virtue of its colonial status, regardless of its domestic capabilities (empirical statehood). International society (primarily the major powers) was in turn expected to foster the independence of the former colonies and guarantee their survival as independent states, however disorganized or illegitimate the governments of these 'ramshackle states' may be.[87] Positive sovereignty, enjoyed by developed states, presupposed capabilities enabling governments 'to be their own masters', provide political goods to their citizens and maintain relations with foreign governments.[88]

Decolonization, then, produced a new category of sovereign entities displaying a distinctively artificial statehood in which inherent positive qualities no longer served as the basis of sovereignty. The exclusive emphasis on juridical statehood meant that sovereignty was henceforth 'not acquired internally but conferred externally'.[89] Bull and Watson referred to them as 'states that are not states in the strict sense, but only by courtesy'.[90] A further implication of the concept of statehood becoming so 'juridicized' is that a 'protracted anarchy' can be recognized as a state; entities that have by all reasonable standards ceased to function as states are guaranteed their statehood.[91] To put it differently, 'once a state is duly baptized and confirmed as a sovereign', the world community relaxes or even ignores the requirement of domestic political supremacy, to quote Fowler and Bunck.[92] Consider the recent cases of Somalia, Liberia and Sierra Leone.

In all the years before the Second World War there had been no special international regime catering for small or weak states. What would in an earlier era have provided *prima facie* grounds for denying membership of the international community of states, has under the new sovereignty regime become an entitlement to material assistance from abroad, what Jackson depicted as 'sovereignty plus'. The modern world community is therefore not merely a civil association of all states, but also 'a joint enterprise association to assist its poorer members' by practising 'affirmative action' (for example trade concessions, debt relief and development aid).[93]

These contrasts lead us to another patently double standard. It is between states 'whose legal international personality masks a general state of domestic collapse', and a group of 'fully-functioning and self-contained states... quarantined as pariahs, excluded from the mainstream channels of international diplomacy, existing in conditions beyond the pale of normal international intercourse'.[94] The first category of course refers to what

Jackson depicted as quasi-states, whereas the other class consists of contested states. The latter collection of 'would-be states in a legal fog'[95] are mostly far stronger in empirical statehood than scores of today's quasi-states but they are excluded from conventional inter-state relations because the world community does not recognize their rights of statehood. This brings us to the vexed question of recognition as a criterion of statehood.

Recognition

Since ours is not a study in international law *per se*, there is no need to join what Crawford called 'the great debate' over the nature of the recognition of states, waged between the proponents of the constitutive and declaratory theories or doctrines respectively.[96] We need to note the contending views only briefly, before focusing on state practice and the implications of non-recognition.

Under the declaratory theory an entity, once it displays the minimum characteristics distinctive of statehood (a territory, population, government and a capacity to maintain relations with other states), is automatically a state and an international subject. 'Recognition can only mark the willingness of other states to have relations with it; absence of recognition does not of itself deny statehood'. The constitutive theory by contrast maintains that an entity meeting these basic requirements 'is not a state and thus not a member of the international community until it is "constituted" as such through the actions of other members of the international community recognising it as a state'. Without recognition an entity is not a state and cannot have international personality.[97]

Although the declaratory doctrine is supposed to be predominant in scholarly circles and also in state practice, the very existence of contested states points to the influence of the constitutive theory in world politics. A 'near affirmation' of the constitutive doctrine is found in the Guidelines on the Recognition of New States in Eastern Europe and the Soviet Union, adopted by the European Community (EC) in 1991, and in the Europeans' accompanying Declaration on Yugoslavia. Going well beyond the factual Montevideo criteria, the EC decided that recognition of new states emerging from the disintegration of existing countries in the region would depend also on the nature of their political structures and practices. The aspirant states were expected to respect established borders, observe human rights and democracy, uphold the rule of law, guarantee minority rights, commit themselves to settle disputes peacefully, and accept nuclear non-proliferation. While the EC was not necessarily suggesting that an entity could not be a state until these conditions were complied with, member states gave notice that they 'would not *treat* a territory as a state'[98] until it abided by norms of behaviour judged essential for the community of European states.[99] The US has followed a similar approach in relation to the republics of the disbanded Soviet Union. This dynamic indicates a new chapter in the doctrine of recognition and the formation of states in international law: Allen described it as 'a more prescriptive approach, premised on the ideological aspirations of the predominant international actors'.[100]

Such prescriptiveness is not new. The major European powers conditioned the recognition of states emerging from the Ottoman Empire in the 19th century on guarantees of the civil and political rights of their religious minorities. This applied, among others, to Greece, Romania, Serbia and Montenegro. After the First World War the great powers again demanded the protection of minority rights as a prerequisite for the recognition of East and Central European states and their membership of the League of Nations.[101] Since the end of the Cold War the international trend towards 'conditioned' recognition has become more pronounced with external demands for democratic institutions and processes, the protection of minority rights and even prescriptions about economic management.[102]

The application of these 'subjective' criteria confirms Fawcett's observation that recognition is 'a political act of government' and 'a matter not of duty but of discretion'.[103] In exercising their discretion political office-holders take a range of factors into account, including what Clapham called 'current international mythologies of legitimate statehood'.[104]

The recognition we have been dealing with is of a *de jure* nature and should be distinguished from *de facto* recognition. The latter may be granted when the recognizing state judges that an aspirant state meets some but not all the requirements of statehood. Hence the notion that *de facto* recognition 'indicates general reluctance on the part of the recognizing state to bring about the whole range of legal effects that would follow from a standard de jure recognition'.[105] *De facto* recognition is provisional and may be withdrawn if the remaining criteria are not complied with. Should these conditions be satisfied, *de jure* recognition may follow.

The granting of *de jure* recognition to a state can take many forms. It could consist of a formal statement (for example congratulating a new state on attaining independence), an official letter to the newly recognized state, a declaration before a national court, or it could be inferred from the establishment of full diplomatic relations. Acts that usually do not imply recognition include participation in a multilateral conference with an unrecognized state, the appointment of representatives not enjoying diplomatic status, the maintenance of unofficial and informal contacts, and the institution of extradition procedures.[106]

What is the legal status of polities that are denied *de jure* recognition but otherwise comply with the formal criteria of statehood? In terms of the widely held declaratory theory recognition is not a precondition for an aspirant state becoming a subject of international law; an entity should merely be able to demonstrate that it is not subordinate to another authority, meaning it should enjoy sovereignty.[107] Given their problematic international status due to collective non-recognition, it would be safer to say that contested states are 'to a limited extent endowed with international legal personality and thus the capacity to become bearers of rights and obligations'.[108] Non-recognizing states, according to Crawford, are not legally permitted to act as if the entity in question was not a state. In practice states do not regard others lacking formal recognition as being exempt from international law. They moreover interact with such entities, even to the extent of joint membership of inter-governmental organizations.[109] This is not to deny that full recognition can have major legal, political and material benefits for a state, such as becoming a party to international agreements, opening diplomatic representation, gaining access to the public goods distributed by the likes of the World Bank and the International Monetary Fund, and making the state's voice heard in multilateral forums.[110]

We also need to deal with the matter of collective recognition extended by inter-governmental organizations. None is more important than the UN, the universal forum of states. The UN Charter mentions the word 'state' no less than 34 times – without providing any definition thereof – and stipulates that only states qualify for membership of the world body.[111] Requiring a substantive decision by the Security Council (meaning the approval of all five permanent members) plus a two-thirds majority in the General Assembly, admission to full UN membership is tantamount to collective *de jure* recognition.[112] The community of states thereby signals its readiness to treat the new member as a full-fledged state with all the attendant rights, duties and responsibilities, both within the UN and beyond. Admission to the UN is also likely to facilitate the entry of the new state into other multilateral organizations.[113] Not surprisingly UN membership is commonly viewed as the 'birth certificate' of a state.[114] Far from applying the formal (Montevideo) qualifications of statehood to the host of applicants in the 1960s – specifically that of effective government – the UN opted for 'casual recognition at entry'. The new international sovereignty regime, dedicated to the elimination of colonialism, would not have permitted anything less than 'run-of-the-mill' admission-*cum*-recognition.[115] Admission to membership of regional organizations such as the EU, North Atlantic Treaty Organization (NATO), Organization (previously Conference) for Security and Cooperation in Europe (OSCE) and AU – usually following on UN membership – amounts to further joint *de jure* recognition of a new entrant's statehood.[116] Although collective recognition is the hallmark of confirmed statehood, allowance should be made for states that choose to remain outside the UN, like Switzerland did until 2002, without compromising their full-fledged statehood.

There is, conversely, the reality of collective non-recognition of a prospective state. The League of Nations, for instance, refused to recognize the independent statehood of Manchukuo. UN member states collectively decided not to recognize the purported statehood of Katanga, Biafra, Rhodesia, South Africa's four homeland states and the Turkish Republic of Northern Cyprus. These instances of joint non-recognition, we noted earlier, were based on a set of peremptory norms (*jus cogens*) that variously prohibit aggression, the systematic violation of human rights, and the denial of self-determination.[117] It would be appropriate to speak of 'regimes of non-recognition' in these cases, meaning that non-recognition was deliberately extended 'from a unilateral basis to a broader representation of the international community'. Such regimes are formed when states wish to prevent the formalization of a legal status, such as an entity's claim of statehood.[118]

The question of non-recognition also arises, in different form, in the rare instance of an entity not claiming to be a state, even if it satisfies the basic criteria of statehood. This is the situation of Taiwan. Crawford's conclusion is straightforward: 'Taiwan is not a State, because it does not claim to be'.[119] In such a case there ought not to be any need for other states to decide individually or collectively on extending *de jure* recognition. What complicates matters, though, is that Taiwan insists on exercising the rights that states enjoy in international law.

Attributes and categories of contested statehood

Since contested statehood is marked by a deficit in *de jure* recognition, we need to elaborate on the reasons for the denial of such recognition. We begin by measuring contested states against the standard requirements of statehood in international law.

First, all contested states have settled populations, but some controversies arise. In the case of secessionist entities, questions are often asked about the inhabitants' actual support for unilaterally breaking away from original states. A different problem that applies in Palestine and Western Sahara is the absence of large numbers of the population; these people are stranded in refugee camps in neighbouring countries. These are admittedly political rather than legal concerns.

Turning to territory, in the second place, we have recorded that final, settled borders are not required for statehood. The boundaries of contested states are, however, disputed in a very fundamental way: since their right of existence as separate, independent states is challenged, their borders are not internationally recognized as legal and legitimate frontiers separating them from other states. Instead, the territories in contention are widely regarded as integral parts of existing states.

Third, the governments of many contested states may well comply with the criterion of effectiveness in terms of their control over territory and people and some even live up to democratic standards. The challenge facing the rulers of contested states is that their right to govern is widely disputed – a corollary of the rejection of these states' right of independent existence. So even if it manifestly possesses empirical statehood, a contested state still lacks juridical statehood conferred from outside through *de jure* recognition.

Contested states in the fourth instance typically have the ability and desire to enter into the standard array of relations (diplomatic, economic, cultural and military) with full-fledged states. Confirmed states, however, deny them the opportunity to engage in normal international interactions by refusing them *de jure* recognition.

The fifth element of statehood, sovereignty, is also hotly disputed in the case of contested states. They as a rule enjoy internal sovereignty, having detached themselves from any larger (foreign) constitutional arrangement and formalized their independent status through their own constitutions. However, confirmed states challenge the self-declared states' exclusive right to create and operate their own institutions of government separate from their original states. In international law, the latter's insistence on a right to rule the break-away territories derogate from the purported states' formal independence. What detracts from their actual independence in international law is the substantially illegal origins of several contested states: they owe their existence to the violation of peremptory international norms such as those prohibiting aggression and racial discrimination. What further compromises the actual independence of many contested states, is their subjection to control or strong influence from outside or at least heavy dependence on a foreign country. That external party is usually the creator or patron state, like Turkey in the case of Northern Cyprus.

While these five grounds already explain why contested states lack *de jure* recognition, other factors support the international rejection of their claims to statehood. The general commitment to maintaining the territorial integrity of states – a hallowed principle of international law – provides a powerful argument against recognizing break-away states. It is a long-standing fear among states that legitimizing secession could set off an unstoppable process of balkanization of existing states into ever smaller and more unviable new polities. What is more, such fragmentation is in many cases bound to be accompanied by violent domestic conflict, as in former Yugoslavia. Another very real obstacle faced by many a contested state is the original state's implacable opposition to the former's separate existence. The central state's objection to the new entity could take the form of overt military action or subversion and will as a matter of course include attempts to prevent the contested state from engaging in conventional state-like international interactions. In so doing the original country becomes what will be called the veto state of the new contested entity. Scores of other states are likely to take their cue from the original state when reacting to the contested entity. Horowitz referred to this as the international law doctrine 'forbidding recognition of secessionist units whose establishment is being resisted by the central government'.[120]

Given the range of external challenges confronting contested states, we can agree with Kurtulus that they 'have a legal status that is uncertain, an international standing that is indefinite, a legal existence that is often relative, and a security situation that is at times precarious'.[121]

While formal international recognition is the most obvious component of statehood lacking among today's contested states, it must be reiterated that the recognition deficit varies. Several levels of formal recognition, based on existing state practice, can be distinguished; in practice a purported state can fall in more than one category. *De facto* recognition is omitted here because all contested states experience some degree of factual recognition.

Titular recognition, first, refers to the wide formal acceptance (at multilateral level) of an entity's *right* of or title to statehood, as in the cases of Palestine and Western Sahara. They are, however, severely constrained by external powers in exercising the domestic rights and responsibilities of modern states. Because Palestine and Western Sahara possess the juridical shell of statehood but lack the empirical substance thereof, they are states in little more than name. The international contestation over their conceded statehood lies in the two entities' failure to form functioning states. They also lack the formal birth certificate of confirmed statehood, namely full UN membership.

Partial recognition means that a wannabe state receives *de jure* recognition from a minority of existing states and lacks UN membership. Kosovo and Taiwan are current examples. In the 1930s and early 1940s the Japanese 'puppet' state of Manchukuo fitted the category. Apart from Japan, it was recognized by only Germany, Italy, Poland, Hungary and the Vatican and was excluded from the League of Nations.[122]

The third, paltry recognition, occurs when a contested state is recognized by only a handful of existing countries, as Nigeria's break-away region of Biafra managed in the late 1960s. Tanzania, Zambia, Gabon, the Ivory Coast and Haiti formally recognized the entity's self-declared statehood.[123] The lowest form of paltry recognition is where a contested state gains formal recognition from a single confirmed state that is not its creator or patron state. The Republic of Ichkeria (Chechnya) was recognized by Afghanistan only.

If its patron or creator state is the only confirmed state recognizing a contested state, we can refer to patron recognition. This fourth form of recognition applies to the Turkish Republic of Northern Cyprus, which has been recognized by Turkey only. South Africa's former homeland states of Transkei, Bophuthatswana, Venda and Ciskei, fell partly in this category because South Africa was the only confirmed state granting them *de jure* recognition. In August 2008 South Ossetia and Abkhazia joined these ranks when Russia recognized both.

Abkhazia, South Ossetia and South Africa's Bantustans each had one foot in a fifth category, namely peer recognition where contested states recognize each other. The two remaining Eurasian entities of Nagorno Karabagh and Transdniestria have peer recognition only.

Finally, zero recognition means that an entity's purported statehood is not formally recognized by either confirmed states or fellow contested states (if the latter exist at the time). Somaliland is in this position, with Katanga and Rhodesia two earlier examples.

Apart from the key characteristic of a lack of formal international recognition, we will be applying also other criteria for including a presumptive state in this inquiry. It must have declared its independence, typically in a unilateral fashion or in conjunction with its creator or patron state, or at least asserted its right to be treated as full-fledged state by others; the entity tries to play the role of a confirmed state in world politics; it meets most of the Montevideo criteria of statehood or, if not, enjoys a generally recognized right of statehood; and it has been in existence for at least three years. The latter requirement on the one hand precludes wannabe states of a 'flash in the pan' variety and on the other ensures that we have enough substantive information to understand the domestic and international conduct of the chosen entities.

Alternative designations

The subjects of our investigation deserve to be called 'states' because nearly all of them satisfy the basic, formal requirements of statehood in international law save for recognition, they aspire to confirmed statehood, and they in many ways act like typical states. It is equally appropriate that we qualify their statehood because of its highly disputed nature and their consequent relegation to life in international limbo. As Bull noted, a polity that claims sovereign statehood 'but cannot assert this right in practice, is not a state properly so called'.[124] For that reason the concept of contested states has been introduced and is preferable to several alternatives.

- *Non- or unrecognized states* imply that the polities concerned enjoy no recognition at all. We have already identified different levels of formal recognition found in practice. In addition all aspirant states receive some *de facto* recognition.
- The term *de facto states* used by Pegg, Lynch and Bahcheli *et al*[125] is problematic because it suggests that these entities are denied *de jure* recognition, receiving *de facto* recognition only. That is not necessarily the case.
- A *statelike entity*, as conceived by King,[126] has a population and a government exercising sovereign control over a territory 'but without the imprimatur of international recognition'. This designation tends to overlook the possibility of limited *de jure* recognition if not *de facto* recognition as well.
- The notion of *quasi-states* is widely associated with Jackson's work, which we have cited extensively. Deficient empirical statehood – a feature of

quasi-states – is not necessarily characteristic of contested states; they lack juridical statehood. Another application of the term quasi-states – also inappropriate for our purposes – is to defenceless states of earlier eras, such as the Venetian Republic, Malta and Belgium.[127] However, Kølsto, for one, applied the designation quasi-states to 'unrecognized, *de facto* states'.[128]

- *Nominal states* would not be helpful either because these are typically Global South countries enveloped – like Jackson's quasi-states – in a shell of juridical statehood but lacking substantive government capacity.
- To refer to *pseudo-states* would be derogatory, suggesting that the polities concerned are all sham or unauthentic creations as opposed to 'genuine' states. True, several contested states (Northern Cyprus and South Africa's homeland states, among others) were artificial, illegitimate creations, but not all of them have such dubious origins (consider Somaliland, for instance). On the other hand several confirmed states enjoying *de jure* recognition are 'sham' states in terms of empirical statehood. What Cohen conceived as pseudo-states – 'ravaged by civil wars, unable to maintain a minimum of social cohesion'[129] – also resemble Jackson's quasi-states.
- *States-within-states* is too wide a concept because it includes national sub-units that may not have any aspirations to sovereign statehood – even if they maintain effective control over territory and possess state-like political structures.[130]
- Entities labelled as *near-states* display many attributes of state sovereignty 'but lack full standing as states'. The deficit would typically relate to one of the Montevideo criteria of statehood – not specifically that of international recognition. These *sui generis* entities constitute a mixed bag, including the Vatican and the Palestinian territories.[131] As such the term is not precise enough for our purposes.
- *Nations without states* likewise refer to cultural communities agitating for either group autonomy or secession and statehood as expressions of self-determination.[132] Contested states, however, demand more than autonomy within an existing state.
- *Areas of special sovereignty*, as Somaliland has been depicted,[133] fail to capture the 'stateness' of the entities under consideration.
- *Non-state actors* would be a singularly inappropriate designation because it too denies the 'stateness' of the polities we are studying. Moreover, a range of inter-governmental and non-governmental actors can be included under the rubric of non-state actors. Contested states have more in common with (confirmed) states and identify with them rather than with non-state entities.
- *Proto-* and *semi-states* hold some attraction, but fail to highlight the contested nature of our entities' purported statehood.

Conclusion

The main category of actors in this inquiry has intentionally been called 'states' to underscore their desire for internationally recognized statehood and to acknowledge their compliance with the standard criteria of statehood. But we cannot simply follow the 'science of duckology' and declare that 'if a creature quacks like a duck, waddles like a duck and paddles like a duck, it must be duck'. The subjects of our inquiry indeed speak like states and act like states but are not accepted into the fold of confirmed states. They lack conventional international recognition as a result of serious challenges to their right of statehood or in some cases the exercise of a conceded right of statehood. Hence the qualification 'contested' statehood.

This introductory chapter identified three other categories of actors prominent in the international politics of contested statehood. One group comprises the confirmed states constituting the international community. Another consists of what could variously be termed the creator, patron or protector states of each contested state. Where the latter has indeed been created by another state – as witnessed in Manchukuo and South Africa's four homeland states – it is appropriate to speak of an external creator that would typically play the roles of patron and protector of the contested state too. Where a contested state is the product of unilateral secession there is no creator state involved, but there may well be a patron or protector state that is vital to the survival of the pretender state. The last type of actor is the veto state, usually the entity from which the contested state has seceded. The veto state thus represents the *ancien régime* from which the contested state unilaterally divorced itself. Its veto role is focused on obstructing the contested entity's bid to gain international acceptance. Put differently, the veto state is the contested state's principal nemesis and blackballer, bent on keeping its illegitimate offspring cabined and confined so as to force it back into the fold. Veto states could also have their own patron states that provide crucial support in resisting contested states. Greece's backing of the Republic of Cyprus against Northern Cyprus is a case in point. In this instance Greece is simultaneously playing the role of external veto state.

2
Origins of Contested Statehood

The excursion into international law in the first chapter may tempt one to proffer a straightforward explanation for contested statehood: the entities were conceived and born in sin. As the products of illegal actions under international law – aggression, occupation and racial discrimination – the putative states may not join the community of confirmed states. This certainly applies to several contested states, but by no means all. In fact unilateral secession, which can be driven by factors wholly unrelated to the above offences, is the single most common origin among our selection of contested states. Given its prevalence, secession justifies considerable attention in this chapter. Thereafter other origins of contested statehood are identified. Our starting point, however, is the notion of self-determination – the holy grail of all contested states, regardless of origin. They all justify their claims to statehood in the name of this principle of international law and canon of world politics. What is meant by self-determination and what is its relationship with the controversial notion of secession?

Conceptions of self-determination

The idea of self-determination, which in its simplest form means to determine one's own fate, has its political roots in both nationalism and liberalism. The nationalist idea is that the state should coincide with a community displaying a sentiment of national or group identity, linked to a shared territory, language or religion. Such a people or ethnic group has a right to detach themselves from multinational states or empires and form their own independent national states. The right of the citizens to rule themselves – which in practice means choosing their own government – is in turn an old liberal principle articulated in, among others, the English Bill of Rights (1689), the American Declaration of Independence (1776) and the French Declaration of the Rights of Man and of the Citizen (1789). In combination these two strands of thought helped to shape what has for over a century been both a prominent theme in international political discourse and a powerful force in world politics: the notion of self-determination.[1]

In the early 20th century American President Woodrow Wilson was the most eminent advocate of self-determination. His Fourteen Point 'program of the world's peace', announced in the US Congress in 1918, is commonly regarded as the blueprint for modern self-determination. However, that term did not appear in Wilson's peace plan; his plea for free and unmolested 'opportunity of autonomous development' for subject populations nonetheless captured the essence of what he subsequently began calling self-determination. Wilson had mainly the East European 'nationalities' of the Ottoman, Russian, German and Austro-Hungarian empires in mind for autonomous development.[2] In championing self-determination the American leader embraced both the normative principle of nationalism (every nation is entitled to its own state) and the liberal principle that the people in such a national state should be free to choose their own political leadership.[3] Despite Wilson's role as a founding father of the League of Nations established in 1919, its Covenant made no mention of self-determination.

After the First World War self-determination found expression in especially the newly liberated territories of Europe and Asia. The former non-European colonies of Germany were conspicuously excluded from an entitlement to self-determination, most of them being taken over by new foreign masters. Bolshevik Russia practised self-determination by relinquishing control over adjacent small nationalities in Finland and the Baltic states (but in some cases reasserted authority in the name of proletarian self-determination within the Soviet Union).[4]

On the whole the world community seemed unenthusiastic about any wide-ranging application of Wilson's notion of self-determination. It would have required the fragmentation of scores of multinational states to create true nation-states. And dozens of new states may in turn have intensified international rivalry and fomented instability. Furthermore, self-determination through territorial dismemberment overlooked other means of domestic conflict settlement and peaceful coexistence.[5] In an entry in his diary in December 1918, Wilson's Secretary of State Robert Lansing recorded his concerns about the contagious effects of self-determination:

> The more I think about the President's declaration as to the right of 'self-determination', the more convinced I am of the danger of putting such ideas into the minds of certain races. It is bound to be the basis of impossible demands. What effect will it have on the Irish, the Indians, the Egyptians, and the nationalists among the Boers? Will it not breed – rebellion? The phrase is simply loaded with dynamite. It will raise hopes which can never be realized. It will, I fear, cost thou-

> sands of lives ... What calamity that the phrase was ever uttered! What misery it will cause![6]

While the radicalism of Wilsonian self-determination severely restricted its practical application in the inter-war years, its propagation of the democratic prescription of government by and for the people inspired oppressed communities far and wide. Coupled to this notion was the conviction that people ought to be treated equally, 'and that since some peoples have the benefit of statehood, others should be entitled as well'.[7]

The norm of self-determination, Okafor observed, is on the one hand normalizing and stabilizing by justifying sovereign statehood for an entire population of a state. On the other hand, it is revolutionary and destabilizing when invoked to challenge the structures of statehood and to protect sub-state groups.[8] Its dualism – both supporting and challenging statehood – helps to explain self-determination's contentiousness and indeterminacy in international law and world politics.[9] Thus the Badinter Commission, tasked with assisting the EU in formulating policies towards the unravelling of Yugoslavia, noted that 'international law as it currently stands does not spell out all the implications of the right to self-determination'.[10]

The Charter of the United Nations contains a few references to self-determination. One of the purposes of the UN (articles 1 and 55) is the development of friendly relations between nations 'based on respect for the principle of equal rights and self-determination of peoples'. There are also implicit references to the application of self-determination in non-self-governing territories (articles 73 and 76). Through the UN Charter the principle of self-determination found its way into international law and its legal status has been affirmed in state practice.[11] As the International Court of Justice ruled in 1995, the right of self-determination was an essential principle of international law and an *erga omnes* obligation.[12] Enshrined in the international legal and also moral order, self-determination 'shines like a beacon in the night', Pegg wrote, pointing the way to aspirant state-founders across the world.[13]

Several major international declarations and conventions adopted since the 1960s have given further content to the principle, especially regarding the 'self' in self-determination and the forms of 'determination'. The UN General Assembly initially set the tone, steering the notion of self-determination 'away from the realms of Wilsonian idealism towards minorities', and applying it to so-called saltwater colonialism.[14] We are dealing here with what has been called the classical theory of self-determination, defining a people in terms of territorial criteria. Self-determination occurs within the confines of an existing state or territorial unit, preserving its territorial integrity. Where statehood has been conferred, the entire people occupying that territory already enjoy sovereign independence – rendering secession a logical impossibility.[15]

The 1960 UN Declaration on the Granting of Independence to Colonial Territories and Peoples acknowledged the right of all peoples to self-determination, in terms of which they freely determine their political status and freely pursue their economic, social and cultural development. Any attempt to disrupt the national unity or territorial integrity of a country was deemed irreconcilable with the principles enshrined in the UN Charter. The Declaration clearly limited self-determination to the right of the majority in an internationally recognized political entity – in this case colonies – to determine their political status. That status could take the form of independence, integration or association with another state, providing it was a voluntary choice by the people of the territory concerned and expressed through 'informed and democratic processes'.[16] The international normative and legal framework of the time clearly favoured self-determination *à la* independence, as the frenzy of state-making through decolonization in the 1950s and 1960s testifies.

Both UN human rights covenants of 1966 – on Civil and Political Rights and on Economic, Social and Cultural Rights, respectively – reaffirmed the rights of all 'peoples' to self-determination, using the same words as the 1960 anti-colonial declaration. Even so, the two covenants suggest that the right of self-determination extended beyond the colonial situation and included the right to free, fair and open participation in democratic processes of governance.[17]

The Declaration on Principles of International Law concerning Friendly Relations and Cooperation among States, adopted by the UN General Assembly in 1970, essentially reiterated what the preceding documents laid down on self-determination. It is worth underlining the statement that '[t]he establishment of a sovereign and independent State, the free association or integration with an independent State or the emergence into any other political status freely determined by the people constitute modes of implementing the right to self-determination by that people'. Independent statehood was therefore not the only form of self-determination; apart from association and integration, the door was left open for a variety of other (unnamed) political arrangements freely chosen by a people.

The 1970 Declaration added an important safety clause that would protect certain states against claims to self-determination involving territorial fragmentation: these were existing states that complied with the principle of equal rights and self-determination (as set out in this and earlier UN declarations) 'and thus possessed of a government representing the whole people belonging to that territory without distinction as to race, creed or colour'. Apart from people subjected to colonial rule, those living under racist regimes by implication had a right of self-determination too.[18] In the latter regard the drafters of the Declaration had white-ruled South Africa and Rhodesia in their sights, where the black majorities were denied self-determination.

As regards secession, the Declaration on Principles of International Law stipulated that '[e]very State shall refrain from any action aimed at the partial or total disruption of the national unity and territorial integrity of any other State or country'. This echoes the language of traditional international law, which opposed the break-up of an established state in the name of the self-determination of sub-national groups. Their right to secede from their existing state was not conceded. Even so the Declaration left secessionists with some room for manoeuvre. According to Okafor, secession was deemed illegitimate 'unless in the case of the secession of a sub-unit from a state that does not behave in accordance with the tenets of "democratic" governance'.[19] This more permissive view of secessionist self-determination gained considerable ground in subsequent years. As Tappe put it, international law underwent 'a process of metamorphosis', marked by a gradual acceptance of some right of secessionist self-determination.[20] Some theorists dubbed it the romantic theory of self-determination (as distinct from the classical theory mentioned above), defining the 'self' as 'a group linked by a common history and culture and bound to a national ideal that the nation should be autonomous, united and distinct in its recognised homeland'.[21]

With its Helsinki Declaration of 1975, the Conference on Security and Cooperation in Europe followed the new trend among international organizations and judicial institutions to reconceptualize the right of self-determination in the context of a post-colonial world. By then decolonization had largely run its course in Africa and Asia. Elaborating the principles underlying relations between the more than 30 participating states, the Helsinki Declaration proclaimed that

> all peoples always have the right, in full freedom, to determine when and as they wish, their internal and external political status, without external interference, and to pursue as they wish their political, economic, social and cultural development.[22]

Instead of being confined to the right of colonial peoples to independence, self-determination was clearly evolving into a right of all peoples to be involved in decisions affecting their future.[23] Nearly two decades later the Vienna Declaration and Programme of Action, adopted at the UN's World Conference on Human Rights in 1993, reaffirmed that all 'peoples' have a right of self-determination, by virtue of which 'they freely determine their political status, and freely pursue their economic, social and cultural development'. At that stage, as Falk famously remarked, it was already 'too late to put the genie of self-determination back in its colonialist bottle'.[24] UN adviser Nicholas Kittrie highlighted the post-colonial appeal of self-determination when he posed the rhetorical question: 'Who is to tell the Bosnians, the Palestinians, Kurds, Druze, Scots, Basques, Quebecois and Bretons that they are not a people and are not entitled to self-determination?'[25]

These reformulations of self-determination have nonetheless been open to divergent interpretations. In terms of one construction, self-determination embodies nothing more than a procedural right: 'entities have a right to see their position taken into account whenever their futures are being decided'. It may not involve a right to secede or even to autonomy, 'but it does amount to a right to be taken seriously'. Self-determination should therefore be treated not as an enforceable right 'but rather as a more open-textured principle'.[26] A more permissive reading of the Helsinki Declaration and other international documents issued since the early 1970s holds that if a state consistently violates the individual and collective rights of ethnic minorities, such groups may invoke the right of self-determination. It would allow them to demand internal reforms such as autonomy or minority protection or to seek external remedies like merging with an existing state, joining a confederation with one or more other states, or independent statehood.[27] According to the widely quoted Capotorti definition, a minority is a numerically inferior and non-dominant group whose members display ethnic, religious or linguistic features different from those of the rest of the population of a state, and who maintain a sense of solidarity aimed at preserving their culture, traditions, language and religion. Minorities were of course at the heart of the Wilsonian conception of self-determination.[28] Ardent secessionists will obviously favour the latter interpretation – as in the case of Eritrea's divorce from Ethiopia – over the view that counsels disgruntled communities to embrace a procedural norm that hopefully entitles them to be consulted by those in power.

Implicit in the preceding discussion is that self-determination has internal and external dimensions. The former involves the choice of a suitable form of government, whereas the external component refers to the selection of an international status.[29]

For most of the 20th century the essence of external self-determination was the right of a people to be free of alien or colonial rule and to decide freely under what sovereignty they wished to live. The choice of international status was typically that of independent statehood. It was given effect after both world wars in former colonial empires, including those of the Turks, British and French. Other forms of external self-determination, like confederating or associating with existing states, were also recognized in international law but seldom implemented.

Internal self-determination, enshrined in the international conventions cited, refers to the right of a people to freely choose their own rulers and form of government and to freely pursue their economic, social and cultural development – meaning without foreign interference and in accordance with democratic procedures. A Unesco conference in 1989 adopted the so-called Kirby definition of a 'people' eligible for internal self-determination.

It is a group of individuals displaying some or all of the following features: a shared historical tradition; racial or ethnic identity; cultural homogeneity; linguistic unity; religious or ideological affinity; territorial attachment, and a common economic existence.[30] (Note the striking similarity with the Capotorti definition of a minority cited earlier.) In the UN, Liechtenstein has since the end of the Cold War been a prominent exponent of internal self-determination *à la* autonomy. 'It allows for a degree of self-expression which can be sufficient to reflect a community's sense of identity', Prince Hans-Adam II told the General Assembly in 1993, without threatening the territorial integrity of established states.[31]

The international legal and political discourse reveals a clear preference for internal over external self-determination. Whereas the latter compromises the territorial unity of an established state, internal self-determination is confined to the restructuring of political power within a state.[32] Internal self-determination finds expression in a variety of constitutional arrangements that accommodate population diversity in a democratic manner while preserving the territorial integrity of the state. Since our interest is at this stage confined to external self-determination – which allows for the establishment of independent states – we need not delve any deeper into internal self-determination; many of the domestic options are examined in Chapter 3 as alternatives to sovereign statehood.

In sum, self-determination has over the years acquired many different 'faces'. These include the right to be liberated from colonial domination (Ghana, Nigeria, Indonesia and dozens of others); the right to remain a dependent territory (Puerto Rico); the right to dissolve an established state peacefully to create new states (the former Soviet Union and Czechoslovakia); the disputed right to unilateral secession (Bangladesh and Eritrea); the right of divided states to reunite (Vietnam and Germany); the right of limited autonomy (the Basque region and Catalonia); minority rights (recognized in several international conventions), and the right of internal self-determination (the freedom to choose a government).[33]

We now turn to the third and fourth of these 'faces', acknowledging that the principle of self-determination is still 'pervading the consciousness of numerous subjected communities' around the world and 'has become a constant force for secession and for its legitimization'.[34]

The meaning of secession

The word 'secession' has featured more than once in our discussion of self-determination. So close is the connection between the two that they have been portrayed as Siamese twins.[35]

Derived from the Latin word 'secedere' (literally, to go apart), secession is the act of withdrawing from, say, a political alliance, religious body or federation. A group of Presbyterians who broke away from the Church of

Scotland around 1733 constituted themselves as the Secession Church. The first political use of the (English) term is found in a statement by Thomas Jefferson in 1825 that the American colonies had seceded from the union with Britain. A new secessionist crisis broke out in 1860–1 when 11 Southern states withdrew from the Union to establish the Confederacy. This move caused the American Civil War, also known as the War of Secession.[36]

The type of political secession that interests us is 'the formal withdrawal from an established, internationally recognized state by a constituent unit to create a new sovereign state'.[37] While secession is in most instances used as a mode of gaining independent statehood, some communities secede from one state in order to become part of another; consider the case of Transylvanians wishing to exit Romania to join Hungary. Such secessionist-irredentist claims fall outside our inquiry. Either way, secession involves a claim to territory but is not designed to overthrow an existing government. Instead, secessionists want to restrict the jurisdiction of the (original) state so that it does not extend to their group and the territory they occupy.[38]

Involving the territorial fragmentation of an established state in order to create a new one (or more states) on the original national territory, secession can occur with or without the consent of the government of the existing state. These respective routes to statehood, both of which are acknowledged in international law,[39] may hold vastly different implications for the emerging states. Consensual secession means that the present government and the secessionists agree to the break-up of the existing state and its replacement with two or more sovereign entities. Such a mutually agreed divorce can also be regarded as an act of state partition. To avoid confusion, 'partition' is the preferred term for consensual dismemberment, while 'secession' will wherever possible be confined in this study to a unilateral (non-consensual) break-away from an existing state. Because the parties involved agree to partition, international recognition of the new states should be unproblematic. Restricting ourselves to 20th century examples of partition, reference can be made to Panama's break with Colombia in 1903, Norway's divorce from Sweden in 1905, Finland's detachment from the Russian Empire after World War I, Iceland's separation from Denmark in 1944, Senegal's departure from the Mali Federation in 1960, the dissolution of the United Arab Republic in 1961 into the constituent states of Egypt and Syria, and Singapore's withdrawal from the Federation of Malaysia in 1965. More recent examples are the so-called velvet divorce between the two former component units of Czechoslovakia in 1993 and Montenegro's withdrawal from the Union of Serbia and Montenegro in 2006.

Some national constitutions have at times incorporated a right of 'secession'. The 1931 Constitution of China recognized a right of secession for all national minorities. The 1975 Constitution of the People's Republic of China (PRC) by contrast alluded to the 'inalienable parts' of the national territory. The Constitution of the Union of Burma (1947) also acknowledged a right of secession, but the procedural requirements were virtually impossible to meet and the regional states most likely to opt out were pointedly excluded from the right of self-determination. Burma's 1974 Constitution omitted any such rights. The 1977 Constitution of the Soviet Union enshrined 'the right of free secession' for all union republics, providing specific rules of procedure were honoured. The Yugoslav Constitution likewise granted component units the right to exit the federation, but this could only be done with the consent of all six republics and the autonomous provinces.[40]

At least three states still make formal provision for territorial fragmentation. Ethiopia's constitution (1994) provides that 'every nation, nationality and people in Ethiopia has an unconditional right to self-determination, including the right to secession'. The prescribed procedure is that the legislative body of the group involved must approve secession by a two-thirds majority and the group has to accept withdrawal from Ethiopia by means of a majority vote in a referendum. Partition may also take place in Sudan under the terms of the Comprehensive Peace Agreement concluded between the central government and the Sudan People's Liberation Movement in January 2005. The people of southern Sudan have the right to decide by referendum, within six years, whether they wish to remain part of the existing state or become independent. The possibility of negotiated divorce exists also in Canada. In 2000 its Parliament adopted the Clarity Act setting out the procedures to be followed when a province no longer wishes to be part of Canada. The same year Quebec's National Assembly enacted a declaration affirming the province's freedom to determine its own future.[41]

There is a rationale behind an opt-out provision: 'this demonstrates a government's confidence that it will adopt policies that will not lead to a ruinous exit'. For their part prospective partitionists, realizing they have meaningful leverage over the national government, need not fear marginalization.[42] And should the authorities fail to accommodate particular communities, the latter would have good reason to exercise their right of separation from the state.[43]

Because secession means that a group or region exits an existing state against the wishes of the national government, those breaking away typically issue a unilateral declaration of independence to announce their secession and founding of a new state.[44] Four elements are needed to reach that point. First, there has to be a distinct community (in terms of objective features such as culture, language, religion or race as well as a shared sense of distinctiveness), smaller than the national population, which threatens to withdraw from the state. The second requirement is a geographical territory on which the community intends establishing its own state. Third, leadership is necessary to present demands for secession and organize actions. Finally, discontent with its prevailing circumstances motivates the community to demand change.[45] Perhaps timing could be added as another variable. Common sense would suggest that secessionists would prefer to launch a break-away bid when the central state's internal power is weak (especially under conditions of serious domestic strife) and its external standing low (due to the domestic situation). Usually, however, secession is resisted by the central authorities who may resort to force to keep the state intact. Their use of force may of course be a response in kind to the actions of the secessionists.[46] Hence Crawford's definition of secession as 'the creation of a State by the use or threat of force and without the consent of the former sovereign'.[47]

Examples of successful secession – with the separatists eventually prevailing in the hostilities (or the national government abandoning its forcible repression of the break-away bid) and receiving *de jure* international recognition of their statehood – are scarce. The only cases over the last 40 years are Bangladesh, Eritrea, East Timor and the constituent units of the former Yugoslavia. Unsuccessful attempts at secession are more numerous, among them Tibet (China), Kashmir (India), Katanga/Shaba (Congo), Biafra (Nigeria), Karen and Shan States (Burma), Bougainville (Papua New Guinea), Chechnya (Russia) and Republika Srpska (Bosnia and Herzegovina).[48] Entities whose unilateral proclamations of independent statehood are still being contested internationally include Abkhazia, South Ossetia, Nagorno Karabagh, Transdniestria and Somaliland.

A special type of (non-consensual) secession occurs when a foreign power excises a slice of territory from an established state and creates a new client or puppet state in the severed area. It is an action typically accompanied by armed conflict and the military occupation of the area in contention; such instances of state-making may well be part of war-making. Examples include Manchukuo between 1932 and 1945, Slovakia and Croatia during Nazi occupation, and the Turkish Republic of Northern Cyprus. As we noted in Chapter 1, states created through an illegal act of aggression face virtually insurmountable problems in gaining formal international recognition.

Finally, secession – like self-determination – remains an ambiguous and controversial notion. It can be interpreted variously 'as self-emancipation from tyranny and as a challenge to the integrity of the polity'. The history of the United States, paradoxically, exemplifies both. Its Declaration of Independence justified secession on the grounds that 'when a long Train of Abuses and Usurpations...evinces a Design to reduce them [a people] under absolute Despotism, it is their Right, it is their Duty, to throw off such Government, and to provide new Guards for their future Security'.[49] The Civil War, in turn, was fought primarily to suppress the Southern states' secession.[50] In the case of contemporary states born of secession, the world community mostly supports the presumption that their emergence is not a justified act of liberation from oppression but an unwarranted assault on the territorial integrity of one of their peers.

International responses to secession

Secessionists, then, face daunting odds when trying to generate international support for their cause. We explore the parameters within which this attempt is made, beginning with two seminal interpretations of the international law of secession.

The first is provided by the African Commission on Human and People's Rights, which in 1996 gave its verdict in a secessionist dispute between the central government of Zaire and one of the constituent units of the state, Katanga/Shaba (the very entity that broke away in the early 1960s). The leader of the Katangese Peoples' Congress requested the Commission to recognize the independence of Katanga and help effect the withdrawal of Zaire from Katanga. The Katangese claimed that Zaire had violated article 20 of the 1981 African Charter on Human and Peoples' Rights. The clause *inter alia* guarantees the right of self-determination to both 'colonized and oppressed peoples' – hence the claims to a right of secession. Citing the absence of concrete evidence of human rights violations to the extent that 'the territorial integrity of Zaire should be called into question', and the absence of evidence that the people of Katanga were denied the right to participate in government (enshrined in article 13(1) of the African Charter), the Commission held that 'Katanga is obliged to exercise a variant of self-determination that is compatible with the sovereignty and territorial integrity of Zaire'.[51] The Commission's findings nonetheless suggested that article 20 of the African Charter allows, in the context of regional international law applicable to Africa, 'a limited treaty-based entitlement to secession in some highly exceptional cases'.[52]

In 1998 the Supreme Court of Canada gave its opinion on Quebec's right of unilateral secession under Canadian constitutional law and international law. The Court maintained that 'international law expects that the right to self-determination will be exercised by peoples within the framework of existing sovereign states and consistent with the maintenance of the territorial integrity of those states. Where this is not possible, in the exceptional circumstance...a right of secession may arise'. The latter would apply 'where a people are oppressed, as for example under foreign military occupation; or where a definable group is denied meaningful access to government to pursue their political, economic, social and cultural development'. The Court, not surprisingly, found that such exceptional circumstances 'are manifestly inapplicable to Quebec under existing conditions'.[53]

In summary, the African Commission on Human and Peoples' Rights and the Canadian Supreme Court affirmed the existence, in two non-colonial settings, of 'a limited international legal entitlement to secede'. It applies only in the highly exceptional circumstances of an oppressed people (living under an undemocratic regime that is not representative and commits flagrant human rights abuses) and a people denied effective participation in the political and economic life of the state. It should be emphasized that neither case acknowledged a general right of secession in every conceivable situation for any disaffected sub-national group.[54] The traditional presumption against secession continues to prevail in international law.[55]

In the practice of states a right of secession is contested even more strongly than in law. As UN Secretary-General Boutros Boutros-Ghali warned in *An Agenda for Peace* (1992), 'if every ethnic, religious or linguistic group claimed statehood, there would be no limit to fragmentation, and peace, security and economic well-being for all would become ever more difficult to achieve'.[56]

Among political theorists views on the justifiability of secession are more diverse than in either law or politics: anti-secessionists oppose a right of secession, except under stringent conditions; pro-secessionists support it, subject to certain conditions; and others support or oppose secession based on a balance of factors.[57] These views have found expression in theories variously labelled as liberal *versus* communitarian,[58] remedial right only *versus* primary right,[59] and just-cause *versus* choice theories.[60] Another theoretician has reinterpreted and applied the principles of *jus ad bellum* to secession.[61]

The following set of prerequisites for secession draws on a host of scholarly writings falling into the above categories. Many of the aspects deal with the intolerability of the *status quo* and the dim prospects of any meaningful improvement in the fate of an aggrieved group. As such these are the 'push' factors driving the disaffected community to sever their links with an existing state and declare their area a separate state under their exclusive control.[62]

- Secession should have a just cause, meaning that the injustice being remedied or prevented is grave enough to justify secession from a parent state. Among such causes are genocide, cultural extinction (also called ethnocide), oppression (which could take such forms as exploitation, marginalization, powerlessness and harassment), deliberate and systematic discrimination (including 'discriminatory redistribution' by the state), forcible assimilation, illegal occupation and annexation of territory by a foreign power, and the wanton breach of the terms of a constitutive (federal) pact. Secession could thus be driven by considerations like the need for physical survival, the preservation of a cultural inheritance and a quest for rectificatory justice (reappropriation by legitimate owners of property seized illegally). The former Yugoslav republics of Slovenia, Croatia, Macedonia and Bosnia and Herzegovina seceded on the basis of their being denied the proper exercise of their right of democratic self-government and, in some instances, subjection to aggression and crimes against humanity. The three Baltic republics reclaimed their independence from Russia on the grounds of rectificatory justice, but since Moscow concurred we are dealing here with partition, not secession.

- Where secession is motivated by a need for cultural self-preservation, the culture in question must be seriously threatened; less drastic means of preserving the culture than secession must be inadequate or unavailable; and the particular culture must meet minimal standards of moral decency (unlike the Nazi and Khmer Rouge cultures).
- Secession is a final resort solution, followed only when it is abundantly evident that all other peaceful and amicable options (including federalism, autonomy and minority rights) cannot remedy or prevent injustice.
- Secession is the only way in which the minority concerned can exercise its right of self-determination in a democratic fashion.
- The internal and external legitimacy of the central government has been widely questioned due to its authoritarian and repressive nature.
- Independent statehood can only be achieved through a legitimate authority, which calls for a secessionist leadership that is manifestly representative of the population of the break-away territory.
- Evidence of extensive, genuine support among members of the disaffected group for breaking away is required.
- The group should have historic claims to the territory on which it intends forming its state and constitutes a numerical majority in that area.
- The new state has to be constituted on a democratic basis, guarantee individual and minority rights on its soil, accept appropriate international obligations, respect applicable international conventions, and recognize the territorial integrity of other states.
- The putative state should have a relatively effective central government that has provided order over a significant period (say at least three years) in terms of functioning police, military and judicial systems. This is a particularly relevant consideration where the aspiring state has broken away from a country that has slid into anarchy and chaos, as Somaliland did from Somalia. An effective government may also help to keep international terrorists at bay since the latter are known to prey on fragile states.
- The emerging state has reasonable prospects of survival and economic prosperity, instead of becoming another basket case.
- The bid for independence has a fair chance of success in terms of international recognition of the new state. Otherwise, the choice of secession would be unjustified, condemning a people to fight a lost cause.
- The principle of proportionality should be upheld, meaning that the anticipated costs of secession are not disproportionate to the benefits (both material and moral).

- The remainder state's economy will not be substantially weakened by the envisaged break-up.
- The minimization if not prevention of violence during the process of dismemberment must be of major concern to the secessionists. There should also be reasonable prospects that the fragmentation of the existing state will enhance the chances of lasting peace between and within the new and old states.
- A final consideration is that international recognition is more likely if secession leads to the complete dissolution of the predecessor state, rather than only a partial disruption of its territorial integrity. There is then no longer an existing state whose consent is needed for any political reconfiguration. Such dissolution, causing the *de facto* and *de jure* disappearance of a pre-existing state, occurred in the former Soviet Union, Czechoslovakia and Yugoslavia.

Although a secessionist entity might improve its chances of international recognition by meeting the criteria just listed, there is no guarantee that the world community will oblige. As we know only too well, recognition is a matter of political discretion, not a legal or moral duty. The original state's role is critical in this respect. Whenever that state persists in its opposition to the secession of one or more of its regions, Crawford found, break-away bids attracted virtually no foreign support or recognition. Indeed, no new state created since 1945 outside the colonial context has gained membership of the UN in the face of the predecessor state's opposition, with the qualified exception of the former Yugoslav republics. This experience led Crawford to conclude that state practice since the Second World War reveals clearly 'the extreme reluctance of states to recognise or accept unilateral secession outside the colonial context' – a practice that has been 'powerfully reinforced' in the post-Cold War era. True, international law allows for the acknowledgment of political realities once the independence of a seceding entity is firmly established and in relation to the territory under its effective control.[63] *De facto* recognition is indeed what contested states enjoy, but the first prize of collective *de jure* recognition and UN membership eludes them.

For separatists bent on creating their own states, consensual partition offers a far better route than confrontational secession because it avoids bloodshed and virtually guarantees confirmed statehood. Various procedures could be laid down for such a separation. These include weighted majorities in referendums on the proposed divorce, and waiting periods. Separatists could also be subjected to special costs, such as compensating the remainder state for investments lost due to the break-up and paying an exit fee or 'secession tax'.[64] Carefully designed procedural hurdles 'can make secession sufficiently difficult to avoid unacceptable risk of premature exit or strategic bargaining by minorities, while still making secession possible under appropriate conditions'.[65] Hedging the right to break away can be done through a state's constitution, as in the case of Ethiopia, by ordinary laws or even through a formal agreement, as in the peace accord concluded between the Sudanese government and southern rebels in 2005.

Other origins of contested statehood

Among our ten contemporary case studies, the four Eurasian entities of Nagorno Karabagh, South Ossetia, Abkhazia and Transdniestria as well as Kosovo have secessionist origins. Somaliland is the product of secession-*cum*-reversion, having broken away from Somalia to return to its former sovereign status. The Turkish Republic of Northern Cyprus (TRNC) has never been recognized as a state in international law because it was supposedly created through Turkey's illegal use of force in 1974. While troops from mainland Turkey were still occupying Northern Cyprus when the TRNC was proclaimed in 1983, one should not overlook the secessionist element in the unilateral declaration of independence. As such the TRNC was the product of the dual transgressions of aggression-*cum*-occupation and secession.

Taiwan is a hold-out against the communist revolution that had swept Nationalist rule aside in mainland China in 1949. For the PRC, Taiwan is nothing more than a rebellious province of China destined to be unified with the mainland. The Republic of China (ROC), by contrast, does not regard itself as a sub-unit of China but as a sovereign entity with a long history of confirmed statehood.

Western Sahara went through a process of self-decolonization by declaring itself independent after Spain withdrew from the territory. A large number of states, mainly in Africa, recognized the statehood of the Sahrawi Arab Democratic Republic (SADR). The problem, though, is that the bulk of the territory of Western Sahara remains under Moroccan occupation and the SADR's government languishes in exile.

The government of Palestine had remained in exile for the first six years after the unilateral declaration of statehood in 1988. In 1994 the leadership of the Palestine Liberation Organization returned to the Palestinian territories and established a government there. Although Palestine's right of statehood was universally recognized and it maintained diplomatic ties with scores of states, it still lacked the final baptism of full UN membership. Meanwhile the translation of Palestine's acknowledged right of statehood into a functioning state enjoying domestic sovereignty (*à la* Krasner) remained fraught with controversy, not least because of Israel's occupation of Palestinian land.

Conclusion

The pursuit of self-determination since the First World War has produced scores of new states. Most of them emerged from the liquidation of colonial empires and others from the territorial fragmentation of existing states. Virtually all the entities thus created were readily admitted to the ranks of confirmed states as their statehood was generally recognized. Nearly two dozen others with aspirations of statehood have over the last 90 years or so failed to gain international recognition – even though they too invoked the right of self-determination to justify their quest for sovereign independence.

The contested statehood of the wannabe states mentioned in our inquiry reveals different causes, but secession is the single most common one. Those whose 'birth defects' related to aggression, occupation or racial discrimination have singularly failed to persuade the world community of their right of statehood. Even secessionist entities claiming grave injustice in their predecessor states have by and large been denied *de jure* recognition. The ingrained presumption against secession that pervades international law and world politics, together with the opposition of original states to break-away bids, create a decidedly hostile external environment for new states born of secession. Secession, therefore, is a likely route to contested statehood.

3
Alternative Destinations for Contested States

The previous chapter provided a theoretical introduction to contested states' origins, the first phase of their life cycle. We now proceed with a theoretical outline of the other two stages. In dealing here with the second phase, the focus will be on how the international community responds to the existence of contested states. It is after all these reactions that create the unfavourable external environment in which contested states find themselves. In trying to survive such adversity, contested states place heavy emphasis on state- and nation-building – the twin endeavours common among new states, especially those emerging from violent conflict. But however successful such projects, very few contested states will be allowed to advance to confirmed statehood for reasons mentioned in Chapter 1. Over the long run the *status quo* satisfies neither contested states nor the community of confirmed states. For one thing, the deprivations of isolation will prevent most contested states from achieving sustainable economic growth. The world community is in turn concerned about the combustible potential of the unresolved conflicts between contested states and their countries of origin. So although all of today's contested states have been in existence for well over ten years and many could survive several more years, they are all ultimately transient phenomena expected to disappear.[1] This leads us to the third and final phase of the life cycle: where might contested states 'disappear' to? The bulk of Chapter 3 is devoted to possible answers.

Points of departure

A wide range of alternative destinations for contested states – other than restoring the *status quo ante*, maintaining the *status quo* and gaining full recognition – will be presented in two broad categories: options of an inter-state character and others of an intra-state nature. The adoption of many of these alternatives will require a flexible approach to three powerful ideas at the heart of the quest for statehood among sub-national groups, namely nationalism, self-determination and sovereignty. Nationalism, to begin with, should be separated from the state. As it is, all nationalisms do not aim at sovereign statehood for the groups involved; a nationalist is not *ipso facto* a separatist. There are many political forms other than an own nation-state (narrowly defined) to advance communal interests.[2] Second, nationalists could paint themselves into a corner if they conceive of self-determination as having an external dimension only, that is independent statehood. They need to work with the notion of internal self-determination, which can be expressed through a variety of political arrangements, including territorial or cultural autonomy. Sovereignty, finally, should be treated not as the exclusive preserve of the central authorities of the state, but instead as a collection of functions exercised at different levels of society. The 'unbundling' of sovereignty has shifted it from the centre to sub-national authorities and even to individuals.[3]

Keating drew these threads together in his portrayal of new minority or regional nationalisms as being 'post-nation-state in inspiration, addressing a world in which sovereignty has ceased to be absolute and power is dispersed'. To promote their nationalist programmes, these groups act at different levels. They are located within state political systems, international regimes and the international order generally. 'The most successful are those able to play in all these arenas simultaneously. This requires access to the state and to the international regime, as well as links with domestic and international economic actors.'[4]

Such alternative conceptions of nationalism, self-determination and sovereignty are already well developed in the theory and practice of conflict prevention and resolution.[5] Many of the options we will record are indeed drawn from the scholarly literature in these fields.

The alternatives listed could be employed for both remedial and preventive purposes: they provide existing contested states and their major external stakeholders with possible ways out of the present impasse, and they offer aspirant state founders with alternatives – short of sovereign independence – to the *cul-de-sac* of contested statehood. First, though, typical foreign responses to contested states will be identified.

International reactions to contested states

The ways in which confirmed states could deal with contested states can be placed on a continuum ranging from the one 'extreme' of military action to suppress a unilateral bid for statehood to the other 'extreme' of *de jure* recognition. For contested states the latter reaction is obviously the most desirable yet the hardest to attain, whereas the military response is the least preferable.

The ingrained international hostility to secession usually means that the state experiencing a break-away bid can count on the backing of its peers in preserving its territorial integrity. The most drastic external support would be military intervention on the side of the original state to restore the *status quo ante*. Such military action could be taken by states individually or collectively under the authority of a multilateral organization.

The next response is the international isolation of a contested state. This reaction may accompany a predecessor state's military response to a secessionist bid, or isolation may be pursued as an alternative to the use of force. We are referring to the deliberate, orchestrated international ostracism of a contested state after its declaration of independence. The extreme form of political isolation is the general non-recognition of an entity's claims to statehood. From this rejection flow various kinds of diplomatic isolation, such as the absence of official bilateral representation and exclusion from inter-governmental organizations. Economic isolation typically involves the application of sanctions aimed at restricting the flow of goods, capital and technology to and from a contested state. Such measures could be authorized by the UN Security Council or some regional organization or be imposed by states individually. Ostracism can also extend to the military domain, which means that a contested state faces restrictions on importing arms and military equipment and engaging in other military relations with foreign states. Socio-cultural isolation covers a wide field, from sports and academic boycotts of a contested state to restrictions on its nationals' ability to travel abroad.

Foreign indifference to the existence of contested states is an option located towards the middle of our continuum of responses. In what amounts to benign neglect, confirmed states simply ignore the putative state. They neither apply punitive measures against the non-recognized polity nor seek to engage it diplomatically, economically or otherwise. Their interactions are minimal, rarely extending beyond a modest amount of trade. It is an easy and inexpensive response for states that are geographically distant from the contested entity (and its original state) and have little to do with either.

Engagement, next, implies others' limited acceptance of a contested state.[6] In rare cases states might regard such *de facto* recognition as a forerunner of *de jure* recognition. However, engagement is in most instances deliberately tentative and restricted, informed by a variety of considerations. One is obviously the factual existence of the aspirant state, to which might be added its stability and durability. Engagement could also be motivated by such instrumental factors as strategic and military importance, economic gains and domestic political motives. Affective factors like ethnic identity, religion, ideology and humanitarian concerns can also come into play.[7]

The forms of engagement can conveniently be placed in the same broad categories as those of isolation. Obviously political and diplomatic engagement will be facilitated if the original state does not deliberately block or strenuously object to such interactions.[8] But even without the predecessor state's approval, others could conduct government-to-government talks and establish reciprocal representative or liaison offices.[9] Alternatively diplomatic involvement – whether bilateral or multilateral – could be designed to promote a resolution of the conflict between a contested state and its original state.[10]

Economic engagement in the form of trade, investment and technology transfer may be relatively uncontentious, unless the UN Security Council has ordered economic sanctions against a contested state. While many confirmed states may be wary of promoting trade with a contested state, they may adopt a *laissez-faire* approach by allowing their nationals to conduct commercial relations with a non-recognized state at their own risk. Where extensive economic ties exist, these may serve as a platform for representative offices. Apart from mere material gain, external economic involvement could be used to support conflict resolution initiatives at the political level. Ending the economic isolation of a contested state could make it more amenable to finding a peaceful settlement of its conflict with its former central state. Economic engagement may in some instances also help to free the political economy of a contested state from the grip of criminal elements.[11]

Most confirmed states would shy away from overt military ties with a contested state, not least for fear of antagonizing the original state. The major exception is of course the contested entity's patron state. An entirely different form of military engagement would be participation in an international peacekeeping mission in a contested state or on its border with its original state. Normal socio-cultural engagement could also be problematic. A contested state's lack of formal recognition and diplomatic ties as well as its general isolation may make it an unattractive destination for tourists, sportspeople, artists and other visitors from abroad.

The final external response on our continuum is *de jure* external recognition of a secessionist entity's claims to statehood. While this is the grand prize cherished by contested states, the record shows it is very rarely achieved; few if any of today's contested states are likely to reach confirmed statehood.

Inter-state options

Options of an inter-state character involve a contested entity and at least one confirmed state. Most of the eight alternatives would leave contested states with a high level of autonomy and the retention of several features of statehood. As mentioned, straightforward *de jure* recognition of existing contested states is not included in the inventory because it is in most cases a remote possibility. Conditional recognition is, however, considered in the section entitled 'International status'. We will not pay attention to suzerainty – the creation of a vassal state – because the institution has fallen into disuse.[12] A very different scenario also excluded from the survey is what could be depicted as denationalization through globalization: a process which, according to some observers, could replace group-based loyalties and emotional attachments to a particular territory with a new stateless, global 'identity'.[13] While this may yet prove a powerful force in some societies, it is a long-term process largely beyond the control of conflicting parties. Our interest is in immediate, manageable plans to resolve and prevent conflicts over statehood.

Confederations

Although confederations should strictly speaking also be excluded – their constituent members are fully independent states[14] – there have been some interesting developments worth noting. The first is that successor states born of agreed partition may well form themselves into a confederation, thus acknowledging both the individual independence and mutual interdependence of the new polities. The Commonwealth of Independent States (CIS, established in December 1991 by 11 former Soviet republics, with another joining later) embodies these very considerations.

As part of a bold plan for lasting peace in conflict-ridden Central Africa, Griggs has proposed 'a confederated Great Lakes Region composed of tribes, city-states and other grassroots structures that give freer play to both local, regional, and global scales of human organisation'. His grand scheme for resolving conflict over boundaries in the area rests on the recognition of state borders as 'soft, flexible, and mobile' and on more decentralized planning by the countries involved. Griggs' 'geography of loosely aligned states, regions and city-states' would include Zaire, Rwanda and Burundi, and possibly also Uganda and Tanzania.[15] With such an array of constituent elements, this would be a highly unconventional confederation. Griggs' proposal could nonetheless offer novel alternatives to independent statehood for separatist groups in several of the states just mentioned.

A less unorthodox but still ambitious confederation has been mooted for Central Asia. Following the dissolution of the Soviet empire, Turkish President Suleyman Demirel spoke hopefully of a revived Turkic commonwealth extending from the Adriatic to China. It would join Turkey in a confederation with five former Soviet republics whose official languages have Turkic roots: Kazakhstan, Kyrgyzstan, Uzbekistan, Turkmenistan and Azerbaijan.[16] If the Turkish Republic of Northern Cyprus were to join – an exceedingly unlikely prospect – it would reduce the isolation caused by the territory's contested statehood.

Another unconventional confederation – with an inter-state character of sorts – has been suggested by Galtung. He made a case for a confederation of autonomies of peoples of the same nation across the borders of the states in which they live. This could apply to the Kurds, for instance, and so possibly avert a secessionist bid and the emergence of another contested state. Relations between the Catholics in Northern Ireland and the Irish Republic may also develop in the direction of a confederation of autonomies.[17]

Condominiums

Historically condominiums were established to resolve territorial disputes between states, but the arrangement might help to settle a particular type of contemporary ethnic-*cum*-territorial conflict. There are two basic forms of condominium. One provides for territorial self-government in the specific area, with final authority vested in the condominium powers. This arrangement applies to the Franco-Spanish condominium of Andorra, the oldest and most successful living example. Since acquiring statehood in 1278 Andorra's rights and freedoms have been jointly guaranteed by its two neighbours, France and Spain. Under its 1993 constitution Andorra became a parliamentary democracy and sovereignty is shared between the Andorran people and the country's two 'co-princes' – the President of France and the Bishop of Urgell in Spain – who jointly remain head of state.[18] The other model involves a non-territorial division of the disputed territory, with each foreign power retaining supreme authority over its respective subjects while exercising equal dominion or sovereignty through an autonomous local administration. An example is the Anglo-French South Pacific condominium of New Hebrides, which existed from 1906 until 1980 when the territory became the independent state of Vanuatu.[19]

Condominium is a rare option that involves compromising territorial claims at both inter- and intra-state levels. It would only be relevant for a multi-ethnic contested state that is claimed by two or more existing states that may also have kinship ties with local communities.[20] The sole candidate among contemporary contested states that could remotely have qualified is Kosovo, if Serbia and Albania had been prepared to exercise joint jurisdiction over the territory (with its concurrence, of course). Kashmir, designated by the UN as an occupied territory whose final status has yet to be decided, could in theory qualify for a condominium under the joint jurisdiction of India and Pakistan. However, this would be exceedingly difficult to achieve given the historic enmity between the two powers, compounded by pro-independence sentiments in the Indian-controlled part of the divided territory.[21]

Free association

Originally conceived by the UN to cater for dependent territories regarded as too small and poor to become economically viable and politically stable independent states, associated statehood is based on a contractual protective relationship between such an entity and an adjacent, larger and more advanced state. The non-self-governing territories could then enter into a 'free association' with an established state as an expression of self-determination.[22] One precondition is that the association must be the result of 'free and voluntary choice by the peoples of the territory concerned expressed through informed and democratic processes'. Another requirement is that the associated territory has the right to determine its internal constitution without foreign interference, but allowance is made for 'consultations as appropriate or necessary' under the terms of the association agreement.[23] The reserved powers of the larger state (the principal) – usually defence and foreign affairs – should not give that party substantial discretion to intervene in the domestic affairs of the junior partner (the associate).[24]

In due course most of the dependent territories in free associations have advanced to independent statehood – while retaining their associated status. They have joined the UN and regional organizations, where they exercise their rights independent of their principals. Several associated states have also established their own diplomatic networks and acceded to multilateral treaties. By contrast the Cook Islands and Niue, associated with New Zealand, do not seem interested in independence or UN membership, but are nonetheless keen to play an active role on the international stage.[25] As Crawford pointed out, it is possible for an entity that is substantially dependent under its constituent instruments – as with an associated state – 'to acquire a measure of independence through independent action and the acceptance by other States of its capacity for independent action'.[26]

Apart from the association of the Cook Islands and Niue with New Zealand, other examples are the former West Indies Associated States (six states – Antigua, Dominica, Grenada, St Kitts-Nevis-Anguilla, St Lucia and St Vincent – associated with Britain); the Associated State of St Kitts-Nevis-Anguilla (also with Britain); the Freely Associated States of Micronesia (being the Federated States of Micronesia, Republic of the Marshall Islands and Republic of Palau, associated with the US); the Commonwealth of Puerto Rico (also associated with the US), and the Commonwealth of the Northern Mariana Islands (the US). All these arrangements comprise several 'substantial elements'. The first, already alluded to, is significant powers of self-government. Associated states usually control such matters as education, taxation, infrastructure and the judicial system. Second, the associate always has the unilateral right under international law to withdraw from the association arrangement. Third, the inhabitants of an associated state may enjoy citizenship rights in the larger state. Fourth, the stronger partners typically provide economic assistance to the weaker. Finally, the principal usually assumes responsibility for the defence of its associate.[27]

Could associated statehood be applied to contested states? The attraction of free association lies in its intermediate status between independence and integration.[28] As such the formula involves a compromise: on the one hand the original state will not be fully restored through the complete reintegration of the contested state, and on the other hand the contested state will have to scale down its ambitions of full-fledged independence. The contested state will moreover have to accept the status of junior partner in an unequal power relationship. It will nonetheless be assured of substantial self-government, enjoy international status even to the extent of qualified independence and membership of the UN, and be permitted to engage in foreign relations of its own. This application of associated statehood differs from the conventional format in that it involves only two parties (the contested state and the original state) and it is not of the 'saltwater' variety (where the senior partner is located overseas).

A potential problem area is that the associate has the unilateral right to terminate its free association with the principal. This means that the erstwhile contested state could withdraw from the arrangement, reassert its earlier independence and treat its former principal as a foreign state. It is a possibility with which the senior partner will have to contend and – if it regards the association arrangement as important enough – try to prevent such a contingency by making it worth the associate's while to remain in what is usually designed as a voluntary but durable partnership.[29]

The Hong Kong option

There are some parallels between the associated status just discussed and that of the Hong Kong Special Administrative Region of the People's Republic of China. The former British colony has a novel constitutional arrangement inconsistent with conventional notions of sovereignty: it is not juridically independent, yet boasts a distinct international legal status recognized by states.[30] An outstanding feature of Hong Kong's present order is its powers in foreign relations; the region enjoys 'probably the most extensive external autonomy that has ever existed in an autonomous region in the world, historical or current', according to Xu and Wilson.[31] A 'one state, two systems' formula comparable to that of Hong Kong within the Chinese state is what Beijing has long proposed for Taiwan. The latter has steadfastly rejected unification as long as mainland China remains under communist dictatorship. 'Self-government through an autonomous arrangement', also resembling that of Hong Kong, has likewise been mooted for Tibet by groups opposed to Beijing's direct rule over the territory.[32]

Protected states and protectorates

Protected statehood can also be regarded as a form of associated status, but the former usually involves two states only and they may be geographically proximate. According to Shaw, a protected state 'retains its status as a separate state but enters into a valid treaty relationship with another state affording the latter certain extensive functions possibly internally and externally'.[33] Because of this transfer of authority to another state, protected states have been variously portrayed as 'non-fully independent territories', 'semi-sovereign states' and 'a new form of international person, a sort of pre-state'. Examples include Morocco's earlier relationship with France under a bilateral treaty of 1912, Malaya, the British-protected Trucial States in the Persian Gulf, and the Indian territories of Bhutan and Sikkim.[34]

The division of powers between protector and protected states can vary. The latter may simply be obliged to take note of the advice of the protecting state, or it may involve 'a form of diplomatic delegation subject to instruction', as with Liechtenstein. Because Liechtenstein had surrendered sovereign powers to neighbouring Switzerland, it was considered incapable of discharging the international obligations imposed by the Covenant of the League of Nations and accordingly denied membership. Even so, Liechtenstein was in many respects treated as a sovereign state. In 1990 it joined the UN. Switzerland still conducts Liechtenstein's routine diplomatic affairs; the two countries maintain uniform customs, immigration and border policies; and Liechtenstein uses the Swiss currency.[35]

We should distinguish between a protected state and a protectorate. Mostly internal colonial arrangements, protectorates came about through treaties of protection between a colonial power and tribal entities that were not states. While legal personality may be involved under a protectorate arrangement, separate statehood is not. Somaliland was proclaimed a British protectorate in 1884. The territory retained this status until 1960, when it became independent for a few days prior to unification with the former Italian colony of Somaliland to form the new sovereign state of Somalia. In 1991 Somaliland issued a unilateral declaration of independence – and promptly became a contested state. Bechuanaland was first placed under British colonial protection in 1885, achieving independence in 1966.[36] A colonial background also shaped the status of Mayotte as a French overseas *Collectivité départementale*. Part of the Comoros archipelago, Mayotte is an integral part of the French Republic with representation in both the National Assembly and the Senate in Paris, as well as in the European Parliament. Executive power in Mayotte is exercised by the President of the locally elected General Council. A protective relationship of sorts also applies to Réunion, elevated to an Overseas Department of France in 1974, with the status of a region.[37]

With colonialism over, the notions of protected states and protectorates may seem outdated. They have, however, lately reappeared in the guise of *de facto* trusteeships. These are not the old UN trusteeships provided for in the Charter, but transitional administrations usually authorized by the Security Council. Resembling protectorates, the new form of trusteeship is a temporary measure designed to either prepare a dependent territory for *de jure* statehood or, conceivably, create conditions for the restoration of the legal sovereignty of a collapsed state. Namibia and East Timor were placed under UN administrations during their transitions from external occupation to sovereign independence, while Kosovo was placed under *de facto* UN trusteeship in 1999 pending a decision on its final status.[38] Kosovo's assumption of independence in February 2008 has not ended the UN presence there.

International status

Under this rubric we will be recording several proposals that involve foreign parties in creating or upholding an international status for particular entities. First, international status can be given to sub-national units like cities and regions. Examples of 'internationalized territories' include the Free City of Danzig (1450–1793, 1919–39), the Free City of Cracow (1815–46), the international zone of Tangier (1923–56), the Memel Territory (1924–39), and the Free City of Trieste (1947–75). An international status has also been proposed for Jerusalem to break the deadlock caused by rival Israeli and Palestinian claims to jurisdiction over the holy city. International status might be considered for contested cities and regions elsewhere, whether the contestants are from rival states or from opposing factions within the same state.[39]

The second proposal, Gottlieb's, calls for an international status for nations lacking their own states. At one level his scheme provides for the granting of 'a formal non-territorial status and a recognized standing internationally' for such nations. That standing would be analogous to the position that the Maastricht Treaty has afforded regions in the European Union. Gottlieb envisaged that non-territorial communities could be granted similar standing in other regional organizations like the Council of Europe and the Organization for Security and Cooperation in Europe.[40] At another more ambitious level Gottlieb argued for the formal extension of the existing system of states to allow for a parallel international system of nations. Participating nations would be accorded a new international legal standing that does not require the creation of new sovereign states. Under this proposal the UN General Assembly would create a novel status of 'Associated People of the United Nations' for nations that are democratically organized on a non-territorial basis. The member nations should gain the right to become parties to different types of treaties, address selected UN organs and participate in the work of international bodies.[41]

A third and entirely different kind of international status has been proposed for and indeed applied to some aspirant states. It goes by various names, including 'earned recognition', 'qualified independence' and 'conditional statehood'. In a preparatory phase the entity would be groomed for sovereign independence, as in the case of contemporary *de facto* trusteeship. To ensure internationally recognized independence the entity should make adequate provision in its laws and political structures for upholding specific standards of conduct. These could relate to observing democracy, individual human rights and minority rights; respecting international borders; resolving disputes peacefully; combating international terrorism, and preventing the proliferation of weapons of mass destruction. Former republics of the Yugoslav federation gained internationally recognized statehood under such conditions.

Conditional statehood could, in the fourth place, extend beyond a purported state's pre-independence obligations to include post-independence commitments as well. The latter could be formalized in an international accord freely concluded between the emerging state and foreign parties, possibly acting under the aegis of a multilateral organization. The agreement could provide for external monitoring of the actual observance of pre-independence undertakings and ways of dealing with non-compliance. Proposals to this effect have been made for Kosovo and Nagorno Karabagh, as our case studies will record. A related fifth type of international status allows for direct foreign involvement in the authority structures of a new state. Krasner called it a system of shared sovereignty, which should be based on a voluntary agreement between the parties involved.[42] In both the latter arrangements, which could be combined in practice, the new entity would enjoy international legal sovereignty but its autonomy would be restricted. A further external element that could be added to both formulas would be international guarantees of statehood. Foreign parties thus act as the guarantors of the new country's independence by protecting it against external and internal threats. Such provisions could be open-ended or limited in duration by means of a sunset clause in the relevant agreements.

While exceptional, conditional statehood is not unknown. Consider the restoration of Austria's independence in 1955 under the Austrian State Treaty concluded by the four occupying powers. They agreed to withdraw, while Austria by law became a permanently neutral state. Cyprus can rightly be called an 'international state' because it was given independence in 1960 by three foreign powers – Britain, Greece and Turkey – who under a formal treaty also served as guarantors of its independence.[43] Particular versions of conditional independence might in at least some cases offer a way out of the impasse in which contested states and their opponents find themselves.

Regional entities

So-called regional states or region-states come in two shapes, neither of which constitutes a separate new state but their creation involves international cooperation. The more ambitious version is an economic zone composed of two or more whole states (say, the US, Canada and Mexico, or the states of West Africa). The lesser form joins adjacent regions located in different states together in an economic unit. Examples of the latter type are found in the Baltic region, the Barents Sea area (linking the north-western regions of Russia with Finland and Sweden), both banks of the Rhine River, the Vienna-Budapest-Prague triangle, the two sides of the Alps in France and Italy, and both the French and Spanish parts of the eastern Pyrenées. Whether on an inter-state or sub-state basis, the purpose of economic integration is the development of the region.[44]

Herbst has in turn proposed that foreign donors should devise aid projects in Africa 'with a true regional scope and which allocate funds to recipients irrespective of the country they are in'. By treating sections of Africa as regions instead of using existing states as the 'unit of analysis', donors could according to Herbst advance the development of a new intellectual framework for considering alternatives to the current state system in Africa. This quest is motivated by the need to replace Africa's dysfunctional states (what others have called failed or quasi-states) with more viable units – which may not necessarily be sovereign states.[45] If a rebellious region could be involved in – and derive both material and symbolic benefits from – a transnational economic zone or a regional development area, it may go some way towards dampening secessionist fervour and preventing the emergence of a contested state.

Should an economic region have a largely homogenous population, the entity could at the same time constitute a transnational cultural domain.[46] This resembles Gottlieb's idea of a national home, being an entity with defined geographic frontiers that extends across state borders. Members of the same ethnic group living in adjacent independent states could thus be drawn together in a national home. They would retain the citizenship of their existing states while enjoying the nationality of their common group, thereby expressing the shared identity of the inhabitants of the national home. The central governments of the states involved would decide on the delegation of powers to the national home. The most obvious candidates for a national home are the Kurds. Again, the option is proposed as an alternative to all-out statehood for the Kurds at the expense of the territorial integrity of their existing countries of residence.[47] Abdullah Ocalan, jailed leader of the Kurdistan Workers' Party, a rebel movement in Turkey, evidently had a similar scheme in mind with his Declaration of Democratic Confederalism in Kurdistan, issued in 2005. He proposed that the Kurdish areas of Turkey, Iran Iraq and Syria be united in a cross-border 'confederation'. Although the entity should have a name and its own flag, Ocalan emphasized that it would not be a sovereign state – a recognition of the fierce opposition of the four states involved to the creation of a Kurdish state out of slices of their national territories.[48] The term 'confederation' is then a misnomer for what amounts to a transnational cultural domain.

The notion of a 'Europe of the Regions' combines regional integration and sub-national autonomy. It is based on the principle of subsidiarity, meaning government tasks should be performed at the level closest to the people – embodied in the 1992 (Maastricht) Treaty on European Union. Should subsidiarity be applied fully, Europe's 'nations without states' could gain a new international status: the English, Scots and Catalonians, among others, would 'sit at the same table enjoying a similar degree of political autonomy' while most of their policies are decided by a European Parliament in which they are all represented.[49] Such a scenario embodies two important developments. First, it is indicative of the rise of nations without states as global political actors in the 21st century, functioning within international or supranational political and economic institutions.[50] The second development concerns a redefinition of independence and sovereignty on the part of long-standing nationalist movements in the Western world in particular. Doyle referred to a new 'cosmopolitan nationalism' and 'flexible sovereignty' guiding political movements that have converted themselves from nationalist-separatist parties in the traditional mould to regional-autonomy parties. The Scottish, Catalan and Basque communities, to name a few, have political vehicles sharing a vision of national self-determination that is comfortable with European integration, open to a globalized world, and articulates a relative conception of sovereignty which accepts that key economic, monetary and possibly security policies will no longer be decided at the level of the independent state.[51]

Talbott drew on 'the great experiment in Europe' in arguing that the rise of interdependence between states offered a better remedy for separatist conflicts than did secession. This alternative is 'to combine the promotion of democracy on the part of the central government with an effort to help would-be break-away areas benefit from cross-border economic development and political cooperation'. The protection of the rights of minorities through a democratic order provided the best insurance against separatism. Once they feel secure in their identities and neighbourhoods – as many European minorities do – groups in Asia, Africa and elsewhere should feel confident enough to seize the opportunities offered by porous borders and interlinked economies – the products of globalization 'and its sub-phenomenon, regionalization'.[52]

Territorial rightsizing

A final and very different inter-state alternative is the so-called rightsizing of existing states. By adjusting established international frontiers, a region may be excised from one state and added to an adjacent country, or neighbouring states could exchange portions of territory. This could be done to (re)unite members of a particular ethnic group, especially if they had previously formed part of a single political entity. Thus a group may wish to leave an existing political union not to form their own, but to join another. An illustration of such a mixed secessionist-irredentist claim is the Transylvanian people of Romania, who desire becoming part of Hungary. More ambitiously, boundary adjustments could be designed to achieve greater correspondence between state frontiers and ethnic identities.[53]

Africa is arguably the continent most in need of territorial rightsizing. 'There is nothing remiss about altering state frontiers in the nobler interests of domestic tranquillity and economic growth, which are now so scarce in these [African] lands', Chege wrote in 1991.[54] Another African intellectual, Mazrui, made the bold claim that over the coming century 'the outlines of most present-day African states' will change in one of two major ways. First, ethnic self-determination will create smaller states, as in the case of Eritrea's divorce from Ethiopia. This separation broke the post-colonial taboo of officially endorsed secession. Second, regional integration will lead Africa towards larger political communities and economic unions. These two factors, he foresaw, will loosen the 'bondage of boundaries' in the continent.[55] Wole Soyinka, the Nigerian author and Nobel laureate, joined in with an impassioned plea to Africans to 'sit down with square-rule and compass and redesign the boundaries of African nations'. The horrors of the Rwanda genocide made it abundantly clear that Africans 'cannot evade this historical challenge any longer'.[56] A more specific proposal 'to disassemble African states and reconfigure them' was made by wa Mutua in the mid-1990s. Motivated by the need to 'legitimize the African state and avoid its demise', wa Mutua's radical new cartography envisaged the 53 existing African states being compressed into 14 larger entities.[57]

Herbst made a case for 'greater flexibility in national design' as a means towards increasing the congruence between the way power is actually exercised in Africa and the design of political units. He acknowledged that there are few 'natural' borders in Africa that correspond with ethnic, economic or geographic realities. Herbst was also sensitive to the concern that the recognition of new African states born of redrawn boundaries could set off a fragmentation process producing ever-smaller polities. However, 'the reality of disintegrating, dysfunctional African states stands in such contrast to the legal fiction of sovereign states', he countered, that 'experimentation with regard to new states' was warranted. The borders drawn arbitrarily during the scramble for Africa were no longer tenable and the time was ripe to discard the 'dogmatic devotion' to inherited boundaries. To prevent an uncontrollable proliferation of new African states, Herbst proposed strict criteria for state recognition.[58]

Territorial adjustments are admittedly easier advocated than executed, especially in Africa. The Cairo Resolution, adopted by the Organization of African Unity in 1964, proclaimed that 'the borders of African States, on the day of their independence, constitute a tangible reality' and member states had a duty to respect inherited colonial boundaries.[59] At stake is also a principle of international law. In implementing the right of self-determination, the 1970 Declaration on Friendly Relations among States read, no action may be taken 'which would dismember or impair, totally or in part, the territorial integrity or political unity of sovereign and independent States'. However, if rightsizing is not of an order that would require massive population transfers and leave the affected state(s) severely dismembered and impoverished, this option could lead the parties involved to an amicable parting of the ways and avoid the emergence of contested states.

Intra-state arrangements

The next set of alternatives contains ways of accommodating population diversity, especially in what Lijphart termed deeply divided or plural societies, marked by pronounced cleavages along religious, ideological, linguistic, cultural, ethnic or racial lines 'into virtually separate subsocieties'.[60] These are essentially compromise options that may resolve ethnic conflicts and forestall secessionist bids. A good many of the alternatives provide for some form of power-sharing, that is the involvement of representatives of all significant communities in political decision-making. This is not coincidental: 'one common feature marking those societies that have been able to remain peaceful despite conflicts of language, religion, or ethnicity', Bogdanor observed, is that none followed the Westminster model of majority rule. Instead, they opted for power-sharing, often not only in parliaments and cabinets but also in the civil service, judiciary, police and military.[61] Alternatively, communities could be granted substantial powers of self-government or autonomy. The intra-state alternatives would thus restore or preserve the territorial integrity of the original state and preclude independent statehood for sub-national groups while allowing for a meaningful improvement in their position. Many of the options overlap or are complementary, allowing for a combination of arrangements in practice.

A return to the *status quo ante* through a contested state's reincorporation into its original state does not feature among the intra-state alternatives. We should acknowledge, though, that the restoration of the old order may occur if a contested state is militarily defeated by the original state (like Katanga and Biafra) or lacks the material resources and political will to continue its rebellion. With our focus now on compromise solutions, this zero-sum outcome (like conventional recognition) is by definition precluded from the range of alternatives to the *status quo*. Since we are interested in arrangements that accommodate demographic diversity, we should also rule out measures to eliminate ethnic differences, including genocide (the mass-extermination of an ethnic collectivity), forced mass-population transfers (ethnic cleansing) and compulsory assimilation (the merging of differences to create a common ethnic identity).[62] For the same reason we exclude 'control regimes' in the shape of coercive domination (like apartheid in South Africa and previous Serb policy in Kosovo) and co-opted rule (as in colonial regimes).[63]

Federalism

It is appropriate to begin with federalism, one of the most familiar political formulas for the accommodation of population plurality. Multinational federations, which are especially relevant for our purposes, belong to what Lijphart termed an incongruent type of federation. This is where internal boundaries tend to coincide with ethnic borders. (In congruent federations the territorial components display social and cultural characteristics that are similar in each unit and in the federation as a whole.)[64] One of the attractions of federalism is that it offers a group that constitutes a minority in the population at large but a majority in a specific territorial area the opportunity to exercise some local autonomy or self-government, meaning the group has the authority to conduct its own internal affairs, particularly in the realms of culture and education. Another is that federal-based recognition of minority groups allows for the management of inter-group conflicts that could otherwise culminate in violence, territorial fragmentation and the proliferation of 'mini-statelets of limited viability'. Finally, the preservation of minority group rights through a federal arrangement can be defended as a counter to cultural assimilation into a majority community.[65]

An essential feature of a federation is that the central and provincial or regional governments have separate spheres of power, but may also have concurrent powers.[66] All the component units of a federation may have equal powers, or the national constitution can provide for an asymmetric arrangement. In the latter case some provinces have greater powers than others, whether in recognition of their separate identities and distinct interests or simply to pre-empt secessionist pressures. The Basque region and Catalonia in Spain and Tatarstan in Russia are examples of such federal units. The Russian case is particularly interesting given the size and diversity of its self-styled 'democratic federate rule-of-law state'. The country is home to over 60 officially recognized minority nationalities and Russia comprises no fewer than 89 'federal subjects', of which 21 are higher-status ethno-republics and 68 are lower-level subjects (regions, territories, autonomous districts and the federal cities of Moscow and St Petersburg). The accommodation of national minorities occurs largely through representation at the ethno-republic level. Such is the extent of asymmetry that dozens of its 89 constituent units enjoy varying degrees of privileged status, none more so than Tatarstan. Among the other contemporary federations catering for population diversity are Belgium, Switzerland and Canada.[67]

In both asymmetrical and some 'standard' federations, the component units have become energetic actors on the world stage, even enjoying the status of persons under international law.[68]

A moot point about federalism in general and the decentralization of power to ethnically-based regions in particular, is whether this arrangement would inflate or deflate ethnic nationalism and thus encourage or erode demands for separate statehood. Some scholars maintain that federalism tends to reduce nationalism; others argue the very opposite, while a third position holds that the strength of nationalism is not determined by federalism *per se*.[69] While federalism's mixed record as a device for regulating conflict in multinational states could deter some rulers, choosing this option may be a risk worth taking if other alternatives hold less promise of preserving peace and territorial unity.

For a disaffected community, federalism means – as with our other intrastate alternatives – renouncing claims to full statehood. Very few federations allow constituent units the option of divorce. Although Russia's original Federal Treaty of 1992 gave ethno-republics the right to secede, the 1993 federal constitution conferred no such right. Chechnya and Tatarstan are the only two republics that have since 1991 sought independence from Moscow, whereas their counterparts agitate for greater autonomy only.[70] Ethiopia's current federal constitution is exceptional in acknowledging 'an unconditional right to self-determination, including the right to secession' for 'every nation, nationality and people' in the country.

Other forms of territorial autonomy

It is possible for a self-defined community to enjoy autonomy within a state framework without a full-blown federation being created. Territorial autonomy can be implemented to varying degrees, ranging from administrative autonomy (executive discretion within the framework of central laws) to full self-government (where a group elects its own legislature and assumes responsibility for most of the executive and administrative functions normally undertaken by central state institutions).[71] Autonomy arrangements go by several other designations too, including devolution, decentralization, self-rule and cantonization. The latter is of course associated with Switzerland – admittedly a federation – and involves 'a micropartition in which political power is devolved to (conceivably very small) political units, each of which enjoys mini-sovereignty'. The cantons are built on the recognition of ethnic diversity and permit asymmetrical relations among themselves and between cantons and the federal government. Cantonization is similar to but not coterminous with federalism as a device for managing ethnic heterogeneity. For one thing, the regions or provinces in federations are normally far larger than cantons.[72] Whatever the designation and scale of the units, we are in essence dealing with the devolution of political power to a political entity that is substantially controlled by an ethnic minority and by and large corresponds with their historical territory (for example, Scotland and the Basque region).[73]

Among the rights and powers that communities can exercise are those relating to political matters (including the choice of a people to be ruled by leaders of their own community, and the structures of representative government), economic and financial affairs (natural resources, infrastructure, industry, tax collection and the like), judicial administration and law enforcement (courts of law and police service), socio-cultural interests (education, language, museums, religion and other aspects related to the protection of collective identity and dignity), international involvement (representation in some global and regional organizations and participation in international conferences), and care for the natural environment.[74]

Practical examples of extensive communal autonomy abound. The Sami people of Finland not only enjoy regional autonomy through their elected parliament, but they also have the authority to represent the community at the international level. Only four subject-matters are excluded from the jurisdiction of the Crimean autonomous republic in Ukraine: national defence, monetary policy, the maintenance of national frontiers, and certain aspects of international relations. Greenland's home rule embraces far reaching domestic and foreign aspects. The territory has, for instance, withdrawn from the EU, while Denmark remains a member. In Britain, powers have been devolved from the centre to Northern Ireland as well as Wales and Scotland. In the latter case this move was not unrelated to the presence of a vocal independence movement. Among the other communities for which autonomy arrangements have been made, are the Inuits in Canada, Kuna Yala in Panama, the indigenous people of the Chittagong Hill region in Bangladesh, the German community in South Tyrol, the German minority in Belgium and national minorities in Estonia.[75] In the Union of the Comoros the three constituent islands enjoy considerable autonomy, each with its own president, government and legislative assembly. The islands freely administer their respective affairs, establish their own fundamental laws and are financially autonomous. The position of President of the Union (head of state) rotates between the three islands.[76]

It should be reiterated that, despite enjoying extensive autonomy, the particular community or region remains an integral part of the state concerned, is represented (whether as a group or as individual citizens) in the national legislature and is firmly integrated into the national economy. The purpose of giving the community maximum autonomy is not to encourage centripetal forces, but instead to steer it away from 'the slippery slope to state-shattering secession'.[77]

Non-territorial autonomy

Up to now we have focused on territorially-based autonomy for specific minorities. While perhaps less fashionable and appealing, powers of self-government need not be territorially bound; they can be exercised by members of a community regardless of where they live in the state. This is known as group or cultural autonomy, non-territorial autonomy or, where appropriate, corporate federalism.[78] The idea is often traced back to the *millet* system of autonomy for religious groups in the Ottoman Empire. In the late 19th century Austrian social democrats Karl Renner and Otto Bauer proposed a democratic version of cultural autonomy in the Habsburg monarchy. Their plan, never implemented, combined the conventional territorial principle of representation with a 'personality principle'.[79] Russia is one country that nowadays acknowledges the rights of cultural autonomy of communities not represented as constituent federal units. Its dispersed German minority exercises such rights, but has also been allowed to establish two culturally autonomous districts within Omsk and Altai.[80] In their post-1919 constitutions Latvia, Lithuania and Estonia guaranteed a measure of cultural and educational autonomy to national minorities. Upon regaining their independence in 1990 and 1991, the three Baltic states reintroduced some of these provisions.[81] Non-territorial autonomy has proven successful in India, Belgium and the Netherlands too, and has been proposed as a supplement to territorial divisions of power for communities living geographically interspersed in Northern Ireland, South Tyrol-Alto Adige and some parts of Central and Eastern Europe.[82]

Consociational democracy

Based on the recognition of ethnic pluralism, consociational democracy is designed to secure the identities, rights, freedoms and opportunities of all ethnic groups and to create institutions that allow them to enjoy the benefits of equality. It rests on four basic principles: government by grand coalition involving parties from different segments of society; segmental autonomy, especially in the cultural domain; proportionality in political representation, civil service employment and the allocation of public funds; and minority vetoes on issues vital to minorities. Classic examples of consociation include Switzerland, Austria, the Netherlands and Belgium; more recently a consociational model was introduced in Bosnia and Herzegovina under the Dayton Peace Agreement (1995). The fact that this system failed in Cyprus, Lebanon, Fiji and Malaysia suggests that particular societal conditions need to exist for consociational democracy to succeed. These include overarching loyalties binding the different groups together, a small number of competing political parties in each segment, roughly equally-sized segments, and a tradition of compromise among political elites.[83]

Given its stringent conditions for success, consociational democracy may have limited relevance for the conflict situations on which our inquiry focuses. Other less demanding techniques of power-sharing could be more appropriate in addressing the political marginalization and alienation of communities.

Multiculturalism

Advocates of multiculturalism like to remind us of the established fact that no contemporary state is entirely homogenous 'as a single culture and breeding population'; most states contain no fewer than five ethnic groups. While sharing the same territory, different groups may wish to maintain their distinct cultures. The classic model of multicultural politics is to be found in the late Austro-Hungarian Empire. In some regions every citizen had the right to freely choose his or her own ethnicity, and each ethnic community was guaranteed representation in the provincial parliament in proportion to its share of the population – regardless of where the members were located territorially.[84]

Multiculturalism is the foundation for the notion of cultural liberty, as propounded by the UN Development Programme in its *Human Development Report 2004*. Cultural liberty is said to be about 'allowing people the freedom to choose their identities – and to lead the lives they value – without being excluded from other choices important to them', for instance in education, health and employment. This requires states to recognize cultural differences in their constitutions, laws and institutions. They should also devise policies to ensure that the interests of particular communities are not ignored or overridden by the majority or by dominant groups. The Report singled out five key areas requiring multicultural policies. In the domain of political participation, multicultural democracy requires effective mechanisms for power sharing or self-government. Specific policies are also needed to ensure religious freedom, legal pluralism, the use of various languages, and advance justice and equality in the socio-economic sphere.[85] Most of these prescriptions also feature under our other intra-state alternatives already recorded.

Further options

For the sake of brevity other known techniques for the political accommodation of demographic plurality are listed in point-form only.

- Cultural recognition has been portrayed as a 'soft' option in a state's recognition of internal diversity. It presupposes a unitary state that merely acknowledges certain cultural traits as 'specific characteristics of a territorially-based national minority'. A minimal degree of decentralization may be permitted and a regional language (if it exists) may be promoted. This had applied by and large to Scotland prior to the election of its newly created Parliament in 1999.[86]
- Another soft option is what Kymlicka and Norman called symbolic recognition of the worth, status or existence of groups within the broader state society. It involves various forms of group recognition in the institutions, symbols and political culture of the larger state, such as the name of the state, its flag, the national anthem, the coat of arms, its public

holidays, and the portrayal of different groups' histories in schools and textbooks.[87]

- A more substantive alternative is the observance of universally recognized minority rights as enshrined in, among numerous other documents, the UN Declaration on the Rights of Persons belonging to National, or Ethnic, Religious and Linguistic Minorities (1992). These typically include the minority's right to enjoy its culture, use its language, profess and practise its religion, and participate effectively in public life and in all decisions affecting the particular group. The full observance of minority rights, through a democratic political order, may prevent political disaffection that could feed secessionist drives.[88]
- Non-territorial electoral constituencies, which have been proposed in Canada among other places, reminds one of the Austro-Hungarian formula. A Canadian electoral reform commission recommended it as a means of guaranteeing representation to aboriginal people, wherever they lived in Canada. It is an arrangement that could conceivably work for other minorities living dispersed outside the 'home' region of the group, as the Tamils in Sri Lanka. By voting as a single constituency, a community would be fairly represented in the legislature – and so possibly leave it with less incentive to engage in secessionist politics.[89]
- Special representation rights could include measures to make political parties more representative of minority groups, the reservation of a certain number of seats in the legislature for minorities, or separate electoral rolls for different communities.[90]
- Weighted majorities in the legislature may be required when deciding issues affecting the interests of particular groups. This so-called suspensive veto has been used in Belgium and Cyprus.[91]
- Regular weighted referendums increase a minority's chances of influencing decisions on matters of major importance to the group. In a referendum featuring, say, 20 propositions and voters having 20 votes each, they are allowed to 'spend' their votes as they please. A voter could, for instance, cast all 20 votes in support of a proposition about which he or she feels very strongly.[92]
- A group veto right and a right of nullification are further constitutional devices to protect minority interests. The former grants a group the right to veto legislation (for example, an attempt to elevate another group's language to the official national language), while the latter allows a group to void legislation in only its jurisdiction (for instance, a tax law amounting to discriminatory redistribution).[93]
- Local secession involves a territorial divorce from a subordinate political unit to create a new one. The Swiss Constitution permits cantons to split into 'half-cantons' (but not to exit the Swiss Confederation).[94]
- More ambitious internal territorial adjustments could also be made to end or prevent turf battles between ethnic groups. A recent move in this

direction was the plan devised by the UN Secretary-General's Special Representative for Iraq to resolve disputes over the borders of the autonomous Kurdistan Region.[95]

Conclusion

Three main considerations informed the survey of alternatives to contested statehood. The first is that very few contested states will receive unqualified *de jure* recognition and join the community of confirmed states. Second, life in international limbo cannot (beyond the short term) satisfy either contested states or the international community. Third, while forcible reincorporation into their original countries may be the fate of some contested states, it is an unattractive option because of its violent nature.

Fortunately there is a wide spectrum of conceivable alternative destinations for contested states, opening up possibilities for peacefully resolving the problems of existing contested states and preventing the emergence of more such entities in future. The variety of options means there is no need for a one-size-fits-all approach in dealing with contested states. The differences in the entities' domestic and external situations would in any case militate against a standard settlement formula. The relevance of several of the proposals has been supported by findings of the Center for International Development and Conflict Management. Where self-determination conflicts have been settled, provision was made for improved access of aggrieved groups to government decision-making, for regional autonomy, the devolution of central power and the redrawing of internal boundaries.[96]

All the alternatives we have identified involve compromises since they fall short of the first preferences of contested states (full international recognition of their statehood) and of original states (a return to the *status quo ante*). Finding an appropriate compromise solution depends on a host of domestic and international variables with which the parties involved have to contend. The dynamics of each contested state will be probed in the case studies presented in Part II.

Part II
Case Studies

4
The Eurasian Quartet

The life cycles of the four contested states of Eurasia reveal striking similarities in respect of their origins, current existence and possible future status. Abkhazia, South Ossetia, Transdniestria and Nagorno Karabagh are moreover located in the space of the former Soviet Union but none are formally part of Russia. The foursome owed their contested statehood to the dissolution of the Soviet Union, taking up arms individually to break free from successor states they considered alien, unrepresentative and repressive. The post-Soviet states involved are Georgia (in the cases of Abkhazia and South Ossetia), Moldova (Transdniestria) and Azerbaijan (Nagorno Karabagh). For these reasons it makes sense to examine the Eurasian quartet – incidentally among the youngest of today's contested states – as a group.

Abkhazia

The territory of Abkhazia, extending over roughly 8,600 km^2 (slightly smaller than Cyprus), is located at the western end of Georgia and has a coastline on the Black Sea. In the north and northeast the Caucasus Mountains separate Abkhazia from Russia. Beyond these incontestable geographic markers, other basic features of Abkhazia's existence are hotly disputed. The Abkhazians insisted that they had never chosen to become part of Georgia in the 20th century but were forced to do so when the Soviet Union's borders were demarcated. They portrayed themselves as a distinct community with an ancient culture: their language differed from Georgian, being related to the Adyghe people of the Northwest Caucasus; whereas the Georgians followed the Christian Orthodox religion, Abkhazians were nominally Muslim; and they had an ancestral link to the Abkhazian territory based on three millennia of continuous occupation.[1] Their struggles against foreign occupiers over the centuries have moreover forged Abkhazian self-identity and nationhood. The Georgian historical narrative by contrast emphasized that the rulers of Abkhazia had for generations until 1810 maintained nominal or effective union with kingdoms and princedoms of Georgia.[2]

The year 1810 marked Abkhazia's absorption into the Russian Empire as a protectorate enjoying the status of a sovereign principality. Russia's revocation of Abkhazia's autonomy in 1864 sparked the first major Abkhazian revolt against the imperial power. Another occurred in 1877. Russia's response to such challenges was severe repression combined with the expulsion of Abkhazians from their homeland. Between 120,000 and 200,000 of them fled to the Ottoman Empire.[3] A new period of repression in Abkhazia began in the wake of the 1917 Russian revolution. Abkhazia joined the Union of United Mountain Peoples of the Caucasus, which was in 1918 remade into the North Caucasian Republic with Abkhazia one of its constituent units. Shortly thereafter the Georgian Democratic Republic was proclaimed. Within weeks Georgia invaded Abkhazia and subjected it to harsh military rule until 1921.[4]

If the period 1918–21 kept reminding the Abkhazians of the horror of Georgian rule, the years 1921–31 were regarded as the source of their contemporary statehood. An independent Soviet Socialist Republic of Abkhazia did indeed exist – but from only March to December 1921. Abkhazia possessed such trappings of statehood as its own flag and emblem and the right to adopt its own laws. The Georgian Soviet Socialist Republic (SSR) even recognized the independence of Abkhazia, the two having equal status. At the close of 1921, however, Stalin compelled Abkhazia to join the Georgian SSR under the Union Agreement that provided for a confederal formula of sorts. It was an asymmetrical arrangement in that Abkhazia delegated some of its powers to Georgia and did not have membership of any regional or international organization separate from Georgia. Even so Abkhazia's constitution of 1925 defined it as a sovereign state and subject of international law. That formal status could not prevent Abkhazia's further demotion in 1931 to an autonomous republic within Georgia.[5] Abkhazians still resent the latter move as forcible incorporation into Georgia on Stalin's orders.

The 'systematic assault on Abkhazian culture' between the 1930s and the 1950s was another vivid memory that has kept shaping the community's political preferences. A campaign driven by Josef Stalin (a Georgian) and Lavrenti Beria (also a Georgian who was Communist Party boss in Georgia in the 1930s and later KGB chief) aimed at obliterating the Abkhazians as a cultural community. The means included the forced exile of Abkhazians and the compulsory resettlement of Georgians, Armenians and Russians in Abkhazia, thereby reducing the ethnic Abkhazians' share of Abkhazia's population from 28 per cent in 1926 to 13 per cent in 1950. All schools using Abkhazian as the medium of instruction were closed and Georgian made the compulsory language of teaching, Abkhazian-language radio broadcasts were stopped and Abkhazian newspapers and journals ceased publication. The process of 'Georgianization' even extended to the methodical assassination of virtually the entire political and intellectual elite of the

Abkhazian community. Economic discrimination gave Abkhazia a smaller *per capita* share of the state budget and relatively lower capital investment than Georgia.[6]

Following the deaths of Stalin and Beria in 1953 the Georgianization campaign was reversed as the Abkhazian language was reintroduced into teaching, broadcasting and publishing. The new flexibility was seized by the Abkhazians to stage a number of protest rallies between the 1950s and the 1970s demanding Abkhazia's exit from the Georgian SSR. That possibility was not entertained by either the Georgian or Soviet authorities, who sought to placate the Abkhazians through major capital investment in infrastructural projects and affirmative action programmes.[7] The calculated beneficence failed in this purpose as Abkhazians' demands for political reforms intensified, especially in the new political space opened up by President Mikhail Gorbachev in the 1980s. The Georgians likewise exploited the unprecedented degree of freedom extended by Moscow to push their own independence agenda. The scene was set for a serious clash of nationalisms.

Secession and war

The Georgian Supreme Soviet threw down the gauntlet in November 1989 by asserting Georgia's sovereignty, including its right to secede from the Soviet Union. The announcement was based on the conviction that Georgia's union with the USSR constituted an 'annexation' brought about by military force and occupation. In August 1990 the Abkhazian Supreme Soviet followed suit by declaring the territory's sovereignty – a proclamation promptly ruled null and void by the Georgian legislature. The next step towards the looming showdown was the all-union referendum of March 1991 on the question of the Soviet Union's continued existence. Whereas the Georgians boycotted the poll, just over half the Abkhazian electorate participated – and 98 per cent of them supported the retention of the USSR. Georgians took the verdict as confirmation of the Abkhazian complicity in Russia's subversion of Georgia. Abkhazian voters, by contrast, feared that being part of an independent Georgia would leave them more vulnerable to persecution and even liquidation than before. By in effect supporting the Union Treaty, Abkhazians expressed a preference for staying in the Soviet Union – but leaving Georgia. This choice, the Abkhazians asserted, was permitted under the 1990 Soviet law on withdrawal from the USSR.[8]

A fortnight after the Soviet referendum, a Georgian national referendum was held to decide the issue of independence. This time Abkhazian voters opted for a boycott, but again 98 per cent of those who voted supported 'the restoration of the independence of Georgia' based on the independence declaration of 1918.[9] In April 1991 the Georgian Supreme Soviet duly proclaimed the republic's independence. Not only was Abkhazia left stranded inside a Georgia that had unilaterally declared its independence, but the protective umbrella of the Soviet Union was folding up. The Abkhazians' sense of foreboding was strengthened after the newly installed military rulers in Tbilisi in 1992 announced the reintroduction of Georgia's 1921 constitution. Concerned that this move would result in the abolition of Abkhazia's autonomous status, the Abkhazian Supreme Soviet proposed a federal or confederal link with Georgia. Eliciting no response from Tbilisi, the Abkhazian legislature in mid-1992 reintroduced its 1925 constitution, in effect declaring Abkhazia a sovereign entity no longer part of Georgia.[10]

The mounting tensions culminated in open warfare when Georgian troops invaded Abkhazia in August 1992. They soon took the capital Sukhumi, where the invaders made a point of attacking government buildings and major cultural centres. The Georgians also destroyed infrastructure and private property over a wide front, plundered farms and plantations and killed about 5,000 people.[11] Thanks to Russian military assistance and the involvement of mercenaries from a shadowy militarized political organization called the Confederation of the Peoples of the Caucasus, Abkhazian forces managed to turn the tide and recapture lost territory. By the end of 1993 the war was effectively over, but it was only in May 1994 that the two sides signed a peace agreement under UN auspices with Russian facilitation. Apart from a ceasefire, the accord provided for the separation of forces and the deployment of peacekeepers. The Commonwealth of Independent States Peacekeeping Forces (CISPKF), composed entirely of Russians, were deployed in a strip of territory between Georgia and Abkhazia in June 1994. The United Nations Observer Mission in Georgia (UNOMIG) was also created under the peace agreement and mandated by the Security Council to monitor the ceasefire and observe the operation of the peacekeepers.[12] In addition Georgia and Abkhazia have since the end of 1993 engaged in negotiations under the Geneva Peace Process, producing a number of bilateral agreements on such matters as the return of refugees, the creation of a joint coordinating council between the two parties, and measures to stabilize conditions on the two sides of their *de facto* border. Chaired by the UN and again facilitated by Russia, the latter initiative included observers from the OSCE and the Group of Friends of the UN Secretary-General (comprising representatives from Russia, America, Britain, France and Germany).[13] The UN's ongoing engagement with the issue of Abkhazia since then has also taken the form of fact-finding missions to the territory, the Secretary-General's appointment of a special envoy to Georgia, the provision of humanitarian aid by UN specialized agencies, and the Security Council's adoption of a series of resolutions designed to end the conflict.[14]

Despite steps towards peace, the war of 1992–3 has left a lasting legacy of bitterness and mistrust between Georgia and its break-away region, thus bedevilling the search for a durable solution to the secessionist conflict. During the hostilities both sides committed atrocities such as ethnic cleansing and indiscriminate attacks on civilians. Neither side has since investigated war crimes or crimes against humanity, thus adding to the mutual antagonism.[15] For the Abkhazians the travails of the war reinforced their historical sense of vulnerability and persecution at the hands of the Georgians. By attacking their country, they believed, the Georgians had forfeited any moral right to rule Abkhazia.[16] The territory's future could therefore not be a continuation of the past. As Abkhazian Foreign Minister Sergei Shamba vowed in 1997, 'we have no intention of giving up our independence'. Under 'the alternative scenario', as he called it, 'there exists a real threat of annihilation for the Abkhazian race'.[17]

Ethnic Georgians also suffered grievously in the war: between 10,000 and 30,000 of them may have died and between 250,000 and 300,000 were forced out of Abkhazia, most of them seeking refuge in Georgia proper.[18] This exodus more than halved Abkhazia's pre-war population of approximately 525,000 (of whom roughly 45 per cent were Georgians, 17 per cent ethnic Abkhazians and the remainder comprising various other groups).[19] While Abkhazia has since 1994 allowed about 45,000 ethnic Georgians to return to its Gali region (their main historical area of settlement), Sukhumi feared that a wholesale return of Georgian refugees would again reduce the ethnic Abkhazians to a tiny minority in their 'own' country.[20]

For the Georgians the war confirmed their suspicions that the conflict over Abkhazia was a direct consequence of Russia's ambitions to retain hegemony in its 'near abroad' through a policy of divide and rule. As President Mikheil Saakashvili saw it, the conflicts in Abkhazia and also South Ossetia were political rather than ethnic in nature, imposed on Georgia by 'post-Soviet forces, the remnants of the old Soviet imperial mentality'. Their purpose was 'to seize control of at least some of the neighbouring territories – Georgia was the most attractive to gobble up – or, at the very least, to create problems for Georgia'.[21] Such a view by implication denied that the Abkhazians were pursuing a legitimate quest for self-determination, but were instead mere pawns in a strategy orchestrated in Moscow. This explains why Georgia tended to treat Abkhazia 'as a subject to be disputed with Russia, not a negotiations partner in its own right'.[22]

State-building and foreign relations

The Abkhazians have since the war set about building a state they hoped would be worthy of international recognition – or at least attract recognition for being an enduring reality that cannot be ignored or wished away. The state-building project received a measure of external endorsement through the Declaration on Measures for a Political Settlement of the Georgian/Abkhazian Conflict signed between Abkhazia and Georgia in April 1994 in the wake of the war. Known as the Moscow Agreement, the accord allowed Abkhazia its own constitution and legislation 'and appropriate State symbols, such as anthem, emblem and flag'.[23] Towards the end of

1994 Abkhazia duly adopted a new constitution to replace the one inherited from its days as an autonomous republic of the Georgian SSR. Although the 1994 constitution declared that Abkhazia was a sovereign state, the government made it clear at the time that it was not proclaiming independence from Georgia. It seemed a case of claiming a right of full statehood, but deciding not to exercise it at that stage. In October 1999, however, Abkhazia held a referendum on independence in accordance with the provisions of the constitution. The magical 98 per cent of the electorate reportedly approved independent statehood, which was formally declared later that same month.[24]

The declaration of independence came shortly after the gravest crisis between Georgia and Abkhazia since the war of the early 1990s. In May 1998 the two countries fought their own six-day war provoked by an attack of Georgian guerrillas on an Abkhazian guard post. In the now familiar pattern fighting was followed by talking, with the parties first concluding a ceasefire treaty and then the Agreement on Peace and Guarantees for Preempting Armed Clashes. Neither party evidently sought an all-out war to the finish. That has not meant peace, however, because armed skirmishes between the two sides have flared up sporadically.[25] The most serious situation of late occurred in July 2006 when Georgian military units were deployed in the Kodori Gorge, ostensibly to dislodge militias and restore Tbilisi's writ over the area. Abkhazia was outraged, not least because the Moscow ceasefire agreement of 1994 had declared the Valley a demilitarized area, off limits to troops from both Georgia and Abkhazia.[26]

President Vladislav Ardzinba made diplomatic recognition of Abkhazia a primary goal after his re-election as head of state in October 1999. Not even Russia seemed keen to oblige, but left the door ajar. 'Why can Albanians in Kosovo have independence, but South Ossetia and Abkhazia can't?' Russian President Vladimir Putin asked in 2006. 'What's the difference?' International opinion, the Russians knew, was emphatically opposed to independence for Abkhazia. The UN Security Council in resolution 1752 of 13 April 2007 reaffirmed 'the commitment of all Member States to the sovereignty, independence and territorial integrity of Georgia within its internationally recognized borders'. So solid was the international front on this issue that Sukhumi's appeals to the UN to participate in Security Council sessions dealing with Abkhazia fell on deaf ears. Conventional wisdom held that Moscow's ambivalent position on Abkhazia's statehood was designed to give it a bargaining chip in dealing with Georgia, and possibly also a means of retribution against Western powers favouring Kosovo's independence.[27]

To undermine whatever international legitimacy the Abkhazian government in Sukhumi may have enjoyed, Georgia set up a rival government in 1995. Initially based in Tbilisi, the so-called government of Abkhazia was in 2006 relocated to the Kodori Gorge, a part of Upper Abkhazia under Georgian control. Although it had the trappings of authority – a council of ministers, various ministries, a tax agency and a police force – the parallel government was nominally in control of only about 17 per cent of Abkhazian territory and its 'subjects' were Georgian refugees from Abkhazia. If the Sukhumi government was a client of Russia, that based in the Kodori Gorge was a wholly owned subsidiary of Georgia.[28]

On the economic front Abkhazia had been severely weakened by the war of 1992–3 and the embargo imposed by the Commonwealth of Independent States (CIS) in January 1996 under pressure from Georgia.[29] Previously one of the most prosperous regions of the Soviet Union, over 70 per cent of Abkhazia's territory was affected by the hostilities. The trade embargo aggravated matters by retarding economic rehabilitation and development. The situation improved in 1999 when Russia suspended its trade sanctions against Abkhazia. Russia became not only Abkhazia's main trading partner but provided an economic lifeline. In March 2005 the Abkhazian Prime Minister revealed that the country's budget had in recent years existed on paper only; it could not have survived without subsidies from Moscow.[30] Still, Abkhazia possessed some valuable economic assets. It was well endowed with natural resources (including oil, gas, coal and water), had a sound agricultural base, boasted modern deep-sea harbours, maintained good rail and road connections with Russia, and showed great tourism potential. These attributes could go some way in offsetting the economic restraints of a modest population size of between 160,000 and 220,000.[31]

There were also other aspects of empirical statehood that supported Abkhazia's claims to independence. The government exercised effective control over its territory (save for the portion under Georgian rule), the entity displayed relative political stability, the different ethnic groups (Abkhazians, Armenians, Russians and Georgians) co-existed peacefully, and Abkhazia had proven its ability to defend itself.[32] We should also take note of the entity's democratic, multiparty political system, as witnessed in the keenly contested presidential election of 2004–5 that was won by opposition candidate Sergei Bagpash. As the Abkhazian Foreign Minister put it in March 2007, 'our objective is to show everyone that we meet modern European standards'.[33]

What may not exactly qualify as a modern European standard, however, is Abkhazia's integration with Russia. As President Ardzinba acknowledged, his country pursued a common defence and foreign policy with Russia, relied on Russian help to guard its state borders, used the Russian currency, accepted Russian pensions, and used its passports. The controversial issuing of Russian passports to Abkhazians has been underway since 2000. By 2006 over 80 per cent of the Abkhazian population had already received such documents. Georgia denounced what it called annexation by 'passportization' as illegal and a violation of its sovereignty. The Georgians were concerned that the presence of a large number of Russian passport-holders in

Abkhazia would give Moscow a pretext to intervene in the name of protecting its citizens in the so-called near abroad. The Abkhazians by contrast took a pragmatic view of their use of Russian passports: Abkhazian passports were worthless for international travel and Abkhazians refused to use Georgian travel documents.[34] Nor did the Abkhazian leadership see any irreconcilable conflict between existing links with Russia and closer ties with Europe. 'Abkhazia is a part of Europe and we have the right to integrate into European society', Foreign Minister Shamba proclaimed in early 2007. He even hinted at some kind of association with the European Union.[35] Moscow, meanwhile, treated the Eurasian entities as states by allowing them to maintain resident missions in the capital, hold meetings on Russian soil and enjoy access to its leadership (including Putin).[36]

Next to the existential relationship with Russia, Abkhazia's foreign policy has of necessity focused on ties with South Ossetia, Transdniestria and Nagorno Karabagh. Their presidents have held summit meetings and the foreign ministers have met on several occasions.[37] Transdniestria and Abkhazia have established diplomatic relations[38] while Abkhazia and South Ossetia in September 2002 signed a defence treaty for mutual protection against Georgian 'aggression' and followed it up with an agreement on cooperation in September 2005.[39] The four entities were evidently keen to coordinate negotiating positions in talks with their former central governments in Georgia, Moldova and Azerbaijan, to support each other's claims to full statehood, and to expand ties between their own governments, military establishments and business sectors.[40] Their solidarity was expressed in the Declaration on Principles of Peaceful and Fair Settlement of Conflicts on the Territory of Moldova, Georgia, Armenia and Azerbaijan. Signed in June 2007 by Abkhazia, South Ossetia, Transdniestria and Nagorno Karabagh, the Declaration emphasized that conflicts should be resolved by peaceful means based on 'respect to all sides' and 'unconditional recognition of the right of nations to self-determination'.[41] The ties between the four contested states were institutionalized with the establishment in July 2006 of the Commonwealth for Democracy and Rights of Nations. The multilateral forum was founded by the presidents of Abkhazia, South Ossetia and Transdniestria, while Nagorno Karabagh was still contemplating involvement. An Inter-parliamentary Assembly for Democracy and Rights of Nations was subsequently established under the auspices of the Commonwealth and was open to parliaments of the four contested states and from confirmed states.[42] Finally, Abkhazia was the only one of the four Eurasian contested states whose name appeared on the membership roster of the Unrepresented Nations and Peoples Organization (UNPO).

Abkhazia's life in international limbo took on a new character in August 2008 when it, along with South Ossetia, was granted *de jure* recognition by Russia. This followed in the wake of Georgia's reckless armed incursion into South Ossetia (see below). Russia's move was strongly condemned by

NATO, the EU and individual Western powers, which vowed to respect Georgia's territorial integrity. Georgia, outraged by Russia's recognition of the two secessionist enclaves' purported statehood, showed no intention of releasing its rebellious regions into independence.

Alternative futures

In ruling circles and at grass-roots level in Abkhazia, by contrast, sovereign statehood commanded overwhelming support.[43] As President Bagpash reiterated in December 2006, it was 'an objective reality' that Abkhazia and Georgia 'cannot exist within the borders of a single country'.[44] This 'reality', Foreign Minister Shamba explained in a statement addressed to the UN in April 2007, was based on 'a consistent policy of Georgian leaders aimed at actual genocide of the Abkhazian ethnos' during the communist era. In the same appeal the Foreign Minister also justified independence for Abkhazia and the other Eurasian contested states as 'a logical conclusion' of the still incomplete process of creating new states in the wake of the implosion of the Soviet Union.[45] Their shared fate was highlighted again in June 2007 when the presidents of Abkhazia and South Ossetia appealed to the UN to place them in line for international recognition after Kosovo because they have 'just as strong grounds to demand independence as Kosovo'.[46] Earlier, Bagpash claimed that 'if Kosovo is recognised, Abkhazia will be recognised in the course of three days. I am absolutely sure of that'.[47]

While over-optimistic about the timing, Bagpash's prophesy was fulfilled six months after Kosovo's second unilateral declaration of independence in February 2008 and its prompt recognition by scores of Western countries. Recognition by Russia meant that Abkhazia and South Ossetia could add patron recognition to the peer recognition with which they had to be content until then. While no doubt a diplomatic breakthrough for South Ossetia and Abkhazia, they may well discover that the proverbial swallow of Russian recognition does not make a diplomatic summer of collective recognition. Given Georgia's rejection of statehood for the two entities and Western backing for this position, it is unlikely that many countries would follow Russia's example. If confirmed statehood continues to elude Abkhazia and assuming that the *status quo* of contested statehood is untenable over the long run, what other status options may be available?

Abkhazian leaders have repeatedly spoken in favour of 'associate membership' of the Russian Federation and the territory's parliament addressed a similar proposal to Moscow.[48] Advocates of this option evidently did not have full integration with Russia in mind. The Abkhazian Foreign Minister in 2006 likened it to the arrangement between the US and the Marshall Islands.[49] That the envisaged associated status would be reconcilable with Abkhazia's sovereignty is further borne out by Sukhumi's appeals to Moscow for the recognition of Abkhazian statehood.[50] We are thus dealing with associated statehood voluntarily entered into by two sovereign states and recognized in international law. Georgia has rejected an associate relationship between Abkhazia and Russia with the same vigour as it has opposed independence for the entity.

Georgia's position on the future of Abkhazia was shared by the international community. The UN has repeatedly endorsed the principles enumerated in the so-called Boden Document, compiled in 2001 by the Secretary-General's Special Representative for Georgia. Entitled Basic Principles for the Distribution of Competencies between Tbilisi and Sukhumi, the document envisioned Abkhazia as a so-called sovereign entity within the state of Georgia, with the division of competencies determined by means of a 'federal agreement'. By advocating a federal formula, the Boden Document tried to strike a balance between the principles of national self-determination and territorial integrity. Georgia welcomed the proposals, whereas Abkhazia dismissed them out of hand.[51]

Adamant that Abkhazia was historically and legally an integral part of Georgia, President Saakashvili even set 2009 as the target date for effecting reintegration.[52] He referred to his preferred formula variously as a 'new, joint-state model of ethnic and civil cooperation'[53] and 'autonomous development and real self-government' for Abkhazia.[54] In March 2008 Saakashvili made a more elaborate offer of 'unlimited autonomy, wide federalism and very serious representation in the central governmental bodies of Georgia', all under international guarantees. The package included a new post of vice president for an Abkhazian; an Abkhazian right to veto national laws affecting their constitutional status and the preservation of their language and culture; Russian involvement in mediating conflicts, and a joint Georgian-Abkhazian-controlled free economic zone.[55]

Before there could be any positive movement on Saakashvili's bold settlement plan, a new crisis broke. It did not concern Abkhazia in the first instance; the entity served as the stage on which a new showdown between Georgia and its Western backers on the one hand and Russia on the other was played out. Incensed by NATO's commitment to Georgia's future membership and by Kosovo's Western-supported independence, Russia retaliated by intensifying its manipulation of the conflicts in Abkhazia and South Ossetia. In March 2008 Russia formally withdrew from the 1996 CIS accord on measures to regulate the Abkhazian conflict. One of the measures involved sanctions against Abkhazia, which Russia had already suspended in 1999. In April Putin announced Russia would strengthen official ties with Abkhazia. Moscow's next step up the escalation leader was to deploy more troops in Abkhazia, ostensibly in accordance with its peacekeeping mandate – but without Georgia's approval.[56] For good measure the Kremlin warned that it was ready to use military force to protect its 'citizens' in Abkhazia (and South Ossetia) should hostilities break out.[57] Georgia had meanwhile been making its own military preparations for a possible confrontation with Moscow. By June 2008 this escalation 'brought Georgia and Russia closer to war than ever before', the International Crisis Group warned.[58]

Two months later war indeed broke out between Russia and Georgia, but it was fought over South Ossetia, not Abkhazia. Still, Abkhazia seized the opportunity to drive Georgian troops out of the Kodori Gorge and so – according to Abkhazian thinking – pre-empt a repetition of the South Ossetian war in Abkhazia itself.[59] Abkhazia also benefited from Georgia's invasion of South Ossetia by gaining *de jure* recognition from Russia, as did South Ossetia. This patron recognition may encourage Abkhazia to persevere in its quest for confirmed statehood, or at least encourage it to soldier on in contested statehood. Either way, Georgia's misadventure has probably set back the prospects for a negotiated settlement in Abkhazia.

South Ossetia

Although covering only 3,900 km^2, South Ossetia's small geographic area is by no means the weakest element of its claim to statehood. Size-wise South Ossetia is after all comparable to Cape Verde and much larger than Luxembourg. However, the location and settlement of the territory render claims to statehood rather problematic. Situated on the southern side of the Caucasus, along Georgia's northern border, South Ossetia is surrounded on the east, west and south by Georgia proper and it also borders on Russia's North Ossetian Autonomous Republic. There are thus two Ossetian entities, one in Russia and the other formally part of Georgia. How and when the Ossetian territories were settled, especially the southern portion, is still disputed by Georgians and Ossetians. The Ossetians maintained that both the North and South constituted their historical homeland. Descendants from the Alanian and Scythian tribes of Persia, the Ossetians migrated to the Caucasus over 5,000 years ago. Initially settling in what is now North Ossetia, the Ossetians were later forced to flee south by the invading Mongols. This has prompted the Georgian view that the Ossetians were late arrivals and hence 'guests' in the Georgian-settled South. Be that as it may, one cannot refute the Ossetians' claim that they constituted a distinct cultural group of which their Indo-European language (related to Pushtu and Farsi) was a prime marker.[60]

The facts about local events of the last two centuries are less contentious, but partisan interpretations are still the order of the day. A watershed occurrence was the incorporation of present-day South Ossetia and Georgia into the Russian Empire at the turn of the 19th century. Unlike other peoples of the region, the Ossetians did not resist Russian expansion into the Caucasus; instead, the Ossetians often fought alongside the invaders. This earned them the reputation of loyal citizens of the Russian Empire, but others despised the Ossetians as stooges of the imperialistic Russians.[61] Following the dissolution of the Empire in 1918, South Ossetia became part of the short-lived Menshevik Georgian Democratic Republic. It was an unhappy union, with the Ossetians staging several rebellions against Georgian rule between 1918 and 1921 and agitating for an independent country of their own. The authorities in Tbilisi used military force to crush the uprising, killing as many as 5,000 Ossetians. In 1921 the Red Army seized control of Georgia and installed the Soviet Georgian government, which in turn created the South Ossetian Autonomous Region the following year. The northern kin entity also underwent several status make-overs. In 1918 it joined the Terek Soviet Republic but after the Red Army conquered the region in 1920 North Ossetia was included in the new Mountain Autonomous Soviet Socialist Republic as an *okrug* (a nationality given a measure of administrative autonomy). In 1924 the territory was reorganized as the North Ossetian Autonomous Region and in 1936 became the North Ossetian Autonomous Soviet Socialist Republic.[62]

For most of the Soviet period relations between Georgia's South Ossetians and ethnic Georgians were peaceful, but tensions remained latent. Georgians tended to regard South Ossetia as an artificial creation of the Russians and they also resented the South Ossetians for allegedly being advantaged over ethnic Georgians in fields such as employment. Ossetians in the South for their part felt oppressed by not having an autonomous republic on par with their kin in North Ossetia. But given their modest numbers, the South Ossetians were hardly capable of serious mischief-making against the might of the Soviet state.[63]

Statehood and war

The Gorbachev era and the unravelling of the Soviet Union gave the South Ossetians the political space to assert their claims to an enhanced status. In 1989 the South Ossetian regional council proposed to the Georgian Supreme Soviet that the Autonomous Region be elevated to an autonomous republic. Tbilisi was outraged. Tensions were meanwhile also building up over the language issue, with the Georgian Supreme Soviet in 1989 proclaiming Georgian as the principal language countrywide. This prompted the South Ossetians to declare their native tongue an official language in the autonomous area. Towards the end of 1989 rising tensions between the two communities spilled over into serious violence and casualties, prompting the deployment of Soviet troops to restore peace.[64] The political temperature rose in mid-1990 when the Supreme Soviet of Georgia decided to ban regional parties in the run-up to a parliamentary election. Seeing this as a ploy to disqualify the South Ossetian Popular Front (created in 1988) from the electoral contest, the Ossetians resorted to the drastic step of proclaiming 'sovereignty' in September 1990. In line with the loose Soviet usage of the term, sovereignty in this case did not mean independent statehood, but secession from Georgia while remaining part and parcel of the Soviet Union. The South Ossetians boycotted the national election of October 1990, instead holding their own. The incoming Georgian government raised the ante by declaring the South Ossetian election result null and void, abolishing South Ossetia's autonomous regional status, imposing a state of emergency in the area and installing a Georgian military officer as mayor of Tskhinvali, the South Ossetian capital. Still, a referendum in the city in early 1992 produced a huge majority in favour of breaking away from Georgia and integrating with Russia. The South Ossetian regional council took a similar vote towards the end of that year, heralding the birth of the self-proclaimed state of South Ossetia.[65]

By then South Ossetia was consumed by war, which began in January 1991 when thousands of Georgian troops entered Tskhinvali. In 1992 Russian forces joined the fray in support of South Ossetia. The war took a high toll, with approximately 1,000 people killed, thousands more Ossetians fleeing the South, about 10,000 Georgians and persons of mixed ethnicity displaced from South Ossetia to Georgia proper, and another 5,000 people internally displaced within South Ossetia. There was also extensive damage to homes and infrastructure. The atrocities committed by both sides and the impunity that the perpetrators enjoyed would poison the atmosphere for years to come.[66]

The international character of the conflict was underlined when a ceasefire agreement was signed in Sochi (Russia) in June 1992 – between Georgian and Russian leaders. The Sochi Agreement provided for the establishment of the Joint Control Commission (JCC) comprising representatives from Georgia, Russia, North and South Ossetia plus participation from the OSCE. The Commission's mandate included supervising the peace accord, undertaking economic reconstruction in the so-called zone of conflict (defined as a circle of 15 km radius from the middle of Tskhinvali), and facilitating the return of refugees and internally displaced people. The Sochi Agreement also led to the creation of trilateral Joint Peacekeeping Forces composed of units from Georgia, Russia and Ossetia (in practice mainly the South), operating under Russian command. Among its tasks were the restoration of peace and the maintenance of law and order in the zone of conflict and the security corridor (a 14 km strip of land on both sides of the border of the former South Ossetia Autonomous Region).[67] The peace process set in motion in 1992 subsequently produced a variety of functional agreements, especially at the JCC level. To help create a climate necessary for resolving the fundamental political conflicts, the Memorandum on Measures to Ensure Security and Reinforce Mutual Confidence between the Parties to the Georgian-Ossetian Conflict was signed in 1996. In 2000 Georgia and South Ossetia, with the assistance of the OSCE and EU, agreed to establish a Joint Law Enforcement Coordination Body.[68] Meanwhile, in 1999, the parties commenced negotiations on a political settlement[69] – a process that has still not produced a final settlement.

As in Abkhazia, Russia's footprint was huge in South Ossetia. The rebel territory could from the outset count on Moscow's political backing and as guarantor of its security. Russian military and secret service personnel were said to occupy senior positions in the *de facto* government.[70] Russia also provided direct financial and technical assistance to rebuild the devastated territory as well as humanitarian relief after the war. (Georgia by contrast provided little if any aid to South Ossetia.) Russia has been South Ossetia's benefactor in other ways too, including the payment of pensions to South Ossetians with Russian citizenship, granting the inhabitants Russian passports, and allowing the territory to use the Russian rouble. By 2004 nearly 90 per cent of the Ossetians in the South were by official accounts Russian citizens, whether by birth or through 'passportization'.[71] The people of South Ossetia were probably motivated by more than the familiar pragmatic considerations of a passport worth the name and an insurance policy against Georgian aggression; integration with Russia was a popular option among them.

Echoing his views on the Abkhazian conflict, Georgian President Saakashvili maintained that the 'crisis in South Ossetia is not a problem between Georgians and Ossetians. This is a problem between Georgia and Russia'.[72] Russia had indeed become an active participant in the South Ossetian conflict by providing secessionists with arms, equipment, military training and manpower in the shape of Russian mercenaries. In Georgia's eyes Russia was trying to annex South Ossetia by stealth, as it was allegedly doing in Abkhazia too.[73]

Despite the mistrust between Georgia and Russia, the Sochi peace accord held up remarkably well until the situation in South Ossetia turned ugly in 2003–4. The ostensible cause of the renewed tension was a major anti-smuggling operation launched by Georgian forces in and around South Ossetia in December 2003. Tbilisi reasoned that smuggling sustained the revolt in South Ossetia by holding personal benefits for the rebel leadership and providing them with the means to buy the loyalty of the populace. By stamping out smuggling, Georgia believed, it would snuff out the secession. The South Ossetians, by contrast, saw the operation as a prelude to military action against them and began preparing for such an eventuality. The zone of conflict became remilitarized. Tbilisi combined its anti-smuggling campaign with another measure to curb secessionist fervour in South Ossetia. This was a 'humanitarian offensive' aimed at changing South Ossetian hearts and minds. By introducing social, economic and cultural projects for their benefit, Georgia hoped to win the South Ossetians' favour and turn them against the government of President Eduard Kokoity. Already aggrieved by hardship induced by Georgia's clamp-down on smuggling, the South Ossetians were not taken in by Tbilisi's charm offensive. The unilateral nature and opportunistic impulse of the initiative instead hardened both elite and popular feelings against Georgia. Such sentiments may have helped the pro-Kokoity party win two-thirds of the seats in a parliamentary election in May 2004.[74] All the while tensions between the two sides kept rising.

Armed hostilities broke out at the end of July 2004, and continued sporadically for three weeks before both sides abided by a ceasefire agreement. This time casualties were modest. In November 2004 Kokoity met Georgian Prime Minister Zurab Zhvania in Sochi where they agreed to demilitarize the zone of conflict. However, since 2004 'not a day has passed without shooting or more serious incidents in the conflict zone', the International Crisis Group reported in June 2007.[75] Worse was to follow a year later.

The OSCE and EU, meanwhile, remained engaged in promoting a peaceful settlement between Georgia and South Ossetia and in improving the situation on the ground for the inhabitants of the region.[76] The UN Development Programme (UNDP) has in turn done sterling work with its special project for the rehabilitation of the Tskhinvali region, which included the restoration of basic infrastructure.[77] Even Georgia and Russia entered into agreements on economic reconstruction of the conflict zone.[78] In June 2006 an international donors' conference in Brussels raised nearly 8 million euro to finance the rehabilitation of that zone.[79] It should be stressed that none of the foreign-sponsored initiatives were designed to prepare South Ossetia for independent statehood, but were all aimed at the integrated development of Georgia as a single unit. This tied in with the world community's firm rejection of independence for South Ossetia and commitment to the sovereignty and territorial integrity of Georgia.[80]

If the foreign rehabilitation projects improved the climate for seeking peace in South Ossetia, political actions undermined the gains. In November 2006 the secessionist authorities in Tskhinvali staged an independence referendum alongside the presidential election. It produced the anticipated result, namely a near unanimous 'yes' to the question: 'Do you agree that the Republic of South Ossetia preserve its current status as an independent state and be recognized by the international community?'[81] Like the 1992 referendum, that of 2006 was not endorsed by Georgia or the international community. The Russian Foreign Ministry, however, depicted the vote as a free and democratic expression of the will of the South Ossetians and urged the world community to take account of the referendum results.[82]

In a decidedly provocative move Saakashvili set up a rival government to that of South Ossetian President Kokoity – a stratagem the Georgian leader also employed in Abkhazia.[83] Following an 'alternative presidential election' in November 2006, coinciding with that held by the rulers in Tskhinvali, Dmitry Sanakoev was installed as President of the Alternative Government of South Ossetia. Both Sanakoev and his Prime Minister had previously served in the secessionist government based in Tskhinvali, but in their new guise they pledged allegiance to Georgia and its territorial integrity. As Sanakoev put it, the future of the South Ossetian people was 'only in a democratic and stable Georgia'.[84] The parallel presidential poll was accompanied by a referendum in which voters were asked to pronounce on the start of negotiations with Tbilisi on a federal arrangement for Georgia. Over 90 per cent supported the idea. In April 2007 the rival government's name was changed to the Temporary Administration Unit for South Ossetia, following Tbilisi's decision to accord it official status. Based in the ethnic Georgian village of Kurta in a Georgian-administered part of South Ossetia, the alternative government's power base lay among the 20,000 to 25,000 inhabitants (of whom only 8,000 were said to be ethnic Ossetians).[85] The Sanakoev government has been branded as traitors and puppets by Kokoity's government, which threatened to pull out of the peace process as long as Georgia continued to promote the rival government of South Ossetia.[86]

A far more brazen act occurred in August 2008 when Georgian forces invaded South Ossetia in an effort to regain control of the wayward territory. Saakashvili miscalculated badly, either with regard to Russian resistance or Western assistance.[87] Responding with a massive counter-offensive, Russia not only drove Georgian troops out of South Ossetia but also attacked targets in Georgia proper. Western powers did nothing to prevent Georgian forces suffering a humiliating defeat in the five-day war.[88] Civilians bore the brunt of the hostilities: between one and two thousand of them may have been killed in South Ossetia and up to half of the enclave's population had reportedly fled into North Ossetia. The capital Tskhinvali experienced massive destruction.[89]

An EU-brokered ceasefire, accepted by Georgia and Russia, provided for the withdrawal of Russian troops from Georgia but left Russian forces in effective control of South Ossetia. Provision was also made for international talks over 'security and stability modalities' in South Ossetia and Abkhazia. The agreement made no reference to the preservation of Georgia's territorial integrity.[90] This omission suited Russia, whose EU Ambassador made the derisive remark that 'territorial integrity had become a virtual notion regarding Georgia'.[91] Less than a fortnight after signing the truce with Georgia, Russia recognized the statehood of South Ossetia (and Abkhazia). President Dmitry Medvedev justified this decision on the same grounds as Russia's military response to Georgia's invasion: 'The most important thing was to prevent a humanitarian catastrophe to save the lives of people for whom we are responsible, because most of them they are Russian citizens'.[92] Whereas Georgia had chosen 'genocide' in pursuit of its political agenda in the break-away territory, Medvedev claimed, 'Russia stopped the extermination' through its military action and subsequent diplomatic recognition.[93] By portraying its military campaign as one of humanitarian intervention, Russia was invoking the kind of justification NATO had offered for its military offensive in former Yugoslavia ten years earlier. The Russian Parliament's insistence on the right of self-determination for the threatened peoples of South Ossetia and Georgia likewise echoed Western justifications for recognizing Kosovo.[94] Medvedev indeed related Russia's recognition of South Ossetia and Abkhazia to Western recognition of Kosovo in early 2008. Ignoring Russia's warnings, Medvedev said, Western states had rushed to recognize Kosovo's 'illegal declaration of independence' from Serbia. 'We argued consistently that it would be impossible, after that, to tell the Abkhazians and Ossetians (and dozens of other groups around the world) that what was good for the Kosovo Albanians was not good for them', the Russian President proclaimed.[95] This might be interpreted as a hint that Russia would drop its opposition to Kosovo's independence if Western powers recognized the statehood of South Ossetia and Abkhazia.[96]

The EU, NATO, France, Britain, Germany and the US were quick to denounce Russia's recognition of the two contested states.[97] Secretary of State Condoleezza Rice vowed that America would use its veto power in the Security Council to make sure that any move to gain wider recognition for the two presumptive states at the UN 'simply will be dead on arrival'.[98]

Alternative futures

Russia's formal recognition of the statehood of South Ossetia has by no means settled the issue of its final political status. Although Medvedev urged other countries to recognize South Ossetia and Abkhazia as independent states,[99] it is doubtful whether many would follow suit. This would leave South Ossetia in international limbo, although slightly less isolated than before. The formalization of its ties with Russia may nonetheless make the entity less receptive than previously to engage in serious talks with Georgia on resolving the conflict over its political destination. The trauma South Ossetians endured because of Georgia's ill-considered invasion will probably also harden feelings against any early settlement with their original state.

Apart from a lack of international recognition, the sustainability of independent statehood for South Ossetia can be questioned on other grounds too. After the war of 1991–2 the authorities of South Ossetia had control over the districts of Tskhinvali, Java, Znauri and parts of Akhalgori, leaving the rest of Akhalgori and several ethnic Georgian villages in the Tskhinvali district to the Georgian central government. Tskhinvali and Java were the only large towns in South Ossetia. Add to this that South Ossetia's resident population had dropped from nearly 100,000 in the late 1980s to as low as 65,000 after the war (with even fewer Ossetians remaining in Georgia proper).[100] The patchwork of settlement and fragmentation of authority, together with the smallness of the population, already cast doubt on the justifiability of a final status for South Ossetia offering anything more than local autonomy. The case for separate statehood has certainly not been helped by South Ossetia's puny economy that was predominantly agricultural with some industry around the capital. Trapped in a frozen conflict, South Ossetia has very limited scope for normal economic interaction with the outside world. Georgia has since the war maintained a *de facto* embargo against South Ossetia – in contravention of the Sochi Agreement – thereby reducing their formal economic ties to a minimum. Trade with Russia was by contrast extensive. The Roki tunnel, linking South Ossetia with the Russian Federation *via* North Ossetia, was one of the former's main economic assets; Tskhinvali reportedly generated up to one-third of its budget by levying customs duties on freight traffic using the tunnel. Given the constraints on legitimate free trade, South Ossetia has not surprisingly developed an illicit shadow economy in which smuggling, drug trafficking, counterfeiting of money, illegal arms trading and kidnapping thrived. Due to disagreements between South Ossetia and Georgia over customs control, smuggling proceeded largely unhindered. Law enforcement officers from the two sides as well as Russian customs officials and peacekeeping troops were thought to participate in the illegal business dealings.[101]

In due course its contested statehood and the attendant deprivations may compel South Ossetia and its Russian patron to seek alternatives to the *status quo* through negotiations with Georgia. What options might then be explored?

The Saakashvili government has been firmly committed to the reintegration of both South Ossetia (which Tbilisi called the Tskhinvali region and considered part of the Georgian province of Shida Kartli) and Abkhazia into Georgia. Saakashvili even promised that South Ossetia, like Abkhazia, would be reunified with Georgia by the time of the presidential election in 2009.[102] Saakashvili's political formula for South Ossetia resembled that proposed for Abkhazia. In January 2005 he offered South Ossetia 'a distinctly broader form of autonomy than it had in Soviet times and than North Ossetia has in the Russian Federation'. The plan provided for an executive branch and legislature to deal with culture, education, social and economic policy, public order and local self-governance, and a three-year transition to the proposed autonomous status.[103] International opinion, expressed through the UN, OSCE and EU, also favoured this future for South Ossetia. President Kokoity, however, rejected the autonomy proposal.[104] Tskhinvali likewise dismissed a plan Saakashvili put forward in April 2007 to create 'appropriate conditions' for a peaceful settlement in South Ossetia. The Georgian President envisaged the establishment of a transitional administrative unit to cooperate with Tbilisi in promoting the economic rehabilitation of South Ossetia, ensuring the representation of all interests and determining the area's final status. That status, according to Saakashvili's proposal, would involve 'European-style autonomy... guaranteeing political self-governance and preservation of national identity and cultural rights of ethnic Ossetians'.[105]

Supported by their kinsfolk in the North (numbering about 700,000), the South Ossetians maintained that their nation had been divided unjustly and against their will between the Georgian and Russian republics during the Soviet period – hence denying them their right of self-determination as a people. Comparing their situation to the division between East and West Germany and North and South Korea, the Ossetians claimed a right to reunite, seeing this as a (delayed) expression of self-determination. 'It is high time to stop dividing Ossetia into North and South. There is one big and unified Ossetia', Kokoity asserted in 2004.[106] It is no coincidence that Putin drew the same analogy between the two Ossetias and the two Germanies.[107] A reunited Ossetia – that might be called 'Alania', the ancient name used by the Ossetian people – would remain part of the Russian Federation; there has been no serious talk in either the South or the North, much less in Moscow, of an independent greater Ossetian state. Indeed, Kokoity was openly committed to the unification of North and South Ossetia within the Russian Federation.[108] In mid-2006 Kokoity announced his government's intention of requesting the Russian Constitutional Court that Russia annex his statelet because 'South Ossetia joined the Russian Empire together with North Ossetia as an indivisible entity and never left Russia'.[109]

A related alternative would be for South Ossetia to be absorbed into Russia as a distinct unit, separate from the North. In the early 1990s, when the South Ossetian legislature was still dominated by representatives from the Soviet period, this was indeed the Ossentians' preferred destination. One consideration that might still favour the option is that the Caucasus Mountains present a formidable natural barrier to North-South unification.[110]

Despite all its support for South Ossetia, Moscow has not consented to the territory's integration into the Russian Federation. In response to an inquiry about the legality of incorporation, the Russian Constitutional Court in June 2004 declared that discussions about South Ossetia had to be held with Georgia – to which the territory belonged – on Tbilisi's initiative.[111] If Moscow abided by this ruling, it could not incorporate South Ossetia unilaterally. It is in any case uncertain that Russia wishes to absorb the entity. Instead, Russia may simply be exploiting the contested statehood of South Ossetia (like Abkhazia's) to gain leverage over Georgia. The unresolved conflicts over South Ossetia and Abkhazia, Moscow may be hoping, would obstruct Georgia's accession to NATO and the alliance's further encroachment into the space of the former Soviet Union. Still, Moscow had a vested interest in the stability and political leanings of South Ossetia because of the entity's strategic location on the border of Russia's volatile North Caucasus region.[112]

Transdniestria

A resolution of the conflict over Transdniestria, the International Crisis Group reported in 2004, 'is vital to remove a potential source of chaos on the periphery of the expanding European Union, to implement an important part of the post-Cold War settlement, and to make Moldova itself a more viable state'.[113] How did Transdniestria, a secessionist region inside Moldova, become such a troublesome entity in Eurasia?

Because the conflict between Transdniestria and Moldova 'is not laden with deep disputes over history'[114] (in contrast with Abkhazia and South Ossetia), we need not trace the evolution of the Moldovan state further back than the Treaty of Bucharest that ended the Russo-Turkish war of 1806–12. Under the peace accord the part of Moldova located between the Prut and Dniestr rivers was annexed by Russia and became known as Bessarabia. The area west of the Prut River joined Romania in 1859. Bessarabia was initially given considerable autonomy in the Russian Empire and ethnic Moldovans constituted nearly 90 per cent of the region's population. In the mid-19th century, however, Russia abolished Bessarabia's local autonomy, replaced the Romanian language (used by Moldovans) with Russian in all legal proceedings, began the active assimilation of Moldovans and encouraged the settlement of Russians and other ethnic groups in Bessarabia. By the turn of the century the Moldovans' numbers had been reduced by nearly 40 per cent, even though they remained the region's largest ethnic group.[115] The First World War and the Russian revolution gave pan-Romanian nationalists in Bessarabia the political space to assert their claims to self-determination in the shape of integration with Romania. A national assembly was formed, which in December 1917 voted to establish the independent Moldovan Democratic Republic of Bessarabia. Extending from the Prut to the Dniestr River, the new entity did not include today's Transdniestria. In March 1918 the infant Republic of Bessarabia united with Romania.[116]

Russia, however, would not acquiesce in the loss of Bessarabia. To highlight their title to the territory, Soviet authorities in 1924 formed the Moldovan Autonomous Soviet Socialist Republic (MASSR) by combining Transdniestria with an area in present-day Ukraine. Ethnic Moldovans comprised only about 30 per cent of the MASSR's total population; Ukrainians accounted for nearly half. The Soviet Union used the MASSR as a base for propaganda and subversion against Romanian-controlled Bessarabia. By holding up the Soviet Union's economic and technological superiority, Moscow hoped to lure Bessarabians back to where they supposedly belonged. While this use of soft power combined with subversion failed to have the desired effect, great power politics gave Moscow the prize it coveted, albeit only briefly. The Molotov-Ribbentrop Pact of 1939 cleared the way for the USSR to demand – with Nazi Germany's blessing – that Romania immediately surrender Bessarabia. This duly happened in July 1940 when the Soviet Union annexed Bessarabia and formed it into the Moldovan Soviet Socialist Republic together with the western part of the MASSR. The very next year the *status quo ante* was restored when the

Romanian army seized control of Bessarabia, courtesy of its German ally. The area of Transdniestria was merely occupied by the Romanians, whereas the remainder of Bessarabia was formally reabsorbed into Romania. As the tide of war changed the Soviet Army in 1944 recaptured Bessarabia, which was promptly combined with components of the former MASSR to constitute the Soviet Socialist Republic of Moldova.[117] This would remain Moldova's political home for the next four decades.

Restored to the Soviet fold, Moldova underwent rapid industrialization and extensive Russification after the Second World War. Between 1944 and 1959 as many as 300,000 Russian-speakers were settled in Moldova, mostly in the more developed Transdniestria and the larger cities on the right bank of the Dniestr River. The influx coincided with the expulsion of over 500,000 Moldovans to other parts of the Soviet Union and the death of another 200,000 during the great famine of 1946–7 (induced by forced collectivization). The Russification policy went hand in hand with the Soviet leadership's encouragement of the formation of a distinct Russian-oriented Moldovan nation, separate from the Romanians. To this end Russian was restored to the language of public life, higher education and inter-ethnic communication, while Romanian was relegated to a kitchen tongue. Romanian, officially called Moldovan, had to be written in Cyrillic script (as opposed to the conventional Latin) and Soviet scholars fabricated the notion that Romanian was fundamentally different from Moldovan so as to provide the foundation for a separate non-Romanian Moldovan nation.[118]

Transdniestria occupied a prominent place in the economic, social and political life of the Soviet Socialist Republic of Moldova. Home to heavy industry and enterprises of the Soviet military-industrial complex, Transdniestria had a concentration of imported Russian workers and hence became more urbanized and Russified than Bessarabia. Transdniestria also had a reputation as a major source for the recruitment of the ruling elite. Russians or Russified Moldovans from Transdniestria dominated state and party structures and occupied the commanding heights of the Moldovan economy.[119] This oligarchical arrangement was bound to cause severe friction. As in several other former Soviet republics, the political liberalization of the Gorbachev period provided an outlet for the pent-up frustrations of Moldova's aggrieved non-Russian communities – and set in motion a train of events that prompted a backlash from Transdniestria.

Towards the PMR

Towards the late 1980s informal pro-reform groups began emerging in Moldova. They pressed for greater cultural and linguistic freedom in Moldova and an end to Soviet policies of Russification. In May 1989 a range of reformist associations joined together in the Popular Front, which soon became the main Moldovan opposition movement. Its agitation was a major factor behind the decision of the Moldovan Supreme Soviet in

August 1989 to make Moldovan (based on the Latin alphabet) the state language.[120] The push for reform also extended to the replacement of old cadres in the spirit of 'perestroika', thereby opening up state and party positions to Romanian-speakers. This process accelerated after the Popular Front's strong showing in the first competitive election for the Supreme Soviet of Moldova in March 1990 and its inclusion in the new government composed almost exclusively of ethnic Moldovans. By 1991 ethnic Moldovans held nearly 90 per cent of leadership posts in the government and public service. Soviet Russification had given way to 'Moldovanization' of power structures as a consequence of democratization and the language law of 1989. These developments together with the Moldovan government's pronounced pro-Romanian agenda and its outspoken support for unification with Romania, caused intense resentment among Moldova's other ethnic groups who feared discrimination and marginalization in the face of resurgent Moldovan nationalism. Above all, they dreaded the prospect of Moldova again (this time with Transdniestria included) becoming part of Romania.[121]

The strongest objections came from the Russian community, who resorted to a 'reactive nationalism'.[122] The backlash was centred on Transdniestria with its large concentration of Russian-speakers who, together with ethnic Ukrainians, comprised 55 per cent of the region's population. In Transdniestria identification with the Soviet Union was greater than elsewhere in Moldova. Transdniestria had moreover never formed part of Romania. It is then understandable that the negative consequences of the shifting balance of power to Romanian-speakers was felt most acutely in Transdniestria, especially by the economic and political elite.[123] Several organizations were formed to protect the interests of Russians (and their Ukrainian and Bulgarian allies) in Transdniestria in particular. The leading movement among them was the Union of Workers Collectives, 'in essence a top-down, pro-Soviet and chauvinist Russian organisation'.[124]

Established in 1989, the Union of Workers Collectives championed a policy of gradual secession from Moldova. It began with a referendum on territorial autonomy in the capital Tiraspol in January 1990 and culminated in September 1990 in the proclamation of the Dniestrian Moldovan Socialist Soviet Republic as a constituent unit of the Soviet Union. The final countdown to a violent showdown had begun. The authorities in the central capital Chisinau made the next move by declaring Moldova independent in August 1991. In September Transdniestria adopted its constitution based on independence from Moldova, and began military mobilization. Igor Smirnov was elected as the first President of the renamed Pridnestrovyan Moldovan Republic (PMR or Transdniestria) in December 1991 in a dual poll in which the electorate also approved the entity's independence.[125] Transdniestria's armed forces immediately launched a 'creeping putsch' by attacking local structures of the Moldovan state such as police stations and local authorities. The process escalated into full-scale war between the forces of Transdniestria and Moldova in the spring of 1992. The Russian 14th Army stationed in Transdniestria – the most powerful military force in all of Moldova – intervened in the hostilities in June 1992 and helped to end the fighting that cost over 1,000 human lives and produced some 100,000 refugees.[126]

The ceasefire agreement of July 1992 was signed by Russian President Boris Yeltsin and his Moldovan counterpart Mircea Snegur. In terms of the agreement Transdniestria would enjoy a special status and was guaranteed the right of self-determination if Moldova changed its statehood. Provision was also made for the creation of a security zone in which peacekeeping forces consisting of Russian, Moldovan and Transdniestrian troops were deployed. A tripartite Joint Control Committee (JCC) was formed to observe the peacekeepers and maintain order in the zone of conflict.[127]

The patron and the peacemakers

The peace arrangements confirmed Russia's role as the *de facto* guarantor of Transdniestria's security and contested statehood. Russian Vice-President Alexander Rutskoi visited Transdniestria in April 1992, in the midst of a state of emergency and without officially informing Chisinau, to express his support for the secessionist cause.[128] After the war of 1992 Russian forces remained involved in Transdniestria through their participation in peace-keeping and in the shape of the 14th Army. In 1994 Russia and Moldova reached an agreement on the withdrawal of the 14th Army within three years, but Moscow cunningly managed to extend the period indefinitely on the basis of a technicality. Russia nonetheless reduced its troop strength to 2,600 by 1999, leaving a force that was not particularly significant in military terms yet large enough to reassure the Transdniestrians.[129] Russia refused to pull its remaining troops out of Transdniestria until a political settlement on the territory's future had been reached.[130] The continued presence of Russian peacekeepers and the 14th Army 'effectively froze the status quo' of *de facto* PMR independence. At the same time the Russians provided a protective shield behind which Transdniestria could develop state-like structures.[131] A positive result of this situation has been the absence of large-scale violence between Moldovan and PMR forces since 1992.[132]

Another of Russia's roles in the PMR has been that of major economic partner-*cum*-benefactor. In 1992 a Transdniestrian cash settlement facility was created with the Russian Central Bank allowing Transdniestrian companies to bypass the National Bank of Moldova for international financial transactions. Generous Russian grants, credits and energy subsidies were also forthcoming, along with material aid ranging from natural resources to food. Ties between the two countries were formalized in a range of economic, scientific-technical and cultural agreements.[133] Special reference should be made to the tangible support provided through the military establishment. The Russian military-industrial sector continued the Soviet-era link with Transdniestria as a site for armament production. The PMR's armed forces had in their formative years drawn heavily on Russian material, logistical, administrative and training support, and scores of demobilized Russian soldiers joined the wannabe state's military.[134] Another familiar but controversial link that bound Russia also to the PMR, was the extension of Russian citizenship.[135]

It would be a mistake to infer that the PMR was a mere pawn of Russia. Instead, it was 'a self-aware political entity with its own interests that it has the ability to advance through lobbying, economic opportunism, political posturing, and creative negotiating'.[136] It can, however, do so only if Russia provided the necessary political space and economic and military backing. Such was the PMR's dependence on Russia that Moscow could indeed pull the plug on the secessionist entity's flirtation with statehood and force it back into the Moldovan fold.

What explains Russia's political, economic and military support for Transdniestria? Russia regarded Moldova as belonging to its sphere of geopolitical interest, which meant that it should integrate into the CIS rather than join West European political and economic structures. Although Moldova's communist-led government had previously been pro-Moscow, the two sides' relations have soured and Chisinau has in recent years expressed an interest in joining the EU.[137] Moscow viewed such a prospect with the same disfavour as that of Moldova uniting with Romania – itself an EU member since 2007. The threat of Russian support for an independent PMR was therefore 'useful whenever Moldova strays too far'. Conversely, Moscow's help in resolving the Transdniestria issue was dangled as a reward for Moldova's compliance with Russia's wishes. The PMR can, of course, provide Moscow with leverage against Chisinau only as long as the territory remained *de jure* part of Moldova.[138] Russia might have calculated that Transdniestria, along with the three other statelets of Eurasia, could offer it pulling power in another area too: by threatening to support the quartet's bid for confirmed statehood, Russia could try to deter Western backing for the independence of Kosovo.[139] If true, the ploy failed because scores of Western states have recognized Kosovo's self-proclaimed independence of February 2008 – without Russian retaliation. An entirely different factor that could have weighed with Russian decision makers is that influential figures among the Russian elite may have been deriving material benefit from involvement in Transdniestria's shadow economy and were therefore keen to retain the *status quo*.[140]

Apart from patron and protector of Transdniestria, Russia has also been acting as a mediator in an international diplomatic initiative to resolve the conflict over the break-away entity's final status. Its two partners have been Ukraine and the OSCE.[141] The latter opened a long-term mission in Chisinau in 1993 to assist Moldova and Transdniestria in pursuing a negotiated lasting political settlement. According to the mission's brief, this would be done within defined parameters: 'consolidating the independence and sovereignty of the Republic of Moldova along with an understanding about a special status for the Trans-Dniestr region'.[142] This mandate neatly encapsulated not only the OSCE's position on the terms of a settlement but that of the international community: independence for Transdniestria was out of the question, but the region could not simply be integrated into a unitary Moldova either; Transdniestria's historical background and socio-economic features had to be considered.[143] Elements of this approach found expression in a 1997 agreement between Moldova and the PMR, brokered by Russia. The accord, called On the Basis for the Normalization of Relations between the Republic of Moldova and Transdniestria, stipulated that the parties would seek to establish 'state-legal relations' within the framework of a common state inside the borders of the former Moldovan Soviet Socialist Republic.[144]

Although not from the outset actively involved in the settlement negotiations, the EU committed itself to cooperate with the mediators in resolving the Transdniestrian conflict. In 2005 the negotiating format expanded to '5+2' talks when the original five parties (Moldova, the PMR and the co-mediators Russia, Ukraine and the OSCE) were joined by the EU and America as observers.[145] By then the EU had already decided that Transdniestrian leaders were 'primarily responsible for the lack of cooperation to promote a political settlement' and consequently in early 2003 imposed a travel ban on President Smirnov, his two sons and 14 other members of the ruling circle. EU associated states (meaning aspirant members) and the US followed suit with similar visa restrictions.[146]

State- and nation-building

Efforts at peacemaking have not held up Transdniestria's state-building project. Shortly after the war of 1992 it already displayed accoutrements of an independent state, including its own constitution, coat of arms, anthem, flag, national bank and currency, border posts, customs service and postage stamps. In the absence of international recognition these were 'important psychological symbols that denoted statehood to many Transdniestrians' – and probably complicated the search for a peaceful end to the stand-off between Chisinau and Tiraspol. Indeed, Transdniestria insisted that a final deal could only be struck between two sovereign states by way of a treaty.[147] As for its political order, the PMR received a 'non-free' grading from Freedom House in its 2007 *Freedom in the World Report*.[148] This corresponded with another reliable assessment that the country 'is controlled by an authoritarian regime with a well-functioning security service that limits political pluralism essentially to the anti-reform, pro-Transdniestrian and Soviet-nostalgic part of the political spectrum'.[149] Smirnov's uninterrupted tenure as President since 1991 (with re-elections in 1996, 2001 and 2006) only reinforced the repressive nature of the regime. State-building has also been accompanied by nation-building, with the PMR leadership trying to fashion a Transdniestrian identity as the basis for statehood. Its core was 'Russo-centric', with genuflexions in the direction of multi-ethnicity and multi-lingualism. (About one-third of the Transdniestrian population were ethnic Moldovans, a slightly larger group than either the Russians or Ukrainians.)[150] On the international relations front, Transdniestria's links with its fellow contested states of Eurasia have been noted earlier in this chapter.

The Transdniestrian economy has been functioning reasonably well, 'or at least little worse than their Moldovan counterparts'. Although it has a relatively small market with only 630,000 inhabitants (comparable to Montenegro but much smaller than Moldova's 4.2 million people) occupying an area of 4,163 km^2 (marginally bigger than Cape Verde), Transdniestria's economy was extremely open. Roughly half its exports went to CIS countries, with Russia, Ukraine and Moldova its three largest trading partners. The PMR has successfully diversified its trade to Western states (including Germany and Greece) and others. Its exports consisted mainly of steel and metal products, mineral products, machines, equipment, textiles and foodstuffs.[151]

Like its counterparts in Eurasia, Transdniestria also had an illicit parallel economy. Its geographic location – a long sliver of land sandwiched between Moldova and Ukraine – placed the PMR at the core of large smuggling rings that connected the Ukrainian ports of Odessa and Illichivsk with markets in Ukraine, Moldova and elsewhere. The beneficiaries included Transdniestrian, Ukranian, Russian and Moldovan government officials, business enterprises and of course criminal organizations, all of whom feared the loss of their ill-gotten gains if Transdniestria became internationally 'respectable' by abandoning its contested statehood. Apart from illegal (contraband) trade in products that were also traded legally, such as fuel, cigarettes, liquor and other standard goods, there was extensive trafficking in drugs, arms and human beings as well as money laundering.[152]

Final status options

The PMR has certainly tried to act the part of an independent state and its Foreign Minister in June 2007 spoke hopefully of 'Kosovo's inevitable independence' setting 'a precedent for unrecognized post-Soviet republics'.[153] Russia's recognition of South Ossetia and Abkhazia raised expectations in Tiraspol that it was only a matter of time before Transdniestria received the same treatment from Moscow.[154] Yet the PMR leadership has long been prepared for other outcomes too – a prudent approach given the implacable opposition of Moldova and the wider international community to independence for Transdniestria.

In a referendum in September 2006 the customary 97 per cent of the territory's electorate voted for independence from Moldova and free association with Russia.[155] Association with the Russian Federation is problematic, however, because of Moldovan and international opposition. Even Russia's position has been ambivalent. On the one hand Moscow has long defended the territory's *de facto* independence, acknowledged Smirnov as 'President of Transdniestria', and declared the 2006 referendum a democratic expression of the popular will of the people of the PMR. On the other hand Russia has never formally recognized the PMR and has supported peace proposals that did not allow for independent statehood.[156]

All parties involved in the settlement initiative seemed to agree that Transdniestria's future lay with Moldova – even Transdniestria itself. In 1997 the two main adversaries signed a memorandum entitled Bases for Normalization of Relations between the Republic of Moldova and Transdniestria, which called for the creation of a 'common state' between them.[157] A more elaborate proposal, known as the Kiev Document, followed in 2002. Here the external mediators for the first time introduced the notion of a federal state in which state-territorial units (especially Transdniestria) would exercise authority over a defined range of matters.[158] Although subsequent negotiations on the Kiev plan became deadlocked, the proposal at least paved the way for the signing of the Protocol on Establishing a Mechanism for the Drafting and Approval of the Constitution of the Federal State by Moldova and Transdniestria in March 2003. It provided *inter alia* for the creation of a Joint Constitutional Commission, which in due course began exploring various constitutional models.[159] Since then status negotiations have focused on the rights and competencies that might be accorded to Transdniestria in a constitutional arrangement providing for power-sharing and minority protection.[160] On occasion Tiraspol has insisted on a loose confederal arrangement between two sovereign states.[161] While this position might be a ploy to formalize the *status quo*, it could alternatively serve as a halfway station to a federal dispensation. Chisinau, in turn, favoured autonomy for Transdniestria within Moldova, granted by law rather under a treaty between sovereign states.[162] Whatever political settlement is eventually reached, it may require an international guarantee to win the trust of Moldova and Transdniestria. The OSCE, Russia, Ukraine, the EU and the US are the obvious candidates to guarantee a final settlement.[163]

In the meantime the lack of mutual trust has been one of the main obstacles to progress in the search for a settlement. Another stumbling block has been that Moldova, for all its insistence on the reintegration of Transdniestria, has not offered an attractive 'home' for the rebel territory. Although freer than the PMR, Moldova has a communist-led government that controlled much of the media and the country was by far the poorest in Europe with a stagnant economy and rampant inflation.[164] In a promising development Smirnov and Moldovan President Vladimir Voronin met in April 2008 for the first time in seven years. They agreed to explore joint projects between their countries, ostensibly to build confidence.[165] It was a timely move: the Russo-Georgian war over South Ossetia four months later showed that Eurasia's so-called frozen conflicts 'are volcanoes that can erupt at any time', Voronin warned.[166]

Nagorno Karabagh

History and geography have also in our final Eurasian case study combined to shape a contemporary contested state. Nagorno Karabagh (literally translated as 'mountainous black garden') is an ancient Armenian-inhabited territory that had in different periods formed part of Armenia. From the 14th to the 18th centuries Nagorno Karabagh was ruled by autonomous Armenian princely dynasties on behalf of the Persian Empire, which was then in control of the area. In 1805 Nagorno Karabagh was annexed by Russia and after the revolution of 1917 became part of the Soviet Union.[167] Due to Soviet machinations Nagorno Karabagh was joined to and became completely enclosed by the territory of Azerbaijan. In the dying days of the Soviet Union both made a bid for independence: Azerbaijan immediately became a confirmed state, whereas Nagorno Karabagh was condemned to contested statehood on the grounds that it was legally part of Azerbaijan.

Given their origins, the fate of Karabagh's population has all along been tied closely to that of their kin in Armenia proper. Two tragedies that befell the Armenians in the late 19th and early 20th centuries influence the larger community's political outlook to this day. It was a period when the Armenian nation, divided between the Russian and Turkish empires, began developing a national consciousness that straddled the imperial divide. In 1894–6 up to 200,000 Armenians living in the Anatolian region of the Ottoman Empire were massacred on the orders of the Turkish Sultan. Barely 20 years later, while the First World War was raging, the Ottoman leadership began another round of genocide against their Armenian subjects, this time exterminating between 1 and 1.5 million of them.[168]

Meanwhile in 1917 the peoples of Transcaucasia had concluded an armistice with the Ottoman Empire, giving Nagorno Karabagh with its 330,000 inhabitants (90 per cent of them ethnic Armenians) *de facto* independence. A formal declaration to this effect was issued by the First Congress of Karabagh Armenians in the then capital Shushi in August 1918. At this time, with the new communist order in Russia in its infancy, Armenia and Azerbaijan also enjoyed brief spells of independence. Towards the end of 1918 the Ottoman army invaded Shushi 'to arrest, pillage, and massacre' until Constantinople's surrender to the Allies forced the Turks to withdraw from Karabagh.[169] Barely a year after the proclamation of Nagorno Karabagh's independence, its rulers entered into a provisional treaty with neighbouring Azerbaijan. In the wake of the massacre of 20,000

Armenians in Shushi in March 1920, in which Azerbaijanis participated, the Karabagh Assembly nullified the treaty and instead proclaimed union with Armenia. For only a few days towards the end of 1920 the Soviet-installed government of Azerbaijan recognized Nagorno Karabagh as part of Armenia, before reversing its decision.[170]

Between 1918 and 1920 Nagorno Karabagh possessed some typical attributes of statehood, although it was not admitted to the League of Nations. Instead, the world body acknowledged the disputed status of Karabagh, refusing to recognize Azerbaijan's sovereignty over the territory. (Neither Armenia nor Azerbaijan joined the League during their short spell of independence.)[171] In 1920 both Armenia and Azerbaijan became 'Sovietized', that is, fully absorbed into the new Soviet empire as Soviet Socialist Republics. The next year Nagorno Karabagh was formally declared part of Soviet Azerbaijan by the Caucasus Bureau of the Communist Party, followed in 1923 by the creation of the Nagorno Karabagh Autonomous Oblast – entrusted with broad autonomy – within Azerbaijan.[172] In deciding the status of Karabagh, the Soviet central authorities were influenced by what would nowadays be called matters of high politics that outweighed the manifest preferences of the inhabitants of the territory and their claims to self-determination. In March 1921 the Soviet Union signed a treaty with the new Republic of Turkey, successor to the Ottoman Empire, in terms of which Nagorno Karabagh would become a subordinate entity inside the Soviet Republic of Azerbaijan. In this way the Soviet rulers hoped to placate the Muslims of Azerbaijan, appease Turkey (whose support for Azerbaijan predated the Soviet era) and so enhance security along Soviet Russia's southern flank. Although the government of Soviet Armenia challenged this move in June 1921 by declaring Karabagh an integral part of its territory, the die had been cast.[173]

In an attempt to separate the two Armenian communities, the Azerbaijanis – with Moscow's blessing – created an artificial buffer between Nagorno Karabagh and Armenia in the shape of the Lachin and Kelbajar districts.[174] This imposed physical separation – which made Karabagh an enclave inside Azerbaijan – added insult to the injury Armenians suffered as a result of Karabagh's incorporation into Azerbaijan. A further source of grievance among Karabagh Armenians was that their share of the territory's population fell from 95 per cent to 75 per cent during the seven decades of Soviet rule. This was due to Baku's deliberate promotion of Azerbaijani settlement in Karabagh as part of a policy of 'cultural de-Armenization' of the region. Azerbaijan furthermore neglected the economic needs of the territory.[175] Local Soviet leaderships in both Nagorno Karabagh and Armenia periodically petitioned Moscow to reconsider the status of the contested territory and the late 1960s even witnessed mass protests in Karabagh over the status issue.[176]

Statehood and war

As in the other Eurasian territories featured in this chapter, the onset of *perestroika* and *glasnost* during Mikhail Gorbachev's tenure as Soviet President unleashed pent-up frustrations and aspirations in Nagorno Karabagh (and Armenia) too. In January 1988 some 80,000 Armenians from Armenia proper and Karabagh signed a petition requesting Moscow to transfer the enclave to Armenia. A month later the Nagorno Karabagh Supreme Soviet voted to unite with Armenia, which in June 1988 agreed to the territory's incorporation. Azerbaijan, not unexpectedly, rejected any such move.[177] The next step in the march towards secession came in December 1989 when the Supreme Soviets of Armenia and Nagorno Karabagh passed a joint resolution supporting their reunification. Without rescinding this resolution, the Karabagh regional council in September 1991 made a provisional declaration of the independence of the Nagorno Karabagh 'Republic' from Azerbaijan, not the Soviet Union. This decision came hard on the heels of Azerbaijan's own declaration of independence. In November 1991 the new state of Azerbaijan revoked Karabagh's autonomous status and followed it up with dissolving Karabagh as a separate territorial entity within Azerbaijan in January 1992.[178] These were largely symbolic gestures by Baku, having no effect on the rebel territory's break-away bid. In a referendum in December 1991 the voters of Nagorno Karabagh had overwhelmingly endorsed independence and based on this verdict a formal declaration of independence was issued from Stepanakert, capital of Nagorno Karabagh, in January 1992. This time it was not merely independence from Azerbaijan that was being proclaimed, but 'real' independence as the Soviet Union had by then ceased to exist.[179]

At the heart of the ongoing dispute over the status of Nagorno Karabagh – and hence the principal reason for its contested statehood – is the unresolved conflict between on the one hand the demand for self-determination clearly expressed by the vast majority of inhabitants of the territory, and on the other Azerbaijan's unambiguous insistence on the preservation of its territorial integrity. Each side therefore based its claims on fundamental principles of international law which, as in Abkhazia, South Ossetia and Transdniestria, collided head-on. Azerbaijan took the view that self-determination did not allow for unilateral secession and could thus not occur at the expense of its territorial unity. The Armenians in Karabagh and Armenia proper maintained that the contested territory had as much right to separate from Azerbaijan as the latter had for seceding from the Soviet Union. The legal grounds were said to be the 1990 Soviet law on withdrawal from the USSR. Armenian nationalists moreover pointed out that when Azerbaijan proclaimed its independence in 1991 it claimed to be the legal successor of the short-lived Azerbaijan Democratic Republic (1918–20) – an entity whose sovereignty over Karabagh had never been recognized by the League of Nations. By this logic the Armenians of Karabagh had in 1991 exercised their right of self-determination over land that had never fallen under the jurisdiction of an independent Azerbaijan. As such Nagorno Karabagh 'did not secede from an existing independent state and has never been part of the post-Soviet Republic of Azerbaijan'.[180]

Human rights concerns also weighed heavily with the Armenians of Nagorno Karabagh, as they typically do with separatist communities. Their grievances dated back to the Soviet era, when the Azerbaijani government had made life a misery for the Karabagh Armenians through socio-economic discrimination and political oppression. When the Armenians of Karabagh sought to achieve self-determination by peaceful means in the final years of the Soviet Union, the Azerbaijan authorities responded with brute force or were at least complicit in acts of violence against Armenians. The first major incident in February 1988 involved the massacre of Armenians in Sumgait, the third largest city in Azerbaijan. Country-wide anti-Armenian riots occurred the following November and in January 1990 another massacre of Armenians took place in the Azerbaijani capital Baku. Operation Ring in 1991–2, a joint military operation by Soviet and Azerbaijani forces, involved the deportation of Armenians from 24 villages in and around Karabagh.[181] In the eyes of the Armenians in Karabagh and Armenia proper these events proved that Baku was bent on cleansing Armenians from all of Azerbaijan, even through acts of extermination – thus conjuring up images of the genocide of 1915. Indeed, most of the 400,000 Armenians living in Azerbaijan fled the country. To be fair, there was also a reverse exodus: 170,000 Azerbaijanis living in Armenia were forced out to Azerbaijan. In August 1990 Azerbaijani forces backed by Soviet troops also drove between 150,000 and 200,000 Armenian villagers out of the northern part of Nagorno Karabagh.[182]

The actual war in Nagorno Karabagh began in December 1991 with an Azerbaijani offensive that included the bombardment of Stepanakert. A second major offensive in the summer of 1992 left roughly half of Karabagh's territory under Azerbaijan's military occupation. The Armenians' counterattack, lasting from October 1992 to September 1993, saw them regain control of most of Karabagh and also occupy 5,500 km^2 of Azerbaijani territory. The Azerbaijanis have in turn remained in control of the entire Shahumian district claimed by Karabagh and parts of two others, amounting to 750 km^2 or 15 per cent of what has traditionally been Karabagh land. The formal ceasefire of May 1994 – brokered by Russia in cooperation with the OSCE – 'froze' this division of the spoils.[183] As usual the human toll of the conflict was high, not least because both sides transgressed the laws of war. By the end of the hostilities in 1994, an estimated 25,000 people had been killed, among them 4,000 civilians, and up to one million were displaced, mostly Azerbaijanis. Among those uprooted were virtually the entire community of 40,000 Azerbaijanis in Karabagh and 90,000 Armenians from the territory.[184]

The ceasefire of 1994 did not provide for a separation of forces or demilitarization. Instead, thousands of troops from the two sides still confronted each other across the so-called line of contact. No peacekeepers have been deployed in Karabagh, leaving it the sole conflict area in the South Caucasus without a foreign peacekeeping mission.[185] A further legacy of the period of intense conflict was the blockade Azerbaijan and Turkey had imposed against Armenia and Nagorno Karabagh in 1991. These two landlocked targets have suffered severe economic deprivation over the 17 years the blockade has been in effect.[186] Although full-scale violence has not recurred since 1994, the underlying causes of the war – at the core of which was the final status of Nagorno Karabagh – have not been addressed. Karabagh therefore deserves the epithet of another 'frozen conflict' in Eurasia.

External involvement

The 'freeze' has not meant an absence of peace initiatives. Already during the war of the early 1990s the OSCE assumed the role of principal mediator. A dozen member states of the OSCE subsequently constituted the Minsk Group that was mandated to ensure the continuation of the ceasefire and to initiate negotiations on a peaceful settlement in Nagorno Karabagh. Co-chaired by Russia, France and the US, the Minsk Group included representatives from Azerbaijan and Armenia. The Minsk Group has since 2004 facilitated a new round of settlement negotiations known as the Prague Process.[187] The UN has not been as directly involved as the OSCE in trying to resolve the Karabagh conflict, but the Security Council has laid down parameters for a settlement in four resolutions (822, 853, 874 and 884) adopted in 1993. Most critically, for our purposes, is that all the resolutions reaffirmed the sovereignty and territorial integrity of Azerbaijan and all other states in the region and the inviolability of international borders. Karabagh was thus by implication recognized as part of Azerbaijan. The series of resolutions furthermore demanded an end to 'all hostilities and hostile acts', called for the withdrawal of armed forces from occupied parts of Azerbaijan and supported the peace process launched by the OSCE. It is instructive that the four resolutions made no reference to the crippling economic blockade of Karabagh and Armenia. UN General Assembly resolutions 49/13 and 57/298 also referred to Nagorno Karabagh as a region of Azerbaijan. The EU, which has kept a low profile in the peace process, has likewise come out in support of the territorial integrity of Azerbaijan and stated explicitly that it did not recognize the independence of Nagorno Karabagh.[188]

The two major 'external' parties to the Nagorno Karabagh conflict were of course Armenia and Azerbaijan. The former was Karabagh's kin and patron state, providing an economic lifeline in the form of an annual 'inter-state loan' that covered up to 80 per cent of the break-away territory's needs and sharing the same currency (the dram), and also supplying military hardware and manpower. In short, Armenia was the guarantor of Nagorno Karabagh's contested statehood. Their domestic politics were probably more intertwined than those of the other Eurasian contested states and their respective patrons: Robert Kocharian, the President of Nagorno Karabagh from 1994 to 1997, became Prime Minister of Armenia in the latter year and President in 1998.[189] Azerbaijan was by contrast Karabagh's *bête noire,* the parent state insisting on the return of its prodigal offspring. In playing the role of veto state Azerbaijan could rely on the unanimous support of the international community, which also rejected confirmed independence for the contested state. Despite the divide between them, Armenia and Azerbaijan have under the Prague Process engaged in several rounds of settlement talks on Karabagh, involving their presidents and foreign ministers. Since signing the ceasefire of 1994, Nagorno Karabagh has been treated as a party to the conflict and accordingly participated in settlement talks.[190]

Because the conflict over Nagorno Karabagh was being played out in the space of the former Soviet Union, Moscow featured prominently in this Eurasian situation too. Its role has at times been ambiguous; during the war, for instance, Moscow provided both Azerbaijan and Armenia with weapons. Since then Russia has been actively involved in the multilateral peace effort, favouring an autonomous status for Karabagh within an unfragmented Azerbaijan. Determined to remain the dominant power in the Caucasus, Russia demanded a hand in shaping the course of events in its near abroad. Karabagh, like Armenia, Azerbaijan and Georgia, served as a buffer between Russia and the two regional powers of Iran and Turkey. Moscow was furthermore keenly aware of Azerbaijan's growing importance as a producer of oil and gas, all the more reason to keep the country within Russia's sphere of influence. The Karabagh conflict offered Moscow useful leverage over Azerbaijan, like the other Eurasian conflicts gave Russia the whip hand over Georgia and Moldova. The presence of Russian troops in Armenia was probably aimed at deterring an Azerbaijan attack on Nagorno Karabagh. All in all, Russia was evidently 'the ultimate arbiter' of the Karabagh situation among the countries of the Minsk Group.[191] The US, also active in the settlement initiative, has likewise followed a rather ambivalent approach to the Karabagh conflict. Washington 'tends to give preferential aid treatment to the Armenians, while providing preferential political treatment to Azerbaijan'. While America subscribed to the preservation of Azerbaijan's territorial integrity and rejected Karabagh's claims to statehood, it allowed the territory's President to visit Washington in 1999, where he met with State Department officials.[192] Turkey, another important external power, has consistently and unambiguously supported Azerbaijan in its struggle to regain control of Nagorno Karabagh. Ankara has provided Baku with diplomatic, economic and military support and has been Azerbaijan's partner in the economic blockade of Armenia and Karabagh.[193]

State-building

In common with other contested entities, Nagorno Karabagh has made a concerted effort to build a working state. It has managed to create a democratic order characterized by a multiparty system with free and competitive elections at national and local levels and the protection of minority rights (only about 5 per cent of the current population were not ethnic Armenians). The incumbent President, Bako Sahakyan, replaced Arkady Gukasyan in October 2007 following the fourth presidential election since 1995.[194] In an earlier exercise in electoral politics in December 2006, 99 per cent of voters approved a draft constitution in which the Republic of Nagorno Karabagh was described as a sovereign, democratic state.[195] Karabagh possessed the usual range of state institutions catering for security and welfare functions, including armed forces that have shown their mettle during the war of the early 1990s. The official welfare services have, however, been hamstrung by the parlous state of Nagorno Karabagh's economy – in part the result of the Turkish-Azerbaijani blockade.[196] On the whole Karabagh has a government that has since the end of the war in 1994 been in effective control of its territory of about 4,400 km^2 (slightly larger than Transdniestria) and of its population of roughly 150,000 (somewhat smaller than that of Sao Tomé and Principe). In these respects Nagorno Karabagh met three of the basic requirements of statehood. As regards a capacity to engage in foreign relations, Karabagh has participated in multilateral settlement talks over the territory's future. In earlier sections of this chapter we recorded that Nagorno Karabagh has been involved in formal relations with Abkhazia, South Ossetia and Transdniestria. These links included the foursome's adoption in 2007 of a declaration on principles for peaceful conflict resolution with their central states, and Karabagh's observer status in the Commonwealth for Democracy and Rights of Nations. In addition Karabagh reportedly maintained representative offices in Russia, Armenia, the US, France, Australia and Lebanon.[197] Karabagh's greatest international handicap is of course that it is not recognized by a single confirmed state – not even by Armenia, which feared that such a move would complicate its own foreign relations.[198]

Searching for a lasting settlement

Although the Karabagh conflict may be called 'frozen', it is far from quiet, not to mention over. 'Today there is neither war nor peace', the International Crisis Group reported in 2005. With ceasefire violations increasing and soldiers and civilians from both sides continuing to die on the line of contact, the Group warned, 'there is a real risk of new large-scale fighting'. Since then sporadic military skirmishes have occurred. It should also be borne in mind that Azerbaijan has reserved the right to use force to restore its territorial integrity.[199] These factors underline the need for a lasting political settlement. What are the conceivable ways out of the conflict?

There is again a range of familiar possibilities. At the one 'extreme' the central state – in this instance Azerbaijan – was adamant that the contested entity was an integral part of its territory. Azerbaijan would remain a unitary republic, as its constitution proclaimed, without any devolution or sharing of power to accommodate the ethnic Armenians of Nagorno Karabagh.[200] At the other end of the spectrum we find an equally vehement demand for Nagorno Karabagh's independence. It was an article of faith among Armenians that Azerbaijan had through acts of omission and commission over many decades forfeited any moral right to rule over Armenians, and that the latter have in turn acquired the remedial right to form their own state – in which they had constituted the majority population since time immemorial – separate from Azerbaijan.[201] Nobel laureate Andrei Sakharov put the choice in stark terms in 1988: 'For Azerbaijan the issue of Karabagh is a matter of ambition, for the Armenians of Karabagh it is a matter of life or death'.[202] Precisely because of existential considerations Karabagh's Armenians claimed independent statehood.

Rare yet authoritative external backing for Karabagh's right of independence has come from the Public International Law and Policy Group, a non-governmental organization consisting mainly of public international lawyers and foreign relations experts. In a report on Nagorno Karabagh released in 2000,[203] the Group argued that the territory qualified for self-determination and the accompanying right of independence in terms of criteria laid down in international law. First, the Armenians of Karabagh constituted a group entitled to self-determination. They met the objective requirement of cultural distinctiveness from Azerbaijanis in terms of history, language, culture and religion and had long been a separate territorial entity (known by the ancient name Artsakh). Second, Nagorno Karabagh has a just claim to remedial self-determination because of Azerbaijan's dismal human rights record in the entity during the Soviet era and thereafter. The prospects for observing human rights and allowing the people of Nagorno Karabagh to pursue their economic, social and cultural development under Azerbaijani rule – even with local autonomy – were therefore poor. Under these conditions the entity's claim to self-determination through independence 'may supersede Azerbaijan's claim to territorial integrity', the Group maintained. Nagorno Karabagh in the third place complied with all the traditional requirements of statehood set out in the Montevideo Convention. We touched on these aspects when considering the territory's state-building project above. Finally, the Public International Law and Policy Group argued that Karabagh's right of independence was consistent with the so-called balancing-of-factors approach. It meant that a *de jure* divorce between Nagorno Karabagh and Azerbaijan would have little adverse effect on the latter. Azerbaijan would lose a mere 2 per cent of its overall population and would not surrender any of its oil fields or have important roads or waterways severed. A negotiated exchange of occupied territories could enhance the security of both Azerbaijan and Karabagh, while an end to further conflict would benefit the entire region. The Group concluded that 'international law provides a firm basis for Nagorno Karabagh's pursuit of independence from Azerbaijan'. It is only fair to add that contradictory readings of international law found no legal grounds for Karabagh's claims to statehood.[204]

Two forms of independent statehood have been advanced for Karabagh. The one is conventional, unfettered independence and the other is conditional independence of the kind proposed for Kosovo. For Karabagh, independence could be conditioned on the prohibition of future unification with Armenia and the guarantee of the rights of non-Armenian communities in Karabagh.[205] The most elaborate formula for the territory's qualified independence has emanated from the Public International Law and Policy Group.[206] Drawing on precedents created in peace processes in Bosnia, Kosovo, Northern Ireland, East Timor and the Middle East, among others, the Group proposed an 'intermediate sovereignty/earned recognition approach' for Nagorno Karabagh. It would consist of two phases. The first, styled 'intermediate sovereignty', would extend over three to five years and include a measure of 'sovereignty' allowing for special relationships with neighbouring states and participation in international organizations, the protection of human and minority rights, and international monitoring of the interim arrangements. In the second period an international mechanism would be used 'to determine whether Nagorno Karabagh had earned international recognition based upon its performance during the interim period of de facto independence'. The wishes of the people of Nagorno Karabagh would be determined through a referendum on independence. While Nagorno Karabagh and Armenia were likely to support this approach, Azerbaijan was bound to reject any blueprint for Karabagh's independence.

Nagorno Karabagh's incorporation into the Soviet Union was formally requested by the Chairman of the Karabagh Supreme Soviet in 1991, but Moscow did not deign to reply. This option seems to have disappeared altogether from the debate about Nagorno Karabagh's final status.[207] Both Stepanakert and Yerevan have also favoured unification between Armenia and Karabagh as a possible free choice of the people of the territory. Lately, however, independence has become the preferred option for both of them. Baku, by contrast, remained as opposed to the incorporation of Karabagh into Armenia as it was to the territory's independence.[208]

Several other status solutions for Nagorno Karabagh, between the mutually exclusive alternatives of incorporation into a unitary Azerbaijan and independence, have been put forward by various parties and interested observers. Predictably an autonomous Karabagh within Azerbaijan is one of them.[209] Azerbaijan President Ilham Aliyev has held out this possibility. 'Our greatest concessions are security guarantees for Nagorno-Karabagh Armenians and our readiness to grant the highest degree of autonomy that exists in the world', he declared in 2005.[210] In similar vein the Minsk Group had in 1997 proposed that Karabagh should become 'a state and a territorial formation within the confines of Azerbaijan', enjoying significant guarantees, rights and privileges.[211] Karabagh's rulers were, however, adamant that Soviet history had shown conclusively that Azerbaijan's offer of broad autonomy was an unworkable option as it allowed a minimal degree of rights while maximizing the territory's vulnerability and insecurity *vis-à-vis* Baku.[212] In this view Karabagh has been supported by Armenia, which maintained that Karabagh cannot be 'vertically subordinated' to Baku. Armenia has furthermore insisted that a final settlement should include security guarantees for the population of Karabagh and provide a permanent territorial link between the territory and Armenia.[213]

The creation of a confederation within Azerbaijan's internationally recognized pre-war borders was mooted by the Minsk Group in 1998 under the rather confusing designation of a 'common state' comprising Azerbaijan and Nagorno Karabagh. Under this formula Karabagh, 'a statal and territorial entity in a form of a Republic', would have extensive powers to conduct its internal affairs and maintain its basic political integrity. Baku would, however, represent Nagorno Karabagh in the UN.[214] Whereas Karabagh President Gukasyan favoured such a 'horizontal or confederative relationship' with Azerbaijan, the latter rejected it.[215]

An alternative to contested statehood that we considered in Chapter 3, namely a protectorate, has also been suggested for Nagorno Karabagh. In this instance the call has been for a dual Azerbaijani-Armenian protectorate over the contested territory.[216] None of the major parties to the dispute have given the idea any serious support.

A land-for-status plan comes in different forms. One proposal is that Azerbaijan would recognize Nagorno Karabagh's *de jure* statehood in exchange for the return of its districts occupied by Karabagh.[217] Under another version Azerbaijan would renounce all claims to Karabagh in exchange for land in Armenia. The latter would involve the strategic Meghri region that would give Azerbaijan a land link with its non-contiguous entity of Nakhichevan (located inside Armenia) and with Turkey.[218] A further possibility is that Nagorno Karabagh would remain part of Azerbaijan but that Armenia would gain land access to the enclave by means of a corridor in the Lachin Strip. This would supposedly bring commercial and cultural benefits to the two Armenian communities. In return for the 'concession', Armenia would be required to transfer its southern province to Azerbaijan to allow the latter territorial access to Nakhichevan and Turkey and so realize the ideal of a pan-Turkic link between the three. While Azerbaijan would probably oppose the first proposal, Karabagh and Armenia are certain to reject the other two.[219]

Conclusion

Abkhazia, Nagorno Karabagh, South Ossetia and Transdniestria represent a microcosm of contested statehood: their life cycles – in terms of origins, current situation and future prospects – display the typical ingredients of this status. They took the secessionist route to statehood, opting for unilateral declarations of independence in the face of violent resistance from their central states. Having existed for between nine and 17 years, the four Eurasian entities have proven their *de facto* statehood. Although becoming well entrenched, they still suffered serious recognition deficits. Russia's *de jure* recognition of South Ossetia and Abkhazia is unlikely to end the pair's contested statehood.

The incendiary potential of the protracted political stalemate over the four wannabe states' final status has drawn major powers and international organizations into the search for peaceful settlements of the inappropriately named frozen conflicts. Proposed solutions cover the familiar spectrum from *de jure* independence to the restoration of the *status quo ante*. In between numerous so-called third-way options have been tabled, including federalism, associated statehood and confederalism. All these try to accommodate current realities on the ground, and reconcile the bedrock principles of the territorial integrity of states and peoples' right of self-determination. Another option that enjoyed considerable support in Abkhazia and South Ossetia was incorporation into Russia. However, the lack of consensus among the parties concerned over acceptable final solutions suggests that Abkhazia, Nagorno Karabagh, South Ossetia and Transdniestria will not exit life in international limbo any time soon.

5
Kosovo

Kosovo has experienced several rounds of contested statehood. The first began in 1991 when the territory seceded from Yugoslavia (effectively Serbia) and declared unilateral independence. Not a single state recognized its purported statehood. In 1999, after NATO's war against Yugoslavia, Kosovo became a ward of the international community. This heralded a new period of international contestation over Kosovo's political fate as its final status was being negotiated by interested parties. Then came Kosovo's second unilateral declaration of independence in February 2008. Although over 40 states including major Western powers had formally recognized its statehood within three months, Kosovo's right of independence has remained contentious – albeit far less so than in the 1990s. Its current spell of self-proclaimed independence admittedly fails to meet our requirement of at least three years' duration, but when Kosovo's earlier experience of life in international limbo is added its inclusion in this inquiry seems justified.

History's stepchild

Serbs and Albanians have for ages been locked in conflict over title to Kosovo. The origins of the dispute can be traced back to the second half of the 12th century, when the Kingdom of Serbia was founded in south-eastern Europe. Kosovo was soon annexed to the expanding Serbian Kingdom, which reached its territorial zenith around 1350. Thereafter Serbia crumbled as the Ottoman Empire expanded northwards. A watershed event in its break-up was the famous battle of Kosovo Polje ('the Field of the Blackbirds') in 1389 between Serb and Ottoman forces. The Turks prevailed, breaking Serbia's military power. Kosovo, the 'cradle of Serbia' and seat of the Serbian Orthodox Church since the late 13th century, was moreover wrested from the Serbs. To rub local salt into the externally inflicted wounds, Kosovo's Albanian population made common cause with their Ottoman co-religionists against the Serbs. Serbia thereafter acknowledged Ottoman suzerainty, until its annexation to the Ottoman Empire in

1459. Serbia's nationalist myth-makers have long seized on the historic 14th century battle to provoke ethnic and religious hatred of the Kosovar Albanians.[1]

The decline of the Ottoman Empire in the 19th century led to the restoration of Serb independence in 1878. The date also marked the launch of an Albanian nationalist movement in Kosovo. While all Albanian territories, including Kosovo, remained part of the Ottoman Empire, the growing Albanian national consciousness found expression in calls for the unification of all Albanian lands in a single Albanian state. This ideal was thwarted by a 1912 agreement between Serbia and Bulgaria that assigned Kosovo to Serbia. The same year the independent state of Albania was proclaimed and granted international recognition in terms of the Treaty of London concluded in 1913. At the end of that year the great powers, under the Protocol of Florence, endorsed Serbia's acquisition of Kosovo. This meant that at least half of the total Albanian population found themselves outside their newly established national homeland of Albania, creating a source of enduring conflict between diaspora Albanians and their local rulers. This also applied to Kosovo, where the Albanian community became deeply resentful of their mistreatment at the hands of the Serbs. To be sure, these feelings were matched by Serb animosity towards the Albanians of Kosovo.[2] With such entrenched ancient hatreds, Kosovo was doomed to protracted inter-communal violence.

The first round of that struggle took place during World War I when Serbia suffered heavily under the aggression of Germany and Austria-Hungary. In this unsettled atmosphere Kosovo witnessed violent clashes between Serbs and Albanians, the latter trying to exploit the vulnerability of their besieged Serb rulers. Afterwards the Entente Powers, far from being concerned about the fate of Kosovo, were keen to reward Serbia for its valiant contribution to the Allied victory. That took the form of support for the establishment in 1918 of a new Serb-dominated Kingdom of Serbs, Croats and Slovenes – with Kosovo remaining part of Serbia.[3] During the interwar period conditions for the Kosovar Albanians, constituting over 60 per cent of the territory's population in 1921, deteriorated. The Albanians' disloyalty during the war was not forgotten by the Serbian authorities. Albanians were given a stark choice: assimilate or emigrate. Assimilation was pursued through such measures as closing down Albanian-language schools in Kosovo and ordering that all official business be transacted in the Serbo-Croatian tongue. Kosovar Albanians who resisted were pressurized to emigrate, which well over 100,000 may have done. To fill their place and change the territory's demography, the large-scale settlement of Serbs and other Slavs in Kosovo was officially encouraged. Not surprisingly armed resistance emerged in the shape of an Albanian guerrilla group called the Kaçak movement. Active from 1918 until the mid-1920s, the rebels were eventually overwhelmed by the brute force of the Serbian authorities. The imposition of a royal dictatorship and the renaming of the state to the Kingdom of Yugoslavia (meaning South Slavs) in 1929 brought no respite for the persecuted Albanians of Kosovo.[4]

The next phase in the struggle for Kosovo coincided with World War II. Axis powers invaded and occupied Yugoslavia in 1941. The country was carved up, with the bulk of Kosovo becoming part of 'greater Albania' under Italian rule while the mineral-rich north-eastern part of Kosovo was placed under German control. The majority of the Kosovar Albanians welcomed the Axis forces as liberators from the yoke of Serbia and took revenge on the Serbs in the territory. The occupying forces permitted Albanian schools and media in Kosovo and also gave the Albanians the right to carry arms. In the wake of the liberation of Kosovo by Yugoslav Partisans in late 1944, the tables were turned and the Albanians again paid dearly for collaborating with the losing side. The retribution to which they were subjected (including massacres) continued the now familiar cycle of grievous ethnic violence in Kosovo.[5]

With the adoption of its first post-war constitution in 1946, Yugoslavia was reconstituted as a federal state comprising six so-called sovereign republics. A special arrangement was made for the Republic of Serbia, one of the six primary units: it had two sub-units, the Autonomous Province of Vojvodina and the Autonomous Region of Kosovo-Metohija, as it was then styled. While both the latter entities enjoyed representation in the federal legislature, they had no independent decision-making authority and their internal affairs (for example education) were determined by the Serbian Republic, not the federal government. The peoples of Yugoslavia were in turn classified as either nations (Serbs, Croats, Slovenes, Macedonians and Montenegrins) or national minorities, subsequently changed to nationalities (encompassing all the rest, including the Albanians). The Kosovar Albanians were thus left without any meaningful autonomy, a feature reinforced by a further enhancement of central power under constitutional amendments in 1953. The Albanians' powerlessness left them vulnerable to persecution at the hands of the Serbian authorities, which continued more or less unabated until a respite in the late 1960s.[6]

Following demonstrations and rioting by Albanians in Kosovo in 1968, ostensibly in support of demands for the territory's elevation to republican status and hence autonomy, the federal and Serbian authorities uncharacteristically made some concessions. These included the founding of the Albanian-language University of Pristina, the establishment of Albanian cultural organizations, and the promotion of educational and cultural exchanges between Kosovo and Albania. Amendments to the federal and Serbian constitutions in 1968 and the adoption of a new Yugoslav constitution in 1974 expanded the independent authority of Kosovo and Vojvodina, allowing them to make their own laws within the framework of the two constitutions and to participate in the federal government in their own right. They were given seats in the Federal Assembly and the federal Constitutional

Court and, like the six republics, the provinces of Kosovo and Vojvodina each acquired a central bank and separate educational, judicial and police services. Redefining the two autonomous entities as constituent units of the Yugoslav federation, Kosovo and Vojvodina achieved the *de facto* status of sovereign republics, except that they were not granted a right of secession. A further landmark feature of the 1974 Constitution was the enshrinement of national distinctions. With the exception of Bosnia and Herzegovina, the republics and provinces were all built on national identity (meaning the majority nation within each unit).[7] As the first article of the Constitution of 1974 put it, Yugoslavia was 'a federal state having the form of a state community of voluntarily united nations'.[8]

The new official recognition of cultural diversity contributed to the major educational and cultural advances that Kosovar Albanians made in the 1970s. Yet they still felt aggrieved at not formally achieving the dual constitutional status of a 'nation' and a 'republic'. This resentment spilled over into sporadic demonstrations and the customary heavy-handed responses of the authorities. In the wake of the death in 1980 of Josip Broz Tito, the founding father of communist Yugoslavia, the ties binding the diverse components of the federation came under enormous pressure. This also affected Kosovo, which witnessed renewed Albanian assertiveness on the one hand and the spill-over of a resurgent Serb nationalism on the other. The Albanian population protested repeatedly against human rights abuses and occasionally called for the unification of Kosovo and Albania proper and even for the independence of Kosovo. The community's major demand between the mid-1970s and the mid-1980s was, however, the relatively modest one of more autonomy for Kosovo within the Yugoslav state.[9]

Another chapter in the Kosovo saga coincided with the leadership of Slobodan Milosevic. Positions on both sides of Kosovo's ethnic divide became radicalized, feeding the spiral of violence. In 1986 Milosevic became leader of the League of Communists of Serbia and from the outset played on Serbs' nationalist sentiments, including their claims to Kosovo. He soon proposed that the autonomy enjoyed by Kosovo and Vojvodina be curtailed and even revoked. Outraged, Kosovar Albanians stepped up their demands for secession from Serbia. Elected President of Serbia in 1989, Milosevic pushed amendments to Serbia's constitution through the republic's legislature and then bludgeoned the Kosovo Assembly into passing constitutional changes that stripped the province of its autonomy and *de facto* republican status.[10] Kosovo descended into turmoil as Albanians vented their anger in public. The federal authorities imposed emergency measures in Kosovo in 1989 and deployed large numbers of federal troops.[11] In this highly charged atmosphere Milosevic addressed a huge Serb rally to commemorate the 600th anniversary of the Battle of Kosovo Polje on 28 June. In an inflammatory nationalistic speech he reaffirmed Serbs' historical claims to Kosovo, giving an intimation of further conflict to come.[12] In his determination to strengthen Serbia's hold over Kosovo, Milosevic inadvertently intensified the resolve of the province's Albanian majority to free themselves from Serbian rule.

The final lap to independence

The year 1990 saw the Serbs and Kosovar Albanians drifting further apart, straining to breaking point the formal ties binding Kosovo to Serbia. The repeal of Kosovo's autonomous status prompted more human rights violations and discriminatory government policies aimed at Serbianizing the province.[13] Amid mass demonstrations and fatal confrontations between police and Albanian protesters, a full-fledged state of emergency was declared in Kosovo in January and federal police and military detachments were deployed in the province. Although federal authorities relaxed the emergency measures in April, their decision to leave matters in Kosovo to the Serbian government and the latter's dismissal of thousands of state employees in the province only aggravated the already volatile situation.[14]

In July 1990 Albanian members of the Kosovo Assembly proclaimed the Republic of Kosovo as an equal member of the Yugoslav Federation, thus separate from but on par with Serbia and the other republics; Kosovo would thus remain within the federal structure of Yugoslavia, not seek independence from it. The Serbian Assembly promptly declared the Albanian proclamation illegal and for good measure disbanded the Assembly of Kosovo.[15] In no mood for compromise, Albanian legislators adopted the Constitution of the Republic of Kosovo in September 1990. Kosovo, in the words of the constitution, was 'a democratic state of the Albanian people and members of other nations and national minorities who are their citizens'. Even so, the 'state' of Kosovo was defined in the constitution as a member of the 'Yugoslav community', confirming that Kosovo was seceding from Serbia but not from the Yugoslav federation.[16] The process of separation continued nonetheless, with an 'underground referendum' on independence for Kosovo held among the local Albanian electorate in September 1991. Kosovo's supposedly dissolved parliament responded to the positive verdict (over 90 per cent in favour) by proclaiming independence the following month. Both the Serbian and Yugoslav authorities rejected the referendum, but the Kosovar Albanians – emboldened by the fragmentation of Yugoslavia – had raised their sights from a restoration of autonomy (as provided by the 1974 constitution) to independent statehood for the territory.[17]

The adoption of Kosovo's constitution had accelerated the development of parallel Albanian institutions of government. These 'underground' structures operated alongside the official Serbian institutions, which were largely ignored or boycotted by the Albanian majority. The Albanians maintained more than a mere shadow cabinet of the kind formed by opposition parties in parliamentary democracies. There was a president (Ibrahim Rugova) and a government of six ministers, five of them living in exile. While the elected Kosovo legislature was unable to hold plenary sessions, several commissions functioned. A particularly noteworthy one was for education, which the Albanians conducted from home or in underground schools. Health care was provided through a network of private hospitals and clinics. There was also an Albanian sports league, cultural associations and media. Underground business firms operated and a form of income tax was levied on Albanian migrants working abroad. Many of these institutions, it should be noted, had already existed before 1990 but acquired a new importance after Kosovo declared independence in 1991.[18] There was apparently also an attempt to create a parallel police force in Kosovo, as witnessed by the conviction of nearly 70 Albanians by a Serbian court in 1995 on such charges.[19] The dual system of government reflected the existence of two separate societies in Kosovo, namely the Albanians constituting about 82 per cent of the territory's population in 1991 (exceeding 90 per cent in 1994) and the Serb minority.[20]

The Serbian authorities were willing to tolerate Albanian self-organization as long as it did not extend to the creation of the institutions of independent statehood. Determined to retain control of traditional state functions, Belgrade refused to recognize the Constitution of the Republic of Kosovo, treated as illegal all actions of the formally disbanded Albanian-dominated legislature, and rejected Albanian-organized elections.[21] Deprived of its autonomy, Kosovo was expected to use the remaining channels of political participation at national level in the shape of a (Belgrade-approved) member in the collective federal presidency as well as representation in the federal Assembly.[22] These structures held no appeal or legitimacy for an Albanian community determined to loosen the constitutional bonds with – and free itself of the bondage of – Serbia and also Yugoslavia. They were obviously inspired by the drives for independence in Slovenia, Croatia and Macedonia (all attaining confirmed statehood in 1991) and the consequent unravelling of the federal state of Yugoslavia.

In a bold act of defiance, Kosovo's alternative government staged presidential and parliamentary elections in May 1992. Although denounced as illegal by the Serbian government, the contest attracted a high voter turnout – almost exclusively Albanian – that gave the process a strong measure of legitimacy. The presence of eight election monitoring teams from abroad added to the credibility of the poll. Rugova, leader of the Democratic League of Kosovo (DLK), was elected President and his party won a majority of seats in the legislature. To drive home the message that they were no longer interested in participating in the politics of Serbia and what remained of Yugoslavia, the majority of Kosovo's Albanians refused to vote in federal and republican elections.[23]

Kosovo met the basic empirical requirements of statehood. It had a defined territory of 10,686 km^2, constituting 15 per cent of the land area of Serbia-plus-Kosovo. This compares in size with Lebanon or Jamaica. Kosovo had a population of approximately two million, including roughly 100,000 ethnic Serbs and far smaller numbers of Bosniaks, Roma, Turks, Gorani and Croats.[24] Kosovo had considerable experience of self-rule and the basic structures of government were in place. The entity was probably capable of engaging in international relations, but collective non-recognition left it in international limbo. A more pressing handicap was Kosovo's severe socio-economic under-development. It was the poorest region in the Balkans and one of the poorest in Europe. Roughly 45 per cent of its inhabitants lived below the poverty line and 14 per cent in extreme poverty. A root cause of the high rate of poverty was unemployment, which at 50 per cent was again the highest in the Balkans. Health indicators were among the worst in Europe, especially with regard to infant mortality (between 18 and 44 per 1,000 births).[25] Kosovo's undecided status, the European Commission observed, hindered badly needed economic and social development.[26]

Contested statehood and war

The Kosovar Albanian leadership was from the outset keen to gain international recognition of their self-proclaimed state. Immediately after the independence referendum in September 1991, Rugova appealed to Lord Carrington in his capacity as chairman of a European Community diplomatic initiative on Yugoslavia to give his 'full and immediate consideration' to the Republic of Kosovo's request to be recognized as a sovereign independent state. Carrington did not deign to reply.[27] President Rugova was received by the Albanian Prime Minister, who went no further than expressing Tirana's unqualified support for Kosovo's eventual (internationally recognized) independence. Kosovo's Prime Minister and his deputy visited several European capitals and also the Vatican, but got little more than polite receptions.[28] Kosovo was tasting the bitter fruits of collective non-recognition.

Although a case could be made in international law for Kosovo's unilateral secession from Yugoslavia – on the basis of systematic oppression and the denial of Kosovar Albanians' right of self-determination[29] – no state was at the time prepared to champion this view. The world community drew a distinction between the legitimacy of Kosovo's claims to statehood and those of the former Yugoslav republics of Slovenia, Croatia and Macedonia, which had been admitted to the UN upon assuming independence. Scores of major powers had already been reluctant to accept the dismemberment of Yugoslavia and appeared even more unwilling to countenance fragmentation-within-fragmentation by supporting a subordinate entity (Kosovo) within a Yugoslav republic (Serbia) to break away. Such a process could moreover encourage imitators beyond Serbia, as restive minorities in Croatia, Macedonia and Bosnia and Herzegovina may wish to create their separate states too. Another consideration behind the international rejection of Kosovo's statehood was the need to avoid alienating Serbia even further. As the major remaining partner in the downsized Federal Republic of Yugoslavia (Montenegro being the junior associate) established in April 1992, Serbia's cooperation was vital in resolving the bloody conflict over Bosnia and Herzegovina's bid for statehood (formally proclaimed in March 1992). In the first half of the 1990s leading powers were indeed heavily preoccupied with addressing the situation in Bosnia and Herzegovina, culminating in the Dayton peace talks in 1995. The fate of Kosovo was not on the agenda at Dayton.

While the international community opposed Rugova's objective of statehood for Kosovo, they commended his commitment to non-violent means. On the home front, however, Rugova had to contend with a rising tide of dissatisfaction over the paltry results of his strategy of passive resistance against Belgrade. Militants impatient with the President's approach formed the Kosovo Liberation Army (KLA) in 1996. Not involved with Rugova's parallel government, the KLA chose armed struggle to settle the final status issue.[30] The uncompromising KLA soon had something to show for its pains: by mid-1998 the movement controlled between 30 and 40 per cent of Kosovo's territory, with a vital corridor to the Albanian border.[31] However, the KLA could not hold on to its gains in the face of a concerted Serbian counter-offensive that had started earlier in the year. Kosovo became engulfed in a vicious war characterized by grave human rights abuses, including ethnic cleansing and mass executions. Between 300,000 and 500,000 people (out of a population of roughly two million) had been displaced by August 1998.[32]

This time the Serbs could not count on an indifferent international community that would allow them to have their way in Kosovo. Towards the end of 1997 the Kosovo issue had at long last made its way on to the international political agenda. The six-nation Contact Group supervising the implementation of the Dayton peace accord for Bosnia and Herzegovina (Russia, the US, Britain, France, Germany and Italy) then for the first time considered the situation in Kosovo as a separate issue.[33] In September the Group laid down the parameters for a peaceful settlement of the conflict over Kosovo: 'We do not support independence and we do not support maintenance of the status quo. We support an enhanced status for Kosovo within the FRY' (Federal Republic of Yugoslavia) that would 'fully protect the rights of the Albanian population'.[34] These guidelines were endorsed by other international bodies like the OSCE, EU, G-8 and the UN Security Council as they became involved in the Kosovo issue in the late 1990s.[35]

Milosevic, elevated to President of Yugoslavia in July 1997, protested vehemently that Kosovo was an internal Yugoslav affair out of bounds to foreigners.[36] It was to no avail. NATO, for instance, in March 1998 declared that its member states and the world community at large had a 'legitimate interest' in events in Kosovo, not least because of their impact on regional stability.[37] The same month members of the Contact Group resorted to mild diplomatic and economic sanctions against Yugoslavia for its 'unacceptable use of force' against Kosovar Albanians.[38] The UN Security Council followed suit with resolution 1160 of 31 March 1998, which imposed an arms embargo against Yugoslavia (including Kosovo) and reaffirmed the now familiar terms for a settlement, namely an 'enhanced status for Kosovo which would include a substantially greater degree of autonomy and meaningful self-administration'.[39] In a subsequent resolution (1199 of September 1998) the Council declared that the worsening security and humanitarian situations in Kosovo threatened international peace and security. The Security Council confronted Belgrade with a set of demands to end the hostilities, allow international humanitarian relief and permit foreign monitoring of developments in the province. The following month Milosevic undertook to implement the demands contained in Security Council resolution 1199, including the creation of an international verification regime to monitor events on the ground in Kosovo.[40]

The next major step in the search for peace in Kosovo was the Rambouillet conference convened by the Contact Group in France in February 1999. Here the parties representing the Yugoslav Federation and Kosovo were presented with an interim settlement proposal that provided for 'substantial autonomy for Kosovo' while maintaining Yugoslavia's territorial integrity, the deployment of a NATO force in the territory and the disarmament of the KLA.[41] Milosevic's refusal to agree to the settlement terms – in effect presented as an ultimatum at Rambouillet – unleashed the wrath of the Western community.

On 24 March 1999 NATO launched Operation Allied Force, 11 weeks of sustained air strikes against targets in Yugoslavia, including Kosovo.[42] While the NATO attacks were in full swing, Serbian security forces stepped up their campaign of mass expulsions and large-scale massacres of Kosovar Albanians. Such was the scale of excesses that the Serbs have been accused of genocide. By mid-May approximately 600,000 ethnic Albanians had fled Kosovo for refuge in neighbouring states. Thousands more were internally displaced and over 10,000 Albanians died in the hostilities.[43]

International trusteeship

The NATO assault ended only after Milosevic in June accepted a package of proposals presented to him jointly by the EU and Russia. In no position to put up further resistance, Milosevic agreed to end violence and repression in Kosovo, the withdrawal of his armed forces from the province, the establishment of international security and civil presences in Kosovo, and the creation of an interim administration allowing the people of Kosovo substantial autonomy within the Federal Republic of Yugoslavia.[44] These terms were confirmed in UN Security Council resolution 1244 of 10 June 1999. While Kosovo's self-declared independence had come to an end, the endgame for Serbian-controlled Kosovo was about to begin.

Resolution 1244 provided for the deployment, under UN auspices and with the cooperation of Yugoslavia, of 'international civil and security presences' in Kosovo. The security presence would take the shape of the Kosovo Force (KFOR), consisting of NATO and non-NATO troops. Its responsibilities included deterring renewed hostilities, demilitarizing the KLA, establishing a secure environment for the return of refugees and displaced persons, and ensuring public safety and order. The main tasks of the international civil component of the UN Mission in Kosovo (UNMIK) included 'the establishment, pending a final settlement, of substantial autonomy and self-government in Kosovo'; performing basic civilian administrative functions; developing provisional institutions for 'democratic and autonomous self-government', protecting human rights, and maintaining civil law and order. Also part of UNMIK's brief was to handle Kosovo's external relations, especially with international organizations entrusted with particular tasks in the territory (the UN and its partners, including the OSCE, NATO and EU).[45]

It was the first time that the UN had assumed such extensive administrative authority in a state or part thereof.[46] (A few months after the approval of resolution 1244, the Security Council created a comparable arrangement for East Timor.) Resolution 1244 placed Kosovo under *de facto* UN trusteeship (or what others called a UN military protectorate) 'for the dual purpose of governing the province and suppressing the territorial dispute' – while leaving aside the vexed issue of the entity's final status.[47] Supreme authority over Kosovo vested in the UN Security Council, while in practice legislative, executive and judicial authority was delegated to UNMIK – the effective government of Kosovo. While UNMIK focused on civil administration, its partner organizations took charge of humanitarian assistance (the UN High Commissioner for Refugees), institution-building (OSCE), economic reconstruction (EU) and security (NATO). A Special Representative of the UN Secretary-General served as overall head of mission.[48]

The 'general principles on a political solution to the Kosovo crisis', enshrined in resolution 1244, explicitly acknowledged the 'sovereignty and territorial integrity' of the Federal Republic of Yugoslavia and other states in the region. This may well have implied that the final settlement alluded to in the resolution would have to be devised within these parameters. If so, both independence for Kosovo and amalgamation with Albania should be ruled out. The 'substantial autonomy and self-government' that had to be developed during the interim period may then have been the final status that at least some of the authors of resolution 1244 had in mind for a Kosovo still legally part of a federal Yugoslavia. Realities on the ground would soon dictate otherwise.

UNMIK's assigned tasks were rolled out in five distinct phases.[49] The first three proceeded relatively smoothly, considering the enormity of the challenges in a deeply divided, war-scarred society. In the first an interim civilian administration was created. The previous Serbian-controlled administration had collapsed as thousands of Serbs, many of them public servants, fled Kosovo under persistent Albanian attacks. To complicate matters UNMIK initially had to contend with two rival Albanian structures of authority: the elected Rugova government of the Republic of Kosovo and the Provisional Government of Kosovo established in 1999 and headed by KLA commander Hashim Thaçi. Both these were dissolved in early 2000, leaving the field to the new interim administration.[50]

The second phase saw the beginning of the gradual transfer of the administration to the local population through the establishment of the Interim Administrative Council on which local Albanian and Serb representatives sat. In the third period municipal elections were held throughout Kosovo (October 2000), followed by a general election (November 2001) for a new Kosovo Assembly. The actual constitution of the elected bodies marked the fourth stage. The freshly elected Assembly convened for the first time at the end of 2001 and in 2002 Rugova was (again) elected President of Kosovo and a ten-member cabinet assumed office. These and other institutions, including courts of law, were established in accordance with the Constitutional Framework for Provisional Self-Government adopted in May 2001. While Albanian parties by and large participated in the new arrangements, Serb politicians in Kosovo boycotted them. In the final phase, when Kosovo's future status had been determined, the provisional institutions and the overall administration of the territory would be transferred to a locally controlled permanent civil administration.[51]

An idea canvassed in UNMIK circles held that Kosovo should have reached a certain degree of 'political maturity' before its end-status could be resolved and the territory could enter the ultimate stage of its transitional process. More concretely, local institutions had to achieve specific standards of democracy, human rights and good governance as a precondition for discussions on Kosovo's final status. This notion of 'standards before status' indeed informed the Constitutional Framework for Provisional Self-Government. The requisite benchmarks were spelled out in an official set of Standards for Kosovo produced by UNMIK in 2003. At the core was the development of a 'truly multi-ethnic, stable and democratic Kosovo' approximating European standards of democracy and market economy. In March 2004 a Kosovo Standards Implementation Plan, defining precise actions to be taken and the conditions under which standards would be met, was announced.[52]

An authoritative assessment of Kosovo's progress in achieving the set standards was released in October 2005. Compiled by Kai Eide, special envoy of the UN Secretary-General, the report presented a very mixed picture of conditions in Kosovo. The economic situation was bleak, respect for the rule of law was insufficiently entrenched and the foundations for a multi-ethnic society were shaky.[53] While an evaluation of the UN's trusteeship falls beyond our remit,[54] it is appropriate to record that the international administration had indeed improved Kosovo in many respects but a major failure was its inability to transform the territory into a tolerant multi-ethnic society respecting the rule of law. This was painfully illustrated by the ongoing inter-communal violence, in which the dwindling Serb community was now the principal victim. The worst incident was a two-day pogrom in March 2004 that left 19 people dead, hundreds of Serb homes damaged or destroyed and 36 Serb Orthodox churches or cultural sites desecrated.[55] Eide duly conceded that standards of implementation in Kosovo had been 'uneven', yet he recommended that 'the time has come to move to the next phase of the political process' because the *status quo* was unsustainable. Nearly six and a half years of international administration was approaching its end.[56]

By then the face of Serbian and indeed Yugoslav politics had changed drastically. Milosevic had been forced to relinquish the Yugoslav presidency in October 2000 and in mid-2001 he was hauled before the International Criminal Tribunal for Yugoslavia in The Hague. While still being tried on charges of crimes against humanity perpetrated in Kosovo and elsewhere in the former Yugoslavia, Milosevic died in detention in March 2006. Milosevic had immediately been succeeded as Yugoslav head of state by Vojislav Kostunica, who presided over the normalization of the country's international relations (including its readmission to the UN after an absence of eight years) and the consolidation of democracy at home. In February 2003 the Federal Republic of Yugoslavia was officially replaced by the State Union of Serbia and Montenegro – with Kosovo still included in the new dispensation as a part of Serbia.[57] A mere three years later Montenegro exited its union with Serbia, opting for independence by mutual agreement. Serbia, which had all along strenuously resisted the fragmentation of the Yugoslav state, had suffered another grievous blow. Now the Republic of Serbia, as the shrunken state called itself, was left to face its most painful and daunting challenge of dismemberment: the likely loss of Kosovo.

The Ahtisaari plan

Both the Secretary-General and the Security Council endorsed Eide's recommendation of advancing to the next phase in designing Kosovo's future. The UN chief appointed former Finnish President Martti Ahtisaari as special envoy for the negotiations on Kosovo's future status. In February 2006 the first round of status talks took place in Vienna.[58] The positions of the two main protagonists remained poles apart, though. The Serbian government still rejected independence for Kosovo, whereas the Albanian-dominated Kosovo Assembly resolved that it would accept only independence as final status. The death of Rugova in January 2006 and his replacement as President by Fatmir Sejdiu in no way weakened the resolve of the Kosovar Albanians to achieve full-fledged statehood.[59] This commitment to independence was reaffirmed in the victory of the Democratic Party of Kosovo, led by former guerrilla leader Hashim Thaçi, in the parliamentary election of November 2007.[60]

After some 14 months of talks chaired by Ahtisaari, the divisions over the future of Kosovo could still not be bridged. In February 2007 Ahtisaari threw down the gauntlet by submitting his far-reaching settlement plan for Kosovo to Ban Ki-moon, Secretary-General of the UN. It consisted of two documents. The brief Report of the Special Envoy of the Secretary-General on Kosovo's Future Status recommended that the territory acquire the status of 'independence supervised by the international community'. The Comprehensive Proposal for the Kosovo Status Settlement spelled out the entity's future system of government, measures for protecting minority communities and mechanisms for international oversight.[61] The proposed mode of governance was based on a familiar set of principles. Envisaged was a multi-ethnic society governed as a constitutional democracy respecting the rule of law, human rights and fundamental freedoms. The rights of members of communities, including their language, culture, education, religion and symbols, had to be protected. Mechanisms such as public representation and veto rights for the non-Albanian community were prescribed. Decentralization would deepen the Serbian community's control over its own affairs. The Comprehensive Proposal furthermore provided for a professional, multi-ethnic security sector comprising police and security forces. In short, the Ahtisaari plan allowed for 'the strongest minority protection regime ever seen in Europe'.[62]

Turning to Kosovo's future international status, the settlement plan contained no reference to either independence for Kosovo or the preservation of Serbian sovereignty over the territory. Union with any state or part of any state was, however, specifically proscribed. This provision ruled out Kosovo's amalgamation with Albania or the joining of Serb-inhabited parts of the territory with Serbia. Kosovo would, however, be awarded such rights of statehood as negotiating and concluding international agreements, acquiring membership of international organizations and adopting its own national symbols (including a flag and anthem). That Kosovo's future international status would be a special one is clear from the provision that '[t]he international community shall supervise, monitor and have all necessary powers to ensure effective and efficient implementation of this Settlement'. A four-fold international presence in Kosovo, to replace the existing UN structures, was recommended. An International Civilian Representative (ICR), also serving as the EU Special Representative and appointed by an International Steering Group comprising major foreign stakeholders, would exercise overall responsibility for the supervision of the implementation of the settlement scheme. This would include the power to nullify decisions or laws approved by Kosovar authorities and to replace officials whose conduct contravened the Status Settlement. The role of an international overseer or governor was modelled on that previously designed for Bosnia.[63] A European Security and Defence Policy Mission would monitor and mentor all matters related to the rule of law, including the police, law courts and penal institutions. An International Military Presence, under NATO command, would be tasked to ensure a safe and secure environment until local institutions were able to assume all security responsibilities. Under a further provision the OSCE would be asked to support the democratic development of Kosovo.

Specific guidelines for implementing the settlement plan were also spelled out. During a four-month transition period UNMIK's existing mandate would remain intact. To ensure the smooth implementation of elements of the plan during this phase, the ICR would monitor the process and make recommendations to UNMIK. During the period of transition the Kosovo Assembly, in conjunction with the ICR, had to adopt a constitution and additional legislation needed to implement the Comprehensive Proposal. UNMIK's mandate would lapse at the conclusion of the transitional phase and all legislative and executive authority vested in UNMIK would be transferred to Kosovar authorities. Within six months thereafter general and local elections were to be held in the territory. The mandate of the ICR would continue until the International Steering Group decided that the provisions of the settlement plan had indeed been implemented.

Finally, Ahtisaari's blueprint for international involvement in Kosovo also provided for socio-economic upliftment. The Comprehensive Proposal for the Kosovo Status Settlement contained elaborate measures to ensure that a future Kosovo would be 'viable, sustainable and stable'.

Stalemate

The Ahtisaari plan's proposed internationally supervised statehood for Kosovo represented a compromise between Kosovar Albanians' demand for outright independence and Serbia's unqualified rejection of this option. Yet the proposal failed to satisfy either of the protagonists. The Albanian community accepted the plan only grudgingly, while Kosovo's Serbs and Belgrade, backed by Moscow, rejected the formula.[64]

An opinion poll conducted by the UN Development Programme (UNDP) in April 2007 had found that 96 per cent of the Albanian community still favoured independence.[65] The US and most EU member states openly backed independent statehood for Kosovo and endorsed the Ahtisaari blueprint. Ranged against this coalition of supporters of independence was an alliance of opponents consisting of Serbs and Russians. In the UNDP survey 82 per cent of Kosovo's Serbs came out strongly against independence for the territory.[66] In Serbia proper a parliamentary resolution of July 2007 gave the government a free hand to protect Serbian sovereignty over Kosovo.[67] The following December the Serbian Parliament reaffirmed that Kosovo was an integral part of Serbia.[68] Russia's view was stated unambiguously by a Kremlin official in June 2007: 'Kosovo is an inviolable part of Serbia and the question of its future status can be resolved only with the agreement of both Belgrade and Pristina'.[69] Russia and Serbia made great play of Security Council resolution 1244's reaffirmation of Serbian sovereignty over Kosovo while the territory's final status was being decided. The resolution furthermore provided for a 'political process' to 'determine Kosovo's future status'. The architects of the resolution had clearly envisaged a negotiated settlement that would then be endorsed by the Security Council. Belgrade and Moscow were adamant that a Kosovo settlement could be reached within this framework only.[70] The two allies seemed determined to prevent any deal that allowed for an independent Kosovo. Russia thus reinforced Serbia's position as a veto state over Kosovo by assuming a similar role itself; it was a unique combination of internal and external veto states.

What explains Russia's opposition to Kosovo's independence? Apart from long-standing solidarity with Serbia, Russia was also concerned about the precedent it would supposedly create for other secessionist communities. As Putin asked, '[i]f people believe that Kosovo can be granted full independence, why then should we deny it to Abkhazia and South Ossetia?'[71] He may as well have added Chechnya, probably Moscow's main concern. Western backing for Kosovo's independence no doubt raised Moscow's hackles. In line with Putin's determination to assert Russian influence as a global power, Moscow would not be dictated to by Western powers on a major political issue of the day, moreover located in an area of geopolitical importance to Russia.

The issue of Kosovo's independence placed Serbia in a double bind, a case of 'damned if you oppose, damned if you approve'. Surrendering the 'cradle of Serbia', given Kosovo's historical, cultural and religious significance for Serbs, may provoke serious resistance within Serbia and among Serbs in Kosovo. A risk Serbia ran in obstructing Kosovo's independence was exclusion from the EU. True, the EU initialled a stabilization and association agreement with Belgrade in November 2007, a typical step towards membership talks,[72] but further progress was unlikely for as long as the Kosovo issue remained unresolved. Should Belgrade agree to Kosovo's independence, the EU may not only allow the accession process to continue, but could even decide to waive the existing precondition of arresting and extraditing suspects indicted by the Yugoslav war crimes tribunal in The Hague.[73] By the end of 2007 the question of whether EU membership could compensate for the loss of Kosovo was already a central – and highly divisive – topic in Serbian political debate.

Given the fundamentally different positions held by Russia and the West on Kosovo's future, the Security Council was left paralysed, unable to endorse Ahtisaari's settlement proposal and revoke resolution 1244 of 1999. In an effort to break the deadlock, the six-nation Contact Group initiated a new round of negotiations between the leaders of Kosovo and Serbia. Beginning in August 2007, the talks were facilitated by a 'Troika' of diplomats from member states of the Contact Group. In December the Group had to concede defeat: it reported to the Secretary-General of the UN that no compromise could be reached on a status settlement for Kosovo.[74]

Contested statehood, again

While the Serbs and Russians were still challenging Kosovo's right of independence, the entity's Albanian government forced the issue by proclaiming Kosovo as 'an independent and sovereign state' on 17 February 2008. Regretting that internationally sponsored negotiations between Belgrade and Pristina over Kosovo's future political status had not produced agreement, the founding document of the new state emphasized that the declaration of independence 'is in full accordance' with Ahtisaari's Comprehensive Proposal for the Kosovo Status Settlement. Kosovo fully accepted the obligations contained in the Ahtisaari plan and the state's future constitution would incorporate all the relevant principles of the blueprint. The founding document specifically welcomed an international civilian mission to supervise implementation of the Ahtisaari plan, an EU-led rule of law mission, and NATO's continuing leadership of the international military force present in Kosovo. The various foreign missions would continue functioning 'until such time as Kosovo institutions are capable of assuming these responsibilities'. On foreign affairs, the independence declaration gave notice of Kosovo's intention to obtain full membership of the EU and other (unnamed) international organizations. A final noteworthy feature of the founding declaration was its observation that 'Kosovo is a special case arising from Yugoslavia's non-consensual breakup and is not a precedent for any other situation'.[75] The latter remark was clearly designed to assuage critics who feared international recognition of Kosovo would open the proverbial Pandora's box full of aspirant states.

Whereas Kosovo's previous proclamation of independence failed to attract any international recognition, the second met a radically different external response. By the end of February Kosovo had received *de jure* recognition from 21 confirmed states, among them 12 EU members (notably France, Germany, Britain and Italy), America, Turkey, Albania, Australia and Senegal. Taiwan, always keen to win friends, recognized Kosovo within days. By mid-June 43 states, with a further eight EU members among them, had formally recognized Kosovo. Japan, South Korea and Liberia were among the non-Western states that joined the list, as were Kosovo's neighbouring countries of Croatia, Slovenia, Hungary and Bulgaria. Muslim states seemed reticent to do likewise: by mid-June Turkey, Afghanistan and Senegal and were the only members of the 60-nation Organization of the Islamic Conference to have recognized Kosovo.[76] The most notable absentees were of course Russia and Serbia, while China's absence might be explained by Taiwan's quick recognition of Kosovo.

Serbia and Russia have not been content to limit their opposition to Kosovo's statehood to merely withholding recognition. Moscow predictably denounced the declaration of independence as illegal and indicated that it would use its veto in the Security Council to block Kosovo's admission to the UN.[77] Belgrade vented its displeasure by annulling Kosovo's independence declaration and filing criminal charges against the entity's leaders for an 'unlawful attempt to bring about the secession of a part of Serbia's territory'.[78] While these were largely symbolic gestures, Serbia also took some concrete steps to undermine Kosovo. Belgrade strengthened its links with Serb-dominated parts of Kosovo by staging local elections there in May 2008 and instructing Kosovo Serbs to form parallel municipal councils based on these elections. UNMIK called the Serb elections illegitimate while Kosovo President Fatmir Sejdiu demanded that the 'illegal' parallel structures be dismantled. Belgrade also encouraged Serbs in Kosovo to maintain their allegiance to Serbia as if they were still its citizens, and to boycott Kosovo's new government institutions. By these means Serbia was suspected of trying to bring about a 'soft' or 'functional' internal partition between Serbs and Albanians in Kosovo.[79]

Undaunted, Kosovo in June 2008 took another major step in formalizing its statehood by introducing a new constitution. Sole decision-making authority was transferred from the UN administration to the governing institutions of Kosovo. However, the international presence in Kosovo would not end. The constitution stipulated that the EU would take over a supervisory role from the UN, as envisaged in the Ahtisaari plan. Russia and Serbia objected that this would be illegal unless authorized by the UN Security Council.[80] To break the impasse and accommodate the 'new reality on the ground' created by Kosovo's constitution, Secretary-General Ban Ki Moon 'reconfigured' the UN mission in Kosovo to allow the EU to deploy its mission under the UN umbrella headed by the Secretary-General's special representative for Kosovo. The arrangement permitted the EU to assume an 'enhanced operational role' in Kosovo 'under the overall status-neutral umbrella of the UN' – a formula clearly designed to address the fears of Russia and Serbia that an EU mission could be biased against Kosovo's Serbs. The EU's main responsibilities would be in the fields of rule of law (through its Rule of Law Mission, EULEX), policing, justice and customs. All this would be done in terms of Security Council resolution 1244, which remained the legal framework for the UN's mandate until the Council decided otherwise. These parameters also applied to KFOR's 17,000 troops whose security mandate would continue in independent Kosovo.[81] By using his authority to reconfigure the UN role in Kosovo instead of seeking a new mandate for an EU role, the Secretary-General avoided a potentially rancorous Security Council session in which Russia could have vetoed implementation of the Ahtisaari plan.

Alternative futures

Kosovo's latest declaration of independence may, unlike the first, prove irreversible and launch the new state on the path to general international recognition. It would nonetheless be useful to compile a short inventory of alternative status solutions that have been proposed for Kosovo.[82] These emanate from various quarters, including the Serbian government and the Contact Group's Troika of diplomats. We list the plans because they add to the diverse range of alternatives to contested statehood and may be of relevance to some other wannabe states. It is then not necessary to assess the merits of the various proposals in the context of Kosovo. Excluded from the survey is of course a return to Kosovo's status as a subordinate unit of Serbia, which had little support outside Serbia and Russia. Since Kosovo's *de facto* status as trusteeship territory was designed as a transitory arrangement only, it cannot be included among final status options either.

- Several proposals revolved around an enhanced status for Kosovo that would grant it some of the substance of independence without actually creating a new state. One variant would place Kosovo more or less on par with South Tyrol-Alto Adige in Italy or the Swedish-inhabited Åland Islands relative to Finland. Another was an 'Ahtisaari-plus' proposal of a loose union or association between Serbia and Kosovo to complement the internal government structures set out in the Comprehensive Proposal. There was also talk of an 'Ahtisaari-minus' status, which accepted the bulk of the plan (including the UN's replacement by the EU) but deferred the determination of Kosovo's final status until a future review. A variation on the autonomy theme placed Kosovo in the same relationship to Serbia as the Serbian enclave (Republika Srpska) *vis-à-vis* Bosnia and Herzegovina. Serbia variously proposed 'more than autonomy, less than independence' for the disputed territory and a 'minimum integration' formula that would leave Kosovo with '95 per cent' jurisdiction over its own affairs. Another of Serbia's proposals was a so-called Hong Kong model of loose integration: Kosovo could enter into direct links with international financial institutions, while Belgrade's powers over the entity would be confined to borders, foreign affairs and defence (although the latter would be delegated to international bodies).

- A different form of association drew on the Basic Treaty concluded between East and West Germany in 1972. This agreement paved the way for the normalization of relations between the two German states and their admission to the UN. Applied to an independent Kosovo, it would involve the signing of an accord on good neighbourly relations between Pristina and Belgrade – without renouncing their fundamental differences over the future status of Kosovo.
- Under a 'formalised regime of special relations' between Kosovo and Serbia, Belgrade would neither govern Kosovo nor maintain a physical presence there but the two sides would 'establish common bodies to implement cooperation'. Kosovo would be entitled to enter into a relationship with international financial institutions, become involved in the EU's Stabilization and Association Process and become fully integrated into regional structures. A related idea was that Kosovo and Serbia establish a coordination council for defence matters and share a foreign ministry.
- A Belgian think-tank advanced the idea of Kosovo being offered 'special status as part of the EU'. By being drawn into the framework of European integration, Kosovo would no longer be subject to the UN's 'legal-procedural conventions regarding international recognition'.
- Another unusual status involved the conversion of Kosovo into a free region on the lines of the free zone of Trieste. It would fall under tripartite supervision by a joint Serb-Albanian commission with the EU serving as guarantor.
- A formal confederal arrangement was also advocated. One version was modelled on the EU-brokered compromise for the transitional State Union of Serbia and Montenegro. Serbia and Kosovo could be joined in a common state for a period of three years after which Kosovo would be entitled to stage a referendum on independence. A suggestion in the same vein granted Kosovo most of the features of statehood – including the right to join the UN – but reserved defence, foreign policy, borders and the status of the Serb minority in the territory for a confederal institution composed of delegates from Serbia, Kosovo and the EU.
- A so-called Andorra solution envisaged an EU-Serbian condominium over a largely autonomous Kosovo.

- Partition came in several variants, of which the most common was dividing Kosovo at the Ibar River. The territory to the north, housing some 40,000 of Kosovo's Serbs, would be joined up with Serbia while the rest of Kosovo would be granted independence. It would simply mean that both sides formally renounced what they in any case did not possess: Belgrade's control over the bulk of Kosovo and Pristina's control over the Serb enclave in northern Kosovo.
- A less drastic form of partition was the 'cantonization' of Kosovo into ethnically homogenous zones, similar to arrangements in Bosnia and Herzegovina. The majority Serb parts in the north could lend themselves to cantons, together with ethnic enclaves elsewhere in Kosovo.
- A 'greater Albania' could be created through territorial 'rightsizing'. It would involve the amalgamation of Kosovo (either as a whole or the bulk of the territory inhabited by ethnic Albanians) with Albania.
- Finally, outright independence within existing borders and without strings attached was the first prize for Kosovar Albanians. Because Serbia and Russia vigorously opposed what they regarded as a zero-sum option, conditional independence for Kosovo was put forward as a compromise. Seven years before the Ahtisaari final settlement plan was produced, the Swedish-initiated Independent International Commission on Kosovo had recommended quasi- or conditional independence. The conditionality would involve a security guarantee provided by NATO and international supervision of human rights protection in Kosovo. Furthermore, Kosovo would be integrated into a Balkan stability pact and eventually also join the EU. Another early version spoke of a multilateral treaty – comparable to the 1955 accord on the re-establishment of an independent and democratic Austria – prohibiting an independent Kosovo joining any other state (read: Albania). Such an agreement would also oblige the government of an independent Kosovo to uphold minority rights and provide for international monitoring of treaty obligations.

Conclusion

Kosovo has experienced two very different spells of contested statehood over the past 17 years. Its first round followed Kosovo's unilateral declaration of independence in 1991, when not a single confirmed state recognized its purported statehood. Worse was to befall the pretender state in the late 1990s when it was the target of a particularly brutal war unleashed by Serbia to bring the break-away province to heel. The enormity of the violence prompted the international community to intervene, both to protect Kosovar Albanians and punish the Serbs. In 1999 international engagement in Kosovo changed to that of UN trusteeship while the entity's final status was being negotiated. Trusteeship of course spelled the end of Kosovo's first period of self-proclaimed independence. Kosovo's route out of the interim status of a ward of the world community was provided by the Ahtisaari plan, a blueprint for internationally supervised statehood. Implementation was, however, delayed by the implacable opposition of Kosovo's two veto states, Serbia and Russia, to any notion of independence for Kosovo. Exasperated, Kosovo threw down the gauntlet with a unilateral declaration of independence in early 2008.

This time Kosovo found its self-declared independence promptly recognized by most EU member states, America, Turkey and a host of others. One reason for the positive international reception was the new state's commitment to implementing the Ahtisaari plan; another was the lack of international sympathy for the obstructive role played by Serbia and Russia. Still, the vast majority of states had by mid-2008 still not recognized Kosovo and Russia may well veto its admission to the UN. This leaves Kosovo's statehood still being contested, although the chances are that the challenge will wane rather than wax. In the meantime the comprehensive international presence in Kosovo should assist the new state in overcoming its severe deficiencies in empirical statehood and so enhance its prospects for stability.

6
Somaliland

At first glance the Republic of Somaliland should have had a smooth passage to confirmed statehood after its unilateral declaration of independence from Somalia in 1991. Unusual among secessionist entities, Somaliland has not been subjected to competing historical claims to its territory by rival ethnic groups, either from within Somaliland or from the central state of Somalia. This is because the former Somali Democratic Republic was a rare African example of a true nation-state: the entire population spoke one language (Somali), practised the same religion (Islam), had a shared social structure (clan families) and engaged in common economic activity (pastoral and agricultural).[1] Somaliland's claims to statehood rested on stronger legal and historical grounds than those of many other contested states. Somaliland moreover broke away from a state that was in the throes of implosion and that has still not been able to rehabilitate itself. Whereas Somalia carries the dubious distinction of the world's longest-limping failed state, the Republic of Somaliland has managed to develop its empirical statehood. Yet Somaliland has been prevented from graduating to confirmed statehood. We need to investigate why the entity has been consigned to international limbo, how it is coping with life on the margins of the world community, and how it might exit this awkward existence.

From colonialism to secession

Because the plight of Somaliland and for that matter Somalia is largely a product of contemporary history, it will suffice to begin our narrative with the advent of colonial rule in the area. In 1884, the year of the Congress of Berlin, the British protectorate of Somaliland was proclaimed over the northern part of the territory inhabited by the Somali people. At roughly the same time France established a colonial presence in an adjacent part of the lands of the Somalis, creating French Somaliland (also known as the French Territory of Afars and Issas, later the Republic of Djibouti). The third European power to occupy Somali territory was Italy, which in 1889 established a protectorate over the larger and more populous southern region.[2] After the Second World War Italy renounced all claims to Italian Somaliland, which was converted into the UN Trust Territory of Somalia in 1950. Italy was charged with administering the territory for a transitional period of 10 years pending independence. During the 1950s British Somaliland was likewise being groomed for statehood. Representatives from the two Somali territories met in April 1960 and agreed to merge into an independent republic.[3] First, though, they became independent briefly as two separate states.

British Somaliland received its independence on 26 June 1960. The UN registered notification of Somaliland's independence and 35 UN member countries, including the five permanent members of the Security Council, immediately recognized the new state.[4] Only a day after independence, however, the new state's legislature decided unanimously to press ahead with the intended merger. On 1 July 1960, when the UN Trust Territory of Somalia also gained its freedom, the legislatures of the two newly independent states held a joint session in Mogadishu where they announced their unification as the National Assembly of the new Somali Republic. The consummation of the union of the two Somali territories on 1 July spelled the end of the independent existence of Somaliland after only four days.[5] A southerner was elected as the first president of the new state while a coalition government comprising parties from the Southern and Northern Regions (as the two constituent units were called) took power.[6]

There had from the outset been several forces at work that would contribute to the subsequent collapse and fragmentation of the Somali Republic.[7] The first was that the country, despite its seemingly homogenous population, was beset by clan rivalries. Based on ancestry, the dozens of clans could be grouped into six major clan-families, namely the Daarood (35 per cent of the national population), Hawiye (23 per cent), Isaaq (23 per cent), Dir (7 per cent), and Digil and Rahanwayan (11 per cent). As Mazrui put it, here was 'a people divided by the same culture'; the combustibility lay at the level of 'subethnicity'.[8] Clan cleavages were in the second place exacerbated by regional divisions. Economic differences, another historical legacy, revolved around the northerners' pastoral nomadism and cattle raising as against the plantation agriculture of people in the southern region. At the political level the Somali leadership tried to accommodate regional and clan interests in central government. The practice of clan-*cum*-regional coalition government was continued by successive civilian rulers in the 1960s. Even so, the Union encountered grave difficulties in amalgamating the constituent units' different administrative, judicial and economic systems. Northerners also complained that their interests were neglected by the Southern-dominated central government in Mogadishu. An abortive military *coup* in December 1961 was symptomatic of the malaise afflicting the infant state.[9]

A third feature that sealed the fate of Somalia was that it did not house the entire Somali nation; there were also sizeable Somali communities in neighbouring Kenya, Ethiopia and Djibouti. The formation of a Greater Somalia that joined together Somalis in the two former protectorates plus those living in the three adjacent countries, became a sacred duty for independent Somalia. Its irredentist dream was symbolized in the five-pointed star on the national flag, representing the five Somali communities. The independence of Kenya in 1963 put paid to any chance of incorporating the Somali-populated Northern Frontier District, while Djibouti's attainment of independence in 1977 likewise thwarted the chances of absorbing former French Somaliland into the Somali Republic. In the mid-1970s Somalia would launch an abortive military offensive to wrest the Ogaden region from Ethiopia, culminating in a devastating defeat at the hands of Ethiopian forces and their Cuban allies in 1978. While the quest for a Greater Somalia had promoted unity within the Somali Republic, its patent failure – especially the humiliation in the Ogaden war – undermined the legitimacy of the government and emboldened a long suffering people to rise up against their rulers in Mogadishu.

The architect of the assault on the Ogaden (1976–8) was General Mohamed Siad Barre, who had seized power in a military *coup* in 1969. Not only was the newly elected civilian government of Abdirashid Ali Shirmake then deposed and the President assassinated, but Barre suspended the 1960 constitution, dissolved the National Assembly and banned existing political parties. As head of the Supreme Revolutionary Council, Barre assumed dictatorial powers. The country was renamed the Somali Democratic Republic, a reflection of Barre's imposition of scientific socialism as the new guiding ideology and of Somalia's decisive lurch towards the Soviet Union in its foreign relations. The new affinity between Mogadishu and Moscow proved rather short-lived, wrecked by Barre's decision to invade Ethiopia against the express wishes of the Soviet Union. His former ally brazenly switched sides to the Marxist government of Ethiopia, which managed to expel the Somali invaders thanks to a massive infusion of Soviet arms and Cuban troops. The Americans stepped into the vacuum left by the Soviets, concluding a defence agreement with Somalia in 1980. The opportunistic friendship with the US could not stem the rising tide of domestic resistance to Barre's rule.

Several clan-based opposition groups emerged from the late 1970s onwards, taking up arms against Barre's government. These movements became major forces in the ten-year civil war that began in 1980. The Somali Salvation Democratic Front (SSDF) was formed in 1978 by rebel military officers belonging to the Majeerteen clan (part of the Daarood clan-family). Based largely in the northeast of the country, it was the first opposition movement committed to overthrowing the government by force. The Somali National Movement (SNM), established three years later by exiled dissidents, drew its support mainly from the Isaaq clan based in the northwest (the former British Somaliland). Ogadeni army deserters created the Somali Patriotic Movement (SPM) in the south in 1985. Finally, the United Somali Congress (USC) was founded by exiled Hawiye notables in 1989. Except for the SSDF which collapsed in the mid-1980s, the other three movements' guerrilla offensives had placed them in control of large swathes of Somalia by the end of the 1980s. The USC's stronghold was in the centre of the country, the SPM held sway in large areas of the south, while the SNM made its presence felt in the northwest.

An SNM offensive in May 1988, during which the rebels briefly held the Northern Region's capital Hargeysa, escalated the low-intensity conflict in the area to a full-blown civil war. In retaliation central government forces bombed civilian targets in the North. By the time the SNM had finally defeated central forces in Somaliland in early 1991, between 50,000 and 100,000 people may have died in the hostilities and another 500,000 displaced. Hargeysa was roughly 90 per cent destroyed.[10] Security forces had reacted with similar ferocity to popular demonstrations in Mogadishu in July 1989, causing about 450 deaths.[11] These harsh responses tended to obscure the fact that Somalia's armed forces and indeed the entire system of government were gradually buckling under the pressures of simultaneous insurgencies across the country, coupled with rising popular disaffection. Towards the end of 1990, the World Bank reported, 'for all intents and purposes the government administration had ceased to function at all'.[12] As the institutions of the state collapsed, Mogadishu was plunged into internecine warfare between remnants of government forces and USC guerrillas. In January 1991 Barre fled the capital and the USC installed itself in power in Mogadishu.

Ali Mahdi Mohamed was named interim President in February. Although he and most other members of government belonged to the Hawiye clan-family, Ali Mahdi's appointment split the Hawiye-based USC into two factions: the opposition group was led by General Mohamed Farah Aidid, a member of the Habar Gidir clan of the Hawiye, while Ali Mahdi and his followers were members of the Abgaal clan. The USC's establishment of a provisional government also placed it on a collision course with the SNM and the SPM. A further cause of conflict was the decision taken at the Burao peace conference of northern clans in May 1991 to dissolve the North-South union of 1960 and 'restore' Somaliland as a sovereign state. Coupled with this unilateral declaration of an independent Republic of Somaliland, SNM leader Abd ar-Rahman Ahmed Ali was elected as interim President of the new state. The USC and its interim government in Mogadishu rejected the North's bid to secede from Somalia and made abortive efforts to engage the SNM in unity talks. At the urging of Egypt, Saudi Arabia and Italy, various Somali factions met in Djibouti in May and June to devise a formula for a national government; this effort was also in vain. In the capital of Somalia things went from bad to worse as clan-based armed formations effectively partitioned the city. All-out civil war completed the collapse of the state of Somalia. All the while the human cost of the mayhem rose. In the first six months of civil war an estimated 14,000 people were killed and a further 27,000 wounded.[13]

Justifications for statehood

The founders of the Republic of Somaliland insisted that theirs was not an act of opportunistic secession precipitated by the anarchy that engulfed Somalia. While there is no doubt that the implosion of the Somali Republic provided an opportune moment for the North to separate from the rest of the country, both historical and contemporary factors weighed with the state creators. To make the point that Somaliland was not conceived and born in secessionist sin but instead represented the restoration of its previous post-colonial status, its leaders and supporters belaboured the territory's earlier separate colonial status, the reasons behind the unification of former British and Italian Somaliland in 1960, and the North's painful experience of life in the union with the dominant South. Its case was unique in Africa, the territory's Foreign Minister declared in 2007, 'because Somaliland was a separate colonial entity from Somalia and was recognised previously as an independent state in 1960 before it joined the disastrous union with Somalia'.[14] In like vein a Somaliland communiqué issued in 2007 stated that the Republic of Somaliland as reconstituted in May 1991 did not secede from the Somali Democratic Republic, but 'is a reversion to the independent state of Somaliland of 1960 within the same agreed borders of the 1960 state'.[15] Far from violating the sanctity of colonial borders in Africa, Somaliland insisted it was merely returning to the borders it had at the time of independence in 1960. In so doing Somaliland could be said to uphold the international law principle of *uti possidetis juris* ('as you possess [in law], so you may possess') and comply with the AU Constitutive Act's prescription regarding 'respect of borders existing on achievement of independence' (article 4).[16]

The new Republic of Somaliland, then, defined itself on the basis of the territory, frontiers and population of former British Somaliland. The British Protectorate had been legalized under international law through a set of treaties and protocols that the United Kingdom concluded with other imperial powers – France, Italy and Abyssinia – between 1888 and 1897.[17] During the 1940s the Protectorate's separate existence was interrupted twice: in 1941 when the Italians conquered the territory and, following their defeat, by the union of British and Italian Somaliland under British military administration. In 1948 the British Protectorate was restored to its separate, pre-war status until granted independence on 26 June 1960.[18]

Why did Somaliland agree to forego its independent statehood in 1960 for the sake of creating a new sovereign entity through a merger with the South? At the time people in both territories widely believed that their act of union was a prelude to the unification of all Somali territories under a single flag – an ideal widely shared in both North and South. The people of Somaliland also hoped for more immediate material benefits: they were keen on retrieving the Haud area, the fertile traditional grazing areas that Britain had transferred to Ethiopia in 1956.[19] We have already noted that none of the other Somali territories joined the process of unification, confining the Somali Republic to the sum of its two original parts.[20]

The Northern Region, despite its initial enthusiasm for unification, soon developed second thoughts. In a referendum on a new constitution for Somalia held in June 1961, voter turn-out in the former British Protectorate was low due to an orchestrated boycott of the poll. Of the ballots cast in the North, over 50 per cent rejected the proposed unitary arrangements. In the Southern Region, by contrast, 1.8 million affirmative votes carried the day.[21] This negative verdict in the former Somaliland was in later years cited as evidence that the union between North and South did not meet the legal requirements set by municipal and international law. In support of the latter argument reference was also made to the dubious legal standing of the actual merger. The *de facto* unification of the two entities in July 1960, it was contended, had never been consummated *de jure* because North and South adopted two distinct acts of union.[22] In the words of Somaliland's Foreign Minister, the union between Somaliland and Somalia was 'only an informal partnership'.[23] Sceptics viewed such arguments, popular in contemporary Somaliland, as *ex post facto* rationalizations for the territory's separation from Somalia in 1991. The unified Somali Republic had after all lasted for three decades.

Another familiar justification for Somaliland's break-away has been mistreatment at the hands of the rulers in Mogadishu. Popular discontent with Barre's dictatorship had become widespread by the late 1970s, most acutely so in the North. The people in the region were subjected to blatant economic deprivation (receiving under 7 per cent of nationally disbursed development assistance), severe restrictions on trade and growing centralization of administrative functions in Mogadishu. Northerners were moreover targeted for harsh repression by government forces, in particular the politically influential Isaaq clan from whose ranks the SNM rebel movement drew most of its recruits.[24] Although the Barre government had also targeted other resistance groups and their followers during the period of insurgency, 'no other Somali community faced such sustained and intense state-sponsored violence' as the people of former British Somaliland.[25]

The deliberate, state-sponsored killing and population displacement that accompanied Somali military operations in the North have been depicted by the government of Somaliland and by human rights bodies as acts of ethnic cleansing, genocide and war crimes.[26] While others may dispute these categorizations, fact is that 'Somaliland continues to define itself with respect to the persecution of northerners under the Barre regime and thus with the generally accepted right to rebellion of a people subjected to the systematic violation of fundamental rights and freedoms'.[27] These arguments seemed to resonate with the AU's Somaliland Fact-finding Mission of 2005. In its report the panel noted that the 'plethora of problems confronting Somaliland [are in part] the legacy of a political union with Somalia, which malfunctioned, [and] brought destruction and ruin, thereby overburdening the population'.[28] Mazrui used a colourful metaphor to make the point that Somalia had forfeited its moral authority to deny Somaliland a separation: 'In a union between two individuals, wife beating can be grounds for divorce. Is it not about time that partner-abuse became grounds for divorce in a marriage between states also?'[29]

When the remainder of Somalia was thereafter plunged into anarchy, there was no effective or legitimate central authority to offer Somaliland any security guarantees to entice it back into the fold. If anything, the collapse of Somalia reinforced the conviction of the people in the North that their safety and survival demanded a formal separation from the South.[30]

It is only fair to record that no fewer than 14 unsuccessful attempts had been made in the course of the 1990s to restore peace and re-establish a functioning central government in Mogadishu. In one of the more memorable efforts, clan leaders meeting in neighbouring Djibouti in August 2000 elected a new president of Somalia, who was to lead the process of forming the Transitional National Government. Lacking legitimacy and authority, the new government failed to bring peace and order to the fractious capital, not to mention the rest of Somalia. In a searing indictment of the 'risible' transitional government, Pham recorded that in three years it went through four premiers, hundreds of cabinet ministers, misappropriated vast amounts of donor funds, and controlled little more than the area comprising the presidential villa in Djibouti.[31]

Another internationally mediated peace effort produced an accord signed by Somali politicians and warlords in Kenya in January 2004. It provided for a set of Transitional Federal Institutions to rule the Somali Republic during a five-year period culminating in national elections in 2009. These included a charter (constitution), federal government and parliament.[32] It is instructive that the Transitional Federal Charter declared that the territorial integrity and sovereignty of the Somali Republic – within the borders created by the act of union in July 1960 – 'shall be inviolable and indivisible'.[33] The Transitional Parliament was duly inaugurated in Kenya in August 2004 and assigned the task of appointing a new Somali president. Two months later Abdullah Yusuf Ahmed was installed in office – in a ceremony held in Nairobi.[34] It was only in 2007 that President Ahmed dared to set foot in Mogadishu after the hold of the Union of Islamic Courts, a group of radical Islamic militias, over the capital had been broken by the Ethiopian forces that invaded Somalia in late 2006. Since Ahmed's return the security situation in Mogadishu has remained fraught as the Ethiopian soldiers failed to root out the Islamic insurgency. The Transitional Federal Government has also been plagued by internal divisions and charges of denying some clans their fair share of the spoils of power.[35] In early 2007 over 1,300 people were killed in the worst fighting Mogadishu had witnessed in 16 years.[36] In another round of fierce fighting a year later, Islamic militants captured a number of key towns from the transitional government and its Ethiopian allies.[37] The fact that Somalia's coastal waters were among the most dangerous in the world because of piracy[38] was another reminder to the world community of the consequences of state collapse. These features merely reinforced Somaliland's determination to go it alone.

Aware that secession is a taboo in Africa, the leaders of Somaliland have been at pains to distance themselves from secessionist movements elsewhere on the continent. As indicated, they portrayed the entity's second declaration of independence in 1991 as 'predicated upon the territory's prior existence as a recognized, independent state'.[39] In this regard Somaliland prided itself on being 'among the first African States to be free from colonial rule'.[40] Instead of an act of secession, Somaliland's (second) independence constituted 'the dissolution of a voluntary union between sovereign states'. The phenomenon of a state exiting a union with another was not necessarily unlawful or unprecedented. During the life of the Organization of African Unity, for instance, Senegal, Gambia, Mali and Egypt were allowed to regain their sovereignty upon the dissolution of unsuccessful unions. By returning to the *status quo ante*, Somaliland's declaration of independence in 1991 therefore did not threaten the territorial integrity and stability of any other African state. As Somaliland maintained, its resumption of sovereign statehood did not alter but instead restored colonial borders.[41]

Predictably, Somaliland's compliance with the Montevideo Convention has been cited in support of statehood. Its territory was defined by three colonial treaties of the late 19th century and comprised a geographic area of 137,600 km^2 (roughly a third of Somali territory), comparable in size to Greece. Somaliland had a coastline of some 850 km on the Gulf of Aden and bordered on the Republic of Djibouti in the west, the Somali-populated region of Ethiopia in the south, and the Puntland region of Somalia in the east.[42] Hargeysa was still the capital of Somaliland and the territory had a current population of anywhere between 2.5 and 3.5 million people (against over eight million in the Somali Republic). The government was in effective control of most of the territory (the exception being the disputed territories of Sool and Sanaag) and hence displayed one of the defining features of a state, namely the maintenance of reasonable order.[43] Finally, Somaliland certainly had the capacity to engage in relations with other states. However, like all contested states, its disputed international status severely circumscribed the utilization of that ability.

For the US and its Western partners, formal ties with Somaliland could allow them to expand their counter-terrorism operations in the area. The Pentagon was particularly concerned about al-Qaeda gaining a foothold in Somalia and suspected the Islamic Courts movement of being affiliated with Osama bin Laden's terrorist franchise. The US military establishment accordingly favoured closer links with Somaliland, even to the extent of formal recognition; the State Department did not share this view.[44]

Economic development has also featured among the justifications for statehood presented by Hargeysa and foreign supporters of Somaliland's cause. An internationally recognized Somaliland, it was suggested, offered the African Union's New Partnership for Africa's Development (NEPAD) the opportunity to advance its goals of good governance and stability in the Horn of Africa.[45] A further argument was that diplomatic recognition would grant Somaliland greater access to sorely needed development assistance from abroad and so stimulate regional prosperity and integration too.[46] Foreign countries have also been called upon to reward Somaliland for its achievements in the face of heavy odds and in sharp contrast to the turmoil in Somalia. Over the same period that Somalia had seen numerous rounds of abortive peace talks, civil war and a failed UN-US military intervention, Somaliland – without foreign intervention, limited international assistance and no formal recognition – 'enjoyed peace, economic growth, and democratic elections'.[47] Even the 2005 AU report acknowledged that compared to 'other regions of Somalia', Somaliland had experienced relative peace and stability and 'made significant headway in the fields of health, education and economic management'.[48] At a meeting of AU foreign ministers in 2006, three African countries – Rwanda, Kenya and Zambia – called for the recognition of the peace and stability Somaliland had established.[49] Although such appeals stopped short of proposing outright recognition of Somaliland's statehood, they were indicative of what some protagonists considered a political duty to give the contested state some acknowledgment and others viewed as a moral imperative.

An extension of the moral argument held that it was manifestly unfair of states to support the 'fictional' Somalia's presence in international forums at the expense of giving 'functional' Somaliland even a hearing.[50] In the same vein it has been said that Somalia could no longer be allowed to veto Somaliland's international recognition. With over a dozen failed peace conferences, five transitional governments and a hugely expensive international peacekeeping mission, Somalia has had more than a fair chance to pull itself together.[51] Leaving discussion of Somaliland's final status in limbo until the situation in Somalia was resolved, the ICG remarked, 'holds Somaliland hostage to events over which it has very little control'.[52]

Features of statehood

Somaliland, as noted, met the basic requirements of statehood in terms of territory, population, government and the ability to engage in relations with other countries. It also displayed such standard symbols of statehood as a flag, anthem, coat of arms and currency.[53] Perhaps its greatest achievement over the past 17 years has been the maintenance of relative peace and stability in contrast to the war and collapse that wracked Somalia. True, Somaliland experienced bouts of political violence in 1991 and 1997, but these were contained reasonably quickly.[54] In 1993 the country successfully navigated its first transfer of power when clan representatives elected Mohamed Ibrahim Egal as President when Ahmed Ali's provisional rule ended.[55] Somaliland's relative tranquillity also owed a great deal to its successful demobilization and disarmament of legions of armed rebels after the declaration of independence.[56]

The same peacefulness has not been evident in Somaliland's relations with neighbouring Puntland, which proclaimed itself an autonomous region of Somalia in 1998. Puntland promptly declared the Sool and Sanaag areas part of its territory based on clan ties. Somaliland by contrast claimed Sool and Sanaag because they were located geographically within the borders of pre-independence British Somaliland.[57] This triggered a fierce turf battle between the two sides. The status of the capital of the Sool region, Las Anod (or Laas Caanood), became the centrepiece of the contest. Initially part of Somaliland, Las Anod was captured by Puntland forces in 2003 and remained under Puntland's heavily disputed control until 2007.[58] In that year forces from Somaliland supported by local militia seized control. Puntland's leaders accused Somaliland of flagrant aggression and vowed to recapture the town, sparking fears of full-scale civil war in the area.[59] To add to Puntland's woes, a chunk of the Sanaag region has seceded from Puntland, declaring itself a self-governing entity called Makhir.[60] To this volatile mix we should add the presence of oil and gas in Puntland, causing tensions between the territory, Somaliland and Somalia over the allocation of exploration rights and ultimately ownership of a potential bonanza.[61] Matters have not been helped either by the fact that the President of Puntland, Abdullah Yusuf, subsequently became President of the Somali Transitional Federal Government and claimed jurisdiction over Somaliland. A former warlord, Yusuf was loathed by the leaders of Somaliland because he had invaded Hargeysa in the late 1990s.[62] It is then not surprising that armed skirmishes between troops from Somaliland and Puntland have continued into 2008, with no resolution of the conflict in sight.[63]

The unsettled relationship between Somaliland and Puntland stood in sharp contrast to the consolidation of a functioning constitutional democracy in Somaliland – something glaringly absent in Somalia and scarce in the Muslim world. The process of democratization began with a referendum on a new constitution in May 2001. Because the constitution affirmed Somaliland's withdrawal from the union with Somalia, many voters took the referendum as a survey of popular opinion on the entity's independence. Of the 1.18 million ballots cast (representing an estimated two-thirds of the eligible voters), nearly 98 per cent supported the new constitution. Equally important is that the referendum had, according to foreign observers, been conducted 'openly, fairly, honestly and largely in accordance with internationally recognized election procedures'.[64] As such the result provided domestic legitimacy to the separate albeit contested statehood of Somaliland. In 2002 credible, competitive local elections were staged, the first in over three decades.[65]

The constitution of 2001 passed its first major test when President Egal died in office a year later. In accordance with the constitution the Vice-President, Dahir Rayale Kahin, immediately took over the reins of power, effecting a smooth transition.[66] A notably free and fair presidential poll, with a large contingent of international observers in attendance, followed in 2003. Incumbent President Rayale won the closely contested election, becoming Somaliland's first popularly elected head of government in over three decades. The country's maiden parliamentary election took place in 2005. The composition of Parliament was a rarity in Africa: opposition parties were in control.[67] Somaliland's leaders had good reason to proclaim to the world that theirs was a government representing the freely expressed will of the people – not only on the question of who should lead them, but also on the critical issue of statehood for Somaliland.[68]

Somaliland's second democratic presidential election is due in the last quarter of 2008, when Rayale's successor is to be chosen. Local government elections will be held around the same time. The fact that the presidential and local elections were postponed more than once – and Rayale's term as a consequence extended beyond the expiry date of May 2008 – sparked considerable controversy in Somaliland. The official reason for the deferments, supported by all three registered political parties, was that more time was needed to complete voter registration.[69]

Somaliland's democratic credentials have meanwhile become tarnished by actual or alleged human rights abuses. In 2007 SHURO-Net, a local human rights network, campaigned for the release of hundreds of citizens (including journalists) jailed on the orders of government security committees without any recourse to the courts.[70] In July of that year three leading figures of the Qaran political association, an emergent but unregistered opposition party, were imprisoned for seditious assembly. They violated a constitutional limitation on the number of political parties (being the three represented in the national legislature). Perhaps sensing the bad publicity generated by the conviction, President Rayale pardoned them five months later.[71] In a further controversial move the Somaliland government expelled 24 Somali journalists from the territory in December 2007. The group, which had previously fled from violence and grave human rights violations in Somalia, were ordered out of Somaliland for allegedly 'endangering the national security' (read: endangering Somaliland's vital relations with Ethiopia by writing articles offensive to Addis Ababa).[72]

The aspirant state's Achilles heel may be its fragile economy. Given the severe environmental conditions – the greater part of the country was dry savannah with no perennial rivers – animal husbandry was the mainstay of the economy. Livestock exports were the principal source of revenue, while remittances from the Somaliland diaspora made a further vital contribution to the economy. An estimated US$ 150 million to 200 million was transferred to Somaliland each year from the ranks of the roughly 500,000 Somalilanders living abroad.[73] Other obstacles to economic growth and to foreign and domestic investment included the paucity of external trade (in part the product of Somaliland's contested international status); the decay of key infrastructure such as roads, ports and airports due to insufficient maintenance funds; and the lack of adequate banking and insurance services.[74] But nature may come to the rescue of Somaliland's rickety economy. The country has some oil and gas reserves as well as rich fishing waters off its coast. A further asset was the deep-water harbour of Berbera, a major port for landlocked Ethiopia's exports and imports and already a sizeable income generator for Somaliland. The two neighbours have concluded the Berbera Corridor Agreement providing for an expansion of their trade relations and the coordination of transportation and taxation matters.[75] Berbera has also been developed as a free zone to which Somaliland hoped to attract major foreign investment.[76]

International reactions

The international response to the (re)birth of Somaliland has been marked by an overwhelming lack of interest. For most of the world community Somaliland, even if its *de facto* existence was noted, simply did not matter. One reason was that Somali territory had lost much of its Cold War strategic significance. Another was that Somaliland may, paradoxically, have become the victim of its own success: its peace and stability amid the turmoil of Somalia did not capture media headlines or arouse humanitarian concerns. More damaging for Somaliland than the isolation of indifference was that several influential states resorted to a 'knee-jerk insistence on the unity and territorial integrity of Somalia as a precondition to peace talks' between North and South. Such prerequisites effectively precluded the Somaliland leadership from meaningful participation in the peace process. This initiative has been driven by the states of the region (under the aegis of the Inter-governmental Authority on Development, IGAD) rather than by the world community acting through the UN. Surrounding countries have displayed very little sympathy for Somaliland's claims to self-determination.

Throughout the 1990s they preferred an empty Somali chair in multilateral forums to Somaliland occupying a new seat in its own right. After the creation of the Transitional National Government (TNG) of Somalia in 2000, these bodies upheld the fiction that the new authority was the sole legitimate international representative of the entire Somalia, North and South. For its part the TNG, however weak and ineffective, immediately claimed sovereignty over the entire Somali Republic, including Somaliland.[77] Without any UN member state objecting, the President of the TNG took Somalia's seat in the General Assembly during the Millennium Summit in 2000.[78] The successor Transitional Federal Government was allowed to retain the Somali seat in IGAD, the AU, UN, Arab League and Organization of the Islamic Conference. For a while Somaliland was interested in obtaining 'special interim international status', comparable to that of the Palestinian Authority, pending *de jure* recognition. Such an arrangement, Hargeysa hoped, would allow Somaliland to access more foreign aid from multilateral and bilateral donors. The proposed formula failed to attract international support.[79]

The AU has sent out mixed signals on the question of Somaliland's final status. On the one hand the continental organization engaged Hargeysa 'within the context of the unity of Somalia', as the head of the AU's Peace and Security Council explained.[80] This view of course endorsed Mogadishu's claims of sovereignty over Somaliland and denied of the latter's right of independent statehood. What is more, collapsed Somalia, an entity devoid of empirical statehood, was placed in the position of veto state over Somaliland. On the other hand the AU's Fact-finding Mission to Somaliland in 2005 reported that the presumptive state's quest for recognition was 'historically unique and self-justified in African political history'. The AU should, the mission recommended 'find a special method of dealing with this outstanding case'. As a guideline, the AU was advised 'to judge the case of Somaliland from an objective historical viewpoint and a moral angle vis-à-vis the aspirations of the people'.[81] In recognition of the decisive role the AU could play in determining the entity's future, Somaliland was keen to join the organization. In 2004 it requested observer status in the AU[82] and the following year Rayale submitted an application for full membership.[83] The issue of Somaliland's future status was discussed by AU foreign ministers in 2006[84] and in 2007 Alpha Konare, Chairman of the AU Commission, told the body's Executive Council that African states had to deal with the reality of Somaliland's existence and address the territory's unsettled international legal status.[85] A divided AU has so far failed to rise to the challenge, preferring a Somaliland left in international limbo to an organization torn by such an emotive issue. Yet the AU was the very institution to which the international community turned for guidance on the future of Somaliland.

Despite its twilight existence, Somaliland's international isolation has been far from complete. Like other contested states, Somaliland has established semi-official ties with several countries, including the US and Britain – thus gaining a measure of *de facto* recognition of its purported statehood. Its most extensive links were with neighbouring Ethiopia, with Somaliland maintaining a liaison office in Addis Ababa and Ethiopia in turn running a trade office in Hargeysa. Ethiopia also allowed Somaliland government officials to enter the country on Somaliland passports. We have already recorded the two neighbours' bilateral agreement on transit trade *via* Berbera; Ethiopia envisaged that up to 20 per cent of its foreign trade would eventually flow through the Somaliland port. Another vital transport link was the regular flights of Ethiopian Airlines between Addis Ababa and Hargeysa. In the field of finance the Ethiopian Commercial Bank has maintained a formal relationship with Somaliland's Central Bank. The two neighbours worked closely on matters of security too. One of the agreements Djibouti concluded with Somaliland was aimed at improving mutual understanding and cooperation and permitted Somaliland to operate a liaison office there. Some African and European countries have allowed entry to Hargeysa's officials using Somaliland travel documents. Among them was South Africa, which also hosted a Somaliland liaison office.[86]

Another indicator of the extent of Somaliland's international interactions was the foreign visits of its leader. President Rayale's recent foreign destinations included Ethiopia, Djibouti, South Africa, Ghana, America, Italy, Norway, Germany and Britain. An official Somaliland delegation led by the Foreign Minister was allowed to meet with representatives from member states on the sidelines of the Commonwealth summit in Kampala in November 2007, courtesy of the host state.[87] The reverse flow of foreign dignitaries to Hargeysa has been modest. A notable recent visitor was the US Under-Secretary of State Jendayi Frazer. Several delegations of foreign parliamentarians have however travelled to Somaliland, including groups from Ghana, Kenya, Britain and the EU. Legislators from Somaliland have in turn been invited to Britain, among other countries.[88]

Somaliland has managed to obtain various forms of foreign aid. There had been some foreign assistance in the reconstruction of Somaliland after the war and UN agencies and international non-governmental organizations have continued to provide humanitarian and development assistance.[89] The UN High Commissioner for Refugees has since 2002 been supporting the repatriation of Somaliland refugees to the territory.[90] The EU, UN and several other donors maintained larger aid programmes in Somaliland than elsewhere in former Somalia and concluded direct cooperative agreements with Hargeysa.[91] In what could be an intimation of greater foreign involvement, representatives from the World Bank, UN and EU attended meetings in Hargeysa in November 2007 on Somaliland's Reconstruction and Development Programme for 2008.[92] The UN Development Programme (UNDP) was indeed set to launch several development projects in Somaliland in 2008.[93] Somaliland's commitment to democracy has meanwhile earned it electoral assistance from the EU, America, Britain, Germany and Denmark, among other donors.[94]

It would be safe to say that the external assistance mentioned has been far below Somaliland's needs – a consequence of its contested statehood. The AU's fact-finding team acknowledged as much in 2005: 'The lack of recognition ties the hands of the authorities and people of Somaliland as they cannot effectively and sustainably transact with the outside to pursue the reconstruction and development goals'.[95]

These instances of limited international engagement with Somaliland have not been translated into anything more than *de facto* recognition of its separate existence. A notable failure has been access to regional and global organizations. At the bilateral level not even immediate neighbours, despite their familiarity with the territory's suffering under Mogadishu and regardless of the kinship ties some of them had with Somaliland, showed any sign of extending *de jure* recognition. Djibouti, for instance, has instead been the principal backer of Somalia's transitional government in the international arena. Egypt's enthusiastic support for the interim rulers in Mogadishu was been matched by its hostility towards Somaliland. Even Eritrea, a recent product of a successful struggle for self-determination, has refused to side with Somaliland lest other African states accused it of fomenting secession elsewhere on the continent. Ethiopia has been equally reluctant to support Somaliland's claims to statehood, even though Addis Ababa maintained fairly wide-ranging ties with Hargeysa.[96]

America likewise followed a policy of non-recognition and engagement towards Somaliland. 'While the United States does not recognize Somaliland as an independent state, and we continue to believe that the question of Somaliland's independence should be resolved by the African Union', the State Department explained in January 2008, 'we continue regularly to engage with Somaliland as a regional administration and to support programs that encourage democratization and economic development in the Somaliland region'.[97] The amount Washington spent on these programmes was exceedingly modest.[98] Britain's policy towards Somaliland was rather confusing. 'The UK does not recognize Somaliland as an independent state', a Minister of State in the Foreign and Commonwealth Office declared in 2008, and offered 'the Somaliland authorities' the gratuitous advice that they 'should negotiate with the Transitional Federal Government to determine their future relationship'.[99] At about the same time a British diplomat sounded a different note by commending Somaliland for its achievements of the last 17 years and declaring that London was ready to strengthen relations between the two countries and to support Somaliland's efforts to promote good governance and economic development.[100] Earlier another Foreign Office official had been even more accommodating: 'Our policy is to do whatever we can to help [Somaliland], short of recognition'.[101]

Explaining external opposition

Why the unanimous international rejection of Somaliland's claims to statehood? One reason, especially pertinent in Africa, was a dogmatic commitment to the sanctity of inherited colonial borders and hence a deep-seated antipathy to secession. This was coupled with an almost pathological fear of setting precedents that would encourage disaffected ethnic minorities to break away from existing states. Africa remained determined to treat the Eritrean case as *sui generis* and hence not applicable to Somaliland or any other unit within an established state on the continent.[102] It is worth noting, though, that the AU's 2005 mission to Somaliland maintained that its case 'should not be linked to the notion of "opening a pandora's box"' – in terms of spawning imitators – but was instead an exceptional instance requiring special treatment.[103]

Another African concern may have been that two Somali states (or even three, if Djibouti was added) could be fierce rivals and draw surrounding countries into their contest – thus jeopardizing regional peace and stability.[104] A related worry was that an independent Somaliland increased the danger of a renewed North-South conflagration because a new government in Mogadishu in effective control of its territory could be expected to claim jurisdiction over Somaliland and even press its demands by forcible means.[105]

Questions have also been raised about the level of popular support for Somaliland's independence, despite the referendum of 2001. The pro-independence constituency was concentrated in the dominant Isaaq clan; other clans appeared more divided on the issue, with some still favouring a united Somalia. The creation of Puntland, discussed earlier, has added to the doubts about political loyalties in the region. Not only was Puntland committed to a federal Somalia, but clans from Somaliland had been prominent in establishing the entity.[106]

A further common argument against Somaliland's statehood was that it lacked economic viability. Poor, underdeveloped and one of the most resource-scarce countries in the world, Somaliland cannot stand on its own feet, it was said. And the world cannot allow the creation of yet another economic basket-case forever dependent on foreign aid. Typical counter-arguments were that Somaliland's economic prospects were no worse than those of Eritrea or Djibouti. Moreover, intrinsic wealth was a lesser determinant of economic success than the quality of political leadership and economic management. The fact that Somaliland has not merely survived for 17 years against immense odds but actually maintained peace and stability and a degree of economic progress, were offered as evidence of its inherent qualities and sustainability as an independent entity.[107]

Although Somaliland has been an island of relative tranquillity in the sea of turbulence that engulfed the old Somalia, the country – like other contested states – could conceivably exercise negative power too. Somaliland could become a spoiler in the neighbourhood if radical Islamic groups were to use its territory as a safe have or transit route to surrounding states. This could happen through acts of omission or commission on the part of the Hargeysa authorities. Omission could flow from Somaliland's limited capacity to monitor and control the activities of such transnational groups, not least because of its exclusion from Interpol and normal intergovernmental intelligence networks. Acts of commission implied active government support for extremist groups, such as providing them with sanctuary and arms. The latter approach would not win Somaliland any respectable foreign friends; instead, it would further reduce the territory's chances of gaining international sympathy and acceptance. On the other side of the ledger, though, Somaliland could try to use its weakness in countering the threat of international terrorism, coupled with its suitable location for intelligence-gathering (on Somalia and other countries in the region), as a lever to extract at least security assistance from major Western powers. More broadly, Somaliland had good reason to argue that it could not be expected to meet the obligations of a good international citizen if it were not treated as one.[108]

What future for Somaliland?

The shaky transitional government in Mogadishu has demanded that Somaliland remain part of Somalia 'forever', to quote interim President Yusuf.[109] The world community for its part has refused to endorse Somaliland's separation from its original state – notwithstanding the protracted anarchy in the South. Somaliland therefore seems unable to capitalize on the South's travails by gaining international support for its statehood; the wreck that is Somalia still acted as an influential veto state over Somaliland. The collapse of authority in the Somali Republic has, however, given the North some breathing space: the international community is unlikely to coerce Somaliland into rejoining the South under prevailing conditions. The implication is then that the future of Somaliland could be settled only once Somalia has been restored to health and was able to engage the North as a credible partner in status talks. That stage may not be reached any time soon. Whether a rehabilitated Somalia would one day agree to partition and international recognition of two Somali states – along the lines of Czechoslovakia's 'velvet divorce' – is questionable.[110] A rebuilt South may indeed become more rather than less assertive in pursuing reunification with the North.

The final status option preferred by Somaliland has consistently been confirmed statehood separate from Somalia. 'Somaliland's desire for international recognition of its independence will not go away', its Foreign Minister asserted in 2007. 'The government and people of Somaliland will continue to press for recognition as long as it takes'.[111] Somaliland's development into 'the largest, wealthiest and best-armed authority within the Somali Republic'[112] has of course encouraged Hargeysa to stick to its guns. The strained personal relations between the leaders of Somaliland and Somalia's Transitional Federal Government have further bedevilled any joint exploration of a common future for the two entities.[113]

Given the poor prospects for a negotiated settlement, the ICG has recommended that the international community devise 'pragmatic responses' to Somaliland's claims to statehood. This is in the place of continuing to 'insist upon the increasingly abstract notion of the unity and territorial integrity of the Somali Republic'. The choice facing the world community in Somaliland was becoming considerably clearer, the ICG argued in 2003: the question 'is no longer whether Somaliland should be recognised as an independent state, but whether there remain any viable alternatives'.[114] In a subsequent report the ICG set out a pragmatic response. The AU was advised to grant Somaliland an interim international status while the organization reviewed the issue of final status. It would be similar to the observer status the AU had given 31 non-African states and the Palestinian Authority enjoyed in the UN. Interim observer status would allow Somaliland to attend open sessions of the AU dealing with the territory's status, and participate in AU meetings to which it was invited but without the right to vote. In short, such interim status for Somaliland would give both sides to the dispute a fair hearing in the AU.[115] A pragmatic approach of a different kind has meanwhile been adopted by Sweden when it decided in 2007 to treat Somaliland as a 'self-governing area' when providing development aid. Stockholm insisted, though, that it was not recognizing the independence of Somaliland.[116]

Finally, various forms of voluntary union between Somalia and Somaliland have been proposed. The options include a confederation, an association of states, a federation and an asymmetrical union.[117] According to one version of a proposed confederation, the two component units' symbols of separate statehood would range from own legislatures, executives, civil services and defence forces to separate UN membership; shared features would include a common currency, joint foreign embassies and common passports. Asymmetrical sovereignty would involve a federation of three or four provinces in the South that would jointly enter into a confederation with Somaliland.[118]

Conclusion

Its secessionist origins have condemned the Republic of Somaliland to contested statehood. The wannabe state has now lived in international limbo for 17 years, unable to secure any formal recognition. But within the constraints of its diplomatic isolation, Somaliland has managed to establish meaningful semi-official links with a number of states and intergovernmental organizations. The domestic transformation Somaliland has undergone in this period has been far more impressive. The war-ravaged former Northern Region of Somalia has established relative peace and order (except for the disputed Sool and Sanaag areas), created a democratic political system (not without blemishes) and recorded progress in economic development (against huge geographic odds).

Somaliland's achievements contrast vividly with the anarchy that has during the same period consumed Somalia, its country of origin. Although devoid of empirical statehood, Somalia has retained its juridical statehood – a feature that has allowed it to effectively veto Somaliland's progress to confirmed statehood. African countries have allowed this absurdity by their dogmatic commitment to the phantom state of Somalia over the factual state of Somaliland. The world community has deferred to the AU in deciding Somalia's international status.

Somaliland's claims to statehood do not rest primarily on the collapse of Somalia, though. Among existing contested states, Somaliland probably has the strongest historical and legal claims to full statehood. Recognition is, however, a political act and those who could give a positive lead in elevating Somaliland to confirmed statehood – the African countries – remained trapped by their self-imposed taboos.

7
Palestine

Unlike most contested states, Palestine has not been suffering from a lack of collective recognition. The right of the Palestinian people to an own state, located in the so-called Palestinian territories and co-existing with the state of Israel, enjoyed universal recognition. The UN similarly recognized the Palestine Liberation Organization as the representative of the Palestinian people. This titular recognition has, however, not been translated into UN membership – the final baptism into the international community – for the self-proclaimed independent state of Palestine. The nature of a future confirmed state of Palestine remains a contentious international issue, especially its status *vis-à-vis* Israel. International controversy has also dogged the first two phases of the life cycle of the purported Palestinian state, namely its origins and the way in which the Palestinian territories have been governed. There is consequently ample reason to treat Palestine as a contested state, albeit a rather exceptional one.

At the mercy of others

The Palestinian national movement, the vehicle for the Palestinian people's quest for statehood, emerged within a broader Arab nationalism that developed in the 19th and 20th centuries.[1] Although stirrings of Arab nationalism could be detected in the wake of Napoleon's invasion of Egypt in 1798, it was the Arabs' experiences of Ottoman rule that provided the spark for their modern nationalism that arose in the latter quarter of the 19th century. Some Arabs clamoured for independence (for example in Lebanon in the 1870s) while others aspired to autonomy or the recognition of their language and cultural rights in the Ottoman Empire. The so-called Arab Revolt of 1916 against the Turks was, however, driven by a desire to create a wholly independent Arab kingdom. To advance their cause, Arabs – including those from Palestine – joined the Allied forces in the war against the Ottoman Empire. With the defeat of the Turks in 1918, Arab expectations of statehood soared. The nearly 700,000 Palestinians, whose territory of 27,000 km^2

had formed part of Ottoman-dominated Syria, shared their Arab brethren's desire for independence and Arab unity. The Arabs' hopes were pinned on the victorious British to help them achieve statehood.[2]

It was not to be. Instead of gaining independence, the Arabs found their lands converted into mandated territories under the newly established League of Nations. Britain was appointed as the mandatory power over Palestine, which had been under British military administration since 1917. The mandate for Palestine, approved by the League in 1922, was unique in that it placed two contradictory obligations on Britain. On the one hand the mandatory power was responsible for developing self-governing institutions and safeguarding the civil and religious rights of all inhabitants of Palestine, and on the other Britain had to create the political, administrative and economic conditions necessary for 'the establishment of the Jewish National Home' in Palestine.[3]

Britain's commitment to a Jewish homeland was first enshrined in the Balfour Declaration of 1917, which was subsequently incorporated into the Palestine mandate agreement. The historic pronouncement of 1917 was a response to representations made to Britain by the Zionist Organization, founded in 1897 to promote the creation of a home for the Jewish people in Palestine. Foreign Secretary Arthur Balfour expressed Britain's support for 'the establishment in Palestine of a national home for the Jewish people', while promising that 'nothing shall be done which may prejudice the civil and religious rights of existing non-Jewish communities in Palestine'.[4] Balfour made no secret of where Britain's priority lay in pursuing these two irreconcilable objectives: 'in the case of Palestine we deliberately and rightly decline to accept the principle of self-determination', he stated in 1919. What is more, in Palestine 'we do not even propose to go through the form of consulting the wishes of the inhabitants of the country' – 90 per cent of whom were Palestinian Arabs.[5] The British were sowing dragon's teeth.

Dr Chaim Weizmann, President of the Zionist Organization, was forthright in his understanding of a Jewish national home: 'To build up something in Palestine which will be as Jewish as England is English'.[6] By contrast the Arab majority in Palestine interpreted Britain's other obligation under the mandate as a pledge of eventual Arab independence. In practice, however, the Palestinian Arabs discovered that when these commitments came into conflict the British rulers gave precedence to their undertakings to the Jews. As increasing numbers of Jews settled in Palestine in the course of the 1920s and 1930s, the Arab community expressed its frustrations in spontaneous protest actions and incidents of violence that were both anti-Zionist and anti-British. More organized resistance took the form of political parties and even guerrilla movements, all of which favoured national independence and opposed Zionism.[7]

Palestinian opposition to British rule reached a climax with the revolt of 1936 to 1939. An intimation of the later *intifadas*, it involved a boycott of

British authority and a general labour and business strike accompanied by sporadic acts of violence and sabotage. The highly effective boycott-*cum*-strike, which paralysed the territory, lasted for six months only but incidents of violence continued until 1939. The Peel Commission, appointed by the British to determine the causes of the boycott, highlighted Arab demands for self-government, the banning of land purchases by Jews and an end to Jewish immigration.[8] Some of these demands were met in a major revision of British policy announced in 1939. Restrictions were imposed on Jewish immigration and on the transfer of Arab land to Jews. More radically, Britain gave notice of its commitment to 'the establishment within ten years of an independent Palestine State...in which Arabs and Jews share in government in such a way as to insure that the essential interests of each community are safeguarded'.[9] The condition attached by the British was that independence could be granted only if relations between Arabs and Jews allowed the withdrawal of foreign authority. A representative Arab body rejected the new policy, instead demanding immediate independence. The Zionists also opposed the revised British policy and some of their armed groups resorted to violent attacks against both the British authorities and Palestinian Arabs. Constituting about 30 per cent of the total population by then, the Jewish community had the manpower, means and motives to press their claims with vigour.[10]

Exhausted by the Second World War, Britain lacked the stamina to continue governing its unruly wards in Palestine on behalf of the international community. The costs far outweighed whatever benefits its stewardship of Palestine held for Britain. In 1947 Britain conceded that 'the Mandate has proved to be unworkable in practice, and that the obligations undertaken to the two communities have been shown to be irreconcilable' – and simply gave the mandate over to the UN.[11] Forced to handle the hot potato, the General Assembly in November 1947 approved a plan to partition Palestine (resolution 181). The decision was far from unanimous: 33 states (including the major powers, among them the Soviet Union) approved the resolution concerned, 13 were against (notably Arab countries) and ten others abstained.[12] Under the partition plan roughly 56 per cent of the total area of Palestine would become a Jewish state accommodating 498,000 Jews and 497,000 Arabs; about 44 per cent was reserved for a Palestinian Arab state housing 725,000 Arabs and 10,000 Jews; and Jerusalem and surroundings (0.65 per cent) would be given a separate and unique international status under UN administration. Provision was also made for an economic union between the two states and the joint management of the City of Jerusalem by a board including representatives appointed by the UN.[13] While the Palestinian Arabs vehemently rejected the partition scheme as a violation of their right of self-determination and weighted in favour of the Jewish minority, the Zionists welcomed the proposal. The Jewish community worked zealously to extend their grip on the allotted land, a process accompanied by a mass exodus of Arabs from the would-be state.[14]

The next major confrontation was not long in coming. It coincided with the proclamation of the state of Israel and the final departure of British troops in May 1948. Military units from seven Arab states attacked Israel in an attempt to strangle the new polity in its cradle. Israel routed the invaders and also managed to extend its territory by a further 4,000 km^2. Arab Palestine was the main loser: Jordan took control of the West Bank, Egypt occupied the Gaza Strip and Jerusalem was divided between Jordan and Israel. About 850,000 Palestinians became refugees, most of them ending up in camps in neighbouring Arab states.[15] This left the Arab Palestinians 'not only a stateless people but the majority of them a homeless people as well'.[16] With most of them already in diaspora by the end of 1948, the Palestinians developed a deep sense of grievance against what they considered an interloper Zionist state created on their historic land.

Enter the PLO

At first the dispersed and dispirited Palestinians had little option but to turn to Arab states to relieve their plight. Apart from humanitarian support involved in hosting refugees, kin states gave the Palestinians a regional platform by allowing their representative to participate in meetings of the Arab League, including the right to vote on matters relating to Palestine.[17] However, rivalries and conflicting interests weakened the resolve of the community of Arab states to advance the Palestinian cause. They moreover lacked the political will and military muscle to free Palestine of Jewish occupation. Recognizing their limitations, the Arab leaders decided to let the Palestinians fight their own corner. At a summit meeting in Cairo in January 1964, the assembled Arab heads of state recommended that the Palestinian people 'assume their duties in liberating their homeland and determining their destiny'.[18] The upshot was the founding of the Palestine Liberation Organization (PLO) by a large representative meeting of Palestinians in Jerusalem in May 1964. The Palestinian National Covenant, the PLO's quasi-constitution, denounced the 1947 partition of Palestine and the establishment of the state of Israel as 'entirely illegal, regardless of the passage of time', committed Arabs to 'purge the Zionist presence from Palestine', asserted that Palestine was 'the homeland of the Palestinian Arab people' and that only Jews who had lived permanently in Palestine before the 'Zionist invasion' would be regarded as Palestinians; the latter stipulation meant that the majority of Jews in Israel would not qualify as Palestinians and therefore had no right to remain.[19]

For the first 30 years of the PLO's existence its leadership was based in exile, unable to exert effective control in Palestine. What is more, the Palestinian people remained dispersed across several Arab states, in addition to those remaining in Palestine and Israel. Even so the PLO in time succeeded in 'putting the Palestinians back on the political map, and bringing them back from the brink of oblivion'.[20] This achievement was in no small measure attributable to the indefatigable Yasser Arafat, elected PLO chairman in 1969. He was also the leader of Fatah, the most powerful of six major guerrilla factions affiliated with the PLO.[21]

Barely three years after its creation the PLO and indeed the Palestinian people suffered a huge setback when Israel, during the Six Day War of 1967, occupied the remaining 20 per cent of the former Palestine mandated territory: the West Bank, Gaza Strip and East Jerusalem. The entire area that the PLO had designated as a future state of Palestine was now in Israeli hands. While excluded from the Palestinian territories, the PLO effectively administered the large refugee camps in Jordan and Lebanon. The liberties the PLO took in Jordan eventually provoked a violent confrontation with that state, leading to the expulsion of PLO forces and their relocation to Lebanon. There they were driven out by Israeli forces in 1982, causing the PLO to move its headquarters to Tunisia.[22]

The 1967 war also had other profound consequences for the Palestinian cause. Israel's victory underscored the need for the Palestinians to do their own international bidding, instead of relying on the now chastened Arab countries. Their principal instrument was the PLO, which managed to elevate the so-called Palestine issue from a humanitarian concern focused on refugees to a people's right of self-determination. One way in which the Palestinians conducted their struggle was through a sustained campaign of violence against Israeli targets in the Jewish state and abroad.[23] The other was the diplomatic route.

In 1974 the PLO achieved a series of diplomatic breakthroughs at the UN. In October the General Assembly through resolution 3210 recognized the PLO as the representative of the Palestinian people and invited the movement to participate in Assembly deliberations during plenary meetings on the Question of Palestine (re-introduced to the General Assembly's agenda after 22 years). As a result Arafat in November 1974 addressed the Assembly, the first representative of a non-state organization to receive such an invitation (except for the ceremonial occasion when Pope Paul VI addressed the body). That same month the Assembly (resolution 3236) acknowledged the Palestinian people as 'a principal party in the establishment of a just and durable peace in the Middle East' and affirmed the Palestinians' inalienable right to 'national independence and sovereignty'. In so doing the Assembly endorsed key tenets of the PLO's programme. In its very next resolution (3237) the General Assembly conferred on the PLO the status of observer so as to participate in the work of the Assembly and all international conferences arranged under its auspices. The PLO subsequently opened a permanent Observer Mission at the UN in New York and another in Geneva.[24]

In November 1975 the General Assembly (resolution 3375) enhanced the PLO's role by calling for its participation 'in all efforts, deliberations and conferences on the Middle East which are held under the auspices of the United Nations, on an equal footing with other parties'. The Assembly also created the Committee on the Exercise of the Inalienable Rights of the Palestinian People and requested the Secretary-General to establish within the Secretariat – a supposedly neutral organ – a Special Unit on Palestinian Rights to assist the PLO.[25] Following the Assembly, the Security Council in December 1975 voted to permit the PLO to take part in Council debates under the procedural rule allowing the body to invite any UN member to participate when its interests are involved. The PLO was to enjoy the same rights of participation as would a member state thus invited. It was the first time that the Security Council extended this prerogative to a national liberation movement.[26] The Economic and Social Council for its part called on the UN's specialized agencies to cooperate closely with the PLO as 'the representative of the Palestinian people' in launching projects for the Palestinians.[27]

The European Community likewise recognized the rights of the Palestinian people and the role of the PLO. In the London Declaration of 1977, the EC stated that the 'legitimate rights of the Palestinians should take the form of a homeland for the Palestinian people'.[28] The EC's Venice Declaration, adopted in 1980, reiterated that the Palestinian people were entitled 'to exercise fully its right to self-determination' and also acknowledged the need to involve the PLO in the search for peace in the Middle East.[29]

Arafat reaped other diplomatic dividends too. In 1979, for instance, he was received by the Austrian Chancellor, the Spanish Prime Minister, and the President and Premier of Portugal. Foreign ministers of several other Western states also met with visiting PLO representatives around this time, indicating the movement's growing international recognition as a legitimate party to the Israel-Palestine issue.[30] By 1980 the PLO had offices in over 80 states. The following year its representative in Moscow received ambassadorial status, with Malaysia and others following suit.[31] Between 1974 and the early 1980s the PLO had indeed achieved unprecedented international recognition for an exiled liberation movement without any control over its would-be state.

It should not be forgotten that the image of a responsible liberation movement engaged in a just struggle was the one side of the Janus-faced PLO. The other was that of a ruthless terrorist organization living by the rule that the end (the destruction of Israel and the liberation of Palestine) justified the means (indiscriminate violence with no regard for human life). Described as 'the pioneer of modern terrorism', the PLO and its associated groups were said to 'hold various records in the field of terrorism' for several years. These distinctions were based on the killing, maiming and destruction caused by such acts as aircraft hijackings, hostage taking, bombings and other armed attacks in scores of countries. Between 1967 and the end of 1980 the PLO had, by its own calculations, carried out 10,000 armed operations. The PLO was moreover 'the pivot of international terrorism' at the time, maintaining active links with the likes of the Baader-Meinhof gang, Red Army Faction, Japanese Red Army and Irish Republican Army.[32]

The PLO's uncompromising hostility towards Israel and the movement's unapologetic practice of terrorism did not endear it to Western opinion, least of all the US. A further alienating factor was the PLO's rejection of UN Security Council resolution 242 that required Israel to withdraw its armed forces from all Arab territories occupied in the wake of the 1967 war. The PLO objected to the resolution's failure to deal with Palestinian rights. The PLO's opposition to 242, shared by Arab states, thwarted US attempts after 1967 to promote a peaceful settlement of the Arab-Israeli conflict. On a bilateral level the PLO deeply mistrusted the US, a committed ally of Israel. American antagonism towards the PLO was in turn reflected in Washington's closure in 1987 of a Palestine Information Office run by American nationals of Palestinian origin since 1978. More importantly, the US opposed the creation of an independent Palestinian state. The Carter administration, for example, insisted that it would not accept Palestinian 'self-determination' if it meant the creation of a Palestinian state on Israel's borders.[33] In like vein the subsequent Reagan Plan for the Middle East proclaimed that 'peace cannot be achieved by the formation of an independent Palestinian state' in the West Bank and Gaza. Instead, the Reagan administration favoured 'self-government by the Palestinians' in those two areas 'in association with Jordan'.[34] As long as America (and Israel) resisted Palestinian statehood, it remained an internationally contested notion.

The Soviet Union had no such reservations about a Palestinian state, even though it had in 1947 supported the UN partition plan that gave birth to the state of Israel.[35] But the PLO's most outspoken foreign backers were developing countries from the Middle East, Asia and Africa. In the latter two continents more states recognized the PLO than Israel; in the Middle East only Egypt had by the end of the 1970s officially recognized Israel's statehood. Regional institutions, notably the Afro-Asian People's Solidarity Organization, Islamic Conference Organization, Organization of African Unity, Non-Aligned Movement and Arab League, were committed supporters of the PLO cause.[36]

Egypt's recognition of Israel came in the wake of the Camp David Agreements concluded between the two countries in 1978 through US mediation. The one accord was a bilateral peace treaty and the other provided for an overall Middle East peace settlement. The latter included a framework for a 'self-governing authority' elected by the Palestinians in the West Bank and Gaza Strip followed by the withdrawal of Israeli forces and civilian administration. The final status of the two territories would be negotiated by Egypt, Israel, Jordan and representatives from the West Bank and

Gaza. The Palestinians, however, feared that the autonomy proposals were designed to swindle them out of independent statehood. This suspicion as well as disagreement over who should represent the Palestinians wrecked the proposed peace deal.[37]

The first *intifada*

On the home front, meanwhile, the outbreak of the *intifada* in December 1987 heralded a Palestinian uprising on a scale not witnessed since the so-called Great Arab Revolt of 1936–9. The *intifada* erupted, coincidentally, exactly 70 years after British forces first occupied Palestine and highlighted issues that had remained unresolved despite the passage of time. Beginning in Gaza, the *intifada* soon spread to the West Bank, effectively engulfing all of Palestine. Apart from being a widespread, popular response to foreign occupation and the denial of Palestinians' self-determination, the *intifada* shared other features with the earlier Arab Revolt. Each lasted for several years; the *intifada* ended only in 1991. In both cases the occupying power used violent repression in a bid to end the uprisings, causing a large number of casualties. Over 5,000 Palestinians were killed by British forces and Jewish militias in the 1930s, while nearly 1,000 Palestinians and fewer than 40 Israelis died during the *intifada*.[38] Initially a spontaneous uprising, the *intifada* was supported and subsequently orchestrated by the PLO.[39] In international consciousness the event gave the Palestinians 'the irrevocable status of a people dispossessed and under a brutal military occupation'.[40] The *intifada* may also have played a role in at least the timing of Jordan's renunciation of all claims to the West Bank in July 1988. This announcement benefited the PLO by eliminating any Jordanian challenge to the movement's claims that it was the sole authentic voice of the Palestinians.[41]

It was during the first *intifada* that the PLO removed two major obstacles to recognition by the West, namely its use of terrorism and commitment to the liquidation of Israel. In November 1988 the Palestine National Council (PNC, effectively Palestine's parliament-in-exile) accepted UN Security Council resolutions 242 (1967) and 338 (1973) as the basis for a comprehensive settlement of the Arab-Israeli conflict. (The former resolution guaranteed the right of all states in the Middle East to live in peace within secure and recognized borders, while the latter called on Israelis and Arabs to give effect to resolution 242.) The National Council announced its willingness to negotiate with Israel in the context of an international peace conference on condition that the Jewish state recognized Palestinian rights. The Palestinians' decision was widely interpreted as a renunciation of the PLO's goal of destroying Israel, and an implicit recognition of the Jewish state's right of existence and hence of a so-called two-state solution involving the co-existence of separate Jewish and Arab Palestinian states.[42]

These watershed announcements were accompanied by the PNC's unilateral declaration of the independence of Palestine, with Jerusalem as its capital. 'The State of Palestine is an Arab state, an integral and indivisible part of the Arab nation', the Palestinian Declaration of Independence read, and 'the state of Palestinians wherever they may be'.[43] The self-proclaimed Palestinian state of 1988 would be created alongside Israel in an area confined to the 22 per cent of the former mandated territory of Palestine, comprising the Israeli occupied West Bank, Gaza Strip and Arab East Jerusalem. The declaration should be seen as a symbolic proclamation of the establishment of an independent Palestine on the basis of the UN General Assembly's partition plan of 1947, rather than a proclamation intended to create the juridical effects of conventional statehood.[44]

The other critical decision taken by the PNC in November 1988 was to reject terrorism 'in all its forms'. This change of tactics was softened by a simultaneous pledge by the Council 'to provide all means and possibilities for the intensification of our people's uprising [the *intifada*]...including the hit groups and the popular army'.[45]

The Palestine National Council's new moderate course was widely applauded abroad. The UN General Assembly, in a resolution adopted in December 1988, acknowledged the proclamation of a Palestinian state and decided that the designation 'Palestine' would replace that of the PLO in the work of the UN. While stopping short of recognizing the phantom state, the Assembly conferred legitimacy on the notion of a Palestinian state. Scores of existing states went much further: within two weeks of its proclamation, the 'State of Palestine' had already been recognized by nearly 70 countries and soon by over 100.[46] Arafat, elected as the first President of the State of Palestine by the PLO's Executive Committee in April 1989, was treated as a head of state by several countries, while others regarded him as at best a president-in-waiting.[47] Western states, among others, maintained that the PNC's declaration of independence had no legal effect because Palestine failed to meet the traditional criteria of statehood. A further accommodation in Western approaches to the PLO nonetheless became evident in 1988. The US ended an official ban on talks with the movement and in December held its first diplomatic exchanges with the PLO in 13 years. At about the same time Britain had its first ministerial-level contact with the PLO.[48]

The PLO's *bona fides* were further enhanced when Arafat in 1989 brought the Palestinian National Covenant in line with the new policy on Israel by declaring that the document's references to the eradication of Israel were obsolete.[49] The PLO's new direction was confirmed in a memorandum sent to the American Secretary of State in 1991: 'Our objective remains to establish the independent Palestinian state on the national soil of Palestine, next to the state of Israel and within the framework of a two-state solution'.[50] By then the PLO knew full well that recognizing Israel's right of existence improved the chances of a Palestinian state being created with general international backing.

Peacemaking and homecoming

Since the PLO's make-over as a respectable international citizen, several Middle East peace initiatives were launched in which the Palestinians featured. The first was the Madrid Peace Conference of 1991, co-chaired by the US and Soviet Union. Although PLO-approved Palestinian delegates participated as part of the Jordanian team, their presence constituted yet further international recognition of the movement's right to be involved in determining Palestine's political fate.[51] The PLO's standing received another boost when Israel in 1993 eventually recognized it 'as the representative of the Palestinian people'.[52] Some analysts read an implicit Israeli recognition of the Palestinians' right of statehood into this move.[53]

It was also in 1993 that Israel and the PLO agreed to a Declaration of Principles on Interim Self-Government Arrangements as part of the Oslo Accords. The two sides concurred 'that it is time to put an end to decades of confrontation and conflict, recognize their mutual legitimate and political rights, and strive to live in peaceful coexistence and mutual dignity and security and achieve a just, lasting and comprehensive peace settlement'.[54] Provision was made for a three-stage process extending over five years. During the first two, Israel would withdraw from designated parts of the West Bank and Gaza (under Israeli occupation since 1967), allowing the establishment of a Palestinian Interim Self-Government Authority. The latter would be an elected body representing the Palestinians in the West Bank and Gaza for a transitional period of five years pending a permanent settlement. Excluded from its jurisdiction were matters to be resolved in permanent status negotiations.[55] During the third stage, scheduled from 1996 to 1999, 'final status' negotiations were to address all remaining matters. These would include the major contentious issues between Israel and Palestine, namely Jerusalem's fate, Jewish settlements in the West Bank and Gaza, the borders of Israel, the situation of an estimated 4.5 million Palestinian refugees, and an eventual sovereign Palestinian state. A series of further agreements between Israel and Palestine flowed from the landmark Declaration of Principles, including the Wye River Memorandum of 1998.[56]

The Oslo Accords afforded the PLO a new lease on life at a time that the movement was facing 'permanent obscurity or worse'. The PLO's ill-advised decision to support Iraq during the Gulf War of 1990–1 offended many Arab states and prompted its principal donors (Kuwait and Saudi Arabia) to cut off further funding. Destitute, the PLO was forced to close several of its offices and terminate many of its activities. Then came the fall of the Soviet Union, which left the PLO without its superpower patron.[57] These realities, together with the fact that its nearly 30 years of struggle had still not liberated Palestine, made the PLO receptive to the compromise solution represented by the Oslo Accords. Although the deal fell far short of the central Palestinian demand of assured statehood, that prospect was plainly part of the package. First, though, the Palestinians would have to serve an apprenticeship of sorts by passing a test of autonomy before proceeding to a higher level of self-determination.[58] The Oslo Accords thus enabled the Palestinians to take their most decisive step towards an own state since 1947.[59]

In 1994 Arafat and the PLO leadership duly went home to Palestine, thereby 'returning the locus of the Palestine question, the arena of Palestinian politics, and the center of gravity of the Palestinian national movement to Palestine'.[60] The *de facto* state of Palestine came into being when the PLO formed a Palestinian government on home soil, known as the Palestine Authority (PA). In elections two years later Arafat won the presidency of the PA and his supporters captured 60 per cent of the seats in the Legislative Council. Formally, the Palestinian government's authority extended over some three million people living in the West Bank and Gaza. Symbols of sovereign statehood were much in evidence, including a national flag and anthem, police force and judicial system, diplomatic corps, Palestinian identity cards and passports, national airline and participation in the 1996 Olympic Games. In July 1998 the UN General Assembly upgraded the PLO's status in the world body by allowing it to participate in general debates, co-sponsor resolutions and raise points of order during discussions on Middle East and Palestinian affairs. Three months later Arafat was allowed to address the Assembly's plenary session under the agenda item 'General Debate'. These additional rights and privileges of participation had previously been exclusive to UN member states. However, the PLO's goal of full UN membership for Palestine as a state remained unfulfilled.[61]

Since the proclamation of independence in 1988, the Palestinian leadership has on a number of occasions threatened to unilaterally declare an independent state of Palestine. This confusing situation seems to acknowledge that the original act had been less than a full assertion of sovereign independence and accordingly produced less than juridical statehood.[62] In terms of international law, the PA possessed only 'some form of limited international personality'.[63]

Ambiguity and fragility

Its ambiguous international status suggested that Palestine was still not a state in the conventional sense. Consider Palestine's questionable compliance with the standard legal criteria of statehood, starting with an independent government in effective control of the purported state. Created in terms of agreements between the PLO and Israel, the Palestine Authority was an autonomous body assigned temporary and limited powers, many of which had to be exercised with the approval or cooperation of Israel. Pending the outcome of permanent status negotiations between the two sides, Israel retained final residual authority in the West Bank and Gaza Strip.[64] On the ground in Gaza and the West Bank, 'the PA's effective mandate remained so circumscribed in practical terms by the realities of external power that its writ on all major issues and most minor ones, was at best tentative'.[65] That power of course belonged to Israel.

Turning to the possession of a defined territory, in the second place, the PA had grave difficulty in proving that it had sovereign title over the territory concerned. Israel retained control over all external borders of Palestine and its airspace and territorial waters. By 1999 the Israelis controlled over 70 per cent of the West Bank and 30 per cent of Gaza. Thereafter Israel continued with its occupation and seizures of Palestinian land for settlements. Palestine furthermore lacked undisputed control over vital resources such as water, and the areas under Palestinian control were highly fragmented and non-contiguous. To add to the complications, the Palestinians' purported state had no fixed national boundaries.[66] Although the total area of the West Bank and Gaza – 6,335 km^2 – was modest and much smaller than Israel (22,145 km^2), it should be noted that 30 UN member states had smaller territories than Palestine. The closest comparison was Brunei, covering 5,765 km^2.

Third, international law required that the government of a state should exercise effective and independent control over a permanent population. Although the PA enjoyed significant powers over Palestinian residents in the West Bank and Gaza, its jurisdiction could not be described as either independent or comprehensive. Through its control of large segments of these two territories, Israel effectively regulated the movement of people and goods between Gaza and the West Bank and within each. What is more, the majority of the people claimed as citizens of Palestine lived outside the entity.[67] By the end of 2005, under 40 per cent of the estimated ten million Palestinians worldwide lived in the Palestinian territories; roughly 11 per cent were in Israel, 30 per cent in Jordan and nearly 5 per cent in Syria.[68]

The final traditional criterion of statehood refers to a capacity to freely engage in international relations. The problem for Palestine was that the matter of foreign relations had – under agreements concluded with Israel – been explicitly reserved for permanent status negotiations. Israel in practice allowed Palestine to engage in limited foreign interaction in such areas as the acquisition of international aid. For the rest international relations were conducted by the PLO rather than the 'State of Palestine'.[69]

In short, Palestine was 'not a state, not sovereign, and under occupation'.[70] Palestine's consolation was that its right of statehood had been generally accepted by the international community – something no other contested state could match.

While Israel's omnipresence was a major factor in Palestine's lack of empirical statehood or domestic sovereignty, a good deal of the blame can be attributed to the Palestinian leadership. As Khalidi recorded, the PLO leaders dominating the PA 'proved to be poorly suited for the task of state building, for transparent governance, or for a stable structure of governance based on law'.[71] Arafat, above all, had much to account for. His authoritarian rule, characterized by the concentration of power in his office, gave Arafat individual control of the bureaucracy, security courts, the fragmented security services and the police force. This made Arafat 'executive administrator, patron, legislator, and judge all in one'.[72] The personalization of power was accompanied by a personality cult built around Arafat. But despite his strongman-image, Arafat was notorious for indecisiveness and impulsive decision-making.[73] As in authoritarian systems elsewhere, Palestine's gave rise to a host of familiar vices such as a lack of transparency and accountability in government, corruption and nepotism, human rights abuses, and violations of the rule of law.[74]

There were also tensions between the previously exiled PLO leadership and the people of Gaza and the West Bank, and the PLO itself was riven by ideologies, personal interests and political loyalties to rival Arab countries. More ominously, Arafat faced a serious challenge to his leadership from Hamas, the military wing of the Islamic Resistance Movement. Hamas and some other militant groups rejected both the PLO's recognition of Israel and the Oslo peace agreements, vowing instead to continue the armed struggle against the Jewish state. For such groups the PLO's most besetting sin was that it had betrayed its credentials as a national liberation movement by allowing the Israeli occupiers to remain in place.[75] Under these inauspicious conditions the Palestinian majority had in the course of the 1990s become 'disillusioned, demoralized, politically paralyzed, and unable to mount any significant action to change conditions on the ground in the occupied territories or internationally'.[76]

The second *intifada*

What added to the Palestinians' sense of despondence was that a final peace agreement with Israel was still not in sight by the turn of the century. In fact, Palestinians came to doubt whether any peace deal based on a two-state model was possible when a growing segment of the Palestinian territories was being absorbed into Israel through settlement and *de facto* annexation.[77] Their frustrations gave rise to the second *intifada*, which broke out in September 2000. Again, Israelis and Palestinians found themselves in a virtual state of war. Nearly 3,000 Palestinians and more than 1,000 Israelis died in the violence.[78] Israel's military forays into the Palestinian territories had by the end of 2002 demolished the PA's security and administrative organs and laid siege to Arafat's Ramallah headquarters;

occupying Israeli forces kept the President of Palestine under house arrest for over a year.[79]

External attempts at peacemaking were not abandoned, though. In 2000 American President Bill Clinton brokered the Camp David peace talks between Arafat and Israel's Prime Minister Ehud Barak. Under the Clinton plan Israel would surrender the majority of its West Bank settlements and relocate its settlers, and share sovereignty over Jerusalem with the Palestinians. The latter would in turn have to accept that most refugees would not be able to return to their original (pre-1948) homes in Israel, but only to a new state comprising the West Bank and Gaza Strip. While the Israeli side was ready for far-reaching compromise, Arafat stone-walled, causing the talks to collapse.[80]

In April 2003 the so-called Quartet (the US, Russia, UN and EU) produced a 'performance-based roadmap to a permanent two-state solution to the Israeli-Palestinian conflict'. Its declared 'destination' was a 'final and comprehensive settlement' of the Israel-Palestine conflict by 2005, allowing for 'an independent, democratic, and viable Palestinian state' living in peace and security with Israel and its other neighbours. The roadmap provided a timeline for implementation consisting of three phases. In the first, terror and violence would be stopped, Palestinian life normalized and Palestinian institutions built. The second phase, called transition, would focus on 'creating an independent Palestinian state with provisional borders and attributes of sovereignty, based on the new constitution [drafted in phase 1], as a way station to a permanent status settlement'. Quartet members would 'promote international recognition' of a Palestinian state, including 'possible' UN membership. The last phase would culminate in a final, permanent status settlement in 2005. Since the Quartet would 'assist and facilitate implementation' of all phases of the plan, the roadmap provided for an internationally supervised transition to independence for Palestine, comparable to what had previously occurred in Namibia and East Timor, among others.[81]

Although Israel approved the roadmap, implementation was threatened by the Jewish state's construction of a 'security fence' in the West Bank. Israel justified erection of the barrier, begun in 2002, as a security measure to prevent Palestinian suicide bombings on Israeli soil, whereas Palestinians saw it as an attempt to annex slices of their land.[82] Arafat was not particularly helpful either. His inability to rein in militants like Hamas (which continued terrorist attacks against Israel) and to stem the rot in the PA, caused the US and Israel to turn their backs on Arafat during the last two years of his life. Instead of negotiating with the Palestinian leadership under Arafat, Israel unilaterally withdrew its settlers from the Gaza Strip and parts of the West Bank – moves ostensibly aimed at imposing Israeli demarcated 'final' borders on Palestine.[83] Arafat's death in November 2004 brought some hope of reviving the peace process.

Exit Arafat, enter Hamas

The mood of anticipation was strengthened by the appointment of the moderate Mahmud Abbas to succeed Arafat as PLO chairman and President of the PA in January 2005. A founding member of Fatah, Abbas had been the leader of the Palestinian delegation in the Oslo peace negotiations and served briefly as Prime Minister under Arafat in 2003.[84] Only weeks after taking office, President Abbas and Israeli Premier Ariel Sharon met at Sharm esh Sheikh, with Egypt's President Hosni Mubarak and King Abdullah of Jordan in attendance. At the summit Abbas announced a ceasefire, while Sharon undertook to halt Israeli military operations in Palestine if militant attacks on Israel stopped. Hamas refused to be bound by the agreement to end hostilities and continued its attacks on Israel, provoking the customary Israeli retaliation.[85] On the domestic front there was no love lost between Hamas and Fatah. Tensions between them had been rising ever since Arafat's demise, causing sporadic armed clashes and politically inspired assassinations. The militancy of Hamas played well with the Palestinian people, who voted the movement into office in the general election of January 2006. To the alarm of Israel and Western states, Hamas swept Fatah from power in the Legislative Council by winning 74 of the 132 seats against Fatah's 45. In March Hamas's first Cabinet under Prime Minister Ismail Haniyeh was inaugurated.[86]

Far from ending the political schism between the two movements, the voters' verdict intensified the mutual hostility. Palestinians faced the spectre of civil war as fighters of Hamas and Fatah battled it out in the streets of the West Bank and Gaza. *The Economist* summed up the dire situation within Palestine at the end of 2006: 'things have never been so volatile, the guns so plentiful and the forces so large as now'.[87]

In a desperate effort to steer Palestine out of the crisis, Saudi Arabia brokered a ceasefire (the Mecca Agreement) between the two rival groups in February 2007. That same month Abbas eventually managed to persuade Hamas and Fatah to join a national unity government under a power-sharing arrangement. Hamas held 12 cabinet posts, Fatah six, and independents and smaller parties seven. The two main parties were also represented on a new national security council.[88] The Mecca ceasefire failed to stem the tide of violence, though. After a particularly intense round of fighting between Hamas and Fatah in the Gaza Strip in June 2007, leaving as many as 100 Palestinians dead, Haniyeh's faction dislodged officials loyal to Fatah and seized control of authority structures in Gaza. This illegal take-over of the government of Gaza, a *coup d'etat* of sorts, caused President Abbas to dissolve the government of national unity (and hence dismiss Prime Minister Haniyeh) and impose a state of emergency. Following a brief spell of ruling the West Bank and Gaza by presidential decree, Abbas in June appointed Salam Fayyad as prime minister and mandated him to form a new government. All the while armed clashes between Hamas and Fatah continued.[89]

The advent of Hamas created a huge new stumbling block on the boulder-strewn road to peace between Palestine and Israel and the formal establishment of a Palestinian state. Israeli officials feared that Gaza could be turned into a Taliban-like Islamic stronghold or 'Hamastan' – 'a kingdom of thugs, murderers, terrorists, poverty and despair'.[90] Some of these apprehensions were confirmed by the continuous barrage of rocket and mortar fire from Gaza into Israel after Hamas took over.[91] Add to this Haniyeh's uncompromising rejection of talks with Israel. 'The option of the resistance and jihad is the shortest way to liberate Palestine, and to restore Jerusalem and Palestinian rights. Not the path of negotiations', he declared in December 2007.[92] The previous April Haniyeh made the categorical statement that 'the issue of recognition of Israel has been settled once and for all...Recognition of Israel is out of the question'.[93] America and the EU greeted Hamas's assumption of power with the suspension of their aid to Palestine until Hamas met three conditions laid down by the Quartet group: the recognition of Israel, adherence to agreements previously concluded between Palestine and the Jewish state, and the renunciation of violence against Israel. Haniyeh, however, vowed that Hamas would not comply with any of the conditions.[94]

Siding openly with the moderate Abbas and Prime Minister Fayyad in their power struggle with Hamas, the Americans and Europeans resumed their assistance to the PA. The intention, shared by Israel, was to 'shower love, money and weapons' on Abbas so that the West Bank would prosper under PA control.[95] Gaza would by contrast be punished – and further impoverished – by tightening the already severe sanctions imposed in the wake of Hamas's election victory. The PA also turned the screws on Gaza by boycotting the judicial, security and other government agencies and restricting ties with the Hamas government.[96] The assumption was that the suffering population would turn against Hamas and re-embrace the more moderate Fatah.

The strategy soon failed. Hamas immediately stepped into the vacuum created by the boycotters and managed to establish a virtual monopoly on the use of force and open political activity in Gaza. While economic conditions in Gaza indeed became desperate, popular anger was directed as much against Fatah, Israel and their Western backers as against Hamas. Fatah thus failed to gain from Hamas's losses. Punishment through isolation did not stop the armed attacks between Islamic militants in Gaza and Israeli forces either.[97] Alarmed by the turn of events in Gaza, Egypt brokered a ceasefire which Israel and Hamas signed in June 2008. Under the terms of the truce Israel would also relax its blockade on Gaza.[98] If honoured, the six-month truce would save lives and bring relief to the besieged people of Gaza. It was, however, not meant to address the fundamental issues of power and governance in the Palestinian territories.

Meanwhile, at the height of the Gaza crisis in November 2007 yet another international peace conference took place. Convened by US President George W Bush in Maryland, the palaver was attended by Abbas and Israeli Prime Minister Ehud Olmert. The occasion produced little more than a Joint Understanding in which Olmert and Abbas recommitted themselves to 'the goal of two states, Israel and Palestine, living side by side in peace and security'. They agreed to immediately start bilateral negotiations leading to a peace treaty resolving all 'outstanding issues' before the end of 2008. This would involve the immediate implementation of their respective obligations under the roadmap of 2003.[99] Months later there was still little evidence of progress, leaving a confirmed Palestinian state a distant dream.

Economic costs of political conflict

Dependence on foreign aid and on Israel rendered the Palestinian economy highly vulnerable to external political manipulation. Over the past 15 years or so, Palestine drew the highest *per capita* foreign aid in the world. The PA had reportedly received $350 million in 2005 and $738 million in 2006. The major donors have been the US, EU, Japan and Arab countries.[100] Israel, in turn, was Palestine's principal trade partner. Over 95 per cent of Palestinian trade was conducted with the Jewish state, with their bilateral trade worth an estimated $2 billion annually.[101] This utter economic dependence on Israel was exacerbated by the fact that up to 40 per cent of the PA's budget emanated from the transfer of taxes and duties collected on its behalf by Israel.[102]

The Palestinian economy has been in decline for most of the present decade. The downturn began with the eruption of new hostilities with Israel in 2000. The following year Palestine's economy contracted by 17 per cent, increasing to 27 per cent in 2002. After a moderate recovery between 2003 and 2005, the economy shrank again in 2006 by six per cent. According to the World Bank, 2007 recorded zero growth and the Palestinian economy was likely to remain stagnant in 2008. Since 1999 the territory's gross domestic product (GDP) *per capita* had dropped nearly 40 per cent. The Palestinian figure of under US$1,130 in 2006 compared poorly with Israel's $27,000.[103] Palestine's economic woes were also evident in increasing poverty resulting from rising unemployment. From only 10 per cent prior to the second *intifada*, unemployment in the West Bank and Gaza Strip grew to roughly 23 per cent by 2006. Gaza was worst off with an unemployment rate of 33 per cent in 2006. The proportion of Gazans suffering 'deep poverty' (based on a budget for food, clothing and housing only) increased from nearly 22 per cent in 1998 to 35 per cent in 2006; for the West Bank the corresponding 2006 figure was 13 per cent.[104] Such has been the magnitude of the deterioration that Palestine's economy may well have suffered longer-term structural damage.[105]

A confluence of three factors accounted for Palestine's protracted economic woes: the suspension of direct foreign aid in the wake of Hamas's election victory in 2006, the increase in Israeli settlements in the Palestinian areas, and Israel's restrictions on movement in and access to those territories.[106]

With over 90 per cent of its foreign aid emanating from the West and Japan, the interruption of this flow in the wake of Hamas's election victory left Palestine in a financial crisis.[107] Israel in turn punished Hamas by stopping the transfer of tax and customs revenue collected on behalf of the PA; by early 2007 Israel was withholding the bulk of $800 million thus collected.[108]

As regards Israeli settlements in the West Bank, there had been 149 by mid-2007, East Jerusalem included. An additional 100 or so illegal outposts were maintained without the approval of the Israeli government. The settlement population of roughly 450,000 represented an increase of over 60 per cent on the number at the time of the Oslo Accords in 1993. Israel may have confiscated up to 50 per cent of West Bank territory for existing and future settlements, outposts, restricted military zones and other purposes.[109] In Gaza, by contrast, Israel unilaterally closed its settlements in 2005, evacuated its settlers and withdrew troops, thus ending almost 40 years of military occupation.[110]

Israel has long been controlling the flow of people and goods to, from and within the Palestinian territories, but imposed a far stricter 'closure regime' in 2000 in response to the second *intifada*.[111] In the West Bank Israel maintained a staggering 600-odd checkpoints and roadblocks by late 2007.[112] Particular reference must be made to Israel's security barrier in the West Bank. The 'seam zone' along the wall has been proclaimed a closed area for an indefinite period. Comprising approximately 8.5 per cent of the West Bank, the zone had housed 50,000 Palestinians in 38 towns and villages.[113]

Israel defended its restrictions on movement on the grounds of countering insurgency and terrorism targeted against its settlements in the Palestinian territories and in Israel proper. While Israelis may have been left safer, the Palestinians have suffered grievously. A study sponsored by the New Israel Fund and the British embassy in Tel Aviv found that the security wall 'almost totally ignores the daily needs of the Palestinian population', while focusing on the desire 'to maintain the fabric of life of Israeli settlers'.[114] Although an Israeli official gave the assurance that '[w]e have no interest in seeing a failed Palestinian economy',[115] that may be the very result of Israel's closure policy. It has constricted the movement of goods between the Palestinian territories and Israel, effectively separated economic and social interaction between the West Bank and Gaza Strip, and fragmented the Palestinian economy. The West Bank itself has been split up 'into ever smaller and more disconnected cantons'[116] which, in Khalidi's words, 'resemble open-air prison camps'.[117]

Tiny Gaza (comprising 365 km^2 and 1.4 million Palestinians) – economically far weaker than the West Bank (5,970 km^2, 2.4 million Palestinians) – suffered a further blow after Hamas took control of the Strip in mid-2007. Gaza became virtually cut off from the West Bank and indeed most of the outside world as Israel imposed an economic blockade against what it designated a 'hostile territory'.[118] The restrictions have caused the suspension of over 90 per cent of Gaza's industrial activities, transforming the area into 'a consumer economy driven by public sector salaries and humanitarian assistance only'.[119]

In the World Bank's assessment, the combination of Israel's settlements and closure policy and the suspension of foreign aid 'placed an already-fragile Palestinian economy in a downward cycle of crisis and dependence'.[120] This situation of course undermined Palestine's development of empirical statehood and invariably conjured up familiar doubts about its viability as an independent state. Israel's role in causing economic havoc in the Palestinian territories in turn raises serious questions about the Jewish state's commitment to Palestine's independence. Israel is obviously well positioned to play the role of veto state over an aspirant Palestinian state.

Alternative futures

Today Palestinians no longer face the problem of convincing the international community of their legal, political and moral right to an own state. The universal recognition of their right is typically couched in terms of a two-state arrangement: an independent Palestinian state peacefully coexisting with Israel.[121] (Israel's right of existence may not enjoy the same global acceptance.) Yet the Palestinians have to prove to an increasingly sceptical world that they are capable of governing a modern state. Their record since 1994 has not been encouraging, even when making due allowance for the unique challenges of building a state under conditions of partial occupation by a hostile power. Israel's consolidation of its hold over the West Bank and East Jerusalem has equally called the prospects of a two-state solution into question – if by a 'State of Palestine' is meant 'a viable, contiguous, sovereign, independent state on the entirety of the 22 percent of mandatory Palestine constituted by the Palestinian territories occupied by Israel in June 1967'.[122] After all, a two-state outcome and peace between Israelis and Palestinians are hardly conceivable if Israel refused to give up the West Bank and share Jerusalem with a state of Palestine.[123] Although it may be premature to consign the two-state formula to the dustbin of irretrievably lost opportunities, it is only prudent to consider alternative political destinations for the Palestinians.

One of the older options has been dubbed the 'Bantustan plan'. It envisaged Israelis and Palestinians living under Israeli sovereignty, with the Palestinians of the West Bank and Gaza Strip given only civil autonomy.

For the rest the Palestinians (including those who were citizens of Israel) would be 'controlled, economically disadvantaged residents of greater Israel'. The parallel with South Africa's black homelands is readily apparent. Such an arrangement would not appeal to the Palestinians, considering that their claims to statehood have long been endorsed the world community.[124] For Israelis the option of exercising sovereignty over the Palestinian territories may not be attractive either. Apart from dealing with a hostile subject people, Israel would have to contend with a serious demographic challenge too. Current population trends suggest that Israel's Jewish population (presently 5.4 million) and the Palestinian population in historic Palestine (currently 5.2 million) would be equal in numbers by 2010, after which Palestinians will gradually outnumber Jews.[125] Such a scenario would threaten Israel's Jewish and democratic character, it has been said. Hence the growing importance in Israeli thinking of 'demography over geography'.[126]

A second option, fragmented cantons, was also bound to be unpalatable to Palestinians. Even under the Oslo Accords the West Bank in particular resembled 'a crazy patchwork of distributed control'. Since then Israel has ceaselessly expanded its settlements and enclosed them in a network of walls, barriers and fences that will eventually turn the West Bank permanently into numerous small and separate Palestinian cantons surrounded by Jewish settlement blocs. Having effectively annexed large portions of the West Bank, Israel would then leave the remaining pockets of land for the Palestinians to call a 'state', if they so wished.[127] Alternatively, a Palestinian state may consist of three geographically non-contiguous parts or cantons, namely the northern West Bank, the southern West Bank, and the Gaza Strip. (This fragmentation has also been likened to South Africa's Bantustan design.) The people affected could be left with fewer civil and political rights than the Palestinians living in either Israel or Jordan.[128]

A third and entirely different set of proposals involved some form of association between Palestine and Jordan. According to one variant, an increasingly autonomous Palestinian legislature could emerge from successive general elections, asserting its independence from both Israel and an Arafat-type regime and drawing the West Bank and Gaza away from Israel's 'octopuslike grip' towards a confederation with Jordan. A second variant called for the incorporation of the West Bank into a confederation with Jordan. The new binational state would comprise two legislatures, one based in the West Bank and representing Palestinians and the other reserved for East Bank Jordanians. The option implied a permanent separation of the West Bank from Gaza and the end of the dream of an independent Palestinian state. Under this proposal Gaza could perhaps be turned over to Egypt as a protectorate.[129] Lastly, the idea of a joint Jordanian-Israeli condominium over Palestine has also been mooted.[130]

The growing belief among several informed observers that the chances of implementing a two-state arrangement have deteriorated over the years, has prompted renewed consideration of a radical fourth alternative, namely a one-state solution. For some this was the ideal future for Palestine/Israel; for others it was the most likely default outcome. Those taking the latter view did not advocate a one-state option but saw it as the inevitable result of present trends. Israel's policy of settlement-*cum*-annexation was likely to turn the whole of Palestine into an Israeli-dominated polity. It would, however, prove impossible to keep Israelis and Palestinians segregated in a single small land. Nor could Jewish domination be sustained indefinitely when the Palestinians inevitably became the numerical majority in this 'greater Israel'.[131]

Another approach to a one-state model drew on the long-standing Palestinian notion of a unitary state of Palestine, comprising Israel too. Presented as an ideal outcome, it had two variations. One was the PLO proposal of a secular, democratic state extending equal rights to all its inhabitants (Palestinian Arabs and Israelis alike), regardless of religion; Israelis would not receive separate national rights. The other variation, championed by Hamas, envisaged an Islamic state of Palestine in which non-Muslim groups (notably Jews) would be tolerated minorities.[132]

None of the above alternatives to the two-state option will gain the support of both Palestinians and Israelis. This leaves us with the last alternative, the so-called binational approach that was predicated on the recognition of two national communities and hence 'two national realities' in Palestine/Israel.[133]

One of the most elaborate proposals for a binational state was produced by Abunimah in 2006.[134] His point of departure was also that a two-state solution was further away from realization than ever before because of Israel's creeping annexation of Palestinian territory. A further complicating factor was the reality of 'two deeply intertwined populations living on a small piece of land'. Rather than pursue the virtually impossible dream of two distinct ethno-national states, Abunimah set out a model allowing Palestinians and Israelis self-determination within a single democratic state. The main appeal of this option, in Abunimah's view, was that it 'allows all the people to live in and enjoy the entire country while preserving their distinctive communities and addressing their particular needs'. A single state also offered the prospect of resolving three intractable issues: the fate of Israeli settlements in occupied Palestinian territory, the status of Jerusalem, and the rights of Palestinian refugees.

In devising a political system for such an entity, a balance had to be found between the desire of many Palestinians and Israeli Jews for cultural autonomy and self-determination on the one hand and on the other the need for a government that did not encourage ethnic or territorial competition, protected the rights of all citizens and promoted interaction between them. Taking his cue from the Belgian example, Abunimah envisaged separate self-governing regions for Jews and Palestinians, with Jerusalem becoming a binational capital. Alternatively, non-territorial community governments could operate alongside a national government. Both variants pointed to a federal arrangement.[135]

Finally, we note some Israeli perspectives on Palestine's future status. Israelis who assumed that an independent Palestine would be a dysfunctional state hostile to theirs, favour unilateral separation. This meant that Israel would disengage unilaterally from the West Bank (as it had done in Gaza), leading to the establishment of a 'limited, constrained Palestinian state' within borders determined by Israel. This route was likely to create a self-fulfilling prophecy, namely an irredentist Palestinian state locked in continuous conflict with Israel. Alternatively, Israel could combine unilateral moves with negotiations with the Palestinians on less than comprehensive agreements. The latter option could also lead to a Palestinian state, but unresolved issues were bound to make for a strained and unstable bilateral relationship.[136] Reference can also be made to the idea (not confined to Israelis) of limitations being imposed on an independent Palestinian state's military forces and on its freedom to enter into military alliances with other states. These restrictions could be enforced through bilateral arms control agreements that would not undermine Palestine's legal status in the world community. The major reason for such conditional independence would be to address Israel's security concerns – and so presumably improve the prospects for peaceful coexistence between the two states.[137] In the late 1990s Israeli Prime Minister Benjamin Netanyahu indeed favoured a 'state-minus' option for the Palestinians, with restrictions on their freedom of choice in the military and foreign policy domains.[138]

Conclusion

Palestine is a unique contested state in that its right of independent statehood has been collectively recognized by the world community acting through the UN. Equally exceptional among contested states is that the Palestinians' liberation movement, the PLO, was recognized by the UN as the legitimate representative of the Palestinian people. The self-declared state of Palestine has, however, not been treated as a full-fledged state by confirmed states; the Palestine Authority nonetheless enjoys many of the trappings of statehood. More than any other contested state, Palestine has been at the centre of repeated diplomatic initiatives aimed at settling the conflict over its future political status. Still the dispute remains unresolved. One reason is the conflict's multilayered character: at the regional level there is tension between so-called moderate and radical countries over Palestine's co-existence with Israel; at the bilateral plane the Israelis and

Palestinians remain at odds on many key issues surrounding the final status of Palestine, and Israel acts as a powerful veto state through its dual policy of settlements in occupied Palestinian territories and a draconian closure regime; finally, at the intra-Palestinian level fundamental disagreement between Fatah and Hamas has sparked a mini-civil war. All this leaves the Palestinians further away from achieving confirmed statehood than at any time since the conclusion of the path-breaking Oslo Accords in 1993. It will be for future historians to judge whether the Palestinians had snatched defeat from the jaws of victory in the 1990s, condemning themselves to unnecessary contested statehood.

8
Northern Cyprus

The Turkish Republic of Northern Cyprus (TRNC) offers something of a model case study of contested statehood. And it is not primarily because the TRNC is a veteran contested state of 25 years' standing. As mentioned in Chapter 1, the TRNC owed its existence to an act of secession on the part of Turkish-dominated Northern Cyprus and occupation perpetrated by Turkey. Conceived and born in political sin if not outside international law too, the self-proclaimed state was doomed to a life in international limbo. Despite having a powerful patron state in Turkey, the TRNC has been unable to graduate to confirmed statehood. Its original and veto state, the Republic of Cyprus (under Greek Cypriot rule), together with its patron state Greece, have been highly effective in keeping Northern Cyprus at the edge of mainstream international existence. By supporting opposing sides – their respective ethnic kin – Greece and Turkey turned Cyprus into a boxing ring in which they pursued their rivalry through their local proxies. Cyprus has also experienced another more beneficial form of internationalization in the shape of diplomatic settlement initiatives spearheaded by the UN and EU. These efforts together with the recent changes of government in both the TRNC and the Republic of Cyprus have improved the prospects for resolving the conflict on the island. In short, key variables in the actual making and prospective unmaking of a contemporary contested state were at work in Cyprus.

The road to rupture

Like numerous other territories with such a long recorded history, Cyprus had through the ages fallen under the heel of many different rulers. Until its capture by Richard I in 1191, the island had for centuries belonged to the Byzantine (or Eastern Roman) empire. Thereafter it saw a succession of rulers come and go until the Ottoman Empire gained control in 1571. During Ottoman rule the Turkish Cypriot community, followers of Islam, were treated as a privileged minority by for instance paying lower taxes than the island's Greek majority with their Christian Orthodox faith. The Turks' preferred status ended when Cyprus was transferred to Britain in 1878. In 1914 Britain annexed the island and for the next nine years assumed the role of a belligerent occupier of an enemy territory. Under the 1923 Treaty of Lausanne peaceful relations between Turkey and the Allied powers were restored and Turkey recognized Britain's annexation of Cyprus. In 1925 Cyprus became a British colony.[1]

His Majesty's new subjects in Cyprus soon proved every bit as disloyal and restive as imperial Britain's wards in Palestine. Not only were the Greek and Turkish communities deeply antagonistic towards each other, but they were also profoundly dissatisfied with the political status of Cyprus. On the Greek side the domestic leadership of the Orthodox Church had already during the Ottoman era become politically active. The greater freedom offered by British rule encouraged nationalist activists in the Greek community – with the church leadership or ethnarchy in the vanguard – to agitate for both representative government and eventual union (*enosis*) between Cyprus and an independent Greece. *Enosis* was to become a rallying cry for Greek Cypriots opposed to foreign rule. In this quest they could count on Greece's enthusiastic support; mainland and Cypriot Greeks believed that the island was a Hellenic entity destined to be 'redeemed by the motherland'. Fearing that *enosis* would reduce them to a highly vulnerable minority in a Greek state, Turkish Cypriots vehemently rejected union with Greece – and in this stance they could rely on Turkey's backing. Constituting only 20 per cent of the island's population, the Turkish community also opposed representative government for Cyprus on the grounds that they would suffer discrimination at the hands of the Greek majority.[2] Notwithstanding four centuries of coexistence and physical intermingling, the two Cypriot communities remained separate and distinct, divided along language, cultural, religious and also political lines,[3] reinforced by vast numerical inequality, and exacerbated by conflicting external orientations towards two rival 'big brothers' who extended their mutual antagonism to Cyprus. In this charged political atmosphere an *enosis* demonstration in 1931 got so out of hand that the British suspended the legislative council of Cyprus and exiled two bishops.[4]

The *enosis* movement was later led by Archbishop Makarios, who became the dominant political figure in independent Cyprus. It was with Makarios at the helm of the unity movement that Greek Cypriots turned to strikes and rioting in 1954 to vent their opposition to British rule and push their case for self-determination – which meant union with Greece.[5] Fearing a new colonial order under mainland Greece, the Turkish minority in Cyprus sought refuge in a resurgence of Turkish nationalism. Turkey got drawn ever deeper into Cypriot politics, not only to defend the interests of the Turkish community there but to protect its strategic interests by preventing the establishment of Greek sovereignty over the island. The rival nationalisms in Cyprus were united in at least one respect, though: both challenged British rule over the island.[6]

Resigning them to the chasm between Greeks and Turks in their colonial possession, the British made no attempt to inculcate a unifying Cypriot national identity. Instead, Britain preferred to keep the antagonistic groups apart, even setting them up against each other in the tradition of divide-and-rule.[7] Britain could hardly have been surprised, then, when civil war erupted between the island's two communities in 1955. The British themselves became targets of terrorism perpetrated by EOKA (National Organization of Cypriot Fighters), the armed wing of the *enosis* movement. Launched in 1954, EOKA was led by Colonel George Grivas, a retired Greek military officer of Cypriot origin. Greece was widely suspected of having a hand in creating and directing EOKA. In 1956 Makarios was temporarily exiled to the Seychelles for his alleged involvement in EOKA's terrorist attacks.[8]

The Archbishop's confrontation with the colonial authorities merely added to his political credentials. In 1959 he won a resounding victory in an election for the first president of an independent Cyprus. The Republic of Cyprus, proclaimed on 16 August 1960, was a rather unusual creation: it was an 'international state', as Tamkoç called it, 'surrounded by five layers of international documents' (the so-called Zurich and London accords of 1959 concluded by Britain, Greece, Turkey and the two communities of Cyprus).[9] These documents placed important restrictions on the autonomy of Cyprus in both domestic politics and foreign relations. The guarantor powers – Britain, Turkey and Greece – were given considerable formal authority over the affairs of an independent Cyprus.[10]

In terms of the Treaty of Guarantee the independence, territorial integrity and security of Cyprus would be matters of direct concern to the guarantor powers. These three states would guarantee the preservation of the constitutional order of Cyprus. The new state was in turn obligated not to enter into a political or economic union with any country (read: Greece and Turkey). Should the Treaty of Guarantee be breached, the guarantor powers would consult together. If they failed to agree on common and concerted action, each reserved the right to act with the exclusive objective of restoring the *status quo*. The Treaty of Alliance gave Greece and Turkey the responsibility of defending Cyprus. For this purpose they were allowed to station 950 and 650 troops respectively on the island. Under the Treaty of Establishment Britain was to cooperate with Turkey and Greece in the joint defence of Cyprus. Britain was furthermore given sovereign authority in perpetuity over two military base areas. The two remaining documents were the Basic Structure of the Republic of Cyprus and the constitution, the former providing the basis of the Constitution of Cyprus. The Treaties of Alliance and Guarantee were also regarded as integral components of the basic structure of the new state and hence accorded constitutional status.

Being the product of international agreements, the Constitution of Cyprus could only be amended in its key provisions if the three guarantor powers as well as the island's Greek and Turkish communities concurred.[11]

The constitution took as its premise that Cyprus consisted of two distinct ethnic, linguistic and religious groups, each entitled to self-determination. This could not be achieved by way of *enosis*, or by returning Cyprus to its former owner Turkey, or by partitioning the island between Greece and Turkey (*taksim*); one or the other community, supported by either Greece or Turkey, would be resolutely opposed to such arrangements.[12] The compromise formula was that of power-sharing on consociational lines enabling the two communities to exercise their respective rights of self-determination without being dominated by the other.[13] Hence the constitutional stipulation that the Greek President of Cyprus and the Turkish Vice President had identical executive powers with respect to foreign affairs, defence and security. The two incumbents would furthermore exercise veto power, separately or jointly, over laws and decisions of the House of Representatives and over the actions of the Council of Ministers in the areas of foreign affairs, security and defence. Turkish representatives in the legislature also enjoyed a separate vote on amendments to the electoral law and the approval of any law regarding municipalities, taxes and duties. Other constitutional provisions with respect to the Turkish Cypriots' so-called 'immutable partnership status' prescribed a 70–30 communal ratio in the cabinet, parliament, civil service and security forces, and allowed for separate (communal) municipalities in the five largest towns.[14] Because the two Cypriot communities were territorially intermixed, cultural and political autonomy for each could only be granted on a non-territorial basis in the shape of their respective sub-legislatures known as Communal Chambers.[15]

The Constitution of Cyprus not merely entrenched the political separation of the Greek and Turkish communities, but also their connections with their respective mother countries. Under the constitution inhabitants of the island were not designated as citizens of the Republic of Cyprus, but as Greek and Turkish citizens. Their languages were declared the two official languages of Cyprus and the communities were entitled to observe Greek and Turkish national holidays respectively. The constitution also permitted Greece and Turkey to subsidize educational, cultural, sports and charitable institutions in the respective communities. Through these arrangements the constitution in effect stated that there was no Cypriot nation and no need to build one either; instead, the two distinct communities of Cyprus were extensions of larger outside nations that had legitimate interests in maintaining their kin-relationships on the island.[16]

Since the constitutional arrangements represented a grand compromise that fell far short of both communities' wishes, the achievement of statehood was hardly a joyous occasion. 'Probably no people in history have ever viewed their independence with less enthusiasm than the Cypriots',

The Economist observed at the time.[17] Far from creating inter-communal harmony, the very international character of the Republic of Cyprus had from the outset created tension on the home front. Opinion leaders in the Greek community claimed that the new Republic was stillborn because it did not meet a basic requirement of statehood, namely independence. They charged that the Zurich and London accords were imposed on the Greek majority under duress, placed the Turkish minority in a privileged position out of all proportion to their numbers, and created a political order in Cyprus that violated the democratic principle of majority rule.[18] For good measure the leaders of the Greek community left no doubt about their unwillingness to implement constitutional provisions regulating the Turkish community's partnership in public affairs.[19] Even so the international community had no serious reservations about the independence of Cyprus; the UN General Assembly by unanimous vote admitted Cyprus to membership of the world body shortly after the new state was born.[20]

The Greek political leadership's systematic subversion of the constitutional order culminated in what amounted to a *coup* staged by Makarios in December 1963. This triggered a new round of inter-communal warfare, with Greece and Turkey providing military assistance to their respective kinfolk.[21] The Greek side managed to usurp political power and take administrative control, denying the Turkish community their constitutionally guaranteed partnership status in the affairs of state. Due to the collapse of bicommunal government, Turkish Cypriots could no longer take up their positions in the cabinet, parliament and civil service. Although the Greek community was left in exclusive control of the organs of state, their effective authority was confined to the Greek areas of Cyprus; the state's writ did not extend to the Turkish enclaves. These vulnerable parts, surrounded by Greek Cypriot troops, comprised a meagre 3 per cent of the island's territory. Cut off from government funding, the Turkish community was compelled to turn to Turkey for financial assistance.[22]

The international community extended *de facto* recognition to the new Makarios government, which insisted that it was the legitimate ruler of the Republic of Cyprus. And that Republic, the UN General Assembly resolved in December 1965 (resolution 2077), was 'entitled to and should enjoy full sovereignty and complete independence without any foreign intervention or interference'. The Turkish community and its defenders by contrast viewed it as an illegal government (an analogy was drawn with the Smith regime in Rhodesia) whose power grab had wrecked the internationally crafted constitutional order of the Republic of Cyprus. The state was moreover deprived of its *raison d'être*, it was said, because one of the two Cypriot communities (the Turks) could no longer exercise their right of self-determination without being subjugated by the other.[23]

A renewed internationalization of the situation in Cyprus came in the wake of the turmoil at the end of 1963. One manifestation was the deployment of the UN Force in Cyprus (UNFICYP) the following year to prevent the resumption of hostilities and to restore law and order.[24] Another was the Security Council's repeated requests that the UN Secretary-General use his good offices to resolve the Cyprus issue.[25]

In December 1967 leaders of the Turkish community established the Provisional Turkish Cypriot Administration, which they intended keeping in place until all the provisions of the constitution of 1960 were enforced. Given their suffering in the enclaves since 1963, the Turkish Cypriots saw this provisional structure as a vital protective measure, whereas Greek Cypriots suspected it was a calculated step towards fragmenting the island. Turkish Cypriots found little cause for comfort in developments on the Greek side of the ethnic divide, where rival factions clashed over the pace of *enosis*. Makarios and his 'moderate revolutionaries' were bent on leading Cyprus to eventual union with Greece through a gradual process of 'Hellenization' of the island. The militant revolutionaries among the Greek Cypriots were committed to early *enosis* at any price. Their leader was Grivas, the former EOKA militant, who was put in charge of the Greek Cypriot National Guard established after the 1963 *coup*. Either way, Cyprus seemed to have been reduced to a temporary 'puppet state' of Greece pending the achievement of *enosis*. Following the ascendance of a military dictatorship in Athens in 1967, Greece intensified its meddling in Cyprus.[26]

A vicious power struggle between the two factions in the Greek Cypriot community occurred in the early 1970s. In 1974 Makarios accused the Greek military junta of subversive activities by supporting the terrorist campaign that EOKA-B (formed by Grivas in 1971) directed against the island's political leadership.[27] Instead of ending their interference, as Makarios demanded, Greece's military rulers plotted Makarios' own downfall. He was duly deposed in mid-July 1974 by the National Guard led by mainland Greek officers, who installed former EOKA gunman Nicos Sampson as President. It was a breathtakingly brazen act of subversion aimed at accelerating *enosis*.[28]

Having fled Cyprus, Makarios made his way to New York where he appealed for help from the UN Security Council. He charged Greece's military rulers of openly violating the independence of Cyprus and extending their dictatorship to the island by masterminding the *coup*. Makarios insisted that the junta in Athens withdraw Greek officers serving in the National Guard and put an end to the invasion of Cyprus.[29] Just as there was no doubt about its complicity in overthrowing Makarios in 1974, the illegality of Greece's latest involvement was beyond dispute. Under international law this was a clear-cut instance of illegal intervention in breach of the Zurich and London accords that formed the basis of independent Cyprus's constitutional order.[30]

Invasion and fragmentation

The Athens-instigated *coup* in Cyprus provoked a drastic response from Turkey and plunged the island into war. On 20 July 1974, only five days after Makarios was unseated, Turkish troops landed in Cyprus and soon occupied 37 per cent of the island's territory. The legality of Turkey's invasion under international law has long (and inconclusively) been debated by jurists, politicians and other commentators. On the one hand there were those who argued that Ankara's resort to limited force complied with the spirit of article 2(4) of the UN Charter (states may not threaten or use force against the territorial integrity and political independence of another) and article 51 (the right of individual and collective self-defence). On this view Turkey had acted within its right as a protector of the independence and territorial integrity of Cyprus as enshrined in the treaties of Guarantee and Alliance.[31] According to a further justification 'it was imperative that Turkey should take action in order to save the Turkish Cypriot community which was in grave and imminent danger of being annihilated by the Greek and Greek Cypriot armed elements'.[32] The counter-argument held that Turkey had not consulted with its co-guarantors before launching its military invasion, as the Treaty of Guarantee required. Its unilateral action was only permissible under that treaty if it were undertaken to restore the *status quo* in Cyprus – and that would have included the maintenance of the independence, territorial integrity and security of Cyprus as well as the basic political structure of the Republic. Far from bringing about such a situation, Turkey's military action caused a radical change in the state of affairs created by the London and Zurich accords.[33] The unity of the island was destroyed by a territorial division between Greeks and Turks unknown in the history of Cyprus, thereby creating 'two completely independent, physically separated statelets'.[34]

The international community did not approve of Turkey's actions in Cyprus, but pronouncements through the UN were guarded. General Assembly resolution 3212, adopted unanimously on 1 November 1974, called on all states 'to respect the sovereignty, independence, territorial integrity and non-alignment of the Republic of Cyprus and to refrain from all acts and interventions directed against it'. The resolution went on to urge the speedy withdrawal 'of all foreign armed forces' from the island. The Security Council endorsed the Assembly resolution in December 1974. Although Turkey was not specifically mentioned in the Assembly resolution – it could have been addressed to Athens and Ankara equally – the Turks could not read any condonation of their Cypriot operation into the world body's statements. Greek Cypriots and mainland Greeks, supported by international opinion, had no doubt that it was the Turkish invasion of 1974 that had destroyed the Republic of Cyprus of the early 1960s. What this popular view overlooked, though, was that the main cause of the collapse of the 'original' independent Cyprus was the violence that the Greek Cypriots had inflicted on their fellow citizens in the early 1950s.[35] The chickens had merely taken time to come home to roost.

The invasion and war of 1974 had severe political and demographic consequences. About 160,000 Greek Cypriots (one-third of the community) fled their homes in areas occupied by Turkish forces in the north of the island and took shelter in the south. In a simultaneous reverse flow some 45,000 Turkish Cypriots (40 per cent of this community) sought refuge in the north. Soon virtually the entire Turkish Cypriot community had been settled in the north under the protection of thousands of Turkish soldiers. Turkish Cypriots had for the first time established a sizeable, consolidated territorial basis for a separate government. To reinforce their claims to the northern third of the island, the Turkish Cypriot political leadership decided to strengthen the size of their community by recruiting thousands of settlers from Turkey. The resettlement programme helped to increase the Turkish proportion of the island's population from 19 per cent in 1974 to approximately 24 per cent in 1996.[36]

A Turkish Federated State of Cyprus was proclaimed in the north of the island in February 1975, an area by then under the effective and exclusive control of the Turkish Cypriots backed by several thousand troops from Turkey. In announcing the move, the President of the Turkish Cypriot administration, Rauf Denktash, affirmed that the Turkish Cypriots remained resolutely opposed to 'all attempts against the independence of Cyprus, and its partition or union with any other state'. The 'final objective' of his community 'is to unite with the Greek Cypriot community within the framework of a bi-zonal federation'. The Turkish component of a future federation of Cyprus had now been created. At the same time Denktash made it clear that the recent ordeals of the Turkish Cypriots left 'no possibility of their living together with the Greek Cypriot co-founders of the Republic of Cyprus'. There was only one way to ensure 'tranquillity, security and permanent peace' on the island, he insisted, and that was 'for the two communities to live side by side in their respective regions, developing their own internal structure'.[37] To create these structures on the Turkish side, a Constituent Assembly was formed and a new constitution introduced after its approval in a referendum in June 1975.[38] As the Turkish Cypriot Legislative Assembly explained in 1976, they were determined to prevent 'further tyranny and oppression or suppression by the Greek Cypriots', who had planned 'the total annihilation of the Turkish Cypriots'. These 'attempts of genocide' had only been stopped by Turkey's military presence on the island, it was said.[39]

Trading on its international status, the Greek Cypriot government of the island took its objections to the Turkish Federated State to the UN Security Council. In resolution 367 of March 1975, the Council expressed regret over the Turkish community's 'unilateral decision' that tended to 'compromise the continuation of negotiations' between the two Cypriot communities on finding a mutually acceptable constitutional arrangement. In the same resolution the Council entrusted a good offices mission to the Secretary-General in a bid to resolve the Cyprus conflict.

The leaders of the new Turkish Cypriot entity engaged in several rounds of talks with their Greek Cypriot counterparts over the creation of a national government. The Greek side was initially led by Makarios, who was reinstated as President of the Republic of Cyprus in December 1974 but died in 1977. By the time Makarios returned to power, democratic, civilian rule had been restored in Athens too. Although these changes did not bring about a settlement in Cyprus, the two sides made some progress in their talks. The Makarios-Denktash guidelines of February 1977 allocated substantial powers and responsibilities to the two constituent regions in a future constitutional structure.[40] A Ten-Point Agreement concluded in May 1979 under the auspices of the UN Secretary-General stipulated that the independence, sovereignty and territorial integrity of Cyprus 'should be adequately guaranteed against union in whole or in part with any other country and against any form of partition or secession'.[41] The two Cypriot communities were merely (re)committing themselves to the constitutional arrangements under which Cyprus had become independent – but with one major difference: the non-territorial autonomy enshrined in the 1960 constitution had been replaced by territorially based solutions, hence the dual notion of a future bicommunal, bizonal federation.[42]

Enter the TRNC

Driven in part by a desire to overcome their entity's inferior international status, Turkish Cypriot leaders on 15 November 1983 founded the Turkish Republic of Northern Cyprus. The expectation was that the TRNC could henceforth engage the Greek side as an equal negotiating partner or co-sovereign. The purpose of final status talks, the Turkish Cypriot leadership proclaimed, should be the establishment of a new bicommunal, bizonal federal republic by mutual consent.[43] The declaration of statehood reiterated that the Turkish community remained committed to the international accords on which the Republic of Cyprus had been founded and that the TRNC would not unite with any other country (meaning Turkey) except with the southern entity to constitute a federal state. The Turkish Cypriot leadership consequently insisted that the proclamation of the TRNC was not an act of secession or a unilateral declaration of independence in the strict sense of the word; instead, it represented an important step in a process of political and administrative evolution.[44] Yet the emphasis was more on separation than evolution: a 'hard' border separated north from south and Nicosia remained a militarily divided capital with the Turkish Cypriots controlling the northern section of the city (called Lefkosia) while the Greek

Cypriots were in control of the southern portion (called Nicosia). The buffer zone between the two entities was patrolled by UNFICYP troops. The territorial division corresponded with ethnic separation. Fully 99.5 per cent of the island's Greek Cypriots lived in the Greek zone in the south, with the remainder in the Turkish north; 98.7 per cent of Turkish Cypriots resided in the north, with a bare 1.3 per cent south of the line of partition.[45]

The TRNC was immediately recognized by Turkey, but not a single other state has since followed suit.[46] By adopting resolution 541 within days of the proclamation of the TRNC, the UN Security Council condemned the entity to contested statehood. With only Pakistan opposing and Jordan abstaining, the Council deplored the Turkish Cypriot authorities' 'purported secession of part of the Republic of Cyprus'. Their declaration of 15 November 'which purports to create an independent State in northern Cyprus' was incompatible with the international accords that gave birth to the Republic of Cyprus and therefore legally invalid and should be withdrawn, the Council resolved. All states were called upon 'not to recognize any Cypriot State other than the Republic of Cyprus'. The world body has on several occasions reaffirmed its unambiguous rejection of a Turkish Cypriot state and the accompanying bisection of the island.

Under international law a number of objections to separate Turkish Cypriot statehood have been recorded. First and foremost, the creation of the TRNC was the product of Turkey's military invasion and occupation of part of Cyprus. By so doing Turkey had violated the *jus cogens* norm prohibiting aggression. The birth of the TRNC was consequently met with collective non-recognition. The failure of the TRNC to qualify as a (confirmed) state is, according to Dugard, better explained by reference to this non-recognition than in terms of the traditional criteria of statehood.[47] Fowler and Bunck have, however, noted that some states questioned the Turkish Cypriots' independence from Turkey. More importantly, in their judgement, was the inability of the Turkish Cypriots to persuade the world community that they were legally separate (and hence enjoyed *de jure* political independence) from the government of the Republic of Cyprus.[48] A further complicating factor may have been the founding fathers' portrayal of the TRNC's purported statehood as a mere interim phase pending the reunification of Cyprus. Why should others recognize a 'state' that saw no long-term future for itself?

Despite Denktash's pledge that 'we shall keep the door wide open to re-establishing unity under a federal system',[49] the emergence of the TRNC complicated the search for an inter-communal political settlement in Cyprus. With Turkey as its patron state, the TRNC had the confidence to stand up to pressures from the Greek Cypriot side and from foreign powers to seek an early compromise solution. Turkey, for its part, was not in a particularly accommodating mood during much of the 1980s and early 1990s either because of its strained relations with Greece. It is against this backdrop that the Legislative Assembly of the TRNC in 1994 renounced resolutions of 1984 and 1985 which had declared that 'setting up a federal state on the island was the only solution to the Cyprus problem'.[50] The shift away from a federal formula was confirmed by Denktash in 1998 when he proposed a 'confederal structure of two peoples and two sovereign states', along with entrenching the two Cypriot communities' special relationships with their respective mother countries.[51] The Greek Cypriot leadership responded in predictable fashion, branding a confederation as 'worse than partition'.[52] In due course the Turkish Cypriot side would return to their original federal preferences.

International isolation

The TRNC has had to contend with the worst form of diplomatic isolation, namely collective non-recognition of its claims to statehood. It was international punishment for its sinful origins. The TRNC maintained diplomatic ties with Ankara only and failed to gain formal membership of any inter-governmental organization. With Turkey's support the TRNC managed to obtain observer status and hence a platform of sorts in the Economic Cooperation Organization (which included Turkey, Iran, Pakistan and several Soviet successor states) and the Organization of the Islamic Conference (OIC). The latter in 1994 called on its 51 member states 'to increase and expand their relations in all fields and in particular in the fields of trade, tourism, culture, information, investment and sports' with the TRNC, but stopped short of extending formal recognition to the breakaway state.[53] Like other contested states the TRNC maintained semi-official representation abroad, with offices in Washington, New York, London, Brussels, Baku, Islamabad and Abu Dhabi.[54]

Economic isolation accompanied the TRNC's diplomatic ostracism. One of the most harmful measures it experienced was an economic embargo imposed by the Greek Cypriot government. Greece and other European states joined the boycott of goods from Northern Cyprus. Also damaging to the TRNC's economy was the Greek Cypriots' success in getting foreign states (except for Turkey) to ban flights to the territory of the TRNC. This prohibition affected both trade and tourism. Northern Cyprus was furthermore denied access to the kinds of bilateral and multilateral aid freely available to the Greek Cypriot government. This economic isolation of course deterred foreign investors.[55]

True, *per capita* GDP in Northern Cyprus had increased threefold between 1977 and 2002 and annual GDP growth rates from 2001 to 2005 ranged between 5.4 and 15.4 per cent.[56] This gave Turkish Cypriots a standard of living higher than that in mainland Turkey. These achievements had only been possible thanks to generous support from Turkey in the shape of direct aid, loans, subsidies and other grants. Turkey also carried the considerable costs of re-exporting Turkish Cypriot textiles and fruit.[57] No less than 80 per cent of goods exported from Northern Cyprus flowed through Turkey – increasing costs for Turkish Cypriot businesses and reducing their international competitiveness.[58] Economically the TRNC was utterly dependent on Turkey; it even used the Turkish lira as its currency. One disadvantage of this asymmetrical relationship was the TRNC's vulnerability to its patron's macro-economic turbulence and high inflation.[59]

Northern Cyprus's economy made a poor showing against that of its southern neighbour. Take *per capita* GDP: although the available statistics vary considerably, one authoritative source recorded US$23,672 for the Greek south in 2006, against $11,802 for the Turkish north.[60] The economic boom that the Greek Cypriot economy had enjoyed after 1974 was in no small measure due to its confirmed statehood and unfettered access to foreign markets.[61] The international factor gained enormously in salience in the 1990s when the Republic of Cyprus began the process of joining the EU. This development deepened Turkish Cypriots' sense of international isolation and relative deprivation – and eventually encouraged them to reconsider the costs of going it alone.

Still, the TRNC comfortably met three of the Montevideo criteria for statehood. Its population of 264,172 (according to a 2006 census)[62] was much smaller than the south's almost 600,000 people and also modest by global standards. Yet the TRNC's population was larger than that of 21 UN member states, with Barbados the closest comparison. Northern Cyprus's territory of 3,355 km^2 (over one-third of the island's total surface area of 9,251 km^2) was in size between that of Cape Verde and Samoa. The government of the TRNC was firmly in control of this territory, thanks largely to the presence of between 35,000 and 40,000 Turkish troops (about twice the number of local and mainland Greek soldiers in the south). As a bonus, Northern Cyprus obeyed the rules of democracy. We must acknowledge, though, that heavy economic and security dependence on Turkey cast some doubt on the TRNC's domestic sovereignty. Finally, the entity's lack of participation in normal foreign relations was attributable to that familiar curse of contested states, namely the absence of collective recognition.

The EU dimension

In the 1990s the EU factor injected a new dynamic into efforts to resolve the Cyprus conflict. Encouraged by Greece's admission to the European Community in 1981, the Greek Cypriot government in 1990 applied for membership too. At first the EU Commission wanted to see a political settlement in the divided island before commencing accession talks. Brussels subsequently relented, agreeing to reconsider Cypriot membership by January 1995 if no settlement could be reached. The EU made it plain that the accession process would not be derailed by Turkish Cypriot objections to the Greek Cypriot government acting on behalf of all of Cyprus in engaging with Brussels.[63] In 1998 the EU duly agreed to start accession negotiations with the Republic of Cyprus.

The very next year the EU also recognized Turkey as a candidate for membership. This prompted Turkey to embark on a far-reaching process of internal political reform designed to meet the EU's political criteria before talks on membership could commence. Ankara was also under pressure from the EU to adopt a new strategy that could resolve the conflict in Cyprus. Under Prime Minister Tayyip Erdogan, who came into office in 2002, domestic reform initiatives gained momentum and Turkey made a 'historical shift' in favour of the reunification of Cyprus. In December 2004 the European Council rewarded Turkey by deciding to start accession negotiations in 2005. Another encouraging development was the *rapprochement* between Turkey and Greece since 1999, further improving the political climate for a settlement in Cyprus.[64]

The EU had compelling reasons for promoting a settlement. As long as the conflict between its Greek and Turkish communities remained unresolved, Cyprus represented 'a potentially disruptive element inside the European Union'.[65] An isolated and aggrieved TRNC could moreover play the role of 'spoiler' by allowing a 'cynical lawlessness' to take hold in the territory. This could encourage trade in international contraband, including narcotics and human trafficking.[66] Although the EU (supported by the UN) preferred that a reunited Cyprus should join the Union, Brussels gave notice that if reunification could not be achieved before the deadline for the island's accession, the Republic of Cyprus would formally join as the sole legitimate representative of Cyprus as a whole. The Turkish-controlled northern part would then be effectively excluded from EU membership. Neither the EU nor the UN would leave matters to chance, though; the final years before Cyprus's admission to the EU in 2004 saw 'the most concerted and comprehensive' international effort to achieve a settlement since the independence negotiations of 1959–60.[67]

The upshot of the renewed settlement drive was the so-called Annan Plan (named after the UN Secretary-General), of which the first version appeared in November 2002. It was an impressively detailed blueprint for a return to a complex, territorially based power-sharing formula found in some consociational democracies. The plan called for the creation of a United Cyprus Republic, a federal state consisting of two constituent units, the Greek Cypriot community in the south and the Turkish Cypriots in the north. The latter's zone would be reduced from the existing 37 per cent of Cypriot territory to about 28.5 per cent. Under the constitution most powers would vest in the constituent entities, leaving the federal government responsible mainly for foreign relations, federal finance and monetary policy, and citizenship and immigration. The essence the Annan Plan was 'the assurance of bizonality and political equality, the respect of ethnic diversity and human rights and the existence of an independent sovereign state with a single international personality'. To protect the constitutional status of the envisaged republic as well as that of its constituent parts, the plan stipulated that the existing Treaty of Guarantee remain intact. The UN peacekeeping force would also be retained to monitor implementation of the new design. In another provision reminiscent of the qualified independence of the original Republic of Cyprus, the Annan Plan stated that a United Cyprus Republic would not allow its territory to be used for international military operations without the consent of the two constituent units and of Greece and Turkey. Finally, the redesigned Cyprus Republic would be a full-fledged EU member.[68]

The Annan Plan went through no fewer than five revisions in a bid to get it approved by all sides, but each time the Turkish Cypriot leadership balked. On 24 April 2004 the two Cypriot communities held referendums on Annan V under the terms of an earlier agreement providing for such a mechanism. The popular verdicts caused a sensation by overturning the historical pattern in the search for a settlement: 65 per cent of the Turkish Cypriots approved the Annan Plan, whereas no less than 76 per cent of the Greek Cypriot voters rejected it.[69] This time the deal wreckers were on the Greek Cypriot side, exercising their veto power in a most unexpected way. Even so the Greek Cypriots were allowed to join the EU: in May 2004 the still divided island entered the EU under the designation Republic of Cyprus. The TRNC became legally but not practically part of the EU; the benefits of membership would be confined to the Greek Cypriot side.[70] And so the Republic of Cyprus, the exclusive political preserve of Greek Cypriots, reaped another benefit of its confirmed statehood while the TRNC remained condemned to contested statehood.

By supporting the Annan Plan, the Turkish Cypriot electorate rebuffed their long serving leader Rauf Denktash who, as founding father of the TRNC and President since its inception, had resisted several diplomatic efforts at reunification with the Greek south. One reason for the rift was the deteriorating economic situation in the TRNC coupled with the envisaged material advantages of EU membership. These considerations made the Turkish Cypriot community increasingly amenable to bearing the costs of reunification for the sake of EU membership. A related factor was Turkey's own interest in joining the EU and its support for the Annan Plan. This reassured Turkish Cypriots that they would eventually be united with Turkey proper (as with the Greek Cypriots and Greece itself) in an expanded European family. Finally, the Annan Plan appealed to the Turkish Cypriot side because it promised to meet the community's status needs and so allayed many identity-related fears.[71] The new climate of opinion in Northern Cyprus was reflected in the election of Mehmet

Ali Talat as President in April 2005 to succeed Denktash. Talat, a left-winger, was an outspoken supporter of reunification and staunchly pro-European.[72]

Why did the Greek Cypriots so overwhelmingly reject the Annan blueprint for reunification? They judged that the settlement proposals held very few gains for them but considerable costs and risks. By giving the Turkish Cypriots minority vetoes on a range of matters, it was argued, the envisaged power-sharing mechanisms would entrench a 'tyranny of the minority'. Another complaint was that the more affluent Greek community would bear the greatest costs for the island's socio-economic reconstruction. At the heart of Greek Cypriots' rejection of Annan V may well have been 'an unwillingness to share power with the other community on the island'.[73] Indeed, the Greek Cypriot leadership reasoned that Cyprus's membership of the EU and Turkey's aspirations to follow suit would enhance their community's bargaining position and hence secure a more favourable deal for the Greek majority than that offered by Annan V. The President of the Republic of Cyprus, Tassos Papadopoulos, put it bluntly: why should the Greek Cypriots 'do away with our internationally recognised state exactly at the very moment it strengthens its political weight, with its accession to the EU'?[74] We should bear in mind that the Greek Cypriots had gained EU membership without having to make any compromise: they had no real incentive to vote 'yes' in the referendum on the Annan proposals, nor any strong disincentive not to vote 'no'. Not even Greece's backing for the final Annan Plan could sway the Greek Cypriots.[75]

Based on their 2004 referendum result, a clear majority of Greek Cypriots' preferred future for the island may well have been a single, centralized state featuring majoritarian democracy (in which the Greek community would prevail) and giving Greek Cypriots the right to return to the north. The bicommunal and consociational characteristics of the original Cypriot constitution and of the Annan Plan would consequently be weakened if not altogether abolished. Advocates of this outcome believed that the Turkish Cypriots would 'sacrifice' self-rule for the advantages of an undivided Cyprus's EU membership.[76] Indications that absorption into the Greek south's institutions (known as 'osmosis') may well have been Greek Cypriot strategy, were said to be the latter's extension of such benefits as Republic of Cyprus citizenship and passports (by the end of 2006 about 65,000 Turkish Cypriots had already obtained such travel documents), employment, social insurance, education and health care to individual Turkish Cypriots. In February 2008 Turkish Cypriots living in the south could for the first time vote in the presidential election there.[77] Pragmatic or opportunistic 'absorption' was one thing, but it is doubtful whether the majority of Turkish Cypriots or their government would countenance wholesale incorporation into the Greek-controlled Republic of Cyprus.

International rewards

At the international level Northern Cyprus was meanwhile experiencing a welcome form of absorption or what the International Crisis Group called 'a creeping de facto recognition of the TRNC by the rest of the world'.[78] By approving Annan's proposal for reunification in 2004, the Turkish Cypriot community turned their backs on secession and hence removed the rationale behind their enforced isolation.[79] Indeed, the UN Secretary-General, EU leaders and several other governments called for an end to the TRNC's isolation in the wake of the referendums. Another reason for lifting Turkish Cypriots' quarantine, EU foreign ministers declared, was 'to facilitate the reunification of Cyprus by encouraging the economic development of the latter community'.[80] To this end the EU approved a 259 million euro aid package for Northern Cyprus.[81] The European Parliament established a High Level Contact Group for relations with Northern Cyprus, and two Turkish Cypriot parliamentarians enjoyed limited rights of participation in the activities of political groups in the European Parliament. The Council of Europe in turn permitted two Turkish Cypriot observers to its Parliamentary Assembly.[82] The Organization of the Islamic Conference, determined to end the 'unjust isolation' of the Turkish Cypriots, in July 2004 upgraded the Turkish Cypriots' designation from 'community' to 'constituent state' (although the TRNC remained an observer within the organization).[83]

At the bilateral level there were no legal or practical obstacles to states opening branches of their embassies on the northern side of the Green Line dividing the two parts of Cyprus, or expanding links with the political leadership and civil society in the TRNC.[84] President Talat has held formal meetings with members of several foreign governments, including Pakistani President Pervez Musharraf. Northern Cyprus also managed to extend its representative offices (without diplomatic status) to Italy, Germany and Israel, among other countries.[85] Britain, Azerbaijan, Pakistan, France and the US were among the states that allowed entry to holders of TRNC passports.[86] The United Kingdom also gave Northern Cyprus aid worth over £500,000 per annum to help the entity reach EU standards, especially through judicial and civil service reform.[87]

Instances of *de facto* international recognition of Northern Cyprus have been dubbed the 'Taiwan solution'.[88] While there are some parallels (see Chapter 10), the TRNC faced formidable obstacles in engaging in international relations even at the functional (non-diplomatic) level. Procedural, legal and political impediments created by the Greek Cypriots in the EU kept hampering the TRNC's access to international aid, trade, transport and tourism.[89] A different stumbling block has been Turkey's refusal to open its harbours and airports to traffic from the Greek-controlled Republic of Cyprus (as it should have under its obligations to the EU to fully implement the customs union protocol for Cyprus). Ankara insisted that the Europeans first honour their promise to lift the trade embargo against the TRNC and allow commercial air traffic into the territory.[90] The Greek Cypriots rejected any such concession to the Turkish side as long as Ankara remained unwilling to recognize their government as the only legitimate one on the island.[91] There has been a similar lack of progress in encouraging commerce between the two Cypriot entities; neither side appeared keen to allow free trade.[92] This was in sharp contrast to the extensive economic ties between Taiwan and China.

Few if any of the foreign parties extending some form of *de facto* recognition to Northern Cyprus did so with the intention of paving the way for the *de jure* recognition of the entity. Referring to moves to lift the isolation of the Turkish Cypriots, the UN Secretary-General declared in 2007 that 'the objective of such efforts should be to engender greater economic and social parity between the sides by further promoting the development of the Turkish Cypriot community, so that the reunification of the island may occur in as seamless a manner as possible'. He emphasized that foreign economic, social, cultural and other links with Northern Cyprus did not amount to recognition or assistance to secession, which would in any case be contrary to Security Council resolutions.[93]

Renewed settlement efforts

A new settlement initiative was launched only in July 2006 when the presidents of the two Cypriot republics, Papadopoulos and Talat, agreed to a five-point framework for resuming negotiations aimed at resolving the Cyprus conflict. Brokered by UN Under-Secretary-General Ibrahim Gambari, the accord provided for negotiations at two levels: technical committees would tackle day-to-day issues and expert working groups would deal with substantive long-term political matters. The two leaders pledged themselves to the reunification of Cyprus on the lines of a bizonal, bicommunal federation and political equality. They also acknowledged that the *status quo* was untenable and that its prolongation would have negative consequences. Despite the apparent sense of urgency and the subsequent efforts of the UN Secretary-General and his Special Representative to Cyprus, the next 18 months saw precious little progress in implementing the July 2006 agreement. Not even a meeting between the Greek and Turkish Cypriot leaders in September 2007 – their first in 14 months – could break the impasse.[94]

Local and international hopes for a settlement in Cyprus were boosted when Demetris Christofias defeated Papadopoulos in the south's presidential election in February 2008. Leader of the communist AKAL (Progressive Party of the Working People), Christofias pledged to resume talks with Northern Cyprus on reunification. With the previous hard-line nationalist leaders replaced, the two sides in Cyprus for the first time had (leftist) presidents who appeared equally committed to finding a lasting settlement to the decades-old conflict between the island's two communities. Talat and Christofias promptly agreed on a set of confidence-building measures between the two sides and there was also progress in establishing the working groups and technical committees envisaged under the July 2006 agreement. In March 2008 the two leaders met for the first time and agreed to begin preparations for formal reunification talks due to commence in June.[95]

The parameters of a final settlement have been firmly established in earlier agreements, especially the Annan Plan of 2004, and enjoyed broad international support. These outlines were reaffirmed in UN Security Council resolution 1789 of December 2007, namely 'a comprehensive settlement based on a bicommunal, bizonal federation and political equality'. Another basic element has long been the withdrawal of most if not all troops from Turkey stationed in Northern Cyprus.[96] Turkey too backed the Annan formula and served notice that it would brook no major deviation from the plan. In early 2008 President Abdullah Gül insisted that '[a] solution will be based on the equality of the two sides and the existence of two different peoples, two democratic systems and two states on the island'. To expect of either the Turkish Cypriots or Turkey to accept anything less would be 'a futile dream', Gül added. For good measure he warned that Turkey 'as the motherland and the guarantor country' would not 'merely stand by and watch' if Turkish Cypriots lost their right to rule themselves in an equal partnership with Greek Cypriots.[97] Talat in turn pledged loyalty to 'the essence of the Annan Plan',[98] which for him meant 'establishing a new partnership state based on the political equality of the two peoples and the equal status of two constituent states'.[99] Talat was moreover confident that '[w]e will solve the Cyprus problem, and make our country a united country that is integrated with the world and a member of the European Union'.[100] He even ventured to say that 'it won't be a surprise if we solve the problem by the end of 2008'.[101] While such a timeline may be overly optimistic, the prevailing public mood in both parts of Cyprus seemed receptive to a grand compromise over the future of the island. A UNFICYP opinion poll conducted in 2007 found that 66 per cent of the Greek Cypriots regarded a federal solution as tolerable, against 72 per cent of the Turkish Cypriots.[102]

Amid the upbeat expectations, we should be aware of the constraints faced by the negotiators. One is that the Greek Cypriots had in 2004 decisively rejected the Annan Plan – Christofias among them. This verdict still rankled with the Turkish Cypriots. Even assuming that Christofias has since then become more amenable to the Annan formula, he has to contend with the wishes of his partner in the coalition government that is none other than the Democratic Party (DIKO) of Papadopoulos who so fervently championed a 'no' vote in 2004. Greece and Turkey could present further complicating factors if one or both opposed a settlement.

Although the UN Secretary-General's Special Representative to Cyprus said in February 2008 that the world body 'will support good faith efforts on the part of both sides to restart talks and work for a solution' rather than launching a new settlement initiative,[103] the UN may well be compelled to assume a more active role should bilateral talks fail to make progress. The EU in turn can hardly watch from the wings. 'Since the Cyprus problem has turned into a major EU-Turkey and EU-NATO problem', the ICG observed, 'Brussels has both a responsibility and a need to ensure the maximum is done to reach a settlement'[104]. Turkey for its part knew full well that it would not be admitted to the EU as long as it was blamed for partitioning a member state (Cyprus) and occupying part of it. Greece stood to reap political, security and economic benefits from improved relations with Turkey if the Cyprus issue was resolved to their mutual satisfaction.[105] For both Cypriot communities there were sound economic reasons to break the current deadlock and reunify the island. A settlement coupled with EU membership would moreover signal the Turkish Cypriots' complete international rehabilitation. An added benefit for Northern Cyprus could be badly needed EU assistance in curbing organized criminal activity thriving in the entity's isolation.[106]

The EU's influence on settlement talks might be felt in a very different, indirect way too. If the Union were to decide that the final goal of Turkey's accession negotiations was less than full membership, Ankara would have little incentive left to seek an accommodation with EU member countries – least of all with the Republic of Cyprus. Furthermore, as mentioned, Turkey's admission to the EU seemed inconceivable while the *status quo* obtained in Cyprus. For one thing, Turkey's presence in Northern Cyprus may well breach the EU's accession criteria with regard to human rights and security policy. Also bear in mind that both Greece and Cyprus had veto power over Turkey's admission to the Union.[107] If the EU were to shun Turkey, Ankara could retaliate by pushing the TRNC's claims to sovereign statehood. In the process relations between Ankara and Athens were bound to deteriorate – and again cause their mutual antagonism to be played out in Cyprus.[108]

Radical alternatives

Should a settlement based on the Annan plan be rejected by one or both Cypriot communities, some radical final outcomes may present themselves. The Greek and Turkish communities could then be given the option of 'separate self-determination' by the international community.[109] Theoretically the self-determination options could for each side include sovereign statehood, involving the mutually agreed and externally supervised (even guaranteed) partition of Cyprus and the emergence of an internationally recognized Turkish state in the north alongside a confirmed Greek state in the south. Incorporation with their mother countries or some form of association with Turkey or Greece were other possibilities. As regards formal integration with Turkey, this alternative enjoyed only limited appeal among Turkish Cypriots and was not regarded as a desirable option in Ankara either.[110] However, the growing number of mainland Turkish settlers in Northern Cyprus, who had little in common with Greek Cypriots, could have a profound effect on TRNC policies – especially if the immigrants became a majority in the north.[111]

Conclusion

With the perfect vision of hindsight it is easy to see that the Republic of Cyprus (b. 1960) carried the seeds of self-destruction. Its two antagonistic communities regarded themselves as extensions of mainland Greece and Turkey, respectively, and they displayed greater affinity for their mother countries than for Cyprus. The two kin states had few qualms about taking a hand in shaping events in Cyprus to suit their respective national interests. Such external meddling contributed to the present territorial and political division of the island between a contested state in the north and a confirmed state in the south.

With the TRNC having existed for 25 years, the territorial, political, economic and ethnic fragmentation of Cyprus has become deeply entrenched. The situation has moreover proven remarkably peaceful and stable. Yet there was no international constituency for prolonging the prevailing division of Cyprus. An impatient UN Security Council has more than once declared that the *status quo* was unacceptable and that negotiations to reunify the island have been deadlocked for too long. The Greek Cypriots have consistently rejected the right of existence of a secessionist Turkish republic on the island. Since 2004 the minority Turkish community has been prepared to reunite with their former Greek compatriots in a loose federal arrangement. The TRNC has thus signalled its willingness to renounce its claims to sovereign statehood. Add the recent changes of political leadership in both north and south, and the prospects for an amicable reunification of Cyprus currently seem better than in many years. In addition, future inclusion in the EU was for Northern Cyprus a major 'pull' factor towards rejoining a united Cyprus. In return for surrendering its purported statehood, Northern Cyprus would also expect meaningful regional autonomy.

9
Western Sahara

The life cycle of the Sahrawi Arab Democratic Republic (SADR or Western Sahara) reveals striking similarities with Palestine's contested statehood. Neither seceded from an existing state but each declared unilateral independence. Both entities' claims to statehood received wide international recognition and their respective liberation movements enjoyed international legitimacy. However, in neither case has titular recognition been translated into full-fledged membership of the world community. Palestine and Western Sahara furthermore displayed limited domestic sovereignty due to foreign occupation of their territories, with the SADR in an even weaker position than Palestine. Morocco, which has occupied and formally annexed Western Sahara, rejected the entity's right of statehood out of hand, whereas Israel has at least accepted the idea of a Palestinian state. Another parallel is that the SADR's government was based in exile, like the Palestinian leadership before 1994. The two entities have also had to contend with large segments of their populations living as refugees in adjacent countries. Compared with Palestine, the fate of Western Sahara has all a along been a peripheral international issue. In fact, the international community seemed to acquiesce in the *status quo* in Western Sahara. By denying Western Sahara its right of self-determination, Morocco has broken a fundamental principle of international law yet has gone virtually scot-free.[1] For the people of Western Sahara, life in international limbo has been solitary, poor, nasty, brutish – and long.

The colonial background

Located in northwest Africa, Western Sahara covers an area of 252,120 km^2 and borders on the Atlantic Ocean in the west, Morocco in the north, Mauritania in the south and east, and Algeria in the northeast.[2] Western Sahara's subjugation to European colonialism began in 1884 when the largest part of the territory came under Spanish rule, a move ratified by the metropolitan powers at the Berlin Conference of 1884–5. The entity's borders were demarcated in a series of agreements concluded between Spain and France (the other major colonial power in the region) in 1900, 1904 and 1912. As elsewhere in Africa, these lines did not coincide with geographic or ethnic boundaries.[3] It was only in the 1930s that Spain eventually managed to gain effective control of the sprawling territory and its restive nomadic tribes. Thereafter Western Sahara was governed as part of Spanish West Africa (together with Spanish South Morocco and Ifni) until 1958, when it became a Spanish African province (*Provincia de Sahara*) incorporated into metropolitan Spain.[4] In 1962 Madrid divided Western Sahara into two parts for administrative purposes: the northern area, comprising 31 per cent of the land (Saguia el-Hamra), and the southern area (Rio de Oro) extending over the remaining 69 per cent of the surface area. In 1963 Spain at long last created a formal administration in the territory, but without seeking to establish a substantial presence across Western Sahara. Ten years later the Spanish population in the province stood at only about 35,000, half of them soldiers and the remainder including civilian administrators and technicians.[5]

By the late 1950s two important developments had taken place that continue to shape the fate of Western Sahara to this day. The Sahrawis had mounted their first major challenge to Spanish colonial rule in 1957–8, a revolt that was only put down by a joint Franco-Spanish military operation. Inspired by the outbreak of the Algerian war of liberation in 1954 and the achievement of independence by Tunisia and Morocco in 1956, the Sahrawi people showed that they too desired self-determination.[6] A national consciousness overriding the Sahrawis' traditional political loyalties to the family, tribe and Islam was emerging.[7] The other development concerned Morocco's irredentist designs on neighbouring territories. No sooner had independence been achieved when Rabat affirmed its commitment to a 'Greater Morocco', an ideology of territorial expansion conceived by Moroccan nationalists in the early 1950s. Encompassing also parts of Algeria and Mali, the whole of Mauritania and all of Western Sahara, Greater Morocco corresponded with the boundaries of the Almoravid dynasty of the 11th and 12th centuries.[8] The claim to Western Sahara was also based on 'historical ties of a political-religious nature to the Sahrawi population', predating Spain's colonization of the territory. Given this sense of entitlement, the incorporation of Western Sahara became 'an unquestioned and integral part of Moroccan nationalist ideology'.[9] Morocco realized in due course that its territorial designs on other independent African states were doomed, and quietly abandoned its claim to part of Mali, recognized Mauritania in 1969 and in 1972 withdrew its demands on territory under Algerian control. Rabat would not renounce its claims to Western Sahara, though; in fact, compromising its other territorial ambitions was largely done to reinforce its title to Western Sahara.[10]

From the start of the 1960s Spain became increasingly exposed to the pressures of decolonization at the UN. Recall that the world body had in

1960 adopted the celebrated Declaration on the Granting of Independence to Colonial Countries and Peoples (resolution 1514), which prescribed self-determination for all non-self-governing territories based on respect for the territorial integrity of each territory destined for independence.[11] In similar vein the General Assembly in December 1965 passed a resolution that for the first time requested Spain to take immediate steps to decolonize Western Sahara. A year later the Assembly resolved that Spain should arrange, under UN auspices, a referendum in Western Sahara so that the inhabitants could exercise their right of self-determination. In annual resolutions between 1966 and 1974 the General Assembly sought to keep an uncooperative Madrid's feet to the fire of decolonization.[12] Morocco, Algeria and Mauritania jointly and repeatedly declared their support for the Sahrawis' right of self-determination and indeed independence. These solemn commitments by Morocco and Mauritania were soon forgotten by the two countries. Spain, meanwhile, began submitting to international pressure by informing the UN in 1974 that a referendum on independence would be held in Western Sahara the following year.[13]

Spain also encountered indigenous opposition to its rule over Western Sahara. To challenge the colonial masters, the Saharan Liberation Movement (MLS, from its French initials) was founded in 1968. At first the movement opted for a gradualist, peaceful approach aimed at attaining autonomy and equal rights of citizenship for the people of Western Sahara. The Spanish authorities' violent suppression of an MLS demonstration in 1970 radicalized the movement, which then turned to armed struggle as a means of obtaining full independence from Spain. A number of other liberation movements were also formed in Western Sahara between 1969 and 1975, the most important being the *Frente Popular para la Liberación de Saguia el-Hamra y Río de Oro* (Polisario Front). Already at its first national congress in May 1973 Polisario affirmed its goal of independent statehood based on a free and fair referendum. The means to the end were the mobilization of the masses combined with armed struggle against the Spanish authorities. During its first two years the Polisario Front was based in Mauritania, which provided sanctuary and material support for the movement's fighters in their raids against Spanish targets in Western Sahara.[14]

As Spain was preparing to exit Western Sahara, Morocco and Mauritania requested an advisory opinion from the International Court of Justice (ICJ) on the status of Western Sahara – presumably in the belief that the Court would endorse their claims to the territory. Pending the ICJ's verdict, the UN sent a mission of inquiry to the region to study the situation first-hand. Reporting in October 1975, the mission highlighted 'the profound political wakening of the population' of Western Sahara, and 'an overwhelming consensus' among them in favour of independence and against integration with any neighbouring state.[15] Shortly thereafter the ICJ dealt Morocco and Mauritania a further blow by ruling that there was no evidence of 'any tie of territorial sovereignty' between Western Sahara and Morocco or Mauritania. 'Thus the Court has not found legal ties of such a nature as might affect the application of General Assembly resolution 1514 (XV) in the decolonization of Western Sahara and, in particular, of the principle of self-determination through the free and genuine expression of the will of the peoples of the Territory'.[16]

Denied legal sanction for the incorporation of Western Sahara, Morocco turned to mass action to reinforce its territorial claims. On the very day the Court delivered its negative verdict, Morocco's King Hassan II announced that tens of thousands of Moroccans would march on the disputed territory. The so-called Green March took place in early November, with up to 350,000 people peacefully invading Western Saharan soil for several days. While this *coup de théâtre* earned the monarch much-needed political capital at home (there had been bouts of political instability, including two *coup* attempts), the world community was not impressed by the stunt. The UN Security Council denounced the march and called on Morocco to withdraw all the invaders from Western Sahara.[17]

The next step in the unfolding drama was decidedly conspiratorial. On 14 November 1975 Spain, Morocco and Mauritania concluded the secret Madrid Accord under which Spain would relinquish Western Sahara to its two partners and a tripartite transitional administration (representing the three signatories) would be established in the territory until Spain's final withdrawal. Needless to say, the inhabitants of Western Sahara were not consulted at all. The Spaniards duly departed at the end of February 1976. It is instructive that Spain announced it was only ceding administrative authority to Morocco and Mauritania, not transferring sovereignty; the central issue over Western Sahara's final status thus remained unresolved.[18]

Independence *versus* incorporation

Morocco and Mauritania were determined to gain more than administrative responsibility in Western Sahara in the wake of Spain's exit: they wanted to dismember the desert territory and incorporate its parts into their own states. Their stalking horse was the legislative assembly of Western Sahara, called the *djemaa*. In an extraordinary meeting of the *djemaa* convened by Morocco on 26 February 1976, the 65 of the 102 members present voted unanimously to ratify the earlier tripartite agreement and to approve the integration of Western Sahara into Morocco and Mauritania. Through the *djemaa*'s vote, these two states maintained, the Sahrawis had exercised their right of self-determination, expressing a preference for incorporation into the neighbouring countries over independence. Rejecting the assembly's decision, Polisario questioned the composition and legitimacy of the *djemaa*. The movement could also point to the lack of international recognition of the parcelling out of Western Sahara and to the two rapacious states' patent disregard for UN General Assembly resolution 3458B adopted in December 1975. That resolution called for Western Saharan self-determination through consultations facilitated by a UN representative.[19]

The Polisario Front did not wait for such consultations. On 27 February 1976 it proclaimed the establishment of the Sahrawi Arab Democratic Republic. The founding fathers described the new entity as 'a free, independent, sovereign State governed by a national democratic system, of a unionist orientation, progressive and of Islamic faith'. In a typical secessionist idiom, the declaration of independence asserted that the 'peaceful people' of Western Sahara were 'victims of an attempt at extermination, a veritable genocide', presumably plotted by Morocco and Mauritania. Reference was also made to the Sahrawi people's 'liberation struggle' against 'the colonialism of the neighbour "brothers"'.[20] The SADR was to be ruled by an eight-man Polisario government-in-exile (based in Tindouf, southwest Algeria), led by the movement's Secretary-General who served as President of the SADR. Although legislative authority was vested in the National Assembly, the seat of real power was the General Congress of the Polisario Front, which elected the members of the Assembly.[21]

Polisario's unilateral declaration of independence constituted a forceful protest against the emasculation of Western Sahara as a political entity entitled to self-determination. And by creating an exiled government, Polisario hoped to strengthen its position in confronting Morocco and Mauritania on the world stage and soliciting foreign support for the Sahrawi cause. That backing was prompt and extensive. Ten states, nine African plus North Korea, afforded the SADR *de jure* recognition in the course of 1976. By the end of 1980 no less than 43 countries had done so; in 1983 the tally stood at 54 and reached 67 in 1987. The single largest group of supporters of Western Saharan statehood were from Africa, while Latin America and Asia were also well represented. Great powers and other Western states were conspicuous by their absence.[22] Those recognizing the SADR saw its advent as another act of decolonization, albeit effected through the unconventional and widely questioned means of a unilateral declaration of independence. The SADR's backers evidently believed that self-proclaimed statehood was legitimate in this instance.

Despite the founding of the SADR and Polisario's control over a sizeable chunk of Western Sahara, the formal takeover of the territory by Mauritania and Morocco prompted an exodus of Sahrawis in the mid-1970s. Encouraged by Polisario, up to half the population of Western Sahara may have sought refuge in camps around Tindouf to escape from new rulers they feared would be no more benevolent than the departed Spaniards. The Polisario Front managed to exert authority over the refugees and also had considerable success in directing Sahrawi nationalist sentiment towards acquiring an own state.[23] That consciousness drew on a separate identity that was far from an artificial construct: 'their nomadism, as well as their clothing, diet, dialect, poetry, pigmentation, and facial features, clearly distinguish them from their Moroccan counterparts'.[24] The Sahrawi people's direct ancestors came from Yemen and Saudi Arabia in the 16th century and their Hassaniya language was a classical form of Arabic distinguishable from that used in neighbouring countries.[25] There was, in other words, a distinct 'self' that qualified for self-determination.[26]

Within weeks of occupying Western Sahara, Morocco and Mauritania formally demarcated the line of partition that formed their new border in the Sahara; the larger portion, containing the bulk of known mineral reserves, was allocated to Morocco.[27] For Polisario this boundary was no more than an illegitimate line in the sand. The armed struggle that the movement had begun against the Spanish colonialists was simply continued against the new occupiers of Western Sahara. Relying on Algeria and Libya for sanctuary and material support, Polisario managed to increase their fighting strength from roughly 3,000 men in early 1976 to between 8,000 and 10,000 towards the end of 1978. Moving unhindered across large tracts of Western Sahara, Polisario combatants staged several effective attacks against occupying forces and also struck targets inside Morocco and Mauritania (including the latter's capital Nouakchott).[28] In the late 'seventies Polisario exerted effective control over substantive parts of Western Sahara, confining the foreign occupiers to major centres of population (including the capital El Ayoun) and strategic points like phosphate mines.[29]

The ever rising military and economic costs of occupation were a factor in the military's seizure of power in Mauritania in July 1978. The new rulers soon accepted a ceasefire offered by Polisario, withdrew Mauritanian forces from active participation in the war and renounced territorial claims to Western Sahara. Just over a year later Mauritania relinquished its portion of Western Sahara, which Morocco promptly annexed.[30] For the Moroccans the 'decolonization' of Western Sahara was now complete: 'territories and populations torn away by colonial usurpation' had been reintegrated into the Moroccan state.[31] For King Hassan II the full 'recovery' of Western Sahara was a major political triumph and a timely boost to the legitimacy of the Moroccan monarchy.[32] For Polisario the exit of the Mauritanians opened new space for military operations further north in Western Sahara. By the early 1980s, at the height of their military prowess, Polisario forces came close to liberating Western Sahara from Moroccan occupation. However, massive infusions of American and French arms enabled Morocco to turn the tide of war.[33]

Although the UN General Assembly deplored Morocco's unilateral act of annexation and urged it to withdraw from Western Sahara,[34] Rabat moved rapidly to consolidate control over its new acquisition. An ambitious development programme was rolled out over the entire Western Sahara, which incidentally expanded Morocco's territory by nearly one-third but increased its total population only fractionally. Over the next 30 years Morocco spent over $2.4 billion on basic infrastructure, including, airports, harbours, roads, water and electricity.[35] A highly controversial aspect of the annexation was the settlement of large numbers of Moroccan nationals in Western Sahara, reducing the Sahrawis to a minority in their own country. By 2007 Moroccan settlers outnumbered Sahrawis by at least two to one.[36] The orchestrated influx of Moroccan colonists – like Israeli settlers in the West Bank – may well be a transgression of the Fourth Geneva Convention, which prohibited states from resettling their civilian populations in territories acquired by military force.[37]

Morocco also relied heavily on security measures to strengthen its hold over Western Sahara. Initially it deployed 40,000 troops in its segment of occupied Western Sahara. In the 1980s the number increased to 160,000. More than 90,000 of them guarded the 2,500 km long defensive wall – otherwise known as the berm – which Morocco constructed between 1980 and 1987. It cut Western Sahara in two: the one side, consisting of some 85 per cent of the territory, was under Moroccan control, while Polisario controlled the other. With its forts, ditches, minefields, razor wire and electronic surveillance devices, the barrier has kept Polisario fighters out of the bulk of Western Sahara and away from most of the fertile land, phosphate mines, oil reserves and the coastline with its fishing grounds.[38]

Searching for solutions

The Organization of African Unity was compelled to tackle the prickly issue of Western Sahara, not least because a pair of its member states had brazenly violated two of the continental body's most sacrosanct principles: the right of colonial peoples to self-determination and independence, and the acceptance of borders drawn by the colonial powers. A Committee of Wise Men (five heads of state) was appointed in 1978 to investigate the matter. The following year the panel recommended an immediate ceasefire in Western Sahara and the holding of an internationally supervised referendum to allow the people of the territory to exercise their right of self-determination. The ballot should offer them a choice between independence and the *status quo*. An OAU summit in July 1979 endorsed the Wise Men's proposals. The referendum plan came to naught due to Morocco's opposition and deep divisions within the OAU over Western Sahara. This discord was also evident in the slim majority of member states supporting the SADR's admission to the OAU as a full member in 1980. When the SADR took its seat at a ministerial meeting in 1981, the resultant schism plunged the OAU into a severe crisis.[39] In protest against the SADR's admission to the OAU, Morocco withdrew from the organization in 1984 (and has not joined the successor African Union either).[40] The OAU nonetheless partnered the UN in 1985 in a diplomatic initiative to resolve the dispute over Western Sahara. Their endeavours paved the way for the adoption of a major settlement proposal in 1988.[41]

The UN, it will be recalled, had first taken up the issue of Western Sahara in 1965 when the General Assembly called on Spain to decolonize the territory. In December 1975, hard on the heels of the ICJ's advisory opinion on the future status of Western Sahara, the General Assembly by resolution 3458A reaffirmed 'the inalienable right' of the people of the non-self-governing territory to self-determination and requested the Secretary-General to arrange for the supervision 'of the act of self-determination'. In November 1979 the Assembly not merely acknowledged the Sahrawis' inalienable right of 'self-determination and independence', but also 'the legitimacy of their struggle to secure the enjoyment of that right'. Polisario was for the first time in a UN resolution recognized as 'the representative of the people of Western Sahara', which should participate fully in the search for a political solution. The same resolution deplored the worsening of the situation caused by Morocco's continued presence in Western Sahara and again urged an end to its occupation.[42] Similar strongly worded resolutions were passed by the General Assembly in subsequent years. In November 1990, for instance, the Assembly reiterated that 'the question of Western Sahara is a question of decolonization which remains to be completed on the basis of the exercise by the people of Western Sahara of their inalienable right to self-determination and independence'.[43] This unequivocal position of course contradicted Morocco's insistence that the 'question' of Western Sahara had been resolved following its incorporation of the entire territory in 1979, and that Western Sahara 'is and will remain Moroccan'.[44]

Despite these fundamental differences, Morocco and the Polisario Front in 1991 accepted the Settlement Plan for Western Sahara proposed by the UN three years earlier. It entailed a transitional period marked by a ceasefire, repatriation of refugees, exchange of prisoners and a referendum on the future of the territory.[45] The United Mission for the Referendum in Western Sahara (MINURSO), a small multinational military-*cum*-civilian unit, was deployed in the territory's capital in April 1991. MINURSO's mandate, issued by the Security Council, included monitoring the ceasefire concluded between Morocco and Polisario in 1991, checking on the confinement of the two sides' troops to designated locations, and organizing a free and fair referendum.[46]

While the ceasefire has been respected by both parties following the deployment of MINURSO, discord over the qualifications for voter eligibility thwarted MINURSO's arrangements for a referendum and so paralysed the settlement process. In 1997 the UN Secretary-General's Personal Envoy to Western Sahara, former American Secretary of State James Baker, brokered a series of agreements between the Polisario Front and Morocco to revive the referendum process. Again the parties stumbled over the composition of the voters' roll. The central point in contention was the eligibility of Moroccan settlers in Western Sahara. In 2000, when the vote was scheduled to take place, there was a new obstacle: Morocco renounced its earlier support for a referendum on independence. Made by King Hassan II, the pledge died with the monarch in 1999. His successor, King Mohammed VI, flatly rejected independence for Western Sahara and hence any referendum featuring this option.[47] The UN seemed unwilling to confront Rabat over this reversal with its far-reaching consequences for the entire settlement drive.

The next round in the search for peace followed in 2001 when Baker presented his Framework Agreement on the Status of Western Sahara, known as Baker Plan I. Since the blueprint provided for a five-year period of autonomy for Western Sahara under Moroccan sovereignty but did not guarantee a referendum and omitted any reference to independence, Polisario rejected it out of hand.[48] Baker Plan II, styled the United Nations Peace Plan for Self-Determination of the People of Western Sahara, was released in 2003. Not only did it emphasize that Western Sahara's final status would be determined by referendum, but the plan offered three referendum options: independence, autonomy or integration with Morocco. Should no option attract more than 50 per cent of the votes in the first round of balloting, a second round would be held on the two options that had gained most votes.[49] The 2003 plan also provided for a transitional government composed of the Western Sahara Authority (WSA) that would deal with local affairs, while foreign relations, national security and external defence were among the matters over which Morocco would have 'exclusive competence'. The scope of Morocco's proposed authority was predictably problematic, especially when considering that Morocco was also entrusted with 'the preservation of territorial integrity against secessionist attempts'.[50] Polisario's advocacy of independence for Western Sahara could conceivably be interpreted by Rabat as a secessionist bid that would violate Morocco's territorial integrity (since Western Sahara was supposedly an integral part of the Kingdom of Morocco and independence for the territory was out of the question). By the same token Morocco rejected any referendum that included independence as an option. This time Polisario accepted Baker's proposal. Having failed to bridge the divide between the two parties, Baker resigned as the Secretary-General's Personal Envoy in 2004.[51]

All the while the General Assembly kept on extending MINURSO's mandate. Despite the frustrating lack of progress in resolving the conflict over Western Sahara, the UN was not prepared to leave the protagonists to their own devices. According to Peter van Walsum, the Secretary-General's second Personal Envoy to Western Sahara, 'there was a consensus in the [Security] Council that any solution to the problem of Western Sahara had to be found in the framework, or under the auspices, of the United Nations'. Secretary-General Kofi Annan was firm on the parameters within which the world body could assist the search for a solution: 'The United Nations could not endorse a plan that excluded a genuine referendum while claiming to provide for the self-determination of the people of Western Sahara'.[52]

Colonialism, Moroccan style

On the ground, meanwhile, Morocco was literally digging in for the long haul in Western Sahara; allowing the Sahrawi people a free choice of political destination was clearly not a factor in its planning. Rabat's intention was to create an irreversible reality that would compel the international community to acknowledge Moroccan sovereignty over Western Sahara as a *fait accompli*.[53] Reference has already been made to the settlement of large numbers of Moroccan colonists in Western Sahara. To accelerate political integration, the four so-called Saharan provinces were represented in the Moroccan Parliament and also staged local elections under Rabat's control.[54] At another level we should take note of the development of 'a dense network of social and economic bonds' that absorbed Western Sahara into Morocco and lifted the area out of the destitution of the Spanish colonial era. Cherkaoui attributed these advances to Morocco's 'effective policy of affirmative action' in the occupied territory.[55]

As for the territory's oil deposits, Morocco had no qualms about assuming ownership by issuing licences to prospectors. The first permits were awarded to Kerr McGee of the US and French company TotalFinaElf to undertake oil exploration off the coast of Western Sahara. In response to a legal challenge that Polisario had lodged at the UN over these permits, the UN Under-Secretary-General for Legal Affairs in 2002 issued an opinion on the matter. Oil licences were not illegal *per se*, but 'if further exploration and exploitation activities were to proceed in disregard of the interests and wishes of the people of Western Sahara they would be in violation of the principles of international law applicable to mineral resource activities in non-self-governing territories'.[56] Morocco's predictable response was that all its efforts in the territory were to the benefit of the inhabitants. The Polisario Front, by contrast, called on oil companies to suspend their activities in Western Sahara – which TotalFinaElf, among others, eventually did. Polisario itself concluded an agreement with Fusion Oil of Australia to study (at its own expense) geological and geophysical data on 'Sahrawi territorial waters'.[57] The movement judged that, as the legitimate ruler of the SADR, it had the authority to enter into such an arrangement.

Although Morocco has been patently in breach of repeated UN resolutions on the disposition of Western Sahara, it was not alone in swimming against the international tide. France, with its strong historical, cultural and economic ties with Morocco, has been the kingdom's closest ally in the conflict over Western Sahara; Paris has long supported Moroccan jurisdiction over the territory. Even Spain has in recent years inclined to Morocco's position, opposing a referendum and independence for Western Sahara. While the US has avoided legitimizing Morocco's occupation and incorporation of Western Sahara, Washington has been keen not to offend a strategic partner in the Arab world, both during the Cold War and in the present era of global terrorism and Islamic extremism. Indeed, in 2004 the US awarded Morocco 'major non-NATO ally status' and a free trade agreement.[58] Algeria, by contrast, has all along been Polisario's principal foreign backer, both materially and diplomatically.[59] Although Algeria and Polisario were on the right side of international law, their position has not been buttressed by the clout of major powers prepared to enforce UN resolutions in the face of Moroccan intransigence.

In 2005 Rabat had to contend with a new challenge when the indigenous population of Western Sahara embarked on a wave of demonstrations against Morocco's ongoing occupation and the attendant abuse of human rights. Sahrawis even claimed to have launched an *intifada* in their quest for self-determination. Some of the protests turned violent as demonstrators and Moroccan security forces clashed. In the midst of the unrest Polisario threatened to resume its armed struggle, which had been suspended since 1991.[60] The growing militancy was an expression of the Sahrawis' popular frustrations about living as a territorially fragmented population for three decades, experiencing violent repression in their homeland, suffering socioeconomic marginalization due to the 'Moroccanization' of Western Sahara, and being largely ignored by an indifferent world community. These feelings have in turn fed a resurgence of Sahrawi nationalism, both in the occupied territory and in refugee camps in Algeria.[61] The ongoing presence of some 230 MINURSO personnel in Western Sahara has evidently done little if anything to break the cycle of Sahrawi resistance and Moroccan repression, which has continued into 2008.[62]

Issues of state viability

Turning to the future, we need to consider a question frequently asked of wannabe states: could Western Sahara become a viable independent state? None other than James Baker said in 2002 that a 'Sahrawi state within the old Spanish colony would be viable and would contribute to the stability of the Maghreb'.[63] The territory met some basic requirements of statehood. Its population was larger than that of many UN member states: a 2003 estimate put the figure at 261,794, with an additional 165,000 Sahrawis living in refugee camps abroad.[64] Geographically Western Sahara was slightly larger than the United Kingdom and had direct access to the Atlantic Ocean. Its extensive territory was not particularly inviting, though: it consisted of desert terrain, mostly vast rocky plains rather than sand; rainfall was extremely scarce and there was only one river of significance; there was precious little arable land, and the temperature fluctuated between scorching summer days and bitterly cold winter nights. What brightened this forbidding picture is that Western Sahara boasted large deposits of high-grade phosphate. The full exploitation of the phosphate reserves could earn Western Sahara one of the highest *per capita* incomes in Africa, given the smallness of its population. Western Sahara already produced oil, with further extensive exploration underway. Its other natural resources included iron ore, titanium oxide and vanadium, as well as rich fishing grounds off the Atlantic coast.[65]

What also counted in favour of statehood is that the Polisario Front seemed to enjoy general support among Sahrawis in Western Sahara and among the refugee population; it was the principal if not sole liberation movement of the indigenous people of the territory and recognized as such by the UN and the OAU/AU.[66] Although exiled, the SADR's Polisario government has existed for over 30 years. The institutions of the Sahrawi Republic and Polisario were, of course, interwoven. The SADR constitution of 1999 formalized the connection: 'Until the achievement of national sovereignty, the Polisario Front remains the political framework that groups and politically mobilises the Sahrawis, to express their aspirations and their legitimate right to self-determination and independence'.[67] The constitution furthermore decreed that the secretary-general of the movement should also serve as the SADR's head of state. That dual position has been held by Mohammed Abdelaziz since the proclamation of the state in 1976. The Sahrawi National Council, the legislature, would be formed after a Polisario congress. The institutions of the state were extended into society through a network of committees, congresses and councils. The SADR administered the Sahrawi refugee camps in Algeria by means of a hierarchy of provinces, communes and districts. In these refugee communities the SADR took care of such basic functions as health and education.[68]

Polisario maintained a political presence in Western Sahara too. To underline this point, the movement in October 2003 for the first time held its regular congress in the 'liberated territories' of the SADR.[69] In February 2008 the 32nd anniversary of the proclamation of the Sahrawi Republic was celebrated in Tifarti, the SADR's provisional capital located in the 'liberated territories'. (The official capital, El Ayoun, remained under Moroccan control.) At the same time the newly elected Sahrawi National Council was inaugurated in Tifarti.[70]

Another conventional criterion of statehood that the SADR met, was a capacity to engage in foreign relations. The entity's statehood has been recognized by some 80 confirmed states, with African countries prominent among them. The SADR was a member of the OAU and at the founding of the AU President Abdelaziz was elected as one of the five vice-presidents of the new continental body.[71] The OAU's embrace of the SADR was in sharp contrast to the organization's rejection of Biafra's secession in the 1960s and that of Somaliland more recently. The OAU evidently placed Western

Sahara in the same category as the 'salt-water' colonialism of old; as a former Spanish colony, Western Sahara was as entitled to sovereign independence as other former African colonies of European powers.[72]

The Sahrawi Republic maintained diplomatic relations with a large number of countries, mostly in the Global South, including Uganda, Tanzania, Mauritius, Algeria, Angola, Libya, Malawi, South Africa and Venezuela. It also enjoyed semi-official representation in Switzerland, Germany, Belgium, Spain and the Nordic countries, among others. Abdelaziz, widely accepted abroad as the legitimate leader of the colonized Sahrawi people, was experienced in personal diplomacy. He and other SADR representatives have recently visited states ranging from Spain, Italy and Mexico to Senegal and Mauritania.[73] The SADR furthermore had a support network of non-governmental organizations abroad, including the National Algerian Committee of Solidarity with the Sahrawi People, the Task Force of the European Coordination of Support for the Sahrawi People, Western Sahara Resource Watch and the Australia Western Sahara Association. The latter two were in the business of naming and shaming companies that imported phosphate and other minerals from occupied Western Sahara. Various foreign political groupings (like the European United Left) and human rights bodies abroad (for instance Human Rights Watch and Amnesty International) occasionally voiced support for the Sahrawi cause and protested against Morocco's human rights abuses in Western Sahara.[74]

On the debit side, critics have suggested that the Polisario Front had links with international terrorism[75] and that the movement's refugee camps in Algeria were potential recruiting areas for al-Qaeda and other militant Islamic groups. An independent Sahrawi state under Polisario leadership, the American ambassador to Morocco claimed in March 2007, would not only be weak but 'would likely morph into a terrorist-controlled one'.[76] Polisario leaders have also been accused of profiting from illegal trafficking.[77] There was no hard evidence to back up allegations about the Polisario Front's terrorist connections, flirtation with Islamic extremism or involvement in organized crime. Polisario was in fact a secular nationalist movement subscribing to a reasonably liberal strain of Islam. Its current leadership also tended to be pro-Western.[78]

Alternative political formulas

The Polisario Front's first prize has remained a sovereign Sahrawi state recognized by the world community. This position was reaffirmed in the settlement plan Polisario submitted to the UN Secretary-General in April 2007. The movement reiterated its long-standing call for 'the self-determination of the people of Western Sahara' through a referendum, insisting that this was the sole solution to the conflict. The Front based its plan on international law, existing Security Council resolutions and Polisario's previous agreements with Morocco. Despite the zero-sum proposal, Polisario declared its commitment to reaching a negotiated, mutually acceptable settlement. The olive branch held out to Rabat was a pledge to co-operate with Morocco in the economic, social and security domains. The Polisario Front even offered to guarantee Moroccan strategic and economic interests in an independent Sahrawi state[79] – concessions that may point to a form of conditional independence. One can also assume that Polisario would be comfortable with an internationally supervised transition to independence, as previous UN settlement schemes had in fact proposed.

Morocco will still have no truck with the idea of a sovereign Sahrawi state. Rabat preferred the continuation of the *status quo*, meaning a Western Sahara that has been fully absorbed into the Kingdom of Morocco and has thus ceased to exist as a separate political entity. This outcome was, of course, wholly anathema to Polisario. Since 'total victory is impossible and total defeat is unthinkable' for either side,[80] we need to explore compromise solutions between the two mutually exclusive options of independence and incorporation.

The two principal compromise outcomes are sharing Western Sahara or splitting it up.[81] Fragmentation, which has been rejected by both sides, would involve another partitioning of the territory, this time between Morocco and Polisario. The latter's share would become an independent state (a mini-SADR) while the other portion remained part and parcel of Morocco.[82] Sharing the territory could take different forms: Western Sahara could be accorded special regional status within Morocco, but without government autonomy; Morocco could be turned into a symmetrical federation that would provide each region, Western Sahara included, with its own elected government; Western Sahara could receive special autonomy within Morocco; or an independent (or semi-independent) Western Sahara could enter into a confederal arrangement with Morocco. Given the practical constraints, special autonomy may be the most plausible of the four alternatives based on sharing power and territory. It envisaged a quasi-independent Western Sahara with its own locally elected government responsible for domestic affairs and Morocco taking care of foreign relations and defence. This so-called 'third way' solution of course resembled the settlement plan presented by Baker in 2001.[83] More importantly, Morocco's latest settlement formula – presented to the UN chief in April 2007 – provided for special autonomy for Western Sahara.

Morocco's 'final political solution' consisted of a reasonably detailed 'autonomy proposal for the Sahara, within the framework of the Kingdom's sovereignty and national unity'. The government of the envisaged Sahara Autonomous Region would comprise a locally elected legislature and an executive authority elected by the legislature. Sahrawi inhabitants would enjoy majority representation in the regional parliament, while long-time non-Sahrawi residents would be given 'credible legislative representation'.

All residents of the area would at the same time continue to elect representatives to the national legislature in Rabat. The head of government or chief executive would be elected by parliament, invested by the King of Morocco and serve as the representative of the Moroccan state in the region. He would be accountable to the regional parliament. A separate judiciary in the shape of a regional high court would have the final power of interpretation of the region's legislation (but without prejudicing the authority of the Moroccan Supreme Court and Constitutional Council). The regional government would in turn enjoy exclusive control of local administration, police, economic development, trade, investment, tourism, agriculture, taxation, infrastructure, health, education, cultural affairs and the environment. (Under its exclusive powers the regional government may open trade offices abroad). The central government in Rabat would retain exclusive jurisdiction over the 'attributes of sovereignty' (notably the flag, national anthem and currency); matters flowing from the monarch's constitutional and religious prerogatives; national security; the Kingdom's juridical order, and external relations. Where matters of foreign relations had a direct bearing on the prerogatives of the Sahara Region, the central state would exercise its responsibilities in consultation with the regional government. The region may, in consultation with the national government, enter into cooperative relations with foreign regions. Powers not specifically entrusted to the region or the centre would be exercised on the basis of subsidiarity (that is, common agreement). Finally, Rabat's proposal stipulated that the 'autonomy statute' would be negotiated and thereafter submitted to the 'populations concerned' in a free referendum to allow them to exercise their right of self-determination.[84]

The Moroccans have presented their autonomy plan in the same zero-sum fashion as Polisario had done with their settlement proposal. In November 2007 the monarch vowed that 'Morocco, its king and its people, will never accept anything other than autonomy [for Western Sahara], within the framework of a single and unified state'.[85] This was not mere rhetoric: popular opinion in Morocco, manipulated by the monarchy and other political elites, viewed Western Sahara as an inviolable part of the Moroccan state and was dead-set against independence for the territory.[86] 'It's a real national red line', in the words of a Moroccan diplomat.[87] Herein lay possibly the greatest obstacle to Moroccan withdrawal from Western Sahara.[88] It is then understandable that Rabat's settlement plan provided for a referendum on autonomy only; Morocco will not entertain any suggestion of a referendum on independence for Western Sahara. By precluding the option of independence, the electorate would of course not be offered a real choice between alternatives and Morocco's referendum could hardly constitute a legitimate act of self-determination. Here it is worth recalling the UN's 1970 Declaration on Principles of International Law, which identified three modes of implementing the right of self-determination: the creation of an independent state, free association or integration with an independent state, or any other political status freely determined by the people concerned.

Other objections have also been raised against the Moroccan proposal. The entire autonomy plan was based on the assumption that Western Sahara was an integral part of Morocco – a view that has long been rejected by the World Court, UN, OAU/AU and by a representative body of international lawyers. If it adopted the autonomy proposal, the world community would be legitimizing Morocco's acquisition of territory by force – a patent violation of international law. A further practical concern was that authoritarian states had a poor track record in respecting regional autonomy; consider the fate of Kosovo at the hands of Yugoslavia and later Serbia. What added to such apprehensions in the case of Morocco was that the king enjoyed absolute authority under article 19 of the constitution. The autonomy plan's stipulation that the Moroccan state 'will keep its powers in the royal domains, especially with respect to defense, external relations and the constitutional and religious prerogatives of His Majesty the King', could give the monarch wide freedom of interpretation. Finally, Morocco's insistence that the Sahrawis renounce their legal and moral right to genuine self-determination may provoke further conflict instead of promoting a peaceful settlement.[89] The latter concern can of course be addressed by offering the people of Western Sahara a free and fair choice between Morocco's autonomy arrangement and independence; should they then prefer autonomy over independence, it would be a legitimate exercise in self-determination. Considering the high degree of autonomy promised by Morocco, a significant number of Sahrawis may well be attracted to the proposal. In the meantime the US, for one, has welcomed Morocco's autonomy plan as a 'promising and realistic way forward'.[90]

Following the release of their respective settlement plans, Morocco and the Polisario Front held their first direct talks in seven years when meeting under UN auspices in June 2007. A second round, also in the US, followed in August and a third in January 2008. After the latter meeting the UN Secretary-General reported that the two sides' stated positions 'remained far apart' and that 'there was hardly any exchange that could be characterized as negotiations'. They nonetheless agreed on the need to advance the process 'into a more intensive and substantive phase of negotiations'.[91] The Security Council, for its part, continued to call on the parties to resume negotiations with a view to achieving 'a just, lasting and mutually acceptable political solution, which will provide for the self-determination of the people of Western Sahara'.[92]

Actually reaching a solution is much easier said than done. The UN's own record in this regard is rather chequered. When the world body first became engaged in Western Sahara, it defined the question in terms of decolonization; the matter had to be resolved on the basis of the self-determination of the population, exercised through a UN-arranged referendum. As we noted repeatedly, a genuine test of the popular will would require that at least the two main options – independence and integration into Morocco – be presented to the electorate. After more than four decades of involvement, the UN has still not put its chosen doctrine of self-determination into practice by organizing such a referendum for the Sahrawis.[93]

A further constraining factor lay, paradoxically, in the effectiveness of the 1991 ceasefire. The suspension of hostilities meant that for both Morocco and Polisario 'the political cost of maintaining intransigent postures has appeared lower than the potential cost of moving away from them'. This held true even in the face of continuing Sahrawi protests against Moroccan rule. By contrast an unfavourable outcome could have serious domestic repercussions for Morocco because the legitimacy of its domestic order was closely tied to the fate of Western Sahara. The Polisario Front could in turn be devastated by an unfavourable settlement since the achievement of independent statehood has all along been its *raison d'être*. Should the movement renounce independence, its credibility among its followers and foreign backers could suffer. A final settlement producing less than Sahrawi statehood could cost Algeria leverage in its relations with Morocco and cause it to lose face internationally.[94]

Even if the *status quo* were bearable – if not actually advantageous – for the main protagonists, there were also costs for all concerned. This applied above all to the more than 160,000 Sahrawis languishing in refugee camps in Algeria, where they have had to endure 'exile, isolation and poverty' under the authority of an exiled state structure that displayed an authoritarian and corrupt streak. The Sahrawis living under Moroccan control were materially far better off than their refugee kinsfolk, but they faced persistent human rights abuses at the hands of their occupiers.[95] Morocco has been shouldering a heavy financial burden in the so-called southern provinces, especially in the areas of defence and infrastructure, at the expense of its own development. There were also diplomatic costs in terms of Morocco's alienation from the African mainstream and its international image as an occupying power denying Africa's last colony its right of self-determination. Algeria too has incurred financial costs through its aid to Sahrawi refugees and military support for Polisario. The Maghreb region was paying a price for the unresolved conflict in Western Sahara in terms of retarding much needed development in what is a poorly governed part of Africa. Under these conditions illegal trafficking (drugs, cigarettes, fuel and arms) has become a thriving industry in the Maghreb.[96] If all these costs continued to escalate, the stalemate over Western Sahara could become painful enough for the parties to engage in a genuine search for a compromise solution.

What if the UN Security Council remained incapable of fulfilling its responsibility of granting the people of Western Sahara their right of self-determination? One conceivable way out of the impasse would be to create an entirely new negotiating framework. The International Crisis Group has proposed that the Security Council should invite Morocco, the Polisario Front and Algeria – the three principal parties – 'to negotiate a resolution of the conflict on the basis of whatever principles on which they can agree', but without UN mediation. A deal (if it emerged) was likely to be based on either fragmenting or sharing the territory – rather than independence or the *status quo* – and could be submitted to the people of Western Sahara for ratification.[97] This route seems premature at the present stage and could therefore be regarded as a fall-back position if the UN decided to bow out of the peace process.

Conclusion

It is a poor reflection on the international community that Africa's last colony should have gone the route of contested statehood to assert its right of self-determination *à la* independence. The former Spanish colony's right of statehood has been recognized by both the UN and the OAU, but Morocco has prevented its realization. Morocco has exercised its veto power over Western Sahara in a direct, forcible manner by occupying and annexing the territory. With the bulk of their purported land under Moroccan control, the Sahrawi independence movement has had to pursue its cause mostly from exile, where a large segment of the population lived as refugees.

As with Palestine, it would probably require an international diplomatic effort to break the current deadlock over the future of Western Sahara. The optimum outcome Polisario could realistically hope for is conditional independence preceded by an internationally supervised transition to this final status. In combination these two forms of international engagement could help overcome Western Sahara's grave deficit in empirical statehood and at the same time allay Morocco's security concerns. Considerations of domestic legitimacy may, however, compel Rabat to offer Western Sahara at most regional autonomy within the Moroccan state. International opinion is unlikely to demand anything more from Morocco and Polisario may be too weak to extract a better deal.

10
Taiwan

Having arranged our selection of contested states in order of seniority, beginning with the most 'junior' pretender, we have to end with the Republic of China (ROC or Taiwan). With its contested statehood dating back to the late 1940s, the ROC was the doyen of this corps. But longevity was not the main reason why the ROC deserved special attention in this inquiry. Taiwan provided a rich illustration of the diversity among contested states and served as an outstanding example of how such an entity can skillfully exploit its limited international space. Unlike many contested states, the ROC was not a secessionist entity that proclaimed unilateral independence. Instead it owed its contested statehood to revolutionary regime change in mainland China, which reduced the ROC to the last outpost of the *ancien regime*. Even so Taiwan has managed to retain a measure of international recognition, with the result that its diplomatic isolation has not been as severe as that of most other contested states. Not content to be boxed in, the ROC has become a pioneer in the development of semi-official foreign representation as a substitute for normal diplomatic ties. One of the reasons for its success in this endeavour was Taiwan's economic muscle – a feature that has also helped the ROC develop its empirical statehood to a level far superior to that of any other contested state. Its extensive socio-economic ties with its veto state, China, added to Taiwan's uniqueness.

From Sun to Mao

The Republic of China was originally established in mainland China in 1912 following the revolution that overthrew the Manchu Qing dynasty. Sun Yat-sen, leader of the Kuomintang (KMT or Nationalist Party), was the founding father of the new republic. During its first 16 years the poorly governed ROC's reach was confined largely to southern China, with warlords holding sway in much of the north. It was only under Sun's successor, Chiang Kai-shek, that the KMT managed to establish an effective government and extend its writ northwards. However, Chiang's authoritarian government still faced huge challenges in stamping its authority on the entire territory. Apart from diehard warlords and the Chinese Communist Party that instigated a revolutionary war in 1928, the central government had to contend with Japanese aggression. Imperial Japan occupied Manchuria in 1931 and staged a full-scale invasion of China six years later, unleashing the Second Sino-Japanese War. The island of Taiwan, which had been ruled as a prefecture of the Chinese Empire for two centuries before being converted to a Chinese province in 1886, was ceded to Japan in 1895. This was one of the terms of the Treaty of Shimonoseki concluded at the end of the First Sino-Japanese War (1894–5).[1] Despite these assaults on its territorial integrity, the Republic of China was treated as a big power by the League of Nations.

During the Second World War the ROC was preoccupied with the presence of Japanese forces on its soil. By 1940 the invaders had occupied China's main cities, directed the major communication routes and controlled the modern sector of the Chinese economy. Even so the war had by then reached a stalemate, Japan realizing that China was unconquerable.[2] Although it had little to contribute to the overall Allied war effort against the Axis powers, China was regarded as a valued partner. In 1942 the ROC signed the Declaration by United Nations and participated in the Cairo Conference with Britain and the US in 1943. At Cairo the three parties resolved that the territories Japan had 'stolen from the Chinese', including Taiwan and Manchuria, should be restored to China.[3] This intention was confirmed by the US, Britain and the Soviet Union at the Tehran and Potsdam meetings. By so doing the trio of Allied powers acknowledged that Taiwan was part of China.[4]

In 1945 the ROC became a founder member of the UN and moreover one of the five permanent members of the Security Council. The ROC also held early elected membership of the Economic and Social Council, the Trusteeship Council and the International Court of Justice, and joined the UN's specialized agencies. Befitting its great power status, the ROC maintained an extensive diplomatic network with embassies or legations in over 70 per cent of the UN's 59 member states in 1949. Its international standing, however, belied the Nationalist government's struggle for survival against Mao Tse-tung's communist forces in the immediate post-war years.[5]

Three major setbacks

The ROC's period of post-war international glory was brief. In 1949 Mao's rebels defeated government forces and took power in mainland China. The newly proclaimed People's Republic of China presented itself as the successor of the ROC. The Kuomintang government fled to Taiwan, located off southeastern China, in what Chiang Kai-shek and his followers portrayed as a temporary relocation following the communists' illegal seizure of power. The KMT still considered itself the only legitimate government of all China and its stated policy was to recover the mainland from communist control and hence restore the ROC there. This was from the outset a very tall order because the ROC had surrendered over 99 per cent of China's territory – including the capital – and more than 98 per cent of the total population to a rival government.[6] The year 1949 represented a watershed in the history of the ROC because its statehood became contested in both world politics and international law.

Although a number of states quickly switched recognition from the ROC to the PRC, the majority initially supported the ROC's claim to sole Chinese statehood and they accordingly refused to recognize the PRC. Largely because of China's involvement in the Korean War, no state recognized Beijing from the spring of 1950 until mid-1955. In retrospect the mid-1950s had perhaps been a golden opportunity that the ROC had lost to proclaim itself as the sovereign government of Taiwan. The PRC had indicated a willingness to moderate its claims to Taiwan for the sake of constructive relations with the US. If the KMT had at that stage renounced its own claims to mainland China and resigned itself to ruling only Taiwan, non-communist states may have approved the arrangement – which may have allowed them to enter into relations with both Beijing and Taipei.[7]

With its own diplomatic fortunes still seeming reasonably bright, the ROC had little incentive to accept the permanence of communist rule on the mainland. The ROC's most active diplomatic year since the retreat from the mainland came in 1957 with diplomatic missions being established or upgraded in several Latin American, Middle Eastern and African countries. The growth in the ROC's diplomatic network continued into the 1960s, focused on Africa. Of the 23 African nations that achieved independence in the first three years of the decade, 13 recognized the ROC, five the PRC and five recognized neither. The process of expansion climaxed in 1970 when a total of 68 states had diplomatic missions in Taipei.

While the ROC managed to extend its bilateral diplomatic network, its position in the world's principal multilateral body was coming under increasing pressure. Upon taking power on the mainland, the Communist Party lost no time in demanding that it be seated forthwith in the UN, particularly in the General Assembly and Security Council, as the sole legitimate government of all China. At the General Assembly's session in 1950 a proposal to admit the PRC to membership was easily defeated by a vote of 33 against, 16 in favour, ten abstentions and one absence. After 1954 the issue of China's representation made an annual appearance on the Assembly agenda. The principal opponent of these moves – and foremost champion of the ROC's continued presence – was the US. Soviet endeavours in support of its Chinese ally were thwarted by such devices as the requirement of a two-thirds majority in the Assembly to change China's representation. However, Washington could not stem the mounting clamour in favour of Peking's inclusion in the UN. By 1965 a vote on the issue recorded 47 opposing the PRC's admission, 47 supporting it, 20 states abstaining and a further three being absent. At the Assembly's session in 1971, the two-thirds ruling was overturned. A convincing majority of 76 against 35 (with 20 nations abstaining or absent) approved the subsequent resolution (2758 of 25 October) 'to restore all its rights' to the PRC and to recognize its government delegates as 'the only legitimate representatives of China' in the UN, and 'to expel forthwith the representatives of Chiang Kai-shek from the place they unlawfully occupy' in the world body. America's proposal of dual representation – a Security Council seat for the PRC and representation for both the ROC and PRC in the General Assembly – was easily defeated.[8] Its enforced departure from the UN was a second turning point in the ROC's post-war history.

By the time the ROC lost its UN seat it had become virtually impossible for the KMT government to sustain the assertion that it was still the sole legitimate ruler of the entire China. Consider the vast disparities between the two sides of the Taiwan Strait: the PRC was the world's most populous state (1971: 730 million), whereas Taiwan (including the adjacent islands of Penghu, Kinmen and Matsu) then had only 13.4 million inhabitants; in size the PRC ranked third (over 9.5 million km^2 against Taiwan's 35,961 km^2); the PRC had joined the ranks of the nuclear powers in 1964; as an international trading partner the ROC still eclipsed the PRC, but the latter offered enormous potential; and finally, the giant PRC made far more impact on the global political scene than tiny Taiwan. The communist government had moreover proven its durability and its long-term prospects for survival seemed better than those of its Nationalist opponents exiled on Taiwan.

The UN's ejection of the ROC was a major act of collective delegitimization, denying the ROC's right of statehood. The UN expressly rejected the ROC's claim to inclusive (all-China) statehood and by implication also any future claim to exclusive (Taiwan-only) statehood. The world body in effect relegated the ROC to non-state status. Having thus cleared its agenda of the Taiwan issue, the UN signalled that the future of the ROC was to become a domestic Chinese matter – off limits to foreign countries and organizations. The outside world henceforth regarded Taiwan (a designation widely preferred to Republic of China) as an integral part of China and supported Beijing's assertion that Taiwan was a 'renegade' province that would in due course return to the fold. The ROC agreed that there was a single China that included both the mainland and Taiwan. As a consequence Taiwan did not claim statehood separate from that of mainland. Instead, it clung to the illusion that the ROC remained the sole legitimate ruler of all China.

While the majority of states accorded the PRC this exclusive status, the ROC proved that it could not easily be condemned to extinction; it became a contested state. Despite expulsion from the UN and the loss of 13 diplomatic partners to the PRC in 1971, the ROC could take some comfort from the fact that 26 countries continued to recognize its statehood. Taipei nonetheless moved quickly to replace conventional diplomatic ties with an innovative web of semi-official or pseudo-diplomatic representation. This alternative network of bilateral links was inaugurated with Japan after it switched recognition to the PRC in September 1972. Tokyo and Taipei agreed to substitute their embassies with the Interchange Association and the East Asia Relations Association, respectively. These were followed by representative offices in scores of other countries in a variety of guises, like trade missions, cultural centres and even China Airlines.[9]

Still, its exclusion from the UN had undoubtedly accelerated Taiwan's slide into diplomatic isolation. The country was swept out of scores of intergovernmental organizations. Although the ROC had withdrawn under duress from a number of UN specialized agencies well before 1971, the floodgates opened after its ejection from the General Assembly and Security Council. At the end of 1973 the ROC retained membership of only four UN agencies, notably the World Bank and International Monetary Fund. In 1980 the ROC lost its membership of both institutions as well. By the end of the decade the ROC belonged to only ten IGOs, all outside the UN ambit. These included the Permanent Court of Arbitration, International Criminal Police Organization (Interpol) and Asian Development Bank (ADB). Although Beijing in 1983 declared its desire to join the ADB on condition that Taiwan be expelled, it subsequently relented and in 1986 took up membership alongside the ROC, henceforth designated as 'Taipei China' in the organization. The ROC initially resented this name change, but then decided that participation was more important than pride. This reflected the so-called flexible diplomacy associated particularly with President Lee Teng-hui, who assumed office in 1988. One aspect of the new flexibility was that Taipei would not necessarily insist on the designation 'Republic of China' when participating in inter-governmental organizations or conferences. Another element was that the ROC would no longer retreat from multilateral forums to which the PRC had gained admission; instead, Taipei would try to secure or retain a seat of its own.

The United States was the only major power to resist the rising tide of isolation engulfing the ROC – until 1979. In that year America also changed sides, unilaterally terminating an official relationship with the ROC that dated from 1928. This move on the part of the ROC's principal post-war ally was a third watershed event, necessitating a reconfiguration of relations between Washington and Taipei. The US formally spelled out the terms of the new bilateral relationship in the Taiwan Relations Act (TRA) of 1979. In letter and spirit the law signalled America's intention to grant the ROC on Taiwan recognition *sui generis*.[10] Among other sovereign attributes the validity of the ROC's laws and acts was recognized; privileges and immunities were accorded, on the basis of reciprocity, to the two countries' representative institutions (called the American Institute in Taiwan and the Coordination Council for North American Affairs in the US); and the treaty-making capacities of the ROC were acknowledged. The TRA also replaced the 1954 Mutual Defence Treaty in some respects by mandating the US to provide such defence items 'as may be necessary to enable Taiwan to maintain a sufficient self-defense capability'. The US would furthermore maintain the capacity 'to resist any resort to force or other forms of coercion that would jeopardize the security, or the social or economic system' of the island.[11]

Democracy at home, flexibility abroad

While the ROC experienced grave setbacks in its international relations, the domestic situation remained remarkably stable. A smooth transition in leadership took place in 1978 when Chiang Ching-kuo, son of the late Chiang Kai-shek, assumed the presidency. For most of his tenure Chiang junior retained the authoritarian features of KMT rule, but in 1987 he initiated a far-reaching process of political liberalization. The formation of new political parties was permitted following the lifting of martial law in July of that year. In January 1988 the registration of new newspapers was allowed for the first time in four decades. The election of Lee Teng-hui as successor to President Chiang in January 1988 provided further impetus to the process of political reform. Lee became the first native Taiwanese to hold the presidency of the ROC, thus breaking the stranglehold that mainland émigrés had exerted over the island's politics since 1949.[12] Within the first few weeks of 1989 a law was enacted to allow democratic political competition. In 1991 a general election produced an entirely new National Assembly and the next year saw the first fully democratic election of the Legislative Yuan, Taiwan's law-making body. Local and county elections followed in 1993 and 1994 and in 1996 the president of the ROC was for the first time directly elected by the people.[13]

On the foreign relations front Lee, as mentioned, initiated a new pragmatic diplomacy designed to expand the ROC's international ties. Taipei became more flexible on the issue of international recognition by accepting the previously taboo idea of dual recognition. Until then Taipei and Beijing had applied their own versions of West Germany's Hallstein doctrine. This zero-sum approach was the result of the two sides' agreement that there was only one China of which Taiwan was an integral part. Because neither would relinquish its claim to being 'the legitimate guardian of Chinese sovereignty', each insisted that foreign states may recognize and enjoy diplomatic ties with only one of them.[14] Under Lee's new pragmatism the ROC would retain diplomatic ties with states that entered into such relationships with the PRC too, instead of automatically breaking existing links. The Caribbean microstate of Grenada became the first to opt for dual recognition in July 1989, but the PRC angrily rejected the 'Grenadian model' and cut its formal ties with the country. The same fate befell Burkina Faso in 1994 when it tried to maintain formal relations with both the PRC and ROC.[15]

The diplomatic scoreboard compelled Taiwan to become flexible in its foreign relations. In 1988 it had diplomatic representation in only 22 states and a consular presence in two more; 14 countries maintained embassies in Taipei while a further three had consular missions there. This meant that in 1988 only about 15 per cent of all states recognized the ROC. Among this relatively small group only South Korea, Saudi Arabia and South Africa were of significance in world power rankings. By then Taipei's semi-official diplomatic web was already larger than its formal network: 22 countries had established semi-official offices in Taipei while the ROC in turn had similar representation in 40 states.

In another major break with KMT ideology, President Lee in 1991 conceded that the PRC leadership controlled the mainland and that the ROC's jurisdiction was confined to Taiwan (and surrounding islets). Taipei would no longer challenge the Chinese Communist Party's right to rule the mainland.[16] In a further belated recognition of reality, the ROC in 1994 announced that it would no longer attempt to represent China 'in the international community'. But there was a sting in the tail: China comprised 'two essentially equal political entities', Lee proclaimed.[17] Proceeding along this track Lee in 1999 characterized cross-Strait interaction as 'state-to-state or at least a special type of nation-to-nation relations' distinct from ties between a central government and a local authority. For Beijing these statements deviated from the two sides' so-called consensus of 1992 that 'both sides of the Strait adhere to the principle of one China'.[18] What the PRC overlooked, though, was that the parties had also agreed that each could interpret the statement orally and by implication differently.[19]

Its general election of 2000 opened a further chapter in Taiwan's domestic politics and foreign relations. Chen Shui-bian, leader of the Democratic Progressive Party (DPP), was elected President. The KMT, which had ruled the ROC since 1912 – mostly in authoritarian fashion – was defeated by an opposition party priding itself on its democratic credentials and Taiwanese character. In 2004 Chen was re-elected for a second term, a victory at the ballot box that he attributed to the consolidation of 'a rising Taiwan identity',[20] or what others described as the growing potency of Taiwanese nationalism.[21] Four years later Chen's party was defeated by the KMT in both the legislative and presidential elections. In a further setback for the DPP, twin referendums on the country's possible membership of the UN – held at the same time as the presidential poll – failed to pass the required threshold of voters to ensure validity.[22] The election of President Ma Ying-jeou in March 2008, together with the failure of the referendums, immediately raised expectations in Taipei, Beijing, Washington and elsewhere of a new chapter of cooperative instead of confrontational cross-Strait relations. Chen's independence-minded 'adventurism', it was hoped, would make way for a resumption of political dialogue to bring about a *rapprochement* between the ROC and PRC.[23] Before examining Taiwan's international relations, though, we need to consider the constraints imposed by the country's contested status under international law.

Legal wrangles

Both Beijing and Taipei have invoked principles of international law to justify their opposing views on Taiwan's legal status. Scholars and jurists have been equally divided on the matter. Instead of joining the inconclusive debate, let us merely summarize the contending readings of international law on a number of salient questions.

The first and most fundamental issue was whether the ROC on Taiwan, or Taiwan *per se*, qualified as a state under international law. Crawford forcefully expressed one position: 'Taiwan is not a State, because it does not claim to be'.[24] This was based on the notion that a formal declaration of independence provided the best evidence of an entity's assertion of sovereign statehood.[25] The counter-argument advanced by the ROC government in particular, was that Taipei had no need to issue a formal declaration of independence because the ROC had been a *de jure* state since its founding in 1912 – and that the relocation of its seat of government to Taiwan in 1949 and its consequent loss of territory and people did not affect the ROC's statehood under international law.[26]

The notion that the ROC has retained *de jure* statehood regardless of the events of 1949 has been hotly disputed. It was a widely held view in world politics and international law that the PRC in 1949 became the legitimate successor government to the ROC. The PRC has been recognized by the international community as the *de jure* government of the entire China, with its authority extending to Taiwan. The ROC government on Taiwan has as a consequence forfeited its legal status in international law; that government was a rebellious local authority under Beijing's jurisdiction[27] or alternatively a government-in-exile based on Taiwan.[28] We should also recall (see Chapter 1) that if a state has a special claim of right to exercise governmental powers over another territory, the latter's formal independence under international law is called into question. The PRC's claims of the right to rule Taiwan thus derogate from any assertions of formal independence made by the island. The predominant view in the international community was indeed that Taiwan was not a state in terms of international law and that Beijing's notion of 'one China' was both legal and legitimate.[29]

The claim that a Republic of Taiwan would qualify for statehood under international law was equally contentious. Beijing maintained that the

Cairo Declaration of 1943 and the Potsdam Proclamation of 1945 provided for the return of Taiwan to China after World War II. However, the decisions reached at the two conferences were not legally equivalent to international treaties.[30] The matter was not resolved by the conclusion of the multilateral San Francisco Peace Treaty of 1951 and the Sino-Japanese Peace Treaty of 1952 either. Neither accord explicitly awarded sovereignty over Taiwan to any specific state or government. Instead, the two agreements formally nullified the sovereignty that Japan had acquired over Taiwan in terms of the Treaty of Shimonoseki (1895).[31]

Proponents of Taiwan's statehood insisted that its international position cannot be frozen as if it were still 1952. As one international lawyer put it, 'Taiwan has evolved from an occupied territory to a country', enjoying *de facto* but not *de jure* independence. This leads us to the theory of evolved nationhood, which posited that the island had through the dual processes of Taiwanization and democratization developed into a country fully entitled to sovereignty. Advocates of Taiwan's statehood made the further obvious point that the entity met the conventional criteria for statehood set out in the Montevideo Convention.[32] With 23 million inhabitants Taiwan was more or less on par with Saudi Arabia, North Korea and Ghana. Its territorial size of roughly 36,000 km^2 (including Penghu, Kinmen and Matsu) was comparable to that of Guinea-Bissau but slightly smaller than Switzerland. Other international comparisons were even more instructive. In 2006 Taiwan was the world's sixteenth largest exporting country; its *per capita* gross domestic product of $16,030 in 2006 was among the top 25 in the world; it had the sixth-best investment climate among 50 major economies in 2007 (according to market research firm Business Environment Risk Intelligence); Taiwan was ranked sixth in growth competitiveness in 2006 and thirteenth in global competitiveness; and its IT industry accounted for over 60 per cent of major IT products in the world.[33] Apart from its weight in the global economy, Taiwan was also a full-blooded democracy. The 2007 World Democracy Audit ranked the island 39th out of 150 countries, just ahead of South Africa. On a scale of 1 (top) to 7, Taiwan scored 1 for civil liberties and 2 for political rights; it fared less well on press freedom and corruption.[34]

To these features we could add the so-called principle of effectiveness, which required that a state should have exclusive control over a territory for a substantial period of time with the intention of governing that territory as the exclusive sovereign. The ROC has since 1949 'served as the only government of the population [of Taiwan] and has acted as a sovereign nation both domestically and internationally', Hamilton argued.[35] Conversely, the communist rulers of the mainland have never exercised any authority over Taiwan.[36] Under customary international law, Shearer concluded, Taiwan was capable of bearing duties and asserting rights – and thus 'a proper candidate for recognition'.[37]

The international law principle of external self-determination has also been invoked by protagonists of Taiwan's statehood. From this perspective the people of the island were entitled to sovereign independence based on 'the distinct territory they have inhabited for a significant period of time, their preferred form of self-governance, and a distinct socioeconomic system and culture that differ in many substantial ways from those of the mainland'.[38] The one-China principle proclaimed by Beijing and endorsed by the world community at large contradicted the notion of external sovereignty for the people of Taiwan. A White Paper of 1993 expressed Beijing's position in uncompromising terms: 'Taiwan's status as an inalienable part of China has been determined and cannot be changed, and "self-determination" for Taiwan is out of the question'.[39]

Another argument used in support of Taiwan's statehood was that of popular sovereignty. China's claim of territorial supremacy, it was said, blatantly disregarded the will of the people of Taiwan. Thanks to its democratization, popular sovereignty prevailed in Taiwan and had to be taken into account when deciding the island's political future. Moreover, modern international law decreed that the expressed wishes of the people affected should be a determining factor in deciding a territorial dispute.[40] Beijing countered with an alternative interpretation of popular sovereignty. A White Paper of 2000, *The One China Principle and the Taiwan Issue*, contended that popular sovereignty extended to the entire population of a state and could therefore not be asserted by sub-national groups to justify their claims to self-determination. On this view the people of Taiwan on their own had no grounds for exercising the right of self-determination. Furthermore, a democratic process confined to Taiwan could not express the political will of the entire Chinese population.[41]

Finally, there was the controversial issue of Beijing's threat to use force against Taiwan if the latter dared to declare independence or even failed to accept unification talks on China's terms. Since it considered Taiwan an integral part of China, but temporarily in rebellion against the mother country, Beijing insisted that like every sovereign state the PRC was entitled to protect its political unity and territorial integrity – through violent means if necessary. One counter-argument has been that a state's territorial rights may not override the principle of self-determination; the people of Taiwan had a right to exercise at least internal self-determination by choosing their own government.[42] Beijing's self-proclaimed right to use force has also been challenged by reference to international law's prohibition on the use of force in international relations (codified in article 2(4) of the UN Charter). The dispute between China and Taiwan was governed by international law, it has furthermore been argued, especially in view of the pronounced international concern over the matter. A related opinion held that contemporary international law would not allow a state to use force to recapture an area it claimed had belonged to its domain a century ago but which had been effectively independent for over 50 years.[43]

Krasner's categories of sovereignty (see Chapter 1) provide a useful analytical tool to understand the problematic international status of the ROC on Taiwan. The government seated in Taipei exercised effective domestic and interdependence sovereignty and also enjoyed Westphalian sovereignty even if it did not claim independent statehood. What Taiwan lacked was international legal sovereignty.[44] The latter deficit is the hallmark of a contested state. So, however strong Taiwan's claims to statehood may be under international law, the fact is that the vast majority of states have decided collectively that it was not entitled to separate statehood – for reasons that have more to do with China's might than with Taiwan's rights. After all, this is essentially a political rather than a legal dispute.

Bilateral and multilateral ties

Taiwan's modest diplomatic network has not been the result of a lack of interest or endeavour on its part. 'Diplomatic relations form the most clear-cut symbol of our country's sovereignty', a recent Taiwan Foreign Policy Report asserted. It stressed that 'having diplomatic relations are absolutely important still' and that Taiwan was 'going to great pains' to maintain such links.[45] Even so, Taiwan enjoyed full diplomatic relations with only 24 states in 2007; 19 of them had embassies in Taipei, whereas Taiwan had resident embassies in all 24. Its diplomatic partners were concentrated in four regions of the Global South: seven in Central and South America, with Nicaragua, Panama and Paraguay the most prominent; five in the Caribbean, including Haiti and St Lucia; six in the Asia-Pacific area, all of them tiny island states including Tuvalu, Kiribati and Nauru (with Fiji and Papua New Guinea having signed communiqués of mutual recognition with Taipei); five in Africa, among them Malawi, Gambia and Burkina Faso; and only one in Europa, namely at the Holy See.[46] Between 2000 and mid-2007 eight states defected from Taiwan to China: Costa Rica, Chad, Senegal, Grenada, Vanuatu, Dominica, Liberia and Macedonia.[47] In an at times farcical game of diplomatic musical chairs some countries switched their recognition back and forth, depending on the political whims of the party in power and the carrots or sticks displayed by the rival suitors in Taipei and Beijing. Among those migrating have been St Lucia and Nauru.[48]

Determined to keep Taiwan's limited diplomatic web intact, President Chen paid official visits to several of his country's foreign allies, including Palau, the Solomon Islands, Marshall Islands, Kiribati, Tuvalu, the Vatican (in 2005, to attend the funeral of Pope John Paul II), Guatemala, Paraguay, Costa Rica, Nicaragua, Panama, El Salvador, Honduras, Belize, the Dominican Republic, St Vincent and the Grenadines, Malawi, Senegal and Swaziland. Several of his counterparts from these countries visited Taiwan. Chen also managed to visit countries not on Taipei's diplomatic roster, including the US, United Arab Emirates and Libya.[49]

Although Taipei has insisted that it had neither the desire nor the capacity to engage in 'cheque book diplomacy' and openly compete with Beijing for diplomatic partners,[50] the ROC's extensive international assistance programmes can hardly be divorced from the need to win or retain friends and keep Beijing at bay. An International Cooperation and Development Fund was created in 1997 to manage all of the ROC's development assistance programmes abroad.[51] One such was known as the Rong Bang project, a special 'co-prosperity' fund of US$250 million launched in 2005 to encourage Taiwanese entrepreneurs to invest in countries maintaining diplomatic ties with Taipei.[52] In Latin America the ROC's bilateral free-trade agreements with Panama, Nicaragua and Guatemala and its trilateral free-trade pact with El Salvador and Honduras were likewise designed to buttress diplomatic links.[53] Reference can also be made to Taiwan's conclusion of information-exchange agreements with several of its diplomatic allies[54] and the conduct of 'knowledge diplomacy' involving international educational and academic exchanges.[55]

Taiwan's provision of humanitarian aid extended beyond its diplomatic partners. Between 1995 and 2004 Taiwan provided about US$180 million in medical assistance to 95 countries, of which only 26 were diplomatic partners.[56] Food and monetary aid and other forms of humanitarian support have in recent years been given to Indonesia, the Philippines and Laos, among others.[57] Local non-governmental organizations in Taiwan have actively cooperated with the ROC government in humanitarian relief efforts abroad. Taiwan Rescue, a private humanitarian relief organization, for instance assisted victims of the 2004 tsunami disaster in Thailand and elsewhere. Another example is the Taiwan Root Medical Peace Corps, which has provided medical care across the world.[58] The Buddhist Compassion Relief Tzu Chi Foundation has undertaken aid projects in more than 60 countries.[59] By 2006 over 30 charitable organizations had partnered the ROC government in providing humanitarian aid overseas.[60]

'People's diplomacy', distinct from exchanges at government level, has been another instrument of ROC foreign policy. Officially portrayed as the involvement of the Taiwanese people 'in cooperative activities with peoples of other countries through transnational or intersocietal networks', the interaction took place through over 2,000 international non-governmental organizations. By launching 'a series of measures' to promote such exchanges, the ROC's Ministry of Foreign Affairs acknowledged that people's diplomacy was indeed complementary to and even a substitute for conventional diplomatic interaction. Another Foreign Affairs initiative has been the appointment of 'ambassadors-at-large' tasked with promoting international links in their respective fields, such as the business world. By 2006 13 of them were already serving Taiwan in this capacity.[61] Finally, Taipei's alternative diplomatic network also contained a network of 17 overseas cultural centres (mostly in the US) run by the Overseas Compatriot Affairs Commission. An official agency, the Commission maintained close links with nearly 5,000 overseas compatriot organizations and assisted in forming Taiwanese chambers of commerce across the world.[62]

In the absence of formal relations, Taipei has managed to maintain an extensive network of semi-official representative (or trade or liaison) offices abroad, with reciprocal representation in Taiwan. In 2007 the ROC was thus represented in 59 countries, including the majority of EU member states, the US, Russia, India, Indonesia, Turkey, Saudi Arabia, Brazil, Mexico, Canada, Australia, Nigeria and South Africa – indeed in most of the prominent economic players at the global and regional levels. Reciprocally, 48 states without diplomatic relations with Taiwan operated representative offices in Taipei in 2007.[63] Taiwan also maintained a pseudo-official arrangement with the PRC. The Straits Exchange Foundation was established in 1991 to deal with issues resulting from Taiwan's growing commercial ties with mainland China. The PRC's counterpart was named the Association for Relations across the Taiwan Strait.[64] Although all the representative offices (including those styled trade and liaison offices, whether in Taipei or abroad) were supposedly unofficial missions, many were staffed by officials seconded from government agencies. These included foreign and trade ministries. Most of the Taiwanese offices abroad performed some typical diplomatic and consular functions.[65]

Considering that it has entered into material relations with some 140 states, it is reasonable to conclude that Taiwan was 'a unique international entity to which substantive, if less than full, recognition is given in a semi-formal manner'.[66] Taiwan has indeed managed to engage in an array of state-like activities despite the absence of general, formal recognition. These include buying heavy weapons abroad, sending its naval vessels on a world cruise, providing development and humanitarian assistance abroad, concluding agreements with states, and participating in the Olympic Games.[67]

At the multilateral level Taiwan has experienced mixed fortunes. One of its greatest diplomatic breakthroughs was to achieve membership of the World Trade Organization, something the ROC had been aspiring to since 1990 when the General Agreement on Tariffs and Trade (GATT, the WTO's predecessor), was still in existence. It joined the WTO in 2002 under the designation 'Separate Customs Territory of Taiwan, Penghu, Kinmen, and Matsu'.[68] We have already noted that the ROC had previously shown a similar flexibility in accepting the name 'Taipei China' in the Asian Development Bank. Another important multilateral institution linking Taiwan to the outside world was the Asia Pacific Economic Cooperation Forum (APEC), created in 1989. Under the name 'Chinese Taipei' the island joined APEC as a member economy in 1991. The 21 participants were referred to as member economies rather than member states to highlight the body's economic focus. Even so APEC provided channels of communication between governments in the Asia-Pacific region, including those of Russia, America, Australia, New Zealand, Brunei and China. The combined economic power of the participants was formidable: they accounted for 60 per cent of global trade and over half the gross domestic product generated worldwide. China has, however, obstructed Taiwan's participation in APEC by preventing its President from attending summits (forcing Taiwan to send economic officials in his stead) and denying the island the opportunity to host high-level APEC meetings.[69]

In addition to the 'Big Three' in its multilateral portfolio, Taiwan managed to secure associate membership or observer status in more than 20 other inter-governmental organizations and their subsidiary bodies. These included the Inter-American Development Bank and the Competition Committee of the Organization for Economic Cooperation and Development (OECD).[70] We can also record Taiwan's participation since 1992 in so-called post-forum discussions of the 16-member Pacific Islands Forum (PIF). Dialogue partners from outside the region were invited to these exchanges held after the PIF's annual summits of heads of government.[71] While less prestigious than membership of the WTO, ADB and APEC, Taiwan's participation in these other organizations – even in lesser capacities than full membership – highlights some alternative modes of multilateral diplomacy available to entities outside the charmed circle of confirmed states.

In the realm of international sport, Taiwan has since 1984 participated in the Olympic Games under the name 'Chinese Taipei'. Taiwan has been using the same name to participate in the quadrennial World Games (dubbed the 'little Olympics') since their inception in 1981. (The eighth World Games in 2009 will be staged in Kaohsiung, Taiwan's second-largest city.)[72]

Its flexibility on the delicate issue of official title has allowed Taiwan to enter international organizations that may otherwise have remained wholly inaccessible. The designations used helped to deny Beijing and others some grounds for opposing Taiwan's membership; the names avoided the sensitivities around the possible existence of two separate Chinese states and assuaged international concerns that Taiwan was bent on separatism. The names moreover implied that the government seated in Taipei supported the eventual unification of the Chinese nation. At the same time the Taiwanese could read some recognition of their distinct identity in the appellations they used in the WTO, ADB and Olympic movement. It has been suggested that Taiwan's WTO membership (as a separate customs territory) could serve as a precedent for its access to the IMF and World Bank.[73]

Readmission to the UN has been the diplomatic prize most coveted by the ROC. On the face of it Taiwan met the formal criteria for membership set out in the UN Charter (article 4): a peace-loving state that accepted the obligations of the Charter and was able and willing to carry out those commitments. Taiwan was moreover a dynamic democracy and its economy was larger than that of 90 per cent of UN member states. As regards sensitivities about two 'Chinas' being members of the world body, we should bear in mind that divided nations have enjoyed parallel representation; consider the cases of East and West Germany and North and South Korea. Instead of deepening the chasm between the two sides of a divided nation, equal representation in the UN could ease tensions between them and promote conditions favourable to (re)unification or at least to the preservation of peace.[74] Against this background a group of Taiwan's diplomatic partners have since 1993 – no doubt at Taipei's instigation – made an annual ritual of proposing to the UN that the ROC be admitted to membership. In 2004, when the twelfth bid was made, an enraged PRC warned that Taiwan's quest for UN membership was 'pushing cross-Strait ties to the brink of danger and seriously threatening peace and stability in the Taiwan Strait and the Asia Pacific Region'.[75] Without resorting to the same inflammatory rhetoric, other states – including the US – joined China in keeping Taiwan's request off the UN agenda. President Chen Shui-bian's direct plea in 2006 for his country's admission to the world body under the name of 'Taiwan' has been equally fruitless.[76] The PRC's position remained inflexible. 'As a region of China, Taiwan is not entitled to apply for UN membership in whatever name', Beijing's UN representative reiterated in September 2007 when the island's fifteenth consecutive bid for participation was thwarted.[77]

Where admission to full membership has proved unattainable, Taiwan considered alternative 'avenues of access'. In such cases the term 'participation' would be more appropriate than 'membership'. Observership in the UN family was one alternative, providing a 'right of participation' and 'access to fora' but not a right to vote. Observer status did not require sovereignty nor did it impute sovereignty. Precedents have been set in providing observer status to North and South Vietnam, East and West Germany, Switzerland and the Holy See, as well as to a wide range of non-state actors (including Palestine, the African Union and the International Committee of the Red Cross). While there are not technical or legal barriers to UN observer status for Taiwan, Beijing has chosen to erect political hurdles. It has, among other things, claimed that the real motive behind the quest for observership was full parallel membership for the PRC and ROC in the UN.[78]

One of the UN's specialized agencies, the World Health Organization (WHO), has also been in the ROC's sights. The country gave up its membership of the WHO after its expulsion from the UN in 1971. Since 1997 Taiwan has campaigned for observer status in the World Health Assembly (WHA), the highest governing body of the WHO. Although the WHA had extended observership to the Palestine Liberation Organization and the Holy See, Taiwan's quest for the same status has been blocked by the PRC. Japan and the US, among others, have supported the ROC's bid.[79]

The Association of South East Asian Nations (ASEAN) has likewise been on Taipei's diplomatic wish-list. Established in 1967, ASEAN presently has ten member states and pursues mainly an economic agenda. Aware that full membership was beyond reach in this regional body that openly supported the 'one-China' principle (but did not have the PRC as member), Taiwan canvassed the idea of a free trade area (FTA) with ASEAN. This was driven by Taipei's concern that the organization's establishment of FTAs with other countries, notably China, could undermine Taiwan's extensive trade and investment links with ASEAN member states. These countries have, however, shied away from any formal affiliation with Taiwan.[80] Given its diplomatic presence in Latin America, it is not surprising that Taiwan has been interested in obtaining permanent observer status in the Organization of American States (OAS) too.[81]

The EU has not seen fit to offer Taiwan the kind of association the country would prefer with its fourth largest trading partner (after China, the US and Japan). Taiwan has been recognized by the EU as an economic and commercial entity and the Union has maintained a European Economic and Trade Office in Taipei since 2003. The EU's one-China policy may be a major reason behind its exclusion of Taiwan from the Asia-Europe Meeting, an institution composed of all EU members, the European Commission and 13 Asian states. The ROC has similarly been kept out of the EU's Generalized System of Preferences. Taiwan has been talking to the EU since 2002 about a free trade area between them, but its formation still eludes Taipei.[82]

Taiwan has not surprisingly been more successful in gaining membership of international forums of which the members are not sovereign states. According to the Ministry of Foreign Affairs, 2,077 international non-governmental organizations had Taiwanese members.[83] Among them was the Unrepresented Nations and Peoples Organization, to which some other contested states also belonged. A very different non-governmental organization was the Pacific Economic Cooperation Council (PECC), which maintained formal ties with ASEAN. Through PECC Taiwan acquired an 'invisible link' with ASEAN,[84] providing another instance of the 'privatization' of the ROC's foreign relations.

The diplomacy of democracy

Taiwan's conversion to democracy has had a major effect on its foreign policy, especially since Chen assumed the presidency in 2000. The 'democracy-based diplomacy' introduced by Chen was on the one hand an exercise in soft power, designed to persuade the community of democracies that Taiwan deserved to enter their ranks.[85] On the other hand Taiwan assumed a missionary role to spread the gospel of democracy beyond its shores. One of the vehicles used was the Taiwan Foundation for Democracy (TFD). Established by the Ministry of Foreign Affairs in 2002, the Foundation was designed to advance the cause of democracy in the region through an Asia Pacific democratic alliance and allow Taiwan to participate in the global democratic network. The TFD has since spawned three subsidiary agencies, namely the World Forum for Democratization in Asia (which coordinated the work of five regional democracy and human rights advocacy networks), the Initiative and Referendum Institute Asia (the first think-tank on direct democracy in Asia), and the Asia Pacific Democracy Resource Centre (a virtual democracy resource agency).[86] In 2005 the Democratic Pacific Union was inaugurated. Although a non-governmental organization, it was initiated by ROC Vice President Lu Hsiu-lien to advance democracy, peace and prosperity in the Pacific Rim. Over 70 representatives from 26 countries participated in the opening meeting of what Lu hoped would develop into a body discharging government-to-government functions.[87] In yet another move to forge semi-official partnerships with foreign democracies, Taiwan in early 2007 hosted a preparatory conference on the establishment of the Global Forum on New Democracies. Former leaders of five countries, including Poland, South Korea and South Africa, participated in the discussion on creating a forum in which newly formed democracies could share their experiences of democratization and so support their further development.[88]

Its thriving democracy has also given the ROC the self-confidence to present itself as a good international citizen. In the wake of the terrorist strikes against the US in September 2001, Taiwan was quick to reaffirm its tacit alliance with America and portray itself as a democratic member of the world community willing and able to join the fight against international terrorism.[89] Democratic Taiwan has also attempted to distance itself from at least some outcast states. In a press statement of 2001 the Government Information Office noted that 'unlike other pariah states, we have managed to develop and modernise our economy, and even to democratize our polity'.[90] President Chen portrayed Taiwan's democracy and economy as the two blades of its 'diplomatic sword' that could be used to open up the country's international space.[91] Vice President Lu in 2007 emphasized Taiwan's sense of 'global responsibility' manifested in its compliance with international norms and its involvement in humanitarian projects abroad.[92] Taiwan's first National Security Report (2006) was written in the same idiom, calling for a 'flexible and pluralistic' diplomatic strategy based on 'democracy, peace, humanitarianism and mutual benefit'.[93] The Ministry of Foreign Affairs conveyed essentially the same message with its notion of 'substantive diplomacy'. At one level Taiwan hoped to become a 'little sun' in the world at large. 'Since we now have the means to give back to the international community, we take it upon ourselves to be a net contributor to the world community'. At another level substantive diplomacy meant that Taipei had to find its diplomatic 'blue ocean', clearly differentiating its foreign policy from that of China. Instead of engaging in direct diplomatic confrontation with the PRC, Taiwan should invest in sustainable relations with its diplomatic allies and the international community generally through comprehensive partnerships. Such a constructive approach, Taipei hoped, would set it apart from what it portrayed as Beijing's selfish and exploitative relations with foreign states and support for obnoxious regimes.[94]

These Taiwanese initiatives amounted to the development of what Madsen aptly depicted as an 'alternative legitimacy' – based on economic liberalism, democratization and international responsibility – to try to improve the ROC's international position.[95] Conversely liberal democratic states were said to have a moral responsibility to support democratic Taiwan, despite its relative lack of formal legal sovereignty.[96] Taiwan's experience should caution against exaggerating the rewards of this approach: China's veto power has remained a formidable deterrent to especially political and diplomatic interaction with Taiwan. Not even the community of democratic states has been willing to treat democratic Taiwan more kindly than before. The ROC's soft power can hardly compete with the hard power at the PRC's command.

Relations with China

In charting Taiwan's domestic and international course, its leaders have had to tread carefully lest they provoked the PRC into a drastic reaction. President Chen was noticeably cautious in his inaugural address in 2000. In what was dubbed a 'peace offensive', Chen went out of his way to soothe Beijing's apprehensions about the newly elected leader. He would honour a series of commitments (the 'five no's') as long as the PRC 'has no intention to use military force against Taiwan': no declaration of Taiwan's independence; no change in the national title (Republic of China); no constitutional revision to provide for 'state-to-state' relations between the ROC and PRC; no referendum to change the *status quo* (meaning Taiwan's international status); and no abolition of the National Unification Council and the National Unification Guidelines. Chen even declared that 'people across the Taiwan Strait share the same ancestral, cultural, and historical background', thereby implying that the Taiwanese were also Chinese – a message dear to Beijing.[97]

Only two years later Chen sounded a different note by insisting that 'Taiwan is not a part of any other country, nor is it a local government or province of another country' [read: China]. The island could never be another Macau or Hong Kong 'because Taiwan has always been a sovereign state'. His logical conclusion was that 'Taiwan and China stand on opposite sides of the Strait, and there is one country on each side'.[98] In like vein Chen proclaimed in 2004 that 'we should be very confident in saying very loudly to the world that Taiwan is an independent, sovereign country. There is no need to be ambiguous'.[99] That same year Taiwan held a referendum in which voters were asked their views about increased defence expenditure and the creation of a 'peace and stability' framework for cross-Strait relations. Because fewer than the required 50 per cent of the electorate bothered to vote, the referendum was declared void.[100] In 2006 Chen, then in his second term as President, suspended the National Unification Council and the Guidelines for National Unification.[101] We have already noted the failed referendums on UN membership staged by Chen in March 2008. With these moves Chen broke the spirit if not the letter of his 'five no's' of 2000. His justification was that the PRC had not removed its threat of a military attack against Taiwan.[102] Chen nonetheless took care not to burn all Taiwan's bridges to a unified China. 'As long as the principle of democracy is honored and Taiwan's 23 million people's free choice is respected', he declared in 2006, 'we will not exclude any possible form cross-strait relations may take in the future'.[103]

The prospects for narrowing the divide between Taiwan and China have improved since the KMT's return to office in early 2008. In his inaugural speech[104] President Ma Ying-jeou struck a conciliatory tone and pledged better relations with China. He promised to maintain the *status quo* in the Taiwan Strait, based on the principles of 'no unification, no independence and no use of force'. This meant that Taiwan would no longer – as under Chen – challenge the *status quo* by pushing for the independence of Taiwan, and would expect the PRC to at least tolerate the island's *de facto* statehood and also renounce the use of violence against Taiwan. At the same time Ma wished to see a resumption of negotiations between Taipei and Beijing 'at the earliest time possible'. This, he said, should be conducted within the framework of the 1992 consensus on 'one China, different interpretations'. Ma was clearly not prepared to embrace Beijing's interpretation that the one China was the PRC, of which Taiwan was an integral part. Still President Ma spoke hopefully of reaching a 'win-win solution', with the normalization of economic and cultural relations the first-step. He approvingly cited his PRC counterpart Hu Jintao's call in April 2008 for 'building mutual trust, shelving controversies, finding commonalities despite differences, and creating together a win-win solution' across the Taiwan Strait. 'His views are very much in line with our own', Ma observed.

The new President at the same time reaffirmed some familiar Taiwanese markers for amicable cross-Strait relations. Ma was determined to enter into consultations with the mainland 'over Taiwan's international space and a possible cross-Strait peace accord'. He was adamant that 'Taiwan doesn't just want security and prosperity. It wants dignity'. Cross-Strait relations could only advance 'when Taiwan is no longer being isolated in the international arena', Ma added. Yet having demanded for Taiwan the attributes of statehood on the world stage, Ma maintained that what mattered in resolving cross-Strait relations 'is not sovereignty but core values and way of life'. These he identified as freedom, democracy and prosperity. If China continued to move in this direction, Ma argued, it would pave the way for 'the long-term peaceful development' of cross-Strait relations. The latter sentiments, dear to the Taiwanese, could not have warmed the hearts of the PRC leadership.

Still, signs of a thaw in cross-Strait relations were soon evident. Following direct talks between the two sides, the first weekly charter flights between China and Taiwan began in July 2008. The new air link could enable up to 12,000 mainland tourists to visit the island every weekend.[105] For Ma this was only the first step: he soon called for regular passenger flights and direct air and sea cargo links across the Taiwan Strait, and for a rapid expansion in economic relations. Adopting a functionalist approach, Ma argued for 'economic normalization' between Taiwan and China before tackling the more sensitive issues of Taiwan's international space and the conclusion of a peace accord.[106] The political and security questions, rather than economic ties, will be the real test for relations between Ma's Taiwan and communist China.

Harsh veto state *versus* hesitant patron state

In our discussion of Taiwan's problematic international status and hence its troubled foreign relations, Beijing's veto power loomed large. The broad parameters within which this power was exercised were encapsulated in the PRC's so-called three no's policy: no support for Taiwan's independence; no support for 'two Chinas' or 'one China, one Taiwan', and no support for Taiwan's membership of international organizations based on statehood.[107] What motivated China's 'obduracy in trying to block Taiwan from international forums'? Beijing has expressed concern that the island 'is out to "internationalize" its division with the mainland as a first step toward cutting off its legal umbilical cord from [the concept of] China'. Hence the PRC's extreme sensitivity (if not paranoia) that Taiwan's participation in state-related activities would confer sovereignty on the island outside the one-China context. A related worry of Beijing's has been that unfettered Taiwanese participation in international forums would reinforce Taipei's intransigence in refusing to enter into a serious dialogue with the PRC on a peaceful end to their political division.[108] To restrict Taiwan's international room for manoeuvre, China has vetoed its membership of the UN and WHO, among others; limited Taiwan's participation in the likes of APEC; and pressurized (or simply bribed or blackmailed) other states into breaking, curtailing or avoiding ties with the ROC. At the same time the PRC's obstructionist tactics were designed to isolate Taiwan internationally and so coerce it into submitting to the mainland's formula for unification. Beijing could be extraordinarily mean-spirited in its vendetta against Taiwan. It prevented the island from receiving emergency medical assistance from abroad during the devastating earthquake of 1999 and the 2003 SARS (Severe Acute Respiratory Syndrome) crisis.[109] Conversely China blocked the UN from accepting financial aid offered by Taiwan to assist Rwandan refugees and the Turkish Kurds in the aftermath of the invasion of Iraq.[110] It is instructive that Beijing's isolation offensive focused on Taiwan's formal involvement in interstate relations rather than on harming its economy; China after all benefited handsomely from Taiwan's economic strength.[111]

The PRC's veto power over Taiwan has been exercised in other ways too. The missile tests China conducted in 1995–6 and its deployment of hundreds of missiles aimed at Taiwan were designed to deter and intimidate.[112] Another was the PRC's long-standing threat to use force against Taiwan if it opted for independence. In a 1993 White Paper, *The Taiwan Question and the Reunification of China*, Beijing declared that 'peaceful reunification' was its aim but that it was 'entitled to use any means necessary, including the use of military force, to protect its sovereignty and territorial integrity'.[113] One of the bluntest warnings came from China's Defence Minister in 2004: the People's Liberation Army, he said, 'has the determination and ability to resolutely smash any Taiwan independence separatist plot'.[114] The PRC's anti-separation law of 2005 – condemned by the US and Japan – reaffirmed its right to apply 'non-peaceful means' against Taiwan if efforts to effect peaceful unification were 'completely exhausted'.[115] The measure thus gave Beijing the legal pretext for a unilateral and forcible change of the *status quo* in the Taiwan Strait.[116] China was evidently convinced that renouncing the use of force would remove a vital deterrent to Taiwan embarking on a determined move towards independence. The right and ability to apply force over its own territory was for the PRC – as for states generally – an essential attribute of sovereignty. Beijing after all insisted that Taiwan was a renegade province of China and subject to its laws.[117] China also derived veto power from its enormous economic clout. No Asian or European government would recognize's Taiwan's independence, Singapore's Prime Minister Goh Chok Tong said in 2004. 'To do so would earn China's permanent enmity. And China is the economic story of this century'.[118]

A paradoxical feature of cross-Strait relations was Taiwan's close ties with its veto state. In tandem with the start of political liberalization in the late 1980s, the ROC adopted a more open policy towards the mainland. Cross-Strait economic, cultural, educational and people-to-people exchanges expanded dramatically. Between 1988 and 2005 Taiwanese citizens paid over 40 million visits to China, while the reverse flow recorded 1.75 million visits to Taiwan. With their two-way trade exceeding US$116 billion in

2006, China (including Hong Kong and Macau) was Taiwan's biggest trading partner by accounting for 27.2 per cent of the island's total trade (followed by Japan and the US). About 40 per cent of Taiwan's exports flowed to China, while the latter was Taiwan's second-largest source of imports. Conservative estimates put Taiwanese investment in China at over $100 billion, making the PRC the principal destination for ROC investment abroad. In addition over one million people from Taiwan lived and worked in China in 2007.[119] There has also been interaction at the humanitarian level, when Taiwan sent rescue teams and emergency relief to China after the devastating earthquake in Sichuan province in May 2008.[120] Given its scope, Taiwan's social and economic interaction with its veto state is unique among contested countries.

Growing ties across the Taiwan Strait do not mean that Beijing has abandoned its demand for unification (the PRC and ROC cannot 'reunify' if they had not formed part of the same state) in favour of spontaneous integration driven by social and economic forces. In fact, the PRC's communist rulers remain obsessed with unification on their terms. Why? Considerations of prestige and national honour feature prominently. For Beijing unification between the mainland and Taiwan was 'essential to China's recovery from a century of national weakness, vulnerability, and humiliation, and to its emergence as a respected great power'. Another explanation was that the PRC feared that an independent Taiwan could set a dangerous precedent for other potentially secession-inclined regions of the country, like Tibet, Inner Mongolia and Xinjiang.[121]

While there is no doubt that China has been Taiwan's veto state, the US cannot by contrast be designated as the ROC's unqualified patron state. Their bilateral relationship since 1949 has been too complex for such a clear-cut categorization. On the one hand 'US economic, military and political ties with Taiwan remain robust', Hickey wrote in 2006.[122] Their economic links were extensive, encompassing trade, joint-venture partnerships and technology transfers, among other exchanges. The US has furthermore honoured its security commitments to the ROC under the 1979 Taiwan Relations Act. In 2001, for instance, President George W Bush affirmed that America had an obligation to defend Taiwan if attacked by China – and would do whatever it took to back the island in such a contingency.[123] Politically Washington supported Taiwan's bid for membership of the World Health Organization. More importantly, the US acted as a self-appointed guarantor of the *status quo* in the Taiwan Strait, pressuring both sides not to undertake risky unilateral actions that could jeopardize peace and stability in the area. On the other hand America stood firmly by its commitment to a one-China policy and a rejection of Taiwan's claims to sovereignty and independence. For the latter reason Washington has opposed Taipei's quest for UN membership. So while the US has been complicit in keeping Taiwan in the position of a contested state, the superpower has at the same time been trying to constrain the PRC in bullying Taiwan.

What future for Taiwan?

As with our other case studies, we end the discussion of Taiwan by considering alternative futures for the territory. It is fair to say that the *status quo* across the Strait was fraught with the danger of serious conflict because the PRC remained deeply dissatisfied with the prevailing state of affairs, which was also far from ideal for Taiwan. As Wachman put it, cross-Strait relations were marked by a 'worrisome volatility', prompting a fear 'that the slightest diplomatic misstep by Taipei or a miscalculation in Beijing might lead to war' that could escalate to hostilities 'of the worst magnitude'.[124] There were, however, powerful countervailing factors promoting a continuation of the present situation. Repeated opinion polls in Taiwan have shown conclusively that the vast majority of its people preferred the *status quo* to either unification on Beijing's terms or independence for the island.[125] It may be a case of 'rather the devil you know than the devil you don't', but the nearly 60-year stand-off across the Taiwan Strait has cultivated mutual restraint and a remarkable degree of stability. This climate has been conducive to increasing interdependence and shared prosperity. There are risks involved for Taiwan, though: economic dependence on China could leave it vulnerable to political pressure from Beijing. The Democratic Progressive Party was quick to warn President Ma that his economic initiatives with China could increase this very danger.[126]

Despite its sometimes strident rhetoric, Beijing also faced constraints in dealing with its wayward 'province'. In the run-up to the 2008 Olympic Games on its soil, the PRC was extremely reluctant to offend world opinion through some rash action against Taiwan. The international outcry over Beijing's clampdown on protestors in Tibet in March 2008 may have served as a salutary lesson. Over time China has probably also realized that turning the screws on Taiwan tended to be counter-productive by stimulating separatist sentiments there. Another major factor in the equation was the US, a vociferous opponent of unilateral conflict-inducing actions on either side of the Chinese divide.[127]

Since the *status quo* was a default option tolerated in the absence of a mutually acceptable alternative, we need to explore various formulas that have been proposed for a lasting settlement of the conflict between China and Taiwan. An extremely risky alternative would be for the island to declare itself independent as the Republic of Taiwan. This was the so-called two-state model championed by the advocates of Taiwan's sovereign statehood. While this may have been the preferred option for elements in the then ruling DPP, Beijing would have put up fierce resistance – even to the extent of exercising its self-proclaimed right to use force to prevent the permanent separation of Taiwan from the mainland. Taiwan (or the ROC) could theoretically become a *de jure* state under international law if the world community made a collective commitment to protect the island in the event of a formal proclamation of statehood.[128] Such an undertaking was inconceivable in practice.

Under an 'EU model', mainland China and Taiwan would join a confederal system as 'two coequal sovereign entities'. To live up to EU standards the two component units would have to dismantle customs, immigration, travel and communications barriers, adopt a common currency and renounce the use of force in their bilateral relations. Although an EU formula would involve a pooling of sovereignty, Beijing was bound to object to any notion of coequal sovereignty between the PRC and Taiwan.[129]

The principal alternative not involving international legal sovereignty was of course that of unifying the two sides of the Taiwan Strait. This has all along been the PRC's demand and the option previously favoured by the KMT. The two sides have, however, consistently been at loggerheads over the form of unification and the route to that destination.

Beijing's sole formula for unification has for decades been that of 'one country, two systems'. The 'one country' or 'one China' touted by Beijing was naturally the PRC; the ROC would cease to exist. In 1973 the PRC's communist leadership promised that if the KMT facilitated unification, Taiwan would become an autonomous region of China. Its special privileges would include managing its internal affairs; maintaining distinct legal, economic and military systems; and retaining such symbols of sovereignty as the ROC's national flag. Reiterating this arrangement in 1979, Beijing added an assurance to the KMT that it could remain as the government of Taiwan for a long time to come – provided it accepted the sovereignty of the PRC.[130] In 1981 China couched its unification scheme in terms of an autonomous 'special administrative region' that would afford Taiwan essentially the same rights as envisaged in 1973 plus participation in China's central government. The latter would not interfere in Taiwan's local affairs either. This kind of arrangement was incorporated into the 1984 Sino-British Joint Declaration on Hong Kong and the Basic Law of the Hong Kong Special Administrative Region.[131] In subsequent statements Chinese leaders like Deng Xiaoping, Jiang Zemin and Hu Jintao elaborated on the features of the one country, two systems model. It would *inter alia* allow the mainland to practice a socialist system while Hong Kong and Taiwan upheld a capitalist economic order; Taiwan as a special administrative region of China would exercise a high degree of autonomy, enjoy legislative and independent judicial power including that of final adjudication, retain its armed forces and administer its own party, government and military systems; Beijing would not station troops or administrative personnel on the island; and Taiwan would gain even more room than presently to participate in external exchanges.[132] Finally, Beijing's established position was that Taiwan had to accept the one-China principle as a precondition for cross-Strait negotiations on final status. Should Taiwan reject this principle in word or deed, the PRC reserved the right to employ force against the island.[133]

The ROC's National Unification Guidelines of 1991 contained an unequivocal commitment to unification: 'Both the mainland and Taiwan areas are parts of Chinese territory. Helping to bring about national unification should be the common responsibility of all Chinese people'.[134] There the consensus between the two sides ended. Taiwan's blueprint set out a process of peaceful unification that would join the two entities 'under a system of governance that will guarantee democracy, freedom, and an equal opportunity for all to pursue economic prosperity', in the words of an ROC leader.[135] An ROC White Paper of 1994 reaffirmed that unification would lead to the creation of a new Chinese state based on democratic governance and human rights combined with the economic strength of a united China.[136] In Taipei's view a united China would thus have to be a post-communist China. In 2004 President Chen said that one China did not exist at the time but may become a reality in future – but only through negotiations between Taipei and Beijing.[137] Taiwan insisted that talks on unification had to be conducted between equal political entities, not between a central government and a subordinate administrative province.[138] This may well be the position taken by President Ma too.

Taiwan's main political parties have for years rejected Beijing's interpretation of the one-China formula as a zero-sum option and public opinion on the island was also vehemently opposed to Beijing's plans for Taiwan.[139] One objection was that a special administrative region would exist at the pleasure of the central authorities; Taiwan would be at the mercy of Beijing, which moreover had the advantage of preponderant force. Another criticism was that the one-China system was merely transitional, created for the purpose of national unification. Once that goal had been achieved, the rationale for maintaining the arrangement would fall away. It would furthermore appear that Beijing's support for Taiwan's autonomous status stopped far short of regarding it as an enforceable international standard.[140] This meant that autonomy for Taiwan would be a purely domestic matter, leaving the entity entirely dependent on Beijing's benevolence. Finally, Hong Kong's experience as a special administrative region has not inspired confidence in Taiwan; the former British territory has been subjected to various forms of interference from Beijing. Taiwanese also made the point that Hong Kong had never enjoyed the domestic sovereignty long exercised by Taiwan.[141]

Given these fundamental objections from Taiwan, it has been suggested that Beijing should do three things to create a climate conducive to cross-Strait talks: drop its insistence that Taiwan accept the one country, two systems formula as a precondition for negotiations; cease its hostile attitude towards Taiwan, which only hardened feelings against the mainland; and make itself more attractive to the people of Taiwan, who were deterred by the authoritarian and corrupt nature of the communist regime.[142] On the Taiwanese side the prospects for constructive talks with China have improved with the advent of President Ma and a KMT government in 2008. Whether the KMT would be prepared to support unification with an undemocratic China is doubtful, though; the Nationalists too may well insist that a unified China has to be a post-communist state. Even then Taiwan may still claim internal self-determination *à la* territorial autonomy to preserve its particular identity in a larger China.[143]

Conclusion

Being the miniscule left-over of a political order overthrown in China's revolution of 1949, Taiwan's separate political existence and assertions of statehood have been an ongoing affront to the PRC. Obsessed with unifying China, the communist rulers in Beijing have all along tried to cajole and coerce Taiwan into the fold. The PRC has exercised its veto power by keeping Taiwan in diplomatic isolation and threatening to use force if the island dared to declare formal independence. Against heavy odds Taiwan has managed to retain diplomatic links with two dozen states, all of which of course also granted it *de jure* recognition. In addition Taiwan has held on to membership of a few inter-governmental organizations. However modest, these are unusual achievements among contested states.

To enlarge its international space, Taiwan has been ingenious in developing an elaborate network of reciprocal semi-formal representation with virtually all major countries. The ROC has indeed become the world's foremost exponent of such alternative forms of routine inter-state exchanges. Another characteristic that set Taiwan apart from other contested states was its extensive economic ties with its veto state, China, despite their political alienation. The strength of Taiwan's empirical statehood, especially in economic terms, was a further distinguishing feature. Taiwan's establishment of an exemplary democracy should also be recorded.

Despite all these qualities, Taiwan is singularly unlikely to graduate to confirmed statehood. For at least as long as the PRC remained under authoritarian communist rule, Beijing would veto any chance of separate Taiwanese statehood. Should China democratize, the prospects for unification (probably on similar lines as Hong Kong) would improve greatly. For the foreseeable future, though, Taiwan is destined to survive and even thrive at the fringes of the international community.

Conclusion

The life and times of 'states' lacking in conventional international recognition do not arouse much interest among scholars and other observers of world politics. There are far more pressing international issues capturing academic and media attention. Yet the pretender states consigned to the borderland of the world community have an external influence disproportionate to their limited numbers and the smallness of their populations, territories and economies. Much of their influence is negative, the result of the conflict surrounding the origins, ongoing existence and ultimate political destination of today's wannabe states. These unsettled situations are not confined to regional backwaters; one of today's problem areas, Cyprus, is located within the EU's borders. Nor is this a current problem only. Presumptive states denied formal international recognition had existed through much of the 20th century – typically in conditions of grave conflict – and more may emerge in future. These are reasons enough for students of international relations and policy-makers to take contested states seriously.

Our inquiry focused on ten such entities: Abkhazia, South Ossetia, Transdniestria, Nagorno Karabagh, Kosovo, Somaliland, Palestine, Northern Cyprus, Western Sahara and Taiwan. We made passing reference to several earlier cases, namely Manchukuo, Croatia, Katanga, Rhodesia, Biafra, South Africa's four homeland states (Transkei, Bophuthatswana, Venda and Ciskei), Bangladesh, Eritrea, East Timor and Chechnya. Altogether 23 contested states encountered over a period of 80 years thus featured in the present study.

Even if they acknowledged that contested states could undermine peace, security and stability in various regions, some scholars would still ask whether it really mattered – in a globalized world – if a dozen or so entities failed to achieve international recognition of their purported statehood and were compelled to exist as something less than full-fledged states? Are these putative states actually disadvantaged by their indeterminate status? After all, states are losing much of their traditional central authority through the processes of fusion from above and fission from below. Upwards states are pooling sovereignty through multilateral institutions and surrendering some of their autonomy to inter-state bodies with supranational features. Downwards they are devolving authority to sub-national regions and groupings in their midst, which demand the right to take care of their particular interests and to gain independent access to the international arena.

However, the mere existence of contested states speaks to the ongoing allure of separate statehood for communities across the world. While some state founders may have exaggerated expectations of the modern state's ability to provide public goods, collectively recognized statehood still has both symbolic and substantive benefits for the rulers, if not the inhabitants generally. For one thing, global and regional forums where matters of high politics are decided are the preserve of full-blown states. Another consideration is that the development assistance offered by international financial institutions is mostly reserved for standing members of the community of states. Confirmed states jealously protect their community against gatecrashers and imposters, thus barring contested states from this sanctum and the benefits it affords its members.

Our analytical framework was designed to investigate three phases in the life cycle of contested states: why they emerge, how they behave and others deal with them, and where they may be heading to.

Contested states are, then, entities whose claims to statehood are challenged by the world community. The dispute usually concerns the presumptive state's very right of separate statehood or, where that is conceded, the translation of the right into empirical statehood. Either way, contested states lack the birth certificate of 'real' statehood: admission to UN membership. This does not mean that the recognition deficit is identical for all contested states. We identified six different levels of recognition in Chapter 1, from what was called titular recognition – the wide recognition of an entity's title to statehood – to zero recognition.

Contested states are the logical opposites of confirmed states, which enjoy conventional international recognition and hence full membership of the UN. It is to confirmed statehood, the normal international status, that contested states aspire. But because their statehood is internationally contested, the pretenders have been condemned to life in limbo. Again, allowance must be made for variation in the degree of isolation experienced by the unwanted entities. No contested state is entirely isolated from the outside world; they all engage in exchanges with existing states in such fields as trade, transport and communication. Diplomatic contact for the sake of resolving conflicts between original and contested states are common. These interactions constitute a measure of *de facto* recognition of the entities' self-proclaimed statehood.

In Chapter 2 we established that secession is the single most common origin of today's contested states. It applied to Nagorno Karabagh, South Ossetia, Transdniestria, Abkhazia and Kosovo. Somaliland owed its existence to a combination of secession and reversion (to its former status of sovereign statehood). Secessionist drives are typically motivated by an ethnic minority's desire to free themselves of previous, present or potential political repression, socio-economic deprivation, cultural discrimination, or even extermination at the hands of the majority group(s) in control of the central state. In both international law and the practices of states there is however a strong presumption against secession because of its unilateral, state-shattering nature. Secession flies in the face of the principle of territorial integrity enshrined in international law and sanctified in the practices of states. Since secession by definition occurs against the wishes of the central state, it is usually accompanied by violence between the two sides. Even if the break-away attempt cannot be stopped, the original state will as a rule try to prevent its illegitimate offspring gaining international recognition and joining the community of confirmed states. In this capacity the original state can exercise veto power over the aspirant's status ambitions. Where the original-*cum*-veto state relies heavily on a single foreign country in its campaign to cabin and confine the wannabe state, that backer can be designated as an external veto state; the original state is then the internal veto state. Contested states may in turn also have foreign backers or patron states providing vital economic, military and diplomatic support.

Secession is not the only origin of contested statehood. Foreign aggression and occupation, racial discrimination and a denial of self-determination – all transgressions under international law – have also played a role in creating contemporary contested states. In these instances the international community collectively refused to recognize the products of illegal acts, hence condemning the putative states to the periphery of international existence. This left the contested states dependent on their creator or patron states for economic survival and security. The Turkish Republic of Northern Cyprus is a case in point, but there is also an element of secession in its origins. (Manchukuo, Croatia and South Africa's four so-called Bantustans are earlier examples.) Western Sahara and Palestine do not fit into any of the categories mentioned. Their respective rights of statehood have been widely recognized and both declared themselves unilaterally independent, but they have been unable to translate this right into political reality. Taiwan's contested statehood reveals unique origins: it is the last remnant of a Chinese regime that had been overthrown in a communist revolution 60 years ago.

In practice the secessionist route to statehood has seldom led to generally recognized sovereign independence, however strong the political and moral justifications for a unilateral break-away may be. The same goes for pretender states conceived and born in the other sins mentioned. Once consigned to contested statehood, entities rarely graduate to confirmed statehood. Contested statehood is therefore not an antechamber to confirmed statehood or a finishing school for states-in-waiting.

In the second phase in the life cycle of contested states, our analytical framework highlighted international responses to these entities, and the latter's ways of dealing with external adversity. One end on a spectrum of possible external reactions features military intervention on the side of the original state to nip secession in the bud. At the other end we find collective *de jure* recognition of an aspirant state. Between the two extremes, foreign actors can choose among isolation, indifference and engagement. Isolation is widely practised, considering that collective non-recognition – the ultimate form of diplomatic ostracism – is a feature of contested states. Diplomatic isolation can be supplemented by economic, socio-cultural and military isolation, all in a bid to keep the putative state out of the community of confirmed states. Isolation can, paradoxically, be combined with engagement. An example is diplomatic initiatives undertaken by the UN and EU to resolve conflicts between contested states and their original countries, even though these organizations refuse to recognize the statehood of the claimants. Foreign indifference is probably the most common external response, adopted by the majority of states that have little if any direct interest in the fate of contested states. This is not be mistaken for neutrality, though; the world community at large rejects most contested states' very right of statehood.

Condemned to a netherworld, contested states are typically excluded from conventional bilateral diplomatic relations and from multilateral diplomacy. To overcome such handicaps, virtually all of them have developed alternative, semi-official links with confirmed states. These take the form of representative or liaison or trade offices abroad and reciprocal representation from foreign countries. We should add that government representatives from contested states manage to travel abroad on official business, even on the passports of their non-recognized countries. But while no contested state is totally isolated, either diplomatically or economically, none experiences a satisfactory level of involvement in inter-state exchanges; their lack of collective recognition severely circumscribes their international space. As a consequence their economies suffer from external political restrictions on the free flow of trade, technology and capital, and they are usually also denied free access to major national and international aid donors. These deprivations in turn compromise the ability of the mostly small and poorly developed contested states to undertake the dual tasks of state- and nation-building, that is, creating and maintaining the institutions and processes of modern governance on the one hand and on the other fostering a sense of national identity and loyalty among a population that may still contain diverse and antagonistic groups.

The final phase in the life cycle of contested states deals with exit possibilities, which takes us into the risky realm of policy proposals. Our point of departure is that contested statehood is an unnatural status that cannot indefinitely satisfy any of the main parties involved. Contested states are frustrated at having their claims to statehood denied and being relegated to a twilight zone. For the original states the mere existence of contested states tore out of their bodies politic is an affront. The broader world community has no real sympathy for the small group of pretenders trying to squeeze into the community of confirmed states. True, elites in contested states and their associated patron and even veto states may reap material benefits from the *status quo*, especially through the black market with its opportunities for smuggling anything from consumer goods to drugs, weapons and people. Such narrowly based opportunistic advantages cannot offset the diplomatic, economic and security costs borne by the various parties.

A few of today's contested states have a chance of advancing to higher honours. Of our ten case studies, Palestine and Western Sahara have long enjoyed titular recognition, meaning their right of statehood has been recognized internationally (Palestine's by the UN and Western Sahara's by the OAU/AU). Although both face formidable practical obstacles in realizing this right, not least of which is foreign occupation by Israel and Morocco respectively, Palestine and Western Sahara already have international endorsement of their claims to statehood. To overcome the resistance of their respective veto states, both may have to settle for an internationally supervised transition to conditional independence. The first element involves an externally managed process of preparation for independence (through the UN, perhaps with the support of regional organizations) culminating in internationally recognized statehood with strings attached. Those conditions, which could be enshrined in the entities' constitutions and in international agreements, would typically relate to matters such as the maintenance of a democratic order based on respect for individual human rights and minority rights; acknowledgment of existing borders; renunciation of merging with any other state; peaceful resolution of international disputes; opposition to international terrorism, and a commitment to the eradication of weapons of mass destruction. External parties could underwrite and even guarantee the observance of these conditions. Namibia, East Timor and Kosovo are recent cases of internationally supervised transitions to independence, while Austria, Cyprus and several former Yugoslav republics are examples of conditional independence. Kosovo, despite having 'seized' independence while still under international trusteeship, is well on its way to generally recognized conditional independence.

Turning to secessionist entities among contemporary contested states, they deserve a more nuanced international response than the reflexive denunciation of secession as an illegal and illegitimate act. The world community should first establish the reasons why a group or region is driven to the drastic step of breaking away from an existing state. Intolerable conditions created by the rulers of a central state may well force a disaffected community to hive off. These could range from political persecution and socio-economic discrimination to acts of ethnic cleansing and genocide. Before a secessionist group can be expected to return to the fold, the UN or regional organizations may need to help reform the political system of the original state to make it safe and attractive for the prodigal group. In other words, the 'push' factors that prompted a secessionist bid should to be addressed before reunification can take place.

This brings us to the wide range of intra-state alternatives to contested statehood recorded in Chapter 3. While they fall short of separatists' cherished ideal of full-fledged statehood, these options allow for the accommodation of ethnic or group diversity and indeed ethnic nationalism, and could – if freely chosen by the people involved – constitute legitimate, internationally recognized expressions of self-determination. Our inventory included federalism, other forms of territorial and communal autonomy, consociational democracy and multiculturalism. All these are compromise options: the separatists do not get their coveted sovereign state, but the original state cannot merely revert to the old order either.

Although the list of intra-state alternatives is varied enough to prevent a one-size-fits-all approach, the most viable compromise formula for resolving conflicts over contested statehood may be dual-level autonomy. By this is meant self-government, probably territorially based, for the former contested state within its original state, coupled with considerable international freedom of action. The internal element of autonomy is designed to safeguard the group interests of the erstwhile secessionist community and can best be ensured in a democratic political order. Democracies seem less likely to spawn secession than authoritarian systems violating human rights. Regional or group autonomy should be a price that an original state would be willing to pay to restore its territorial integrity. The external component of autonomy would allow the former contested state to maintain a circumscribed but state-like international presence in deference to its earlier 'statehood'. The latter role conforms to a global trend that sees an increasing number of nationalities, religious communities, diasporas and other groups joining states as legitimate actors on the world stage. To reassure apprehensive groups reintegrating with their original countries, autonomy deals may need to be guaranteed by foreign powers or multilateral bodies (as had been done with Cyprus in 1959). Although its democratic qualities are questionable, the so-called Hong Kong option embodies internal and external dimensions of autonomy. Taiwan, although not a secessionist entity, is an obvious candidate for a dual-autonomy arrangement as final status. This formula could also be appropriate for the four Eurasian contested states, Northern Cyprus and perhaps Somaliland. In the latter case Somalia would of course first have to undergo thorough state-rebuilding.

Where exhaustive efforts at state-remaking have manifestly failed to create the conditions necessary for the safe return of a break-away entity, a more radical alternative presents itself. Outside actors could then assist the presumptive state in acquiring confirmed statehood on the grounds that reunification would expose the alienated community to existential danger. Here too an internationally supervised transition to qualified independence may be advisable. Conditional statehood could resemble some of the inter-state options outlined in Chapter 3, such as a confederation and free association. Conditional statehood is another conceivable alternative for Somaliland. An altogether different and extreme remedy for secessionist statehood would be territorial right-sizing, in which a contested entity could for instance be incorporated into its patron or kin state by redrawing international boundaries. This would have happened if Kosovo were absorbed into Albania or Northern Cyprus into Turkey; neither outcome is likely, however.

When dealing with existing contested states, the alternative formulas mentioned would serve remedial purposes. We should also regard the list of options as possible preventive measures that could be explored by states confronted with secessionist revolts. Again the alternatives could be either inter- or intra-state in nature, ranging from territorial right-sizing through transnational economic zones and cultural domains to multiculturalism and minority rights. Although few states may favour it, the constitutional provision of exit mechanisms offers a way of dealing with secessionist pressures and avoiding the emergence of a contested state. These, as we saw in Chapter 2, would make state fragmentation difficult but not impossible. It would happen by consent and hence in a reasonably amicable and orderly fashion – a mutually agreed partition (as in Czechoslovakia) as opposed to heavily contested unilateral secession. Such a parting of the ways could also be effected under international supervision.

There is clearly an array of compromise options offering practical alternatives to the *status quo* of contested statehood, a return to the *status quo ante* (anathema to the contested entity) and conventional international recognition of the contested state (unacceptable to the original state). Identifying the alternatives is not merely an academic exercise. The conflicts surrounding all of today's contested states, even if temporarily 'frozen', compel us to explore alternatives to the *status quo*. This has also been the rationale behind the settlement initiatives that have been undertaken in all the cases considered in our study. Many of the proposals we have just outlined closely resemble the options put forward by intermediaries and other parties involved in these settlement endeavours.

Implementing alternative arrangements is admittedly a tall order. The relative durability of contested states indicates how difficult it is to resolve the underlying conflicts. Apart from a seemingly appropriate political formula, a successful settlement could depend on a host of other variables too. One is an acknowledgment by all parties involved that the costs of the *status quo* outweigh the risks of a settlement. Another variable, difficult to foresee, is changes of government and policy in the states most closely involved, specifically the contested and original states. It is precisely such changes that have given new momentum to the search for solutions in Cyprus and Taiwan.

Changes in the power relationship between a contested and original state constitute a further variable also hard to predict. Take the case of Somaliland and Somalia: as long as the latter remains in a state of collapse, Somaliland faces only mild external pressure for reunification. Should Somalia put its house in order, however, it could drastically change the distribution of power between the two. Not only will Somalia become far more assertive in demanding the return of Somaliland, but it may also appear administratively capable of reabsorbing Somaliland and militarily able to force the issue. Conversely, a marked weakening in the power of an original state, be it Somalia or any other, may improve a contested offspring's chances of survival over the short term at least – but without necessarily offering it a way out of contested statehood.

We conclude with a table highlighting a set of features of the ten contested states examined in Part II. We begin with the birth dates of the entities, followed by their origins or routes to contested statehood. Patron states are recorded next, but it will be noted that not all contested states have such foreign backers. Nor do they all have an original state from which they had broken away. In most instances, as the following column indicates, there is an original state that also acts as veto state obstructing its contested offspring's claims to statehood. In the absence of an original state, the role of veto state is assumed by an adjacent state with which the entity has historical ties. The recognition level, next, underlines the fact that the recognition deficit is not the same for all contested states. Following their *de jure* recognition by Russia, South Ossetia and Abkhazia fall into more than one category. The final column suggests conceivable compromise options for the ten contested states. We thus omit the 'extreme' alternatives of unconditional international recognition on the one hand and a restoration of the old (pre-contested state) order on the other. The *status quo* is likewise disregarded. In the very nature of a compromise, neither the contested state nor its original state achieves its first prize. As a result of such settlements the current clutch of contested states will of course disappear. That, however, may not spell the end of contested statehood as a problem in world politics.

Contested state	Birth date	Origin	Patron state	Original (veto) state	Recognition level	Conceivable compromise formula
Abkhazia	1999	Secession	Russia	Georgia	Peer & patron	Dual autonomy
South Ossetia	1992	Secession	Russia	Georgia	Peer & patron	Dual autonomy
Nagorno Karabagh	1992	Secession	Armenia	Azerbaijan	Peer	Dual autonomy
Transdniestria	1991	Secession	Russia	Moldova	Peer	Dual autonomy
Kosovo	1991	Secession	–	Serbia	Partial	Conditional independence
Somaliland	1991	Reversion & secession	–	Somalia	Zero	Conditional independence
Palestine	1988	Self-proclaimed independence	–	Israel (veto)	Titular	Conditional independence
Northern Cyprus	1983	Aggression, occupation & secession	Turkey	Republic of Cyprus	Patron	Dual autonomy
Western Sahara	1976	Self-decolonization	Algeria	Morocco (veto)	Titular	Conditional independence
Taiwan	1949	Revolution	–	China (veto)	Partial	Dual autonomy

Notes

Introduction

1 *Time*, 24 April 2006.
2 Macmillan, Johannesburg/St. Martin's, New York, 1984.
3 Cambridge University Press, Cambridge, 1990.
4 Macmillan, Houndmills, 1998.
5 Palgrave Macmillan, Houndmills, 2004.
6 *Human Development Report 2004: Cultural Liberty in Today's Diverse World*, UN Development Programme, New York, 2004, pp.1–2.
7 J Joseph Hewitt *et al*, *Peace and Conflict 2008*, Center for International Development and Conflict Management, University of Maryland, 2007, p.14.
8 Scott Pegg, *International Society and the De Facto State*, Ashgate, Aldershot, 1998.
9 Tozun Bahcheli *et al* (eds), *De Facto States: The Quest for Sovereignty*, Routledge, London, 2004.
10 Dov Lynch, *Engaging Eurasia's Separatist States: Unresolved Conflicts and De Facto States*, United States Institute of Peace Press, Washington DC, 2004.

Chapter 1: Confirmed *versus* Contested States

1 Joshua Castellino, *International Law and Self-determination: The Interplay of the Politics of Territorial Possession with Formulations of Post-Colonial 'National' Identity*, Martinus Nijhoff Publishers, The Hague, 2000, pp.77–89; Martin Dixon, *Textbook on International Law*, 4th edition, Blackstone Press, London, 2000, p.105.
2 Malcolm N Shaw, *International Law*, 5th edition, Cambridge University Press, Cambridge, 2003, p.178; Thomas J Biersteker, 'State, sovereignty and territory', in Walter Carlsnaes *et al* (eds), *Handbook of International Relations*, Sage, London, 2002, p.162.
3 Martin Dixon, pp.107–8.
4 Joshua Castellino, p.78; Martin Dixon, p.108.
5 Gianfranco Poggi, *The State: Its Nature, Development and Prospects*, Polity Press, Cambridge, 1990, p.26.
6 Quoted by Chris Brown *et al* (eds), *International Relations in Political Thought: Texts from the Ancient Greeks to the First World War*, Cambridge University Press, Cambridge, 2002, p.364.
7 Lars-Erik Cederman, 'Nationalism and ethnicity', in Walter Carlsnaes *et al* (eds), p.410.
8 Rainer Bauböck, 'Why stay together? A pluralist approach to secession and federation', in Will Kymlicka & Wayne Norman (eds), *Citizenship in Diverse Societies*, Oxford University Press, Oxford, 2000, p.366.
9 Quoted by Alan James, *Sovereign Statehood: The Basis of International Society*, Allen & Unwin, London, 1986, p.2.
10 *The Economist*, 9 September 2006, p.42; Amitai Etzioni, 'The evils of self-determination', *Foreign Policy*, No. 89, Winter 1992–93, p.23.

11 *Vereinte Nationen*, Vol. 56 (1), February 2008, pp.44–6; Jorri Duursma, *Fragmentation and the International Relations of Micro-States: Self-Determination and Statehood*, Cambridge University Press, Cambridge, 1996, pp.133–42.
12 Martin Dixon, p.108.
13 Joshua Castellino, pp.78–9.
14 Martin Dixon, p.108; James Crawford, *The Creation of States in International Law*, Clarendon Press, Oxford, 1979, p.37.
15 Ian S Lustick, *Unsettled States, Disputed Lands: Britain and Ireland, France and Algeria, Israel and the West Bank-Gaza*, Cornell University Press, Ithaca, 1993, p.3.
16 Malcolm N Shaw, pp.179–81.
17 Malcolm N Shaw, p.179.
18 Joshua Castellino, p.79.
19 James Crawford, p.36.
20 Elmer Plischke, *Microstates in World Affairs: Policy Problems and Options*, American Enterprise for Public Policy Research, Washington DC, 1977, p.ii.
21 *Vereinte Nationen*, pp.44–6.
22 Rein Muellerson, *Ordering Anarchy: International Law in International Society*, Martinus Nijhoff, The Hague, 2000, p.165.
23 Thomas J Biersteker, p.165; Jean-Marie Guéhenno, *The End of the Nation-State*, University of Minnesota Press, Minneapolis, 2000, pp.8–9.
24 Gertrude E Schroeder, 'On the economic viability of new nation-states', *Journal of International Affairs*, Vol. 45(2), Winter 1992, pp.549–74.
25 Rik Coolsaet, 'The transformation of diplomacy at the threshold of the new millennium', in Christer Jönsson & Richard Langhorne (eds), *Diplomacy*, Vol. 3, Sage Publications, London, 2004, p.4.
26 Alberto Alesina & Enrico Spolaore, *The Size of Nations*, MIT Press, Cambridge Mass., 2005, p.198.
27 James Crawford, p.42.
28 James Crawford, pp.45–6.
29 Martin Dixon, p.108.
30 Daniel S Papp, *Contemporary International Relations: Frameworks for Understanding*, 2nd edition, Macmillan, New York, 1988, p.456.
31 Samuel P Huntington, *Political Order in Changing Societies*, Yale University Press, New Haven, 1968, p.1.
32 Malcolm N Shaw, p.180.
33 Sheila Harden (ed.), *Small is Dangerous: Micro States in a Macro World*, Frances Pinter, London, 1985, p.17.
34 Robert H Jackson, *Quasi-States: Sovereignty, International Relations, and the Third World*, Cambridge University Press, Cambridge, 1990, pp.24–5.
35 Malcolm N Shaw, p.180; James Crawford, p.43; Martin Dixon, p.109.
36 Quoted by Robert H Jackson, p.38.
37 Rein Muellerson, p.166.
38 Thomas M Franck, 'The emerging right to democratic governance', *American Journal of International Law*, Vol. 86(1), January 1992 , pp.46–91. Also see Morton H Halperin & Kristin Lomasney, 'Toward a global guarantee clause', *Journal of Democracy*, Vol. 4(3), July 1993, pp.60–9.
39 Thomas J Biersteker, p.163.
40 Thomas J Biersteker, p.163.
41 Thomas J Biersteker, p.169.

42 Donald L Horowitz, 'The cracked foundations of the right to secede', *Journal of Democracy*, Vol. 14(2), April 2003, pp.13–14.
43 Rein Muellerson, p.166.
44 James Crawford, pp.47–8.
45 Alan James, pp.24–5, 266.
46 John Dugard, *International Law: A South African Perspective*, Juta, Cape Town, 1994, p.68.
47 James Crawford, p.47.
48 Quoted by Malcolm N Shaw, p.178.
49 Quoted by Michael R Fowler & Julie M Bunck, *Law, Power, and the Sovereign State: The Evolution and Application of the Concept of Sovereignty*, Pennsylvania State University Press, Pennsylvania, 1995, p.10.
50 Nkambo Mugerwa, 'Subjects of international law', in Max Sorensen (ed.), *Manual of Public International Law*, Macmillan, London, 1968, p.253; Hedley Bull, *The Anarchical Society: A Study of Order in World Politics*, Macmillan, London, 1977, p.8; Thomas J Biersteker, p.168.
51 Quoted by Ralph Pettman, *World Politics: Rationalism and Beyond*, Palgrave, Houndmills, 2001, p.148.
52 Nkambo Mugerwa, p.253.
53 Bruce Russett *et al*, *World Politics: The Menu for Choice*, 7th edition, Thomson Wadsworth, Belmont, 2004, p.56; FH Hinsley, *Sovereignty*, CA Watts, London, 1966, p.26; Alan James, p.3 ; Gianfranco Poggi, p.21.
54 KJ Holsti, *Taming the Sovereigns: Institutional Change in International Politics*, Cambridge University Press, Cambridge, 2004, pp.135–6.
55 Alan James, pp.24–5.
56 Stephen D Krasner, 'Problematic sovereignty', in Krasner (ed.), *Problematic Sovereignty: Contested Rules and Political Possibilities*, Columbia University Press, New York, 2001, pp.6–7, 10–11.
57 Nkambo Mugerwa, p.253.
58 Frederick L Schuman, *International Politics: The Western State System and the World Community*, McGraw-Hill, New York, 1958, p.67.
59 James Crawford, pp.52–6.
60 James Crawford, pp.55–6.
61 KJ Holsti, pp.42, 114, original emphasis. Also see Stephen D Krasner, 'Economic interdependence and independent statehood', in Robert H Jackson & Alan James (eds), *States in a Changing World: A Contemporary Analysis*, Clarendon Press, Oxford, 1993, pp.318–19.
62 James Crawford, pp.56–7.
63 Michael R Fowler & Julie M Bunck, pp.37–9.
64 Stephen D Krasner, *Sovereignty: Organized Hypocrisy*, Princeton University Press, Princeton, 1999, p.4.
65 Joshua Castellino, pp.97–9; Herbert Dittgen, 'World without borders: Reflections on the future of the nation-state', *Government and Opposition*, Vol. 34(1), Winter 1999, p.163.
66 KJ Holsti, pp.63, 136, 140; Gianfranco Poggi, pp.21–2.
67 James Crawford, pp.57–8.
68 James Crawford, p.58.
69 James Crawford, pp.106–7.
70 Martin Dixon, p.111; Malcolm N Shaw, p.182.
71 James Crawford, pp.59–60, 108.
72 James Crawford, p.60.

73 James Crawford, p.61.
74 James Crawford, pp.62–5; Joshua Castellino, p.81.
75 Jan Donkers & Minka Nijhuis, *Burma behind the Mask*, Burma Centrum Nederland, Amsterdam, 1996, pp.119–20.
76 James Crawford, p.63.
77 Joshua Castellino, p.81; Martin Dixon, p.111.
78 James Crawford, pp.65–6.
79 Robert Jackson, *Sovereignty: Evolution of an Idea*, Polity Press, Cambridge, 2007, pp.10–11.
80 Malcolm N Shaw, pp.192–3; Nkambo Mugerwa, p.253; Michael R Fowler & Julie M Bunck, pp.12–14.
81 Michael R Fowler & Julie M Bunck, p.21.
82 Stephen D Krasner, *Sovereignty: Organized Hypocrisy*.
83 Quoted by Chris Brown *et al* (eds), pp.322–3.
84 Robert H Jackson, pp.21–25, 43.
85 Bruce Russett *et al*, p.61.
86 Stephen D Krasner, 'Problematic sovereignty', pp.7, 9.
87 Robert H Jackson, pp.24–5, 34, 41.
88 Robert H Jackson, pp.24, 29; Christopher Clapham, 'Degrees of statehood', *Review of International Studies*, Vol. 24(2), April 1998, pp.143–6.
89 Gerard Kreijen, 'The transformation of sovereignty and African independence: No shortcuts to statehood', in Kreijen (ed.), *State, Sovereignty, and International Governance*, Oxford University Press, Oxford, 2002, p.89.
90 Quoted by Gerard Kreijen, p.89.
91 Gerard Kreijen, p.100.
92 Michael R Fowler & Julie M Bunck, p.42.
93 Robert H Jackson, pp.24, 31, 43, 48, 134–6.
94 Barry Bartmann, 'Political realities and legal anomalies: Revisiting the politics of international recognition', in Tozun Bahcheli *et al* (eds), *De Facto States: The Quest for Sovereignty*, Routledge, London, 2004, pp.12–14.
95 Barry Bartmann, pp.12–14.
96 James Crawford, p.16.
97 Ivan Shearer, 'International legal relations between Australia and Taiwan: Behind the façade', *Australian Year Book of International Law*, Vol. 21, 2000, p.113. Also see Martin Dixon, pp.120–1.
98 Martin Dixon, pp.122–3; Malcolm N Shaw, p.185.
99 Olivier Ribbelink, 'State succession and the recognition of states and governments', in Jan Klabbers *et al* (eds), *State Practice regarding State Succession and Issues of Recognition: The Pilot Project of the Council of Europe*, Kluwer Law International, The Hague, 1999, pp.44, 78.
100 Steve Allen, 'Statehood, self-determination and the "Taiwan question"', *Asian Yearbook of International Law*, Vol. 9, 2000, p.204.
101 Stephen D Krasner, 'Explaining variation: Defaults, coercion, commitments', in Krasner (ed.), *Problematic Sovereignty*, pp.330–2.
102 Thomas J Biersteker, p.169; Thomas C Heller & Abraham D Sofaer, 'Sovereignty: The practitioners' perspective', in Stephen D Krasner (ed.), *Problematic Sovereignty*, p.28.
103 JES Fawcett, *The Law of Nations*, Allen Lane, London, 1968, p.41.
104 Quoted by Guido Acquaviva, 'Subjects of international law: A power-based analysis', *Vanderbilt Journal of Transnational Law*, Vol. 38(2), March 2005, p.353.

105 Ersun N Kurtulus, *State Sovereignty: Concept, Phenomenon and Ramifications*, Palgrave Macmillan, Houndmills, 2005, p.125.
106 Martin Dixon, p.119.
107 Guido Acquaviva, p.345.
108 Michael Schoiswohl, 'De facto regimes and human rights obligations – the twilight zone of public international law?', *Austrian Review of International and European Law*, Vol. 6, 2001, pp.45–90.
109 James Crawford, p.23.
110 James Crawford, p.23; Martin Dixon, p.120; Edward Mihalkanin, 'The Abkhazians: A national minority in their own homeland', in Tozun Bahcheli *et al* (eds), p.157.
111 Philip C Jessup, *The Birth of Nations*, Columbia University Press, New York, 1974, p.305; James Crawford, p.129.
112 James Crawford, p.140; Martin Dixon, p.119.
113 Jorri Duursma, p.112.
114 Steve Allen, p.202.
115 Gerard Kreijen, pp.84–7, 98.
116 Robert H Jackson & Alan James, 'The character of independent statehood', in Jackson & James (eds), p.4.
117 John Dugard, pp.74–5.
118 Thomas D Grant, 'Hallstein revisited: Unilateral enforcement of regimes of nonrecognition since the two Germanies', *Stanford Journal of International Law*, Vol. 36(2), Summer 2000, p.221.
119 James Crawford, pp.119, 151.
120 Quoted by Tozun Bahcheli, 'Introduction: A new world of emerging states', in Bahcheli *et al* (eds), p.7.
121 Ersun N Kurtulus, p.105.
122 Mo Shen, *Japan in Manchuria: An Analytical Study of Treaties and Documents*, publisher not mentioned, Manila, 1960, p.300; Philip C Jessup, *The Birth of Nations*, Columbia University Press, New York, 1974, pp.306, 334.
123 John J Stremlau, *The International Politics of the Nigerian Civil War, 1967–1970*, Princeton University Press, Princeton, 1977, pp.127, 141.
124 Hedley Bull, pp. 8–9.
125 Scott Pegg; Tozun Bahcheli *et al* (eds); Dov Lynch, *Engaging Eurasia's Separatist States: Unresolved Conflicts and De Facto States*, United States Institute of Peace Press, Washington DC, 2004.
126 Charles King, 'The benefits of ethnic war: Understanding Eurasia's unrecognized states', *World Politics*, Vol. 53(4), July 2001, p.525.
127 Christopher Clapham, 'Degrees of statehood', *Review of International Studies*, Vol. 24(2), April 1998, p.144.
128 Pål Kølsto, 'The sustainability and future of unrecognized quasi-states', *Journal of Peace Research*, Vol. 43(6), 2006, pp.723–40.
129 Samy Cohen, *The Resilience of the State: Democracy and the Challenge of Globalisation*, Hurst, London, 2003, p.20.
130 Ian S Spears, 'States-within-states: An introduction to their empirical attributes', in Paul Kingston & Spears (eds), *States-within-States: Incipient Political Entities in the Post-Cold War Era*, Palgrave, Houndmills, 2004, pp.16–17.
131 Jacques deLisle, 'Law's special answers to the cross-Strait sovereignty question', *Orbis*, Vol. 46(4), Fall 2002, p.741.
132 Montserrat Guibernau, *Nations without States: Political Communities in a Global Age*, Polity Press, Cambridge, 2000, pp.1–2.
133 National Geographic, *Atlas of the World*, 8th edition, Washington DC, 2005.

Chapter 2: Origins of Contested Statehood

1 Maurice Cranston (ed.), *A Glossary of Political Terms*, The Bodley Head, London, p.92; Roger Scruton, *A Dictionary of Political Thought*, Macmillan, London, 1982, pp.40, 421; Erin Jenne, 'National self-determination: A deadly mobilizing device', and Hurst Hannum, 'Self-determination in the twenty-first century', both in Hannum & Eileen F Babbitt (eds), *Negotiating Self-Determination*, Lexington Books, Lanham, 2006, pp.11, 28 and 61 respectively.

2 8 January 1918: President Woodrow Wilson's Fourteen Points, http://www.lib.byu.edu/-rdh/wwi/1918/14points.html.

3 Maurice Cranston, pp.91–2; William Saffire, *Saffire's Political Dictionary*, Ballantine Books, New York, 1978; Richard Falk, 'Self-determination under international law: The coherence of the doctrine versus the incoherence of experience', in Wolfgang Danspeckgruber (ed.), *The Self-Determination of Peoples: Community, Nation, and State in an Interdependent World*, Lynne Rienner, Boulder, 2002, p.39; Stefan Wolff, *Disputed Territories: The Transnational Dynamics of Ethnic Conflict Settlement*, Berghahn Books, New York, 2003, p.23; Allen Buchanan, *Secession: The Morality of Political Divorce from Fort Sumter to Lithuania and Quebec*, Westview Press, Boulder, 1991, p.48; Margaret Moore, 'Introduction: The self-determination principle and the ethics of secession', in Moore (ed), *National Self-Determination and Secession*, Oxford University Press, Oxford, 1998, pp.2–3.

4 George Barrie, *Self-Determination in Modern International Law*, Occasional Papers, Konrad Adenauer-Stiftung, Johannesburg, 1995, p.4; Paul Johnson, *Modern Times: A History of the World from the 1920s to the 1990s*, Orion Books, London, 1992, pp.41, 74–7.

5 Jan Klabbers, 'The right to be taken seriously: Self-determination in international law', *Human Rights Quarterly*, Vol. 28(1), February 2006, p.187.

6 Quoted by Vernon Bogdanor, 'Forms of autonomy and the protection of minorities', *Daedalus*, Vol. 126(2), Spring 1997, p.86 and Ved P Nanda, 'Self-determination and secession under international law', *Denver Journal of International Law and Policy*, Vol. 29(4), Summer-Fall 2001, p.307.

7 Richard Falk, 'Self-determination under international law', p.31.

8 Obiora C Okafor, *Re-Defining Legitimate Statehood: International Law and State Fragmentation in Africa*, Martinus Nijhoff, The Hague, 2000, p.60.

9 Jan Klabbers, p.188.

10 Quoted by Jan Klabbers, p.198.

11 Malcolm N Shaw, *International Law*, 5th edition, Cambridge University Press, Cambridge, 2003, p.226; Emilio J Cárdenas & María F Cañás, 'The limits of self-determination', in Wolfgang Danspeckgruber (ed.), *The Self-Determination of Peoples*, p.101.

12 Peter Radan, *The Break-Up of Yugoslavia and International Law*, Routledge, London, 2002, p.9.

13 Scott Pegg, *International Society and the De Facto State*, Ashgate Publishing, Aldershot, 1998, p.143.

14 Joshua Castellino, 'Order and justice: National minorities and the right to secession', *International Journal on Minority and Group Rights*, Vol. 6(4), 1999, pp.393–4.

15 Peter Radan, pp.10, 17, 20.

16 Viva O Bartkus, *The Dynamic of Secession*, Cambridge University Press, Cambridge, 1999, p.71; George Barrie, p.6.

17 Steven Wheatley, *Democracy, Minorities and International Law*, Cambridge University Press, Cambridge, 2005, pp.79–80.

18 George Barrie, pp.10-11; Malcolm N Shaw, p.228; Steven Wheatley, p.93.
19 Obiora C Okafor, *Re-Defining Legitimate Statehood*, pp.60, 190.
20 TN Tappe, cited by Obiora C Okafor, *Re-Defining Legitimate Statehood*, p.61.
21 Peter Radan, p.12.
22 Quoted by George Barrie, p.13.
23 Jan Klabbers, p.189.
24 Richard Falk, p.38.
25 Quoted by Karen Mingst, *Essentials of International Relations*, 4th edition, WW Norton, New York, 2007, p.132.
26 Jan Klabbers, pp.189, 199.
27 Donald L Horowitz, 'The cracked foundations of the right to secede', *Journal of Democracy*, Vol. 14(2), April 2003, pp.6–8; George Barrie, pp.13, 28–9.
28 Joshua Castellino, pp.401, 410.
29 Stefan Wolff, *Disputed Territories*, p.23.
30 Unrepresented Nations and Peoples Organization (UNPO), *The Implementation of the Right to Self-Determination as a Contribution to Conflict Prevention*, Report of the international conference of experts held in Barcelona from 21 to 27 November 1998, http://www.unpo:org/news_detail.php?arg=01&par=446, pp.2–19; George Barrie, pp.13, 23; James Crawford, *International Law as an* Open *System*, Cameron May, London, 2002, p.18.
31 UN General Assembly, 48th session, 25 October 1993, Official Records, p.2.
32 Joshua Castellino, p.394.
33 Frederic L Kirgis, 'The degrees of self-determination in the United Nations era', *American Journal of International Law*, Vol. 88(2), April 1994, p.307. Also see Antonio Cassese, *Self-Determination of Peoples: A Legal Appraisal*, Cambridge University Press, Cambridge, 1995, pp.316–17.
34 Viva O Bartkus, p.113.
35 Jan Klabbers, p.205.
36 *Chambers Twentieth Century Dictionary*, Chambers, Edinburgh, 1974; *Collins Concise Dictionary*, Collins, Glasgow, 2004; Donald W Livingston, 'What is secession?', Vermont Commons Blog, November 2005, http://www.vtcommons.org/node/232, p.2.
37 Viva O Bartkus, p.3.
38 Allen Buchanan, *Secession: The Morality of Political Divorce from fort Sumter to Lithuania and Quebec,*, p.10; Alexis Heraclides, 'Secession, self-determination and non-intervention: In quest of normative symbiosis', *Journal of International Affairs*, Vol. 45(2), Winter 1992, p.400.
39 Steven Wheatley, pp.85–6.
40 Quoted by Jorri Duursma, *Fragmentation and the International Relations of Micro-States: Self-Determination and Statehood*, Cambridge University Press, Cambridge, 1996, p.90; Alexis Heraclides, p.407.
41 Ved P Nanda, pp.318–19.
42 Jeffrey Herbst, 'Responding to state failure in Africa', *International Security*, Vol. 21(3), Winter 1996, p.134.
43 Rainer Bauböck, 'Why stay together? A pluralist approach to secession and federation', in Will Kymlicka & Wayne Norman (eds), *Citizenship in Diverse Societies*, Oxford University Press, Oxford, 2000, p.379.
44 James Crawford, *State Practice and International Law in Relation to Unilateral Secession*, Report to Government of Canada concerning unilateral secession by Quebec, 19 February 1997, Tamilnation.org, http://www.tamilnation.org/selfdetermination/97crawford.htm, p.4.

45 Viva O Bartkus, pp.10–11, 14.
46 Metta Spencer, 'When states divide', in Spencer (ed.), *Separatism: Democracy and Disintegration*, Rowman & Littlefield, Lanham, 1998, pp.18–19; Eileen F Babbitt, 'Self-determination as a component of conflict intractability: Implications for negotiation', in Hurst Hannum & Babbitt (eds), pp.116–18.
47 James Crawford, *The Creation of States in International Law*, Clarendon Press, Oxford, 1979, p.247.
48 James Crawford, *State Practice and International Law in Relation to Unilateral Secession*, pp.15–16.
49 Quoted by Viva O Bartkus, p.12.
50 Michael Freeman, 'The priority of function over structure: A new approach to secession', in Percy B Lehning (ed.), *Theories of Secession*, Routledge, London, 1998, p.12.
51 Quoted by Obiora C Okafor, 'Entitlement, process, and legitimacy in the emergent international law of secession', *International Journal on Minority and Group Rights*, Vol. 9(1), 2002, p.50.
52 Obiora C Okafor, 'Entitlement, process, and legitimacy in the emergent international law of secession', p.70.
53 Quoted by Ved P Nanda, pp.315–17; Obiora C Okafor, 'Entitlement, process, and legitimacy in the emergent international law of secession', pp.47–8.
54 Obiora C Okafor, 'Entitlement, process, and legitimacy in the emergent international law of secession', pp.51, 54; Ved P Nanda, p.325.
55 James Crawford, *International Law as an Open System*, p.233.
56 UN Document A/47/277 (1992), para. 17.
57 Percy B Lehning, 'Theories of secession: An introduction', in Lehning (ed.), p.2.
58 Percy B Lehning, 'Theories of secession: An introduction', pp.2–7.
59 Allen Buchanan, 'The international institutional dimension of secession', in Percy B Lehning (ed.), pp.230–6; Allen Buchanan, 'Secession', in Edward N Zalta (ed.), *The Stanford Encyclopedia of Philosophy*, 2003, http://plato.stanford.edu/entries/secession; Allen Buchanan, 'Uncoupling secession from nationalism and intrastate autonomy from secession', in Hurst Hannum & Eileen F Babbitt (eds), *Negotiating Self-Determination*, pp.82–92.
60 Yuchao Zhu & Dongyan Blachford, 'Ethnic disputes in international politics: Manifestations and conceptualizations', *Nationalism and Ethnic Politics*, Vol. 12(1), Spring 2006, p.36; Margaret Moore, pp.5–6; Bruno Coppieters, 'Introduction', in Coppieters & Richard Sakwa (eds), *Contextualizing Secession: Normative Studies in Comparative Perspective*, Oxford University Press, Oxford, 2003, pp.6–7.
61 Bruno Coppieters, 'Secession and war: A moral analysis of the Russian-Chechen conflict', *Central Asian Survey*, Vol. 22(4), December 2003, pp.380–2.
62 Donald L Horowitz, pp.6–12; Morton H Halperin *et al*, *Self-determination in the New World Order*, Carnegie Endowment for International Peace, Washington DC, 1992, pp.76–80; Alexis Heraclides, pp.410–15; Iris M Young, 'Polity and group difference: A critique of the ideal of universal citizenship', *Ethics*, Vol. 99, January 1989, p.261; Frederic L Kirgis, p.308; Ralph R Premdas, 'Secessionist movements in comparative perspective', in Premdas & AB Anderson (eds), *Secessionist Movements in Comparative Perspective*, Pinter Publishers, London, 1990 p.15; William Safran, 'Non-separatist policies regarding ethnic minorities: Positive approaches and ambiguous consequences', *International Political Science Review*, Vol. 15(1), 1994, p.63; Allen Buchanan, 'Self-determination and the right to secede', *Journal of International Affairs*, Vol. 45(2), Winter 1992, pp.353–8; Allen Buchanan, *Secession: The Morality of Political Divorce from Fort Sumter to*

Lithuania and Quebec, pp.40–5, 61–8; Viva O Bartkus, pp.80–91, 117–18, 223–7; Gertrude E Schroeder, 'On the economic viability of new nation-states', *Journal of International Affairs,* Vol. 45(2), Winter 1992, pp.549–74; Metta Spencer, 'Conclusion', in Spencer (ed.), *Separatism,* pp.308–9; Will Kymlicka & Wayne Norman, 'Citizenship in culturally diverse societies: Issues, contexts, concepts', in Kymlicka & Norman (eds), *Citizenship in Diverse Societies,* p.26; John McGarry & Brendan O'Leary, 'Introduction: The macro-political regulation of ethnic conflict', in McGarry & O'Leary (eds), *The Politics of Ethnic Conflict Regulation: Case Studies of Protracted Ethnic Conflicts,* Routledge, London, 1993, p.19; Unrepresented Nations and Peoples Organization, *The Implementation of the Right to Self-determination,* pp.19–21; Oliver P Richmond, 'States of sovereignty, sovereign states, and ethnic claims for international status', *Review of International Studies,* Vol. 28(2), April 2002, p.394; Peter Radan, p.248; Steven Wheatley, pp.88–9; *The Nagorno Karabagh Crisis: A Blueprint for Resolution,* A memorandum prepared by the Public International Law and Policy Group, May 2000, p.31; James Crawford, *State Practice and International Law in Relation to Unilateral Secession,* p.9; Jorri Duursma, p.96.

63 James Crawford, *State Practice and International Law in Relation to Unilateral Secession,* pp.5, 17–21.

64 Allen Buchanan, *Secession: The Morality of Political Divorce from Fort Sumter to Lithuania and Quebec,* pp.132–5.

65 Allen Buchanan, 'Secession', p.2.

Chapter 3: Alternative Destinations for Contested States

1 Pål Kølsto, 'The sustainability and future of unrecognized quasi-states', *Journal of Peace Research,* Vol. 43(6), 2006, p.735.

2 Michael Keating, *Nations against the State: The New Politics of Nationalism in Quebec, Catalonia and Scotland,* Macmillan, Houndmills, 1996, pp.18–20.

3 Unrepresented Nations and Peoples Organisation (UNPO), *The Implementation of the Right to Self-Determination as a Contribution to Conflict Prevention,* Report of the international conference of experts held in Barcelona from 21 to 27 November 1998, hhtp://www.unpro.org/news_detail.php?arg=01&par=446, p.26; Juan Enriquez, 'Too many flags?', *Foreign Policy,* Issue 116, Fall 1999, p.48.

4 Michael Keating, pp.52–63.

5 Emilio J Cárdenas & María Fernanda Cañás, 'The limits of self-determination', in Wolfgang Danspeckgruber (ed.), *The Self-Determination of Peoples: Community, Nation, and State in an Interdependent World,* Lynne Rienner, Boulder, 2002, pp.110–11; UNPO, pp.10, 21.

6 Scott Pegg, *International Society and the De Facto State,* Aldershot, Ashgate, 1998, p.180.

7 Alexis Heraclides, 'Secessionist minorities and external involvement', *International Organization,* Vol. 44(3), 1990, pp.370–1.

8 Scott Pegg, p.182.

9 Alexis Heraclides, p.368; GR Berridge & Alan James, *A Dictionary of Diplomacy,* http://www.grberridge.co.uk/dict_comp_p_t.htm.

10 Dov Lynch, *Managing Separatist States: A Eurasian Case Study,* Occasional Papers 32, Institute for Security Studies, Western European Union, Paris, November 2001, p.31.

11 Dov Lynch, p.31.

12 JL Brierly, *The Law of Nations: An Introduction to the International Law of Peace*, 6th edition, Clarendon Press, Oxford, 1963, p.136; JG Starke, *An Introduction to International Law*, 6th edition, Butterworths, London, 1967, p.108.
13 See Alain Dieckhoff & Christophe Jaffrelot, 'From the nation-state to post-nationalism?' in Marie-Claude Smouts (ed.), *The New International Relations: Theory and Practice*, Hurst, London, 2001, pp.32–5.
14 JG Starke, p.108.
15 Richard A Griggs, 'Geostrategies in the Great Lakes conflict and spatial designs for peace', Center for World Indigenous Studies, 1999, http://www.cwis.org/hutu3_1.html.
16 *The Economist*, 3 June 2006.
17 UNPO, p.22.
18 Stefan Wolff, *Disputed Territories: The Transnational Dynamics of Ethnic Conflict Settlement*, Berghahn Books, New York, 2003, pp.196–7.
19 JG Starke, p.109; Malcolm N Shaw, *International Law*, 5th edition, Cambridge University Press, Cambridge, 2003, pp.206–7; Stefan Wolff, *Disputed Territories*, pp.196–205.
20 Stefan Wolff, *Disputed Territories*, pp.16, 207–9; Clive Parry, 'The function of law in the international community', in Max Sorensen, *Manual of Public International Law*, Macmillan, London, 1968, p.42.
21 James A Paul, 'Nations and states', Global Policy Forum, July 1996, http://www.globalpolicy.org/nations/natstats.htm, p.8; John Gershman, 'Overview of self-determination issues in Kashmir', Self-determination in Focus, 2001, http://www.fpif.org/selfdetermination/conflicts/kashmir.html; Muzamil Jaleel, 'A guide to Kashmir peace plans', Countercurrents.org, 2002, www.countercurrents.org/kashmir-jaleel230603.htm.
22 See the Declaration on Principles of International Law concerning Friendly Relations and Cooperation among States, adopted by the UN General Assembly in 1970.
23 UN General Assembly resolution 1541(XV), 1960; Chimène Keitner, 'Associate statehood: Principles and prospects', Paper prepared for the Faroese Constitutional Committee, March 2003, courtesy of the author, p.5.
24 Masahiro Igarashi, *Associated Statehood in International Law*, Kluwer Law International, The Hague, 2002, p.238.
25 Masahiro Igarashi, pp.258–300, and Joshua Castellino, *International Law and Self-Determination: The Interplay of the Politics of Territorial Possession with Formulations of Post-Colonial 'National' Identity*, Martinus Nijhoff Publishers, The Hague, 2000, p.83.
26 James Crawford, 'Islands as sovereign nations', *International and Comparative Law Quarterly*, Vol. 38(2), April 1989, p.283.
27 Masahiro Igarashi, pp.238–57; Chimène I Keitner & W Michael Reisman, 'Free association: The United States experience', *Texas International Law Journal*, Vol. 39(1), 2003, pp.45–61; Chimène Keitner, pp.6–9.
28 Chimène Keitner, p.5.
29 Chimène Keitner, p.5.
30 Stephen D Krasner, 'Explaining variation: Defaults, coercion, commitments', in Krasner (ed.), *Problematic Sovereignty: Contested Rules and Political Possibilities*, Columbia University Press, New York, 2001, pp.339–40.
31 Xiaobing Xu & George D Wilson, 'The Hong Kong Special Administrative Region as a model of regional external autonomy', *Case Western Reserve Journal of International Law*, Vol. 32(1), 2000, p.6.

32 Eva Herzer, 'Options for Tibet's future status: Self-governance though (sic) an autonomous arrangement', Tibet Justice Center, undated, http://www.tibetjustice.org/reports/AutonomyBooklet.pdf, p.24; Xiaobing Xu & George D Wilson, pp.1–38.
33 Malcolm N Shaw, pp.194–5.
34 Martin Dixon, *Textbook on International Law*, 4th edition, Blackstone, London, 2000, p.114; Malcolm N Shaw, pp.194–5; Nkambo Mugerwa, 'Subjects of international law', in Max Sorensen (ed.), pp.262–3.
35 Malcolm N Shaw, pp.194–5; Eva Herzer, p.24.
36 Malcolm N Shaw, pp.194–5.
37 *Africa South of the Sahara 2007*, Routledge, London, 2006, pp.275–82, 924–6.
38 Stephen D Krasner, 'Sharing sovereignty: New institutions for collapsed and failing states', *International Security*, Vol. 29(2), Fall 2004, pp.99–107; Tonny B Knudsen & Carsten B Laustsen, 'The politics of international trusteeship', in Knudsen & Laustsen (eds), *Kosovo between War and Peace: Nationalism, Peacebuilding and International Trusteeship*, Routledge, London, 2006, pp.1–12; Malcolm N Shaw, pp.207–10.
39 Metin Tamkoç, *The Turkish Cypriot State: The Embodiment of the Right of Self-Determination*, M Rustem & Brother, London, 1988, p.68; Allen Buchanan, *Secession: The Morality of Political Divorce from Fort Sumter to Lithuania and Quebec*, Westview Press, Boulder, 1991, p.46; David J Elkins, *Beyond Sovereignty: Territory and Political Economy in the Twenty-First Century*, University of Toronto Press, Toronto, 1995, pp.244–5.
40 Gidon Gottlieb, 'Nations without states', *Foreign Affairs*, Vol. 73(3), May/June 1994, p.107.
41 Gidon Gottlieb, *Nation against State: A New Approach to Ethnic Conflicts and the Decline of Sovereignty*, Council on Foreign Relations Press, New York, 1993, pp.3, 36–40.
42 Stephen D Krasner, 'Sharing sovereignty', pp.108–15.
43 Metin Tamkoç, pp.70–1.
44 Thomas J Biersteker, 'State, sovereignty and territory', in Walter Carlsnaes *et al*, (ed.), *Handbook of International Relations*, Sage, London, 2002, p.166; J Orstrom Moller, *The End of Internationalism or World Governance?*, Praeger, Westport, 2000, pp.48–50; Gulnaz Sharafutdinova, 'Paradiplomacy in the Russian regions: Tatarstan's search for statehood', *Europa-Asia Studies*, Vol. 55(4), 2003, p.613.
45 Jeffrey Herbst, *States and Power in Africa: Comparative Lessons in Authority and Control*, Princeton University Press, Princeton, 2000, pp.263–4.
46 Charles W Kegley & Eugene R Wittkopf, *World Politics: Trend and Transformation*, 9th edition, Thomson Wadsworth, Belmont, 2004, p.165.
47 Gidon Gottlieb, *Nation against State*, pp.4, 43.
48 'Confederation isn't the solution', Kurdish Media, 26 March 2005, http://www.kurmedia.com/news.asp?id=6479.
49 Montserrat Guibernau, p.172.
50 Montserrat Guibernau, , *Nations without States: Political Communities in a Global Age*, Polity Press, Cambridge, 2000, p.49; J Orstrom Moller, pp.41–7; Alberto Alesina & Enrico Spolaore, *The Size of Nations*, MIT Press, Cambridge, Mass., 2005, p.221.
51 John Doyle, 'New models of sovereignty for contested states: Some empirical evidence of non-Westphalian approaches', in Howard M Hensel (ed.), *Sovereignty and the Global Community: The Quest for Order in the International System*, Ashgate, Aldershot, 2004, p.156.

52 Strobe Talbott, 'Self-determination in an interdependent world', *Foreign Policy*, Spring 2000, pp.152–61.
53 Brendan O'Leary, 'Introduction', in Brendan O'Leary *et al* (eds), *Right-Sizing the State: The Politics of Moving Borders*, Oxford University Press, Oxford, 2001, pp.1–12; Ian S Lustick *et al*, 'Secessionism in multicultural states: Does sharing power prevent or encourage it?', *American Political Science Review*, Vol. 98(2), May 2004, p.209; Allen Buchanan, *Secession*, p.18.
54 Michael Chege, 'Remembering Africa', *Foreign Affairs*, Vol. 71(1), 1991–92, p.153.
55 *The Economist*, 11 September 1993.
56 *The Economist*, 10 September 1994.
57 Makau wa Mutua, 'Why redraw the map of Africa: A moral and legal inquiry', *Michigan Journal of International Law*, Vol. 16(4), Summer 1995, pp.1113–76.
58 Jeffrey Herbst, pp.263, 266.
59 Quoted by Sheila Harden (ed.), *Small is Dangerous: Micro States in a Micro World*, Frances Pinter, London, 1985, p.20.
60 Arend Lijphart, 'Self-determination versus pre-determination of ethnic minorities in power-sharing systems', in Will Kymlicka (ed.), *The Rights of Minority Cultures*, Oxford University Press, Oxford, 1995, p.276.
61 Vernon Bogdanor, 'Forms of autonomy and the protection of minorities', *Daedalus*, Vol. 126(2), Spring 1997, p.66; Arend Lijphart, 'Constitutional design for divided societies', *Journal of Democracy*, Vol. 15(2), April 2004, pp.97, 105.
62 John McGarry & Brendan O'Leary, 'Introduction: The macro-political regulation of ethnic conflict', in McGarry & O'Leary (eds), *The Politics of Ethnic Conflict Regulation: Case Studies of Protracted Ethnic Conflicts*, Routledge, London, 1993, pp.6–17; Stefan Wolff, *Ethnic Conflict: A Global Perspective*, Oxford University Press, Oxford, 2006, pp.140–2; Montserrat Guibernau, p.60.
63 Stefan Wolff, *Ethnic Conflict*, pp.142–3.
64 Cited by Rainer Bauböck, 'Why stay together? A pluralist approach to secession and federation', in Will Kymlicka & Wayne Norman (eds), *Citizenship in Diverse Societies*, Oxford University Press, Oxford, 2000, p.368.
65 Graham Smith, 'Sustainable federalism, democratization, and distributive justice', in Will Kymlicka & Wayne Norman (eds), p.346; Arend Lijphart, 'Constitutional design for divided societies', p.97.
66 John McGarry & Brendan O'Leary, p.33.
67 Graham Smith, pp.346–51; Vernon Bogdanor, pp.67–78; Rein Muellerson, *Ordering Anarchy: International Law in International Society*, Martinus Nijhoff Publishers, The Hague, 2000, p.105; Montserrat Guibernau, pp.50–4.
68 Metta Spencer, 'Conclusion', in Spencer (ed.), *Separatism: Democracy and Disintegration*, Rowman & Littlefield, Lanham, 1998, p.310.
69 Ian S Lustick *et al*, pp.210–11; Rainer Bauböck, pp.378–81; John McGarry & Brendan O'Leary, pp.34–5.
70 Graham Smith, pp.349, 361.
71 Lars-Erik Cederman, 'Nationalism and ethnicity', in Walter Carlsnaes *et al* (eds), *Handbook of International Relations*, p.410; Stefan Wolff, *Disputed Territories*, p.209.
72 John McGarry & Brendan O'Leary, pp.31–2.
73 Will Kymlicka, *Multicultural Citizenship: A Liberal Theory of Minority Rights*, Clarendon Press, Oxford, 1995, p.30; Montserrat Guibernau, pp.37–8; Kenneth McRoberts, 'Managing cultural differences in multinational democracies', in Alain G Gagnon *et al* (eds), *The Conditions of Diversity in Multinational Democracies*, Institute for Research on Public Policy, Montreal, 2003, pp.ix–x; Allen

Buchanan, 'Uncoupling secession from nationalism and intrastate autonomy from secession', in Hurst Hannum & Eileen F Babbitt (eds), *Negotiating Self-Determination*, Lexington Books, Lanham, 2006, pp.92–6.

74 UNPO, pp.2, 3, 7, 16, 18, 19; Wolfgang Danspeckgruber, 'A final assessment', in Danspeckgruber (ed.), pp.352–4; Jorri Duursma, *Fragmentation and the International Relations of Micro-States: Self-Determination and Statehood*, Cambridge University Press, Cambridge, 1996, pp.424–5; Hurst Hannum, *Autonomy, Sovereignty, and Self-Determination: The Accommodation of Conflicting Rights*, University of Pennsylvania Press, Philadelphia, 1992, pp.458–68; Steven Wheatley, *Democracy, Minorities and International Law*, Cambridge University Press, Cambridge, pp.106–9.

75 UNPO, pp.19, 21, 22; Stefan Wolff, *Disputed Territories*, pp.16, 17; Vernon Bogdanor, p.83.

76 *The Europa World Year Book 2005*, Routledge, London, 2005, pp.1286–9.

77 Wolfgang Danspeckgruber, 'A final assessment', pp.352–3.

78 Vernon Bogdanor, p.66; Arend Lijphart, 'Constitutional design for divided societies', p.105; John Coakley, 'Approaches to the resolution of ethnic conflict: The strategy of non-territorial autonomy', *International Political Science Review*, Vol. 15(3), 1994, pp.297–314; Obiora C Okafor, *Re-Defining Legitimate Statehood: International Law and State Fragmentation in Africa*, Martinus Nijhoff, The Hague, 2000, p.61.

79 Rainer Bauböck, p.387.

80 Graham Smith, p.358.

81 Stefan Wolff, *Disputed Territories*, p.210.

82 Arend Lijphart, 'Constitutional design for divided societies', p.105; Rainer Bauböck, p.391.

83 John McGarry & Brendan O'Leary, pp.34–7; Arend Lijphart, 'Self-determination versus pre-determination of ethnic minorities in power-sharing systems', in Will Kymlicka (ed.), *The Rights of Minority Cultures*, Oxford University Press, Oxford, 1995, pp.277–9; Stefan Wolff, *Disputed Territories*, pp.30–1; Donald L Horowitz, 'The cracked foundations of the right to secede', *Journal of Democracy*, Vol. 14(2), April 2003, pp.1–15; Steven Wheatley, pp.161–78.

84 Metta Spencer, 'When states divide', in Spencer (ed.), pp.31, 35.

85 *Human Development Report 2004: Cultural Liberty in Today's Diverse World*, UN Development Programme, New York, 2004, pp.6–9.

86 Montserrat Guibernau, pp.34–6.

87 Will Kymlicka & Wayne Norman, 'Citizenship in culturally diverse societies: Issues, contexts, concepts', in Kymlicka & Norman (eds), p.29.

88 Will Kymlicka, *Multicultural Citizenship*, p.31; Steven Wheatley, pp.155–9; Hurst Hannum, 'Self-determination in the twenty-first century', in Hannum & Babbitt (eds), pp.70–6.

89 Metta Spencer, 'Conclusion', p.311.

90 Will Kymlicka, *Multicultural Citizenship*, pp.31–2; Vernon Bogdanor, p.78.

91 Vernon Bogdanor, p.81.

92 Metta Spencer, 'Conclusion', p.311.

93 Allan Buchanan, *Secession*, pp.143–4.

94 Allen Buchanan, *Secession*, p.15.

95 UN Assistance Mission for Iraq, Press release, 'UNAMI presents first analysis to GOI to help resolve on disputed internal boundaries', 5 June 2008, http://www.uniraq.org/newsroom/getarticle.asp?ArticleID=702.

96 J Joseph Hewitt *et al*, *Peace and Conflict 2008*, Center for International Development and Conflict Management, University of Maryland, 2007, p.14.

Chapter 4: The Eurasian Quartet

1 ICG (International Crisis Group), *Abkhazia Today*, Europe Report No. 176, 15 September 2006, p.3; Edward Mihalkanin, 'The Abkhazians: A national minority in their own homeland', in Tozun Bahcheli *et al*, *De Facto States: The Quest for Sovereignty*, Routledge, London, 2004, p.144.
2 Natalie Sabanadze, 'International Involvement in the South Caucasus', ECMI Working Paper No. 15, February 2002, Flensburg, p.11.
3 ICG, *Abkhazia Today*, p.4; UNPO (Unrepresented Nations and Peoples Organization), *Abkhazia*, 6 August 1991, http://www.unpo.org/member_profile.php?id=3, p.1; Edward Mihalkanin, p.144.
4 ICG, *Abkhazia Today*, p.4.
5 ICG, *Abkhazia Today*, p.4; UNPO, *Abkhazia*, pp.1–2; Natalie Sabanadze, p.12; Oliver Wolleh, *A Difficult Encounter – The Informal Georgian-Abkhazian Dialogue Process*, Berghof Report, No. 12, September 2006 (Berghof Research Center for Constructive Conflict Management, Berlin), p.11.
6 Oliver Wolleh, p.11; Edward Mihalkanin, p.145.
7 Edward Mihalkanin, p.146.
8 Edward Mihalkanin, p.147; ICG, *Abkhazia Today*, p.5.
9 Quoted by Edward Mihalkanin, p.147.
10 ICG, *Abkhazia Today*, pp.4–5; Oliver Wolleh, p.15.
11 Radio Free Europe, *Caucasus Report*, 22 April 2005, pp.5–6, http://www.rferl.org/reports/Caucasus-report/2005/04/12-080405.asp
12 Edward Mihalkanin, pp.148–9; ICG, *Abkhazia Today*, pp.5–6.
13 ICG, *Abkhazia Today*, pp.6–7; Edward Mihalkanin, pp.150–2.
14 Natalie Sabanadze, pp.13–14.
15 ICG, *Abkhazia Today*, p.6; Oliver Wolleh, p.16.
16 ICG, *Abkhazia Today*, p.5.
17 Quoted by Edward Mihalkanin, p.149.
18 Human Rights Watch, *Georgia/Abkhazia: Violations of the Laws of War and Russia's Role in the Conflict*, Helsinki, March 1995, http://www.hrw.org/report/pdfs/g/georgia/georgia953.pdf.
19 Oliver Wolleh, p.17.
20 ICG, *Abkhazia Today*, pp.19, 26; Natalie Sabanadze, p.13.
21 Quoted in ICG, *Abkhazia Today*, p.7.
22 ICG, *Abkhazia Today*, p.26.
23 Internet source, mhtml:file://F:\CASE%20STUDIES?Georgia1.mht.
24 UNPO, 'Act of state independence of the Republic of Abkhazia', 11 October 1999, http://www.unpo.org/content/view/705/236/.
25 Edward Mihalkanin, pp.151–3.
26 UNPO, 'Abkhazia: Visit by new UN Envoy', 1 September 2006, http://www.unpo.org/article.php?id=5301; UNPO, 'Abkhazia: "Spiral of tension" continues', 12 January 2007, http://www.unpo.org/article.php?id=6140.
27 UNPO, 'Abkhazia: UN reports progress', 25 January 2007, http://www.unpo.org/article.php?id=6219.
28 ICG, *Abkhazia Today*, pp.21–2.
29 ICG, *Abkhazia Today*, p.8; Oliver Wolleh, p.18.
30 Radio Free Europe, *Caucasus Report*, pp.5–6.
31 Edward Mihalkanin, pp.154–5; ICG, *Abkhazia Today*, pp.8–17; UNPO, 'Abkhazia signs treaty with Pridnestrovie', 26 December 2006, http://www.unpo.org/article.php?id=6071; Oliver Wolleh, p.17.

32 ICG, *Abkhazia Today*, pp.8, 12; UNPO, 'Abkhazia signs treaty with Pridnestrovie'.
33 Quoted in BBCNEWS, 'Breakaway Abkhazia votes in poll', 4 March 2007, http://news.bbc.co.uk/1/hi/world/europe/6416685.stm.
34 Edward Mihalkanin, p.153; ICG, *Abkhazia Today*, pp.8–10.
35 UNPO, 'Abkhazia: EU explores options', 24 January 2007, http://www.unpo.org/article.php?id=6210.
36 Vladimir Socor, 'A "parallel CIS" in democratic packaging', *Eurasia Daily Monitor*, 19 September 2005 (The Jamestown Foundation), http://www.jamestown.org/edm/article.php?article_id=2370236; Nicu Popescu, '"Outsourcing" *de facto* statehood: Russia and the secessionist entities in Georgia and Moldova', CEPS Policy Brief (Centre for European Policy Studies), No. 109, July 2006, p.5; ICG CrisisWatch, 'Georgia', 1 December 2003, http://www.crisisgroup.org/home/index.cfm?action=cw...; UNPO, 'Abkhazia: Leader says independence inevitable', 23 October 2006, http://www.unpo.org/article.php?id=5674; UNPO, 'Abkhazia: Leaders meet to discuss cooperation', 17 November 2006, http://www.unpo.org/article.php?id=5858.
37 Dov Lynch, *Engaging Eurasia's Separatist States: Unresolved Conflicts and De Facto States*, United States Institute of Peace Press, Washington DC, 2004, p.3.
38 UNPO, 'Abkhazia signs treaty with Pridnestrovie'.
39 Edward Mihalkanin, p.153; UNPO, 'Abkhazia and South Ossetia signed an agreement on cooperation', 20 September 2005, http://www.unpo.org/article.php?id=2982.
40 Charles King, 'Eurasia's nonstate states', *East European Constitutional Review*, Vol. 10(4), Fall 2001, http:/www.law.nye.edu/eecr/vol10num4/features/king.html, pp.4–5; UNPO, 'Abkhazia signs treaty with Pridnestrovie'.
41 PanArmenian.Net, 'Unrecognized states adopt declaration on principles of conflict settlement', 18 June 2007, http://www.panarmenian.net/news/eng/?nid=22691.
42 *The Tiraspol Times*, 17 March 2007, http://www.tiraspoltimes.com/news/group_warns_of_threat...; UNPO, 'Abkhazia signs treaty with Pridnestrovie'.
43 ICG, *Abkhazia Today*, p.1.
44 UNPO, 'Abkhazia: Russian Duma calls for recognition', 10 December 2006, http://www.unpo.org/content/view/5994/236.
45 UNPO, 'Abkhazia: Appeal to UN Security Council', 15 April 2007, http://www.unpo.org/article.php?id=6557. A case for independence was also made by Thomas Kunze & Henri Bohnet, 'Zwischen Europa und Russland', *KASAuslands-informationen*, No. 1/07, February 2007.
46 UNPO, 'Abkhazia: Kosovo's independence will help', 5 June 2007, http://www.unpo.org/article.php?id=6793.
47 Quoted by Nicu Popescu, '"Outsourcing" *de facto* statehood', p.7.
48 Edward Mihalkanin, p.153; UNPO, 'Abkhazia: FC draws statement on Abkhazian, Ossetian independence referenda', 22 December 2006, http://www.unpo.org/article.php?id=6061.
49 ICG, *Abkhazia Today*, p.8.
50 UNPO, 'Abkhazia: Leader says independence inevitable', 23 October 2006, http://www.unpo.org/article.php?id=5674.
51 Oliver Wolleh, p.19; UNPO, 'Abkhazia: UN adopts resolution with focus on Kodori', 18 October 2006, http://www.unpo.org/article.php?id=5646; Eurasia Daily Monitor, 'Moscow kills Boden Paper, threatens to terminate UNOMIG in Georgia', 7 February 2006, http://jamestown.org/edm/article.php?article_id=2370748.

52 ICG CrisisWatch, 'Georgia', 1 June 2004, http://www.crisisgroup.org/home/index.cfm?action=cw...; ICG, *Abkhazia Today*, pp.2, 21.
53 Quoted in ICG, *Abkhazia Today*, p.2.
54 UNPO, 'Abkhazia: Georgia promises autonomy', 28 May 2007, http://www.unpo.org/article.php?id=6760; UNPO, 'Abkhazia and Georgia debate "South-Tirol model"', 13 April 2005, http://www.unpo.org/news_detail.php?arg=03&par=2320.
55 ICG, *Georgia and Russia: Clashing over Abkhazia*, Europe Report No. 193, 5 June 2008, p.18.
56 ICG, *Georgia and Russia*: pp.i, ii, 2, 13–16.
57 *Frankfurter Allgemeine Zeitung*, 30 April 2008.
58 ICG, *Georgia and Russia*: p.23.
59 George Hewitt, 'Abkhazia and South Ossetia: heart of conflict, key to solution', Democracy News Analysis, 19 August 2008, p.5, http://www.opendemocracy.net.
60 ICG, *Georgia: Avoiding War in South Ossetia*, Europe Report, No. 159, 26 November 2004, p.2; GlobalSecurity.org, 'South Ossetia', http://www.globalsecurity.org/ military/world/war/south-ossetia.htm.
61 BBCNEWS, 'Regions and territories: South Ossetia', 4 March 2007, http://news.bbc.co.uk/1/hi/world/europe/country_profiles/3797729.stm.
62 ICG, *Georgia: Avoiding War in South Ossetia*, p.3; Caucasus Foundation, 'South Ossetia', http://www.kafkas.org.tr/english/bgkafkas/bukaf_gosteya.htm.
63 ICG, Georgia: *Avoiding War in South Ossetia*, p.3.
64 ICG, *Georgia: Avoiding War in South Ossetia*, p.3; BBCNEWS, 'Regions and territories'.
65 ICG, *Georgia: Avoiding War in South Ossetia*, p.3.
66 ICG, *Georgia: Avoiding War in South Ossetia*, pp.3, 6–7.
67 ICG, *Georgia: Avoiding War in South Ossetia*, pp.4–5; Dov Lynch, *Engaging Eurasia's Separatist States*, pp.115–16.
68 Dov Lynch, *Engaging Eurasia's Separatist States*, p.116.
69 ICG, *Georgia: Avoiding War in South Ossetia*, p.5.
70 ICG, *Georgia's South Ossetia Conflict: Make Haste Slowly*, Europe Report, No. 183, 7 June 2007, pp.9, 13.
71 ICG, *Georgia: Avoiding War in South Ossetia*, pp.7–8, 18.
72 Quoted in ICG, *Georgia: Avoiding War in South Ossetia*, p.16.
73 ICG, *Georgia: Avoiding War in South Ossetia*, p.16; ICG CrisisWatch, 'Georgia', 1 October 2005, http://www.crisisgroup.org/home/index.cfm?
74 ICG, *Georgia: Avoiding War in South Ossetia*, pp.11–14; ICG, *Georgia's South Ossetia Conflict*, pp.22–3.
75 ICG, *Georgia: Avoiding War in South Ossetia*, p.14; ICG, *Georgia's South Ossetia Conflict*, p.17.
76 ICG, *Georgia's South Ossetia Conflict*, p.20.
77 Natalie Sabanadze, pp.16–17.
78 ICG, *Georgia's South Ossetia Conflict*, p.20.
79 ICG CrisisWatch, 'Georgia', 1 July 2006, http://www.crisisgroup.org/home/index.cfm?action=cw...
80 See, for instance, Portuguese Presidency of the Council of the European Union, 'Statement of the European Union on South Ossetia, Georgia', 12 July 2007, http://www.delvie.ec.europa.eu/en/eu_osce/eu...
81 Quoted in ICG, *Georgia's South Ossetia Conflict*, p.3.
82 Wikipedia, 'South Ossetia', 2007, pp.2, 5; BBCNEWS, 'Regions and territories'.
83 ICG, *Georgia's South Ossetia Conflict*, p.5.

84 Quoted in ICG, *Georgia's South Ossetia Conflict*, p.8.
85 ICG, *Georgia's South Ossetia Conflict*, pp.1, 3.
86 ICG CrisisWatch, 'Georgia', 1 June 2006, http://www.crisisgroup.org.home/index.cfm?action=cw...
87 Tony Iltis, 'Behind the war on South Ossetia', Green Left, 16 August 2008, p.2 http://www.greenleft.org.au/2008/763/39407; George Hewitt, 'Abkhazia and South Ossetia: heart of conflict, key to solution', Open Democracy News Analysis, 19 August 2008, p.5, http://www.opendemocracy.net.
88 'Georgia declares "state of war" over South Ossetia', guardian.co.uk, 9 August 2008, http://www.guardian.co.uk/world/2008/aug/09/georgia.russia2/print; 'Georgia: Russia enters into "war" in South Ossetia', Telegraph.co.uk, 9 August 2008, http://www.telegraph.cu.uk/news/worldnews/europe/georgia/2525400/Georgia-Russia-en...
89 'Georgia declares "state of war" over South Ossetia'; 'Georgia: Russia enters into "war" in South Ossetia'.
90 Tony Iltis, 'Georgia and Russia declare ceasefire', guardian.co.uk, http://www.guardian.co.uk/world/2008/aug/16/georgia.russia2; BBCNEWS, 'Russia signs up to Georgia truce', 16 August 2008, http://news.bbc.co.uk/2/hi/europe/7564776.stm; 'Sarkozy under fire over "foggy" Georgia peace plan', EurActiv, 29 August 2008, http://www.euractiv.com/en/enlargement/sarkozy-fire-foggy-georgia-peace-plan/articl...
91 'Sarkozy under fire over "foggy" Georgia peace plan'.
92 BBCNEWS, 'Russia recognises Georgian rebels', 26 August 2008, http://newsvote.bbc.co.uk/mpapps/pagetools/print/news.bbc.co.uk/2/hi/europe/7582181.sttm.
93 'Russia recognizes South Ossetia and Abkhazia to save people's lives', Pravda, 26 August 2008, http://english.pravda.ru/print/russia/kremlin/106214-russia_ossetia_abkhazia-O.
94 *Frankfurter Allgemeine Zeitung*, 26 August 2008.
95 'Medvedev defends his stance on Georgia', France 24, 27 August 2008, http://www.france24.com/en/20080827-russia-georgia-dmitry-medvedev-defends-decisio...
96 Tony Iltis, p.3.
97 'Russia recognizes Abkhazia and South Ossetia, while the West condemns it', RTTNews, 26 August 2008, http://www.rttnews.com/ArticlePrint.aspx?id=694224; 'Russia faces Western pressure over Georgia', Reuters, 26 August 2008, http://www.reuters.com/articlePrint?articleId=USL768040420080826.
98 'Medvedev endorses Georgia break-up', FT.com, 26 August 2008, http://www.ft.com/cms/s/0043d384-7632-11dd-8a-66...
99 'Russia recognizes Abkhazia and South Ossetia, while the West condemns it'.
100 ICG, *Georgia: Avoiding War in South Ossetia*, pp.4, 6, 8; Kafkas Vakfi; GlobalSecurity.org, 'South Ossetia', 2007, http://www.globalsecurity.org/military/world/war/south-ossetia.htm.
101 ICG, *Georgia: Avoiding War in South Ossetia*, pp.9–11; ICG, *Georgia's South Ossetia Conflict*, p.16.
102 ICG CrisisWatch, 'Georgia', 1 June 2004, http://www.crisisgroup.org/home/index.cfm?...; BBCNEWS, 'Regions and territories'.
103 ICG, *Georgia's South Ossetia Conflict*, p.11.
104 *Time*, 7 February 2005.
105 Quoted in ICG, *Georgia's South Ossetia Conflict*, p.8; Institute for War and Peace Reporting, 'Georgia devises new plan for South Ossetia', 6 April 2007, http://www.iwpr.net/?p=crs&s=f&o=334684&apc_state=henpcrs.

106 Quoted in ICG, *Georgia: Avoiding War in South Ossetia*, p.8.
107 Civil.Ge, 'Putin speaks of S. Ossetia, Abkhazia', 11 October 2006, http://www.civil.ge/eng/detail.php?id=13843.
108 BBCNEWS, 'Regions and territories'; *The Christian Science Monitor*, 5 June 2006.
109 Quoted in *The Christian Science Monitor*, 5 June 2006.
110 Kafkas Vakfi, 'South Ossetia', *Caucasus Today*, undated, http://www.kafkas.org.tr/english/bgkafkas/bukaf_gosetya.htm; ICG, *Georgia: Avoiding War in South Ossetia*, p.8.
111 ICG, *Georgia: Avoiding War in South Ossetia*, p.17.
112 ICG, *Georgia: Avoiding War in South Ossetia*, p.9.
113 ICG, *Moldova: Regional Tensions over Transdniestria*, Europe Report, No. 157, 17 June 2004, p.i.
114 ICG, *Moldova: No Quick Fix*, Europe Report, No. 147, 12 August 2003, p.1.
115 Steven D Roper, 'From frozen conflict to frozen agreement: The unrecognized state of Transdniestria', in Tozun Bahcheli *et al*, p.103; ICG, *Moldova: No Quick Fix*, p.2.
116 Steven D Roper, pp.103–4.
117 Steven D Roper, pp.104–5; ICG, *Moldova: No Quick Fix*, p.2.
118 Steven D Roper, p.105; ICG, *Moldova: No Quick Fix*, p.2.
119 ICG, *Moldova: No Quick Fix*, p.2.
120 ICG, *Moldova: No Quick Fix*, pp.2–3; Steven D Roper, pp.105–6.
121 ICG, *Moldova: No Quick Fix*, p.3; Steven D Roper, pp.102, 106–7; Thomas Kunze & Henri Bohnet, p.6.
122 William Crowther's expression, quoted in ICG, *Moldova: No Quick Fix*, p.3.
123 Steven D Roper, pp.106–7.
124 ICG, *Moldova: No Quick Fix*, p.3.
125 ICG, *Moldova: No Quick Fix*, p.3; Steven D Roper, p.107; ICG, *Moldova: Regional Tensions over Transdniestria*, p.1.
126 ICG, *Moldova: No Quick Fix*, pp.3–4; Transdniestria.com, 2007, http://www.transdniestria.com...
127 Steven D Roper, p.110.
128 Steven D Roper, p.108.
129 ICG, *Moldova: No Quick Fix*, p.4; Steven D Roper, pp.111–12.
130 ICG, *Moldova's Uncertain Future*, Europe Report, No. 175, 17 August 2006, p.3.
131 ICG, *Moldova: No Quick Fix*, p.4.
132 ICG, *Moldova's Uncertain Future*, p.1.
133 ICG, *Moldova: Regional Tensions over Transdniestria*, pp.4, 8, 17; ICG, *Moldova's Uncertain Future*, p.4.
134 ICG, *Moldova: Regional Tensions over Transdniestria*, p.8; Charles King, 'The benefits of ethnic war', p.539.
135 ICG, *Moldova: Regional Tensions over Transdniestria*, p.17.
136 ICG, *Moldova: Regional Tensions over Transdniestria*, p.27.
137 *The Economist*, 12 March 2005; ICG, *Moldova's Uncertain Future*, p.12.
138 ICG, *Moldova: Regional Tensions over Transdniestria*, pp.i, 1–4.
139 *The Economist*, 5 August 2006.
140 ICG, *Moldova: Regional Tensions over Transdniestria*, pp.i, 1.
141 ICG, *Moldova: No Quick Fix*, pp.7–9.
142 Quoted in ICG, *Moldova: No Quick Fix*, p.7.
143 ICG, *Moldova: No Quick Fix*, p.7.
144 Dov Lynch, Engaging Eurasia's Separatist States, pp.112–13.

145 ICG, *Moldova: No Quick Fix*, p.1; Thomas Kunze & Henri Bohnet, p.7; ICG, *Moldova's Uncertain Future*, p.2.
146 ICG, *Moldova: No Quick Fix*, pp.10–11.
147 Steven D Roper, pp.110–11; ICG, *Moldova: No Quick Fix*, p.5.
148 http://www.freedomhouse.org/uploads/press_release/fiw07_charts.pdf2007.
149 ICG, *Moldova: No Quick Fix*, p.27.
150 ICG, *Moldova: Regional Tensions over Transdniestria*, p.13.
151 ICG, *Moldova: No Quick Fix*, p.5; ICG, *Moldova: Regional Tensions over Transdniestria*, p.14.
152 ICG, *Moldova: No Quick Fix*, p.6; ICG, *Moldova's Uncertain Future*, pp.2–4; Steven D Roper, p.115; ICG, *Moldova: Regional Tensions over Transdniestria*, p.15; *NewNations Bulletin*, 19 April 2006, pp.2–4, http://www.newnations.com/newsletterssystem/lt/t_go.php...; *The Economist*, 5 August 2006 & 21 April 2007; Dov Lynch, *Managing Eurasia's Separatist States: A Eurasian Case Study*, Occasional Papers 32, Institute for Security Studies, Western European Union, Paris, November 2001, p.22.
153 UNPO, 'Abkhazia: Call for peaceful settlement of territorial conflicts', 18 June 2007, http://www.unpo.org/content/view/6852/236/
154 *Frankfurter Allgemeine Zeitung*, 28 August 2008.
155 Thomas Kunze & Henri Bohnet, p.6.
156 ICG, *Moldova: Regional Tensions over Transdniestria*, pp.3, 19; ICG, *Moldova's Uncertain Future*, pp.19–20; ICG CrisisWatch, 'Moldova', 1 October 2006, http://www.crisisgroup.org/home/index.cfm?action=cw...
157 ICG, *Moldova: Regional Tensions over Transdniestria*, p.6.
158 ICG, *Moldova: No Quick Fix*, pp.1, 8; Steven D Roper, pp.114–15.
159 ICG, *Moldova: No Quick Fix*, pp.10–13.
160 ICG, *Moldova: No Quick Fix*, p.24.
161 ICG, *Moldova: Regional Tensions over Transdniestria*, p.17.
162 Steven D Roper, p.115.
163 ICG, *Moldova's Uncertain Future*, p.20.
164 ICG, *Moldova's Uncertain Future*, pp.11–13, 17.
165 *Frankfurter Allgemeine Zeitung*, 15 April 2008.
166 *Frankfurter Allgemeine Zeitung*, 28 August 2008.
167 *The Nagorno Karabagh Crisis: A Blueprint for Resolution*, A Memorandum Prepared by the Public International Law and Policy Group, May 2000, p.4, http://www.armeniaforeign ministry.com/htms/blueprint.html; Levon Chorbajian, 'Introduction to the English language edition', in Chorbajian *et al*, *The Caucasian Knot: The History and Geopolitics of Nagorno-Karabagh*, Zed Books, London, 1994, p.4.
168 Levon Chorbajian, 'Introduction', pp.4–5.
169 *The Nagorno Karabagh Crisis: A Blueprint for Resolution*, p.4; Claude Mutafian, 'Karabagh in the twentieth century', in Levon Chorbajian *et al*, pp.114–17.
170 *The Nagorno Karabagh Crisis: A Blueprint for Resolution*, p.5.
171 *The Nagorno Karabagh Crisis: A Blueprint for Resolution*, p.5.
172 Levon Chorbajian, 'Introduction', p.6; ICG, *Nagorno-Karabagh: A Plan for Peace, Europe Report*, No. 167, 11 October 2005, p.3.
173 *The Nagorno Karabagh Crisis: A Blueprint for Resolution*, p.5; Levon Chorbajian, 'Introduction', pp.24, 28: Alexei Zverev, 'Ethnic conflicts in the Caucasus 1988–1994', in *Contested Borders in the Caucasus*, undated, p.2, http://poli.vub.ac.be/publi/ContBorders/eng/ch0102.htm.
174 *The Nagorno Karabagh Crisis: A Blueprint for Resolution*, p.5.

175 Gerard Chaliand, 'Preface', in Levon Chorbajian *et al*, pp.xi–xii; Alexei Zverev, p.2.
176 *The Nagorno Karabagh Crisis: A Blueprint for Resolution*, p.6; Levon Chorbajian, 'Introduction', p.7.
177 Levon Chorbajian, 'Introduction', pp.7–8; ICG, *Nagorno-Karabagh: A Plan for Peace*, Europe Report, No. 167, 11 October 2005, pp.3–4; Dov Lynch, *Managing Separatist States*, p.18.
178 *The Nagorno Karabagh Crisis: A Blueprint for Resolution*, p.8; Levon Chorbajian, 'Introduction', p.2.
179 ICG, *Nagorno-Karabagh: A Plan for Peace*, p.4; *The Nagorno Karabagh Crisis: A Blueprint for Resolution*, pp.7–10.
180 ICG, *Nagorno-Karabagh: A Plan for Peace*, pp.4–5.
181 ICG, *Nagorno-Karabagh: A Plan for Peace*, p.6; *The Nagorno Karabagh Crisis: A Blueprint for Resolution*, pp.7–8; Alexei Zverev, p.8.
182 Gerard Chaliand, p.xiii; *The Nagorno Karabagh Crisis: A Blueprint for Resolution*, p.8; Alexei Zverev, p.6.
183 ICG, *Nagorno-Karabagh: A Plan for Peace*, p.7; Gerard Chaliand, p.xii–xv; Levon Chorbajian, 'Introduction', pp.3, 13; Maria R Freire, 'The search for innovative procedures: The OSCE approach to conflicts in the former Soviet area', in Howard M Hensel (ed.), *Sovereignty and the Global Community: The Quest for Order in the International System*, Ashgate, Aldershot, 2004, p.205.
184 Levon Chorbajian, 'Introduction', p.2; ICG Report, 'Nagorno-Karabagh: Risking war', 14 November 2007, from the executive summary, http://www.crisis-group.org/home/index.cfm?id=5157; ICG, *Nagorno-Karabagh: A Plan for Peace*, p.7; ICG, 'Conflict history: Nagorno-Karabagh (Azerbaijan)', September 2004, http://www.crisisgroup.org/home/index.cfm?action=conflict...; *The Nagorno Karabagh Crisis: A Blueprint for Resolution*, p.8.
185 ICG, *Nagorno-Karabagh: A Plan for Peace*, p.7; Natalie Sabanadze, p.9.
186 *The Nagorno Karabagh Crisis: A Blueprint for Resolution*, p.1; Levon Chorbajian, 'Introduction', pp.16, 18–19; Alexei Zverev, p.11.
187 Richard Giragosian, *The Organization for Security and Cooperation in Europe (OSCE) and the Nagorno Karabagh Conflict: A Compilation of Analyses*, Washington, July 2000, http://www.ancsf.org/files/essaysanalysis/osce_Karabagh.pdf; ICG, *Nagorno-Karabagh: A Plan for Peace*, pp.8–9; ICG Report, 'Nagorno-Karabagh: Risking war'.
188 Nicu Popescu, 'The European Union and the conflicts in the South Caucasus', Caucaz europnews, 1 August 2007, http://www.caucaz.com/home_eng/breve_contenu.php?id=291.
189 Dov Lynch, *Managing Eurasia's Separatist States*, p.18; *The Nagorno Karabagh Crisis: A Blueprint for Resolution*, p.11.
190 ICG, *Nagorno-Karabagh: A Plan for Peace*, pp.2, 10. Also see ICG CrisisWatch, 'Nagorno-Karabagh', for regularly updated information.
191 *The Nagorno Karabagh Crisis: A Blueprint for Resolution*, pp.16–17; Gerard Chaliand, p.xv; Levon Chorbajian, 'Introduction', p.32, *Frankfurter Allgemeine Zeitung*, 28 August 2008.
192 *The Nagorno Karabagh Crisis: A Blueprint for Resolution*, pp.17–18; Levon Chorbajian, 'Introduction', p.31.
193 *The Nagorno Karabagh Crisis: A Blueprint for Resolution*, pp.18–19; Levon Chorbajian, 'Introduction', pp.33–4.
194 *The Nagorno Karabagh Crisis: A Blueprint for Resolution*, pp.11, 37; BBCNEWS, 'N Karabagh elects separatist head', 20 July 2007, http://news.bbc.co.uk/go/pr/fr_/2/hi/europe/6908092.stm.

195 ICG, Sabine Freizer, 'Nagorno-Karabagh: Between vote and reality', 14 December 2006, http://www.crisisgroup.org/home/index.cfm?id=4578.
196 Alexei Zverev, p.17.
197 *The Nagorno Karabagh Crisis: A Blueprint for Resolution*, p.36.
198 Alexei Zverev, p.10.
199 ICG, *Nagorno-Karabagh: A Plan for Peace*, pp.1, 15.
200 ICG, *Nagorno-Karabagh: A Plan for Peace*, pp.12–13; Dov Lynch, *Engaging Eurasia's Separatist States: Unresolved Conflicts and De Facto States*, United States Institute of Peace Press, Washington DC, 2004, p.117.
201 ICG, *Nagorno-Karabagh: A Plan for Peace*, p.6; Gerard Chaliand, 'Preface', in Levon Chorbajian *et al*, *The Caucasian Knot*, p.xiv.
202 Quoted by Levon Chorbajian, 'Introduction', p.1.
203 *The Nagorno Karabagh Crisis: A Blueprint for Resolution*, pp.34–7.
204 See, for example, Azerbaijan International, 'The Nagorno-Karabagh question', Winter 1998 (6.4), http://azer.com/aiweb/categories/magazine/64_folder/64_articles...
205 ICG, *Nagorno-Karabagh: A Plan for Peace*, pp.12–14.
206 *The Nagorno Karabagh Crisis: A Blueprint for Resolution*, pp.2, 38–59.
207 Alexei Zverev, p.10.
208 ICG, *Nagorno-Karabagh: A Plan for Peace*, pp.12, 14.
209 ICG, *Nagorno-Karabagh: A Plan for Peace*, p.13.
210 ICG, *Nagorno-Karabagh: A Plan for Peace*, p.13.
211 Quoted in ICG, *Nagorno-Karabagh: A Plan for Peace*, p.13; Richard Giragosian, p.10.
212 Richard Giragosian, p.11.
213 Richard Giragosian, p.11; Radio Free Europe, *Caucasus Report*, 8 April 2005, p.3, http://www.rferl.org/reports/caucasus-report/2005/04/12-080405.asp.
214 ICG, *Nagorno-Karabagh: A Plan for Peace*, pp.13, 15; *The Nagorno Karabagh Crisis: A Blueprint for Resolution*, pp.15–16.
215 Quoted by Richard Giragosian, p.10.
216 ICG, *Nagorno-Karabagh: A Plan for Peace*, p.13.
217 ICG, *Nagorno-Karabagh: A Plan for Peace*, p.21.
218 ICG, *Nagorno-Karabagh: A Plan for Peace*, pp.13–14.
219 Levon Chorbajian, 'Introduction', pp.29–30.

Chapter 5: Kosovo

1 Dick Leurdijk & Dick Zandee, *Kosovo: From Crisis to Crisis*, Ashgate, Aldershot, 2001, pp.3–7. Also see Noel Malcolm, *Kosovo: A Short History*, Macmillan, London, 1998.
2 Dick Leurdijk & Dick Zandee, pp.10–12; AW Palmer, *A Dictionary of Modern History, 1789–1945*, Penguin Books, Harmondsworth, 1972, p.296; The Independent International Commission on Kosovo, *The Kosovo Report: Conflict, International Response, Lessons Learned*, Oxford University Press, Oxford, 2000, p.33.
3 Dick Leurdijk & Dick Zandee, pp.12–13.
4 Julie A Mertus, *Kosovo: How Myths and Truths started a War*, University of California Press, Berkeley, 1999, pp.285–6; Dick Leurdijk & Dick Zandee, pp.13–14.
5 Julie A Mertus, p.287; Dick Leurdijk & Dick Zandee, p.14.
6 Julie A Mertus, pp.288–9.

7 Julie A Mertus, pp.290–2; Dick Leurdijk & Dick Zandee, pp.15–16; The Independent International Commission on Kosovo, pp.35–6.
8 Quoted by Julie A Mertus, p.292.
9 The Independent International Commission on Kosovo, pp.36–7; Peter Radan, *The Break-Up of Yugoslavia and International Law*, Routledge, London, 2002, pp.196–7.
10 Julie A Mertus, pp.294–6; Dick Leurdijk & Dick Zandee, pp.18–19; Peter Radan, p.197.
11 Julie A Mertus, pp.295–6.
12 Joyce P Kaufman, 'The politics of negotiation: A comparative study of Dayton and Rambouillet', in Howard M Hensel (ed.), *Sovereignty and the Global Community: The Quest for Order in the International System*, Ashgate, Aldershot, 2004, p.138.
13 The Independent International Commission on Kosovo, p.41.
14 Julie A Mertus, pp.296–7; Joyce P Kaufman, p.138.
15 Dick Leurdijk & Dick Zandee, p.19; Juliane Kokott, 'Human rights situation in Kosovo 1989–1999', in Christian Tomuschat (ed.), *Kosovo and the International Community: A Legal Assessment*, Kluwer Law International, The Hague, 2002, p.5; Julie A Mertus, p.297.
16 Quoted by Dick Leurdijk & Dick Zandee, p.19 and by Peter Radan, p.199.
17 Dick Leurdijk & Dick Zandee, pp.20–1; Shkëlzen Maliqi, *Kosova: Separate Worlds*, MM Society, Pristina, 1998, p.184; Michael Waller *et al* (eds), *Kosovo: The Politics of Delusion*, Frank Cass, London, 2001, p.174; Miranda Vickers, *Between Serb and Albanian: A History of Kosovo*, Hurst & Co, London, 1998, p.261.
18 Dick Leurdijk & Dick Zandee, p.21; Shkëlzen Maliqi, pp.182–4; Juliane Kokott, pp.4–6.
19 Julie A Mertus, p.306.
20 Dick Leurdijk & Dick Zandee, p.21; Juliane Kokott, p.4; Miranda Vickers, p.289.
21 Shkëlzen Maliqi, pp.184–5.
22 Julie A Mertus, p.297.
23 Julie A Mertus, pp.301–5; Miranda Vickers, p.260; *The Europa World Year Book 2006*, Routledge, London, 2006, p.3816.
24 European Forum, 'UN envoy Ahtisaari presents "compromise" proposal on Kosovo'; *The Economist*, 4 November 2006.
25 United Kingdom, Department for International Development, 'Kosovo', December 2007, http://www.dfid.gov.uk/pubs/files/kosovo-factsheet.pdf; The World Bank, 'Kosovo: Country Brief 2006', September 2006, http://web.worldbank.org...
26 European Commission, Economic and Financial Affairs, 'Kosovo: An economy on hold', Issue 8, October 2007, http://ec.europa.eu/economy_finance/een/008/article_6170_en.htm.
27 Alex J Bellamy, *Kosovo and International Society*, Palgrave Macmillan, Basingstoke, 2002, p.26.
28 Miranda Vickers, pp.259–62.
29 Juliane Kokott, pp.6–9; Gerd Seidel, 'A new dimension of the right of self-determination in Kosovo?' in Christian Tomuschat (ed.), pp.203–15.
30 Julie A Mertus, p.307; Dick Leurdijk & Dick Zandee, p.22.
31 Michael Waller *et al*, p.175.
32 Julie A Mertus, pp.308–9; Dick Leurdijk & Dick Zandee, pp.22–3.
33 Dick Leurdijk & Dick Zandee, p.27.
34 Quoted by Dick Leurdijk & Dick Zandee, pp.28–9.

35 Dick Leurdijk & Dick Zandee, p.27.
36 Dick Leurdijk & Dick Zandee, p.29.
37 Quoted by Dick Leurdijk & Dick Zandee, p.27.
38 Quoted by Joyce P Kaufman, p.140.
39 Quoted by Dick Leurdijk & Dick Zandee, p.31.
40 Dick Leurdijk & Dick Zandee, pp.33–4; Joyce P Kaufman, pp.137–47.
41 Quoted by Dick Leurdijk & Dick Zandee, pp.34–5.
42 On the legality and legitimacy of NATO's air campaign, see The Independent International Commission on Kosovo, pp.4–5, and Ivo H Daalder & Michael E O'Hanlon, *Winning Ugly: NATO's War to Save Kosovo*, Brookings Institution Press, Washington DC, 2000.
43 *The Europa World Year Book 2006*, p.3822; Tonny B Knudsen & Carsten C Laustsen, 'The politics of international trusteeship', in Knudsen & Laustsen (eds), *Kosovo between War and Peace: Nationalism, Peacebuilding and International Trusteeship*, Routledge, London, 2006, p.13.
44 Dick Leurdijk & Dick Zandee, pp.37–8.
45 Michael Bothe & Thilo Marauhn, 'UN administration of Kosovo and East Timor: Concept, legality and limitations of Security Council-mandated trusteeship administration', in Christian Tomuschat (ed.), p.241.
46 Dick Leurdijk & Dick Zandee, p.105; Lene M Søbjerg, 'The Kosovo experiment: Peacebuilding through an international trusteeship', in Tonny B Knudsen & Carsten B Laustsen (eds), p.71.
47 Tonny B Knudsen & Carsten B Laustsen, 'The politics of international trusteeship', p.15; Peter Radan p.201.
48 Lene M Søbjerg, pp.65–6.
49 Lene M Søbjerg, pp.66–7.
50 Dick Leurdijk & Dick Zandee, p.130; *The Europa World Year Book 2006*, p.3823; The Independent International Commission on Kosovo, p.104.
51 Lene M Søbjerg, pp.66–7; Iain King & Whit Mason, *Peace at any Price: How the World failed Kosovo*, Hurst & Co, London, 2006, pp.270–4; *The Europa World Year Book 2006*, p.3823.
52 Lene M Søbjerg, pp.69–70; Rasmus A Kristensen, 'Administering membership of international society: The role and function of UNMIK', in Tonny B Knudsen & Carsten B Laustsen (eds), pp.141–5.
53 Iain King & Whit Mason, p.vii.
54 See, for instance, Iain King & Whit Mason; Richard Caplan, *International Governance of War-Torn Territories: Rule and Reconstruction*, Oxford University Press, Oxford, 2005; Michael Bothe & Thilo Marauhn, pp.217–42.
55 Iain King & Whit Mason, pp.5, 22–4.
56 Quoted by Iain King & Whit Mason, p.vii; *Kosovo Countdown: A Blueprint for Transition*, Europe Report No. 188, 6 December 2007, International Crisis Group, Brussels, p.5.
57 *The Europa World Year Book 2006*, pp.3817–20.
58 Iain King & Whit Mason, pp.vii, 278; *The Europa World Year Book 2006*, p.3824.
59 *The Europa World Year Book 2006*, p.3824.
60 *The Economist*, 24 November 2007.
61 *Kosovo Countdown*, p.1; European Forum, 'UN envoy Ahtisaari presents "compromise" proposal on Kosovo', 2 February 2007, http://www.europeanforum.net/news/340.
62 Chris Patten, 'A ticking clock on Kosovo', *The Boston Globe*, 10 August 2007.
63 *The Economist*, 9 June 2007.

64 *The Economist*, 24 March 2007.
65 Martin Pabst, 'Der kosovarische Knoten, *Europaeische Sicherheit*, No. 56, December 2007, p.21.
66 Martin Pabst, p.21.
67 Chris Patten.
68 *Frankfurter Allgemeine Zeitung*, 29 December 2007.
69 Quoted in 'Kosova: US President takes strong stance', Unrepresented Nations and Peoples Organization, Abkhazia June 2007, http://www.unpo.org/article.php?id=6821.
70 Kosovo Countdown, p.16; Frankfurter Allgemeine Zeitung, 15 October 2007.
71 Quoted in *The Economist*, 1 December 2007.
72 ICG, 'Serbia: "Double trouble"', 14 November 2007, http://www.crisisgroup.org/home/index.cfm?id=5167&1=1.
73 *The Economist*, 15 December 2007.
74 *Kosovo Countdown*, p.1.
75 BBCNEWS, 'Full text: Kosovo declaration', 17 February 2008, http://newsvote.bbc.co.uk/mpapps/pagetools/print/news.bbc.co.uk...
76 'Who recognized Kosovo as an independent state?' 15 June 2008, http://www.kosovothanksyou.com/... ; IntelliBriefs, 'Whether Kosovo will create a precedent for other territories?', 22 February 2008, http://intellibriefs.blogspot.com/2008/02...
77 *The Economist*, 23 February 2008.
78 *The Economist*, 23 February, 2008.
79 ICG, New Briefing, 'Kosovo's first month', 18 March 2008, http://www.crisisgroup.org...; ICG, 'Reassuring Kosovo's Serbs', 20 March 2008, http://www.crisigroup.org/home/index.cfm?id=5348&1=1; *Frankfurter Allgemeine Zeitung*, 26 March 2008; UN Security Council, Update Report No. 5, 'Kosovo', 13 June 2008.
80 *International Herald Tribune*, 15 June 2008.
81 UN Security Council, Update Report No. 5, 'Kosovo'.
82 The single most comprehensive source on status options for Kosovo is the ICG's report *Kosovo Countdown*, pp.3–6. The alternatives listed in our survey are also drawn from Michael Waller *et al*, p.124; Shkëlzen Maliqi, pp.186–7; Miranda Vickers, p.287; Anna Matveeva & Wolf-Christian Paes, *The Kosovo Serbs: An Ethnic Minority between Collaboration and Defiance*, Bonn International Center for Conversion, Friedrich Naumann Foundation (Belgrade) and Saferworld (London), 2003, pp.47–9; International Crisis Group, Conflict Prevention and Resolution, 1 May 2005, http://www.crisisgroup.org/home/index....; Rasmus A Kristensen, 'Administering membership of international society: The role and function of UNMIK', in Tonny B Knudsen & Carsten B Laustsen (eds), pp.142–3; *The Economist*, 22 July 2006, p.35; Gerd Seidel, 'A new dimension of the right of self-determination in Kosovo?' in Christian Tomuschat (ed.), pp.212–15; The Independent International Commission on Kosovo, p.284; Dick Leurdijk & Dick Zandee, pp.145–8; Miranda Vickers, pp.269–70; Martin Pabst, pp.20–2; *The Economist*, 12 May 2007.

Chapter 6: Somaliland

1 Henry Srebrnik, 'Can clans form nations? Somaliland in the making', in Tozun Bahcheli (ed.), *De Facto States: The Quest for Sovereignty*, Routledge, London, 2004, p.210.

2 *The Europa World Year Book 2005*, Routledge, London, 2005, p.3907; *Somaliland: A Promising Country*, Éditions Couleur Locale, Djibouti, 2004, p.18.
3 *The Europa World Year Book 2005*, p.3907.
4 Edna A Ismail, 'Somaliland – Africa's secret success story', Address by the Minister of Foreign Affairs, Republic of Somaliland, to the South African Institute of International Affairs, Johannesburg, 3 February 2005, p.1; ICG, *Somaliland: Time for African Union Leadership*, Africa Report No. 110, 23 May 2006, p.4.
5 Matt Bryden, 'State-within-a-failed-state: Somaliland and the challenge of international recognition', in Paul Kingston & Ian S Spears (eds), *States-Within-States: Incipient Political Entities in the Post-Cold War Era*, Palgrave Macmillan, Houndmills, 2004, p.170.
6 *The Europa World Year Book 2005*, p.3907.
7 This part draws largely on Deon Geldenhuys, *Foreign Political Engagement: Remaking States in the Post-Cold War World*, Macmillan, Houndmills, 1998, pp.124–31.
8 Ali A Mazrui, 'The blood experience: The failed state and political collapse in Africa', *World Policy Journal*, Vol. 12, Spring 1995, p.30.
9 Hussein M Adam, 'Formation and recognition of new states: Somaliland in contrast to Eritrea', *Review of African Political Economy*, Vol. 21(59) March 1994, pp.24–6.
10 Ministry of Foreign Affairs, *Briefing Paper: The Case for Somaliland's International Recognition as an Independent State*, Hargeysa, August 2002, p.6; ICG, *Somaliland: Time for African Union Leadership*, p.5.
11 Deon Geldenhuys, *Foreign Political Engagement*, p.129.
12 Quoted by Matthew Bryden, 'Somalia: The wages of failure', *Current History*, Vol. 94(591), April 1995, p.146.
13 Deon Geldenhuys, *Foreign Political Engagement*, p.130; *The Europa World Year Book 2005*, p.3908; Ministry of Foreign Affairs, *Briefing Paper: The Case for Somaliland's International Recognition as an Independent State*, p.6.
14 Somaliland Official Website, 'Somaliland Minister of Foreign Affairs welcomes first ever discussion of Somaliland at an African Union summit', 27 January 2007, http://www.somalilandgov.com...
15 Awdalnews, 'Somaliland's communiqué to African leaders' summit in Accra', 5 July 2007, http://www.awdalnews.com/wmprint.php?ArtID=9053.
16 ICG, *Somaliland: Time for African Union Leadership*, pp.15–16.
17 Ministry of Foreign Affairs, *Briefing Paper: The Case for Somaliland's International Recognition as an Independent State*, p.7.
18 U Mattei, 'Patterns of African constitution in the making', in Michael Likosky (ed.), *Transnational Legal Processes*, Butterworths, London, 2002, pp.282–5.
19 Ministry of Foreign Affairs, *Briefing Paper: The Case for Somaliland's International Recognition as an Independent State*, p.3.
20 Matt Bryden, 'State-within-a-failed-state', p.171.
21 Hussein M Adam, p.25.
22 Matt Bryden, 'State-within-a-failed-state', p.170; Hussein M Adam, p.24; Ministry of Foreign Affairs, *Briefing Paper: The Case for Somaliland's International Recognition as an Independent State*, p.3.
23 Edna A Ismail, 'Somaliland – Africa's secret success story', Address to the South African Institute of International Affairs, Johannesburg, 3 February 2005, p.2.
24 Matt Bryden, 'State-within-a-failed-state', p.171.

25 ICG, *Somaliland: Time for African Union Leadership*, p.6.
26 Ministry of Foreign Affairs, *Briefing Paper: The Case for Somaliland's International Recognition as an Independent State*, p.6; Matt Bryden, 'State-within-a-failed-state', p.172.
27 Matt Bryden, 'State-within-a-failed-state', p.172.
28 Quoted in ICG, *Somaliland: Time for African Union Leadership*, p.15.
29 Quoted in ICG, *Somaliland: Time for African Union Leadership*, p.17.
30 Matt Bryden, 'State-within-a-failed-state', p.172.
31 J Peter Pham, 'Significant stakes suggest Somaliland shift for U.S.', World Defense Review, 13 December 2007, p.3. http://worlddefensereview.com/pham121307.shtml.
32 African Union, Report of the Chairperson of the Commission on the Situation in Somalia, Peace and Security Council, Addis Ababa, 29 April 2004, pp.3–4; Peter J Pham, p.3.
33 Quoted in ICG, *Somaliland: Time for African Union Leadership*, p.19.
34 Timothy Othieno, 'Somalia's elections and clan politics: A new opportunity or a temporary ceasefire?' Global Insight (Institute for Global Dialogue), Issue 40, November 2004, pp.1–4.
35 *The Washington Post*, 4 December 2007; Stephanie Hanson & Eben Kaplan, 'Somalia's Transitional Government', Council on Foreign Relations Backgrounder, 12 May 2008, http://www.cfr.org/publication/12475/somalias_transitional_government.html.
36 Reuters AlertNet, 'Somaliland leader rules out reunion with Somalia', 2 May 2007, http://www.alertnet.org/thenews/newsdesk/L02453188.htm.
37 ICG, CrisisWatch No. 57, 1 May 2008, http://www.crisisgroup.org/home/index.cfm?id=5417&1=1.
38 'Somaliland and the African Union', Umrabulo, No. 26, August 2006, http://www.anc.org.za/ancdocs/pubs/umrabulo/umrabulo26art16.html.
39 Somaliland Ministry of Foreign Affairs memorandum, April 2002, quoted in Matt Bryden, 'State-within-a-failed-state', p.170.
40 Edna A Ismail, 'Somaliland – Africa's secret success story', p.7.
41 Ministry of Foreign Affairs, *Briefing Paper: The Case for Somaliland's International Recognition as an Independent State*, pp.9–10; Edna A Ismail, 'Somaliland – Africa's secret success story', pp.2, 7.
42 U Mattei, 'Patterns of African constitution in the making', in Michael Likosky (ed.), pp.282–5.
43 Matt Bryden, 'State-within-a-failed-state: Somaliland and the challenge of international recognition', in Paul Kingston & Ian S Spears (eds), *States-Within-States: Incipient Political Entities in the Post-Cold War Era*, Palgrave Macmillan, Houndmills, 2004, pp.168–70, 178; Ministry of Foreign Affairs, *Briefing Paper: The Case for Somaliland's International Recognition as an Independent State*, p.11; ICG, *Somaliland: Time for African Union Leadership*, pp.4, 11, 13.
44 J Peter Pham, pp.1–2, 4; *The Washington Post*, 4 December 2007.
45 Somaliland Page, 'Somaliland Foreign Ministry welcomes U.S. State Department statement', 8 December 2007, http://somalilandpage.blogspot.co/2007/12/somaliland-foreign-ministry-welcomes-us.ht...
46 J Peter Pham, p.4.
47 Former World Bank economist William Easterly, quoted by J Peter Pham, p.4.
48 AU, Report of the Chairperson of the Commission on the Situation in Somalia, Peace and Security Council, Addis Ababa, 29 April 2004.

49 VOAnews.com, 'Somaliland statehood discussed at AU summit', 5 July 2006, http://www.voanews.com/english/archive/2006-07...
50 J Peter Pham, p.3.
51 'Somaliland and the African Union', Umrabulo No. 26, August 2006, p.2.
52 ICG, *Somaliland: Time for African Union Leadership*, p.17.
53 Farhiya Ali Ahmed, 'Somaliland: Elusive independence', *New African*, No. 447, January 2006, p.35.
54 Carsten Heeger, 'Somaliland (Somalia): Staatszerfall, Staatenbildung und Friedenskonsolidierung', in Mir A Ferdowski & Volker Matthies (eds), *Den Frieden Gewinnen: Zur Konsolidierung von Friedensprozessen in Nachkriegsgesellschaften*, Dietz, Bonn, 2003, pp.217–18.
55 Edna A Ismail, 'Somaliland – Africa's secret success story', p.5.
56 Carsten Heeger, pp.222–4.
57 Alisha Ryu, 'Tensions between Somaliland, Puntland heat up', 15 October 2007, Somaliland News Archives, http://www.mbali.info/newsfile 25.htm; ICG, *Somaliland: Time for African Union Leadership*, p.8.
58 Muhammad S Megalommatis, 'Somaliland and Puntland in war...', 20 September 2007, Somaliland News Archives.
59 Garowe Online, 'Somalia: Protestors oppose arrival of Somaliland delegation..., 1 November 2007, Somaliland News Archives, http://www.mbali.info/newsfile 25.htm; BBC Monitoring International Reports, 'Somaliland forces injure four protestors...', 17 October 2007, Somaliland News Archives; BBC Monitoring International Reports, 'Somalia Puntland vows to recapture...', 22 October 2007, Somaliland News Archives.
60 *The Economist*, 6 October 2007.
61 *The Economist*, 6 October 2007.
62 Abdiqani Hassan, 'Breakaway Somali republic advances into Somalia', 15 October 2007, Somaliland News Archives, http://www.mbali.info/newsfile 25.htm.
63 Reuters AlertNet, 'Ten killed in enclave clashes in Somalia', 14 January 2008, http://www.alertnet.org/thenews/newsdesk/L14657508.htm.
64 Quoted by Matt Bryden, 'State-within-a-failed-state', p.172.
65 Matt Bryden, 'State-within-a-failed-state', p.173.
66 Matt Bryden, 'State-within-a-failed-state', pp.172–3.
67 ICG, *Somaliland: Time for African Union Leadership*, p.7.
68 Matt Bryden, 'State-within-a-failed-state', pp.169, 173; Edna A Ismail, 'Somaliland – Africa's secret success story', p.6; Shannon Field, 'Somaliland – the little country that could', *Global Dialogue* (Institute for Global Dialogue), Vol. 8(2), October 2003, p.17.
69 *The Somaliland Times*, 10 May 2008, http://www.somalilandtimes.net/sl/2008/329/1.shtml.
70 Somaliland Forum, Press release, 3 November 2007, http://somalilandforum.org/sl/2007/11/03/somaliland-forum-press-release-3/; Amnesty International, Public Statement, 'Somaliland: Leaders of new opposition party arrested', 7 August, 2007.
71 Somaliland Forum, Press release, 10 August 2007, http://somalilandforum.org/sl/2007/08/10/somaliland-forum-press-release-2/; Amnesty International, Public Statement, 'Somaliland: Opposition party leaders jailed...', 22 August 2007; allAfrica.com, 'Somaliland frees key political prisoners', 18 December 2007, http://allafrica.com/stories/printable/200712190007.html.

72 Amnesty International, 'Document – Somaliland', 5 December 2007, http://www.amnesty.org/en/library/asset/AFR52/017/2007/en/AFR520172007en.html; Africa News, 'Somalia; Government minister says journalists expelled...', 7 December 2007, Somaliland News Archives.
73 Somaliland: A Promising Country, Éditions Couleur Locale, Djibouti, 2004, pp.5, 29; Carsten Heeger, pp.225–6; Matt Bryden, 'State-within-a-failed-state', p.168.
74 Matt Bryden, 'State-within-a-failed-state', p.169.
75 Edna A Ismail, 'Somaliland – Africa's secret success story', p.9; Carsten Heeger, p.227; Somaliland Official Website, 'Ethiopian delegation arrives...', 15 November 2005, http://www.somalilandgov.com.
76 Somaliland Official Website, 'Somaliland President welcomes...', 24 March 2006, http://www.somalilandgov.com.
77 Matt Bryden, 'State-within-a-failed-state', pp.168, 175–8.
78 Shannon Field, 'Somaliland – the little country that could', p.16.
79 ICG, *Somaliland: Time for African Union Leadership*, p.3; Matt Bryden, 'State-within-a-failed-state', pp.173, 180.
80 Quoted by Farhiya A Ahmed, p.35.
81 Quoted by J Peter Pham, p.3 and in Somaliland Page, 'Somaliland Foreign Ministry welcomes U.S. State Department statement', 8 December 2007, http://somalilandpage.blogspot.com/2007/12...
82 AU, Report of the Chairperson of the Commission on the Situation in Somalia, p.5.
83 IFTIN News, 'Overdue recognition of Somaliland border...', 4 June 2008, http://iftin.net/over.html.
84 VOAnews.com, 'Somaliland statehood discussed at AU summit', 5 July 2006, http://www.voanews.com/english/archive/2006-07/2006-07-05-voa.cfm?CFID=24362...
85 Awdalnews, 'Somaliland's communiqué to African leaders' summit in Accra', 5 July 2007, http://www.awdalnews.com/wmprint.php?ArtID=9053.
86 Matt Bryden, 'State-within-a-failed-state', pp.173–4, 181; ICG, *Somaliland: Time for African Union Leadership*, p.2.
87 The Somaliland Times, 'Somaliland Foreign Minister sets the record...', 24 November 2007, http://www.somalilandtimes.net/sl/2007/405/90.shtml.
88 Information obtained from The Somaliland Official Website, http://www.somalilandgov.com.
89 Matt Bryden, 'State-within-a-failed-state', p.174; Ministry of Foreign Affairs, *Briefing Paper: The Case for Somaliland's International Recognition as an Independent State*, p.11; Farhiya A Ahmed, p.35.
90 UN News Centre, 'UN refugee agency starts final phase of repatriation...', 20 November 2007, http://www.un.org/apps/news/story.asp?NewsID...
91 ICG, *Somaliland: Time for African Union Leadership*, p.2.
92 Somaliland Official Website, 'Somaliland Reconstruction and Development Programme meeting held...' 28 November 2007, http://www.somalilandgov.com.
93 Somaliland Official Website, 'UNDP delegation visits Somaliland', 16 April 2008, http://www.somalilandgov.com.
94 Matt Bryden, 'State-within-a-failed-state', p.174.
95 Quoted in Somaliland Page, 'Somaliland Foreign Ministry welcomes U.S. State Department statement', 8 December 2007.
96 Matt Bryden, 'State-within-a-failed-state', pp.176–7.

97 U.S. Department of State, Office of the Spokesman, 'Somaliland', 17 January 2008, http://www.state.gov/r/pa/prs/ps/2008/jan/99466.htm.
98 See U.S. Department of State, Bureau for African Affairs, 'United States policy on Somaliland', 5 December 2007, http://www.state.gov/p/af/rls/fs/2007/96359.htm.
99 'Q & A: UK Parliament on Somaliland', The Somaliland Times, 8 May 2008, http://www.somalilandtimes.net/sl/2008/329/027.shtml.
100 'President Rayale receives British diplomats', The Somaliland Times, 8 May 2008, http://www.somalilandtimes.net/sl/2008/329/080.shtml.
101 Quoted in ICG, *Somaliland: Time for African Union Leadership*, p.13.
102 Matt Bryden, 'State-within-a-failed-state', pp.178–9.
103 Quoted in 'Somaliland and the African Union', Umrabulo, No. 26, August 2006, http://www.anc.org.za/ancdocs/pubs/umrabulo...
104 Matt Bryden, 'State-within-a-failed-state', p.179.
105 ICG, *Somaliland: Democratisation and its Discontents*, Africa Report No. 66, 28 July 2003, from the executive summary.
106 Matt Bryden, 'State-within-a-failed-state', pp.178, 185; Timothy Othieno, p.6.
107 Matt Bryden, 'State-within-a-failed-state', pp.184–5.
108 Matt Bryden, 'State-within-a-failed-state', pp.182–4.
109 ICG, *Somaliland: Time for African Union Leadership*, pp.13, 16.
110 Somaliland Official Website, 'Somaliland Minister of Foreign Affairs welcomes first ever discussion...', 27 January 2007, http://www.somalilandgov.com/.
111 ICG, *Somaliland: Time for African Union Leadership*, p.4.
112 Carsten Heeger, p.231.
113 ICG, *Somaliland: Democratisation and its Discontents*, from the executive summary, http://www.crisisgroup.org/home/ index.cfm?id=1682&1=1; ICG, 'Somaliland: Alternatives to independence?' 28 July 2003, http://www.crisisgroup.org/home/index.cfm?id=2097&1=1.
114 ICG, *Somaliland: Time for African Union Leadership*, p.22.
115 Reuters AlertNet, 'Somaliland leader rules out reunion with Somalia', 2 May 2007, http://www.alertnet.org/thenews/newsdesk/L02453188.htm
116 ICG, *Somaliland: Time for African Union Leadership*, p.18.
117 Hussein M Adam, p.36.
118 Matt Bryden, 'State-within-a-failed-state', p.186.

Chapter 7: Palestine

1 Jamal R Nassar, *The Palestine Liberation Organization: From Armed Struggle to the Declaration of Independence*, Praeger, Westport, 1991, p.1. Also see Baruch Kimmerling & Joel S Migdal, *Palestinians: The Making of a People*, The Free Press, New York, 1993.
2 Jamal R Nassar, pp.2–5; Paul JIM de Waart, *Dynamics of Self-Determination in Palestine: Protection of Peoples as a Human Right*, EJ Brill, Leiden, 1994, p.103.
3 Quoted by Jamal R Nassar, p.9.
4 Quoted by Jamal R Nassar, p.9 and by Dan Tschirgi, 'Palestine 2003: The perils of de facto statehood', in Tozun Bahcheli *et al* (eds), *De Facto States: The Quest for Sovereignty*, Routledge, London, 2004, p.191.
5 Quoted by Ibrahim Abu-Lughod, 'Introduction: On achieving independence', in Jamal R Nassar & Roger Heacock (eds), *Intifada: Palestine at the Crossroads*,

Praeger, New York, 1990, p.4; Dan Tschirgi, p.191; Jamal R Nassar, pp.7–9; Paul JIM de Waart, pp.101, 108–9.

6 Quoted by Jamal R Nassar, p.10.
7 Jamal R Nassar, pp.10–11; Ibrahim Abu-Lughod, p.5; Dan Tschirgi, p.191.
8 Jamal R Nassar, pp.12–13; Dan Tschirgi, p.193.
9 Quoted by Jamal R Nassar, p.13.
10 Dan Tschirgi, p.194; Jamal R Nassar, p.13.
11 Quoted by Jamal R Nassar, p.13; Dan Tschirgi, p.194.
12 Jamal R Nassar, p.14; Paul JIM de Waart, p.121.
13 Jamal R Nassar, p.14; Shibley Telhami, 'The road to Palestinian sovereignty: Problematic structures or conventional obstacles?', in Stephen D Krasner (ed.), *Problematic Sovereignty, Contested Rules and Political Possibilities*, Columbia University Press, New York, 2001, pp.301–2; Paul JIM de Waart, pp.132–5.
14 Jamal R Nassar, p.15.
15 Dan Tschirgi, p.194; Jamal R Nassar, p.16.
16 Jamal R Nassar, p.16.
17 Jamal R Nassar, p.18.
18 Quoted by Jamal R Nassar, p.20.
19 Quoted by John Laffin, *The P.L.O. Connections*, Corgi Books, London, 1982, pp.40–2 and by Paul JIM de Waart, p.140.
20 Rashid Khalidi, *The Iron Cage: The Story of the Palestinian Struggle for Statehood*, Beacon Press, Boston, 2006, p.165.
21 Don Peretz, *Intifada: The Palestinian Uprising*, Westview Press, Boulder, 1990, p.184.
22 Paul JIM de Waart, p.129; Shibley Telhami, pp.309–11, 315.
23 Dan Tschirgi, pp.195–8.
24 Permanent Observer Mission of Palestine to the United Nations, 'Status of Palestine at the United Nations', undated, http://www.un.int/palestine/status.shtml.
25 Deon Geldenhuys, *Isolated States: A Comparative Analysis*, Cambridge University Press, Cambridge, 1990, p.132.
26 Permanent Observer Mission of Palestine to the United Nations, 'Status of Palestine at the United Nations'; Jamal R Nassar, p.149.
27 Deon Geldenhuys, p.132.
28 Quoted by Dan Tschirgi, p.200.
29 Quoted by Dan Tschirgi, p.200.
30 John Laffin, pp.54–5, 78.
31 John Laffin, p.155; Shibley Telhami, p.313.
32 John Laffin, pp.17–19, 153.
33 Jamal R Nassar, pp.154–6.
34 Quoted by Paul JIM de Waart, p.183.
35 Jamal R Nassar, pp.161–2.
36 Jamal R Nassar, pp.168–9.
37 Geoffrey Aronson, *Israel, Palestinians and the Intifada: Creating Facts on the West Bank*, Kegan Paul International, London, 1987, pp.179–85.
38 Ibrahim Abu-Lughod, pp.3, 6, 9–10; B'Tselem, Fatalities in the first Intifada, undated, http://www.btselem.org/English/Statistics/First_Intifada_Tables.asp.
39 Shibley Telhami, p.315.
40 Edward Said, quoted by Samih K Farsoun & Christina E Zacharia, *Palestine and the Palestinians*, Westview Press, Boulder, 1997, p.299.
41 Dan Tschirgi, p.201.

42 Deon Geldenhuys, p.133; Don Peretz, 1990, p.187.
43 Quoted by Don Peretz, pp.211–14.
44 Rashid Khalidi, pp.194–5.
45 Quoted by Deon Geldenhuys, pp.133–4.
46 Deon Geldenhuys, p.134; Dan Peretz, p.187.
47 Don Peretz, p.187.
48 Tal Becker, *International Recognition of a Unilaterally Declared Palestinian State: Legal and Policy Dilemmas*, Jerusalem Center for Public Affairs, undated, at footnote 2, http://www.jcpa.org/art/becker1.htm; Deon Geldenhuys, pp.133–4.
49 Deon Geldenhuys, pp.133–4.
50 Quoted by Paul JIM de Waart, p.141.
51 Dan Tschirgi, p.202.
52 Israel Ministry of Foreign Affairs, 'Israel-PLO recognition: Exchange of letters between PM Rabin and Chairman Arafat', 9 September 1993, http://www.mfa.gov.il/MFA/Peace...
53 Shlomo Brom, *From Rejection to Acceptance: Israeli National Security Thinking and Palestinian Statehood*, United States Institute of Peace Special Report No. 177, February 2007, p.1, http://www.usip.org/pubs/specialreports/sr177.html.
54 Israel Ministry of Foreign Affairs, 'Declaration of Principles on Interim Self-Government Arrangements', September 13, 1993, http://www.mfa.gov.il/MFA/Peace...
55 Malcolm N Shaw, *International Law*, 5th edition, Cambridge University Press, Cambridge, 2003, p.221.
56 Samih K Farsoun & Christina E Zacharia, p.253; Barry Rubin, *The Transformation of Palestinian Politics: From Revolution to State-Building*, Harvard University Press, Cambridge, Mass., 1999, pp.10–11; Glenn E Robinson, *Building a Palestinian State: The Incomplete Revolution*, Indiana University Press, Bloomington, 1997, p.175; Dan Tschirgi, pp.188, 206; Malcolm N Shaw, p.221–2.
57 Glenn E Robinson, pp.175–6.
58 *Time*, 22 November 2004.
59 See Raja Shehaded, *From Occupation to Interim Accords: Israel and the Palestinian Territories*, Kluwer Law International, London, 1997.
60 Rashid Khalidi, p.172.
61 Dan Tschirgi, pp.188–9; Glenn E Robinson, pp.195–7; Samih K Farsoun & Christina E Zacharia, p.284; Barry Rubin, pp.192–3; *The Europa World Year Book 2006*, Routledge, London, 2006, p.3418; Permanent Observer Mission of Palestine to the United Nations, 'Status of Palestine at the United Nations'.
62 Tal Becker, p.2, from the executive summary.
63 Malcolm Shaw, p.222.
64 Tal Becker, p.2, from the executive summary.
65 Dan Tschirgi, p.189.
66 Tal Becker, p.3, from the executive summary; Dan Tschirgi, pp.206–7; Rashid Khalidi, p.199; Barry Rubin, pp.1–3.
67 Tal Becker, p.4, from the executive summary; Dan Tschirgi, pp.206–7.
68 PCBS, Palestinians in Diaspora and in Historic Palestine End Year 2005, 1 January 2006, p.1, http://www.abudis.net/Pal_demographics.htm.
69 Tal Becker, pp.3–4, from the executive summary.
70 Rashid Khalidi, p.159.
71 Rashid Khalidi, pp.158–9.
72 Samih K Farsoun & Christina E Zacharia, p.280.

73 Glenn E Robinson, pp.181–7; Barry Rubin, p.4.
74 Dan Tschirgi, p.205; Rashid Khalidi, pp.203–4.
75 Samih K Farsoun & Christina E Zacharia, pp.219, 315; Barry Rubin, pp.2, 7, 24; Dan Tschirgi, p.205; Glenn E Robinson, p.191.
76 Samih K Farsoun & Christina E Zacharia, p.304.
77 Rashid Khalidi, p.200.
78 *The Europa World Year Book 2006*, p.3419; Dan Tschirgi, pp.187, 203; *Time*, 22 November 2004.
79 Dan Tschirgi, p.188; *The Europa World Year Book 2006*, pp.3421–2.
80 *The Economist*, 26 May 2007; *Time*, 22 November 2004.
81 BBCNEWS, 'The roadmap: Full text', 30 April 2003, http://news.bbc.co.uk/2/hi/middle_east/2989783.stm.
82 *The Europa World Year Book 2006*, pp.3422–3.
83 *Time*, 22 November 2004.
84 *Time*, 22 November 2004.
85 *The Europa World Year Book 2006*, pp.3424–5.
86 *The Europa World Year Book 2006*, p.3429.
87 *The Economist*, 23 December 2006.
88 *The Economist*, 24 March 2007.
89 World Bank, *Investing in Palestinian Economic Reform and Development, Report for the Pledging Conference*, Paris, December 17th, 2007, pp.5–6; 'Hamas takes control of Gaza', 15 June 2007, guardian.co.uk, http://www.guardian.co.uk/world/2007/jun/15/israel14.
90 Quoted in 'Hamas controls Gaza, says it will stay in power', CNN.com, 14 June 2007.
91 Israel Ministry of Foreign Affairs, 'Terror in Gaza': Eight months since the Hamas takeover', 14 February 2008, pp.1–12 http://www.mfa.gov.il/MFA/Terrorism...
92 Quoted in Israel Ministry of Foreign Affairs, 'Terror in Gaza', p.11.
93 Quoted in Israel Ministry of Foreign Affairs, 'Palestinian PM Haniyeh: Recognition of Israel is out of the question', 3 June 2007, p.1, http://www.mfa.gov.il/MFA/Terrorism...
94 *The Europa World Year Book 2006*, p.3426; *The Economist*, 23 December 2006.
95 *The Economist*, 23 June 2007 and 2 February 2008.
96 ICG, *Ruling Palestine I: Gaza under Hamas*, Middle East Report No. 73, 19 March 2008, from the executive summary, http://www.crisisgroup.org/home/index.cfm?id=5341&1=1.
97 ICG, *Ruling Palestine I: Gaza under Hamas*, from the executive summary.
98 BBCNEWS, 'Israel and Hamas ceasefire begins', 19 June 2008, http://newsvote.bbc.co.uk/mpapps/pagetoosl/print/news...
99 Israel Ministry of Foreign Affairs, 'Joint Understanding on Negotiations', 27 November 2007, http://www.mfa.gov.il/MFA/Peace...
100 Steven Stotsky, 'Will massive infusions of aid rescue the Palestinian economy?' Committee for Accuracy in Middle East Reporting in America, 2 November 2007, pp.1,4, http://www.camera.org/index.asp?x_print...
101 World Bank, *Investing in Palestinian Economic Reform and Development*, p.10; Ziv Hellmann.
102 Dan Tschirgi, pp.206–7.
103 *The Jerusalem Post*, 10 December 2007; World Bank, *Investing in Palestinian Economic Reform and Development*, p.2.

104 World Bank, *Investing in Palestinian Economic Reform and Development*, p.7; Palestinian Central Bureau of Statistics, 'Statistical Abstract of Palestine', No. 8, 15 November 2007, p.2, http:///www.pcbs.gov.ps/Portals/_pcbs/PressRelease…; *International Herald Tribune*, 27 April 2008.
105 *The Economist*, 24 March 2007.
106 World Bank, Investing in Palestinian Economic Reform and Development, pp.5–6.
107 Barry Rubin, p.199.
108 *The Europa World Year Book 2006*, p.3426.
109 World Bank, *Investing in Palestinian Economic Reform and Development*, p.9; World Bank, *Movement and Access Restrictions in the West Bank: Uncertainty and Inefficiency in the Palestinian Economy*, Report of a Technical Team, 9 May 2007, p.2.
110 BBCNEWS, Country profile: Israel and Palestinian territories', 18 December 2007, http://news.bbc.co.uk/1/hi/world/middle_east/country_profiles/803257.stm.
111 World Bank, *Investing in Palestinian Economic Reform and Development*, pp.5–6.
112 *The Economist*, 6 October 2007.
113 *The Guardian*, 9 May 2007.
114 Quoted in *The Guardian*, 9 May 2007.
115 Quoted in *The Guardian*, 9 May 2007.
116 World Bank, *Movement and Access Restrictions in the West Bank*, p.12.
117 Rashid Khalidi, p.202.
118 Ziv Hellmann; *The Economist*, 26 May 2007.
119 World Bank, *Investing in Palestinian Economic Reform and Development*, p.8.
120 World Bank, *Investing in Palestinian Economic Reform and Development*, p.5.
121 Haig Khatchadourian, *The Quest for Peace between Israel and the Palestinians*, Peter Lang, New York, 2000.
122 Rashid Khalidi, p.207.
123 *The Economist*, 26 May 2007.
124 Samih K Farsoun & Christina E Zacharia, p.314.
125 PCBS, Palestinians in Diaspora, p.3; *The Economist*, 26 May 2007.
126 Shlomo Brom, *From Rejection to Acceptance: Israeli National Security Thinking and Palestinian Statehood*, Special Report No. 177, February 2007, United States Institute of Peace, from the summary, http://origin.usip.org/pubs/special-reports/ sr177.html.
127 Rashid Khalidi, pp.213–15.
128 Glenn E Robinson, p.198; Samih K Farsoun & Christina E Zacharia, p.315.
129 Ian Bremmer in *Khaleej Times*, 17 June 2007.
130 Samih K Farsoun & Christina E Zacharia, pp.314–15.
131 Rashid Khalidi, pp.207–8.
132 Rashid Khalidi, pp.208–9.
133 Rashid Khalidi, p.209.
134 Ali Abunimah, *One Country: A Bold Proposal to End the Israeli-Palestinian Impasse*, Metropolitan Books, New York, 2006, pp.12–16, 105, 109.
135 Ali Abunimah, pp.109–12, 116–18.
136 Shlomo Brom, from the summary.
137 Shibley Telhami, p.320.
138 Barry Rubin, p.190.

Chapter 8: Northern Cyprus

1 Florence Elliott, *A Dictionary of Politics*, Penguin Books, Harmondsworth, 1977, p.112; Metin Tamkoç, *The Turkish Cypriot State: The Embodiment of the Right of Self-Determination*, M Rustem & Brother, London, 1988, p.42; Tozun Bahcheli, 'Under Turkey's wings: The Turkish Republic of Northern Cyprus, the struggle for international acceptance', in Bahcheli *et al* (eds), *De Facto States: The Quest for Sovereignty*, Routledge, London, 2004, p.165; Stavros Panteli, *A New History of Cyprus: From the Earliest Times to the Present Day*, East-West Publications, London, 1984.
2 Florence Elliott, p.112; Tozun Bahcheli, p.165.
3 Joseph S Joseph, *Cyprus: Ethnic Conflict and International Concern*, Peter Lang, New York, 1985, p.241.
4 Florence Elliott, p.112.
5 Florence Elliott, p.112.
6 Tozun Bahcheli, pp.165–6; Metin Tamkoç, pp.42–3.
7 Metin Tamkoç, p.42.
8 Metin Tamkoç, p.43; Florence Elliott, p.112.
9 Metin Tamkoç, p.71.
10 Zaim M Nejatigil, *The Turkish Republic of Northern Cyprus in Perspective*, published by the author, Nicosia, 1985, pp.1–3; Florence Elliott, p.113.
11 Metin Tamkoç, p.65.
12 Metin Tamkoç, pp.64, 70; Zaim M Nejatigil, p.1.
13 Metin Tamkoç, p.67; ICG, *The Cyprus Stalemate: What Next?* Europe Report, No. 171, 8 March 2006, p.8.
14 Metin Tamkoç, pp.65, 71; Tozun Bahcheli, p.166.
15 Guy Dundas, 'Cyprus from 1960 to EU accession: The case for non-territorial autonomy', *Australian Journal of Politics and History*, Vol. 50(1), 2004, p.87.
16 Metin Tamkoç, pp.65, 70; Zaim M Nejatigil, p.3; Halil I Salih, *Cyprus: The Impact of Diverse Nationalism on a State*, University of Alabama Press, Alabama, 1978.
17 Quoted by Zaim M Nejatigil, p.1.
18 Metin Tamkoç, pp.65, 71.
19 Metin Tamkoç, p.71; Tozun Bahcheli, p.166; Zaim M Nejatigil, p.3.
20 Metin Tamkoç, pp.70–1.
21 Nancy Crawshaw, 'Cyprus: The political background', in John A Koumoulides (ed.), *Cyprus in Transition 1960–1985*, Trigraph, London, 1986, pp.3–4; Salahi R Sonyel, *Cyprus: The Destruction of a Republic and its Aftermath (1960–1974)*, CYREP, Lefkosa, 2003, pp.37–67.
22 Metin Tamkoç, pp.81–2; Tozun Bahcheli, p.167.
23 Metin Tamkoç, pp.81–2, 133.
24 Nancy Crawshaw, p.3; George S Kaloudis, *The Role of the U.N. in Cyprus from 1964 to 1979*, Peter Lang, New York, 1991.
25 Tozun Bahcheli, p.165; Nancy Crawshaw, p.6.
26 Metin Tamkoç, pp.81–2; Nancy Crawshaw, pp.5–6, 9; Salahi R Sonyel, pp.94–7.
27 Metin Tamkoç, p.82.
28 Nancy Crawshaw, p.9.
29 Metin Tamkoç, p.83.
30 Metin Tamkoç, p.100; Salahi R Sonyel, pp.341–6.
31 Metin Tamkoç, pp.101, 107; Tozun Bahcheli, p.168; Salahi R Sonyel, pp.346–9.
32 NM Ertekün, *The Cyprus Dispute and the Birth of the Turkish Republic of Northern Cyprus*, K Rustem & Brother, Nicosia, 1981, p.32.

33 Metin Tamkoç, p.101.
34 Guy Dundas, p.88.
35 ICG, *The Cyprus Stalemate*, p.8.
36 Tozun Bahcheli, p.168.
37 Quoted by NM Ertekün, p.252.
38 NM Ertekün, p.34.
39 Quoted by NM Ertekün, p.274.
40 NM Ertekün, p.357.
41 Quoted by NM Ertekün, p.360.
42 Guy Dundas, pp.88–9.
43 Zaim M Nejatigil, pp.102–3, 150.
44 Zaim M Nejatigil, p.102.
45 Encyclopedia of the Nations, 'Cyprus', undated, http://www.nationsencyclopedia. com/economies/Asia-and-the-Pacific/Cyprus.html.
46 Tozun Bahcheli, pp.170–1.
47 John Dugard, *International Law: A South African Perspective*, Juta, Kenwyn, 2000, pp.88–9.
48 Michael R Fowler & Julie M Bunck, *Law, Power, and the Sovereign State: The Evolution and Application of the Concept of Sovereignty*, Pennsylvania State University Press, Pennsylvania, 1995, p.52.
49 Quoted by Zaim M Nejatigil, p.107.
50 Quoted by Tozun Bahcheli, p.172.
51 Quoted by Tozun Bahcheli, p.173.
52 Quoted by Tozun Bahcheli, p.173.
53 Final Communique of the twenty-second Islamic Conference of Foreign Ministers, Casablanca, Kingdom of Morocco, 10–12 December 1994, http://www.oic-oci.org/ English/conf/fm/22/final%2022.htm.
54 Tozun Bahcheli, p.170.
55 Tozun Bahcheli, pp.170, 174; ICG, *The Cyprus Stalemate*, p.13.
56 Wikipedia, 'Northern Cyprus', 29 April 2008, http://en.wikipedia.org/wiki/Northern_Cyprus...
57 Tozun Bahcheli, pp.173–4.
58 House of Commons Foreign Affairs Committee, *Visit to Turkey and Cyprus*, Fifth Report of Session 2006–07, The Stationary Office, London, May 2007, p.21.
59 ICG, *The Cyprus Stalemate*, p.27.
60 US Department of State, Bureau of European and Eurasian Affairs, 'Background Note: Cyprus', March 2008, http://www.state.gov/r/pa/ei/bgn/5376.htm.
61 ICG, *The Cyprus Stalemate*, p.2.
62 Turkish Republic of Northern Cyprus Presidency, 'About TRNC', undated, http://www.kktcb.eu/print.php?men=226&submen=0&1n=en.
63 Tozun Bahcheli, pp.176–7.
64 ICG, *The Cyprus Stalemate*, pp.16–17; Tozun Bahcheli, pp.177–80.
65 ICG, *The Cyprus Stalemate*, p.30.
66 *NewNations Bulletin*, 19 April 2006, http://www.lebanonwire.com/0640MLN/06042010NN.asp.
67 ICG, *The Cyprus Stalemate*, p.3.
68 ICG, The Cyprus Stalemate, pp.3–4, 7–9.
69 ICG, *The Cyprus Stalemate*, p.4; Tozun Bahcheli, p.181.
70 Guy Dundas, p.90.
71 ICG, *The Cyprus Stalemate*, p.5; Tozun Bahcheli, pp.182–3.
72 BBCNEWS, 'Turkish Cypriots vote for Talat', 17 April 2005, http://newsvote.bbc.co.uk/mpapps/pagetools/print/news...

73 ICG, *The Cyprus Stalemate*, p.6.
74 Quoted in ICG, *The Cyprus Stalemate*, p.10.
75 ICG, *The Cyprus Stalemate*, pp.8–10.
76 ICG, *The Cyprus Stalemate*, pp.19–20.
77 ICG, *The Cyprus Stalemate*, p.15; ICG, *Cyprus: Reversing the Drift to Partition*, Europe Report, No. 190, 10 January 2008, p.25; *The Economist*, 26 February 2005; House of Commons Foreign Affairs Committee, p.17.
78 ICG, *The Cyprus Stalemate*, p.20.
79 ICG, *Cyprus: Reversing the Drift to Partition*, p.22.
80 Quoted in ICG, *The Cyprus Stalemate*, p.14; *International Herald Tribune*, 17 June 2008.
81 UN, *Report of the Secretary-General on the United Nations Operation in Cyprus*, Security Council document S/2007/699, 3 December 2007, p.3.
82 ICG, *The Cyprus Stalemate*, p.29.
83 ICG, *The Cyprus Stalemate*, p.12; Istanbul Declaration, adopted by the thirty-first session of the Islamic Conference of Foreign Ministers, Istanbul, 14–16 June 2004, http://www.oic-oci.org/english/conf/fm/31/31%20icfm-DECLARATION-eng.htm.
84 ICG, *The Cyprus Stalemate*, p.29.
85 ICG, *Cyprus: Reversing the Drift to Partition*, p.25; David Ravid, 'Turkish Republic of Northern Cyprus to open trade office in Israel', *Haaretz*, 10 March 2008, http://www.haaretz.com/hasen/objects/pages/PrintArticleEn.jhtml?itemNo=962666.
86 House of Commons Foreign Affairs Committee, p.12; *International Herald Tribune*, 1 July 2005.
87 House of Commons Foreign Affairs Committee, p.12.
88 Tozun Bahcheli, p.184.
89 ICG, *The Cyprus Stalemate*, pp.12–15.
90 *The Economist*, 9 December 2006.
91 *The Economist*, 21 October 2006.
92 *Time*, 13 November 2006; ICG, 'Settling Cyprus', 15 February 2008, http://www.crisisgroup.org/home/index.cfm?id=5294&1=1.
93 UN, *Report of the Secretary-General on the United Nations Operation in Cyprus*, p.10.
94 UN, *Report of the Secretary-General on the United Nations Operation in Cyprus*, pp.2–3; ICG, *Cyprus: Reversing the Drift to Partition*, pp.5–6.
95 BBCNEWS, 'Country profile: Cyprus', 28 February 2008, http://newsvote.bbc.co.uk/mpapps/pagetools/print/news...; TRNC Presidency, 'Talat: "We are bound to prepare a plan, which would be acceptable to both peoples"', 26 April 2008, http://www.kktcb.eu/print_news.php?id=303&1n=en; TRNC Presidency, 'President Talat wraps up his contacts in Ankara', 25 April 2008, http://www.kktcb. eu/print_news.php?id=305&1n=en; ICG, *CrisisWatch*, No. 56, 1 April 2008.
96 ICG, *Cyprus: Reversing the Drift to Partition*, p.12.
97 Türkiye Cumhuriyeti Cumhurbaskanligi, 'Speech by H.E. Mr. Abdullah Gül, President of the Republic of Turkey, in honour of H.E. Mr. Mehmet Ali Talat, President of the Turkish Republic of Northern Cyprus, 3 January 2008, p.1, http://www.cankaya.gov.tr/tr_html/KONUSMALAR/03.01.2008.3721.html.
98 TRNC Presidency, 'Talat: "We are bound to prepare a plan"'.
99 TRNC Presidency, 'President Talat's statement on 25 February 2008 on the results of the Greek Cypriot elections', http://www.kktcb.eu/print_news.php?id=242&1n=en.

100 TRNC Presidency, 'Talat: "We are bound to prepare a plan"'.
101 Quoted in BBCNEWS, 'Cyprus leaders seek fresh talks', 25 February 2008, http://newsvote.bbc.co.uk/mpapps/pagetools/print/news...
102 ICG, *Cyprus: Reversing the Drift to Partition*, p.7.
103 Quoted in *International Herald Tribune*, 7 February 2008.
104 ICG, *Cyprus: Reversing the Drift to Partition*, p.9.
105 ICG, *Cyprus: Reversing the Drift to Partition*, pp.17–18.
106 ICG, 'Settling Cyprus', 14 February 2008; ICG, *Cyprus: Reversing the Drift to Partition*, pp.15–18.
107 Guy Dundas, p.91.
108 ICG, *The Cyprus Stalemate*, pp.20–1.
109 ICG, *The Cyprus Stalemate*, p.22.
110 Tozun Bahcheli, pp.182–3.
111 House of Commons Foreign Affairs Committee, p.13.

Chapter 9: Western Sahara

1 Stephen Zunes, 'Indigestible lands? Comparing the fates of Western Sahara and East Timor', in Brendan O'Leary *et al* (eds), *Right-Sizing the State: The Politics of Moving Borders*, Oxford University Press, Oxford, 2001, p.289; Francois Rigaux, 'East Timor and Western Sahara: A Comparative view', in *International Law and the Question of East Timor*, CIIR/IPJET, London, 1995, pp.166–8.
2 John Damis, *Conflict in Northwest Africa: The Western Sahara Dispute*, Hoover Institution Press, Stanford, 1983, p.1.
3 Joshua Castellino, *International Law and Self-Determination*, Martinus Nijhoff Publishers, The Hague, 2000, p.173; Stephen Zunes, 'Indigestible lands?', p.295.
4 Faten Aggad & Pierre du Toit Botha, 'Revisiting the Western Saharan conflict', *Africa Insight*, Vol. 35(1), April 2005, p.66.
5 John Damis, pp.2, 12.
6 Faten Aggad & Pierre du Toit Botha, p.66.
7 John Damis, p.13.
8 Faten Aggad & Pierre du Toit Botha, p.66; John Damis, p.15; Tony Hodges, *Western Sahara: The Roots of a Desert War*, Lawrence Hill, Westport, 1983, p.vi.
9 John Damis, pp.15, 19, 23.
10 Stephen Zunes, 'Indigestible lands?', p.311.
11 Thomas Franck, 'The theory and practice of decolonization – the Western Saharan case', in Richard Lawless & Laila Monahan (eds), *War and Refugees: The Western Sahara Conflict*, Pinter, London, 1987, p.10.
12 Jarat Chopra, *United Nations Determination of the Western Saharan Self*, Norwegian Institute of International Affairs, Oslo, 1994, p.9.
13 Faten Aggad & Pierre du Toit Botha, pp.66–7.
14 John Damis, pp.38–42; Tony Hodges, *Western Sahara*, p.vii.
15 Quoted by Toby Shelley, *Endgame in the Western Sahara: What Future for Africa's Last Colony?* Zed Books, London, 2004, p.171 and by Jarat Chopra, p.10.
16 Quoted by Faten Aggad & Pierre du Toit Botha, p.67; Thomas Franck, pp.11–12.
17 Toby Shelley, p.190; Tony Hodges, *Western Sahara*, p.viii; Faten Aggad & Pierre du Toit Botha, pp.67–8.
18 John Damis, p.74; Faten Aggad & Pierre du Toit Botha, p.67; Tony Hodges, *Western Sahara*, p.viii; Thomas Franck, p.12.
19 John Damis, pp.74–5.

20 Western Sahara Online, 'SADR: Proclamation of the Sahrawi Arab Democratic Republic (February 27, 1976)', http://www.wsahara.net/sadr.html.
21 Western Sahara Online, 'SADR: Proclamation of the Sahrawi Arab Democratic Republic; John Damis, pp.75–6; Timothy Othieno & Siphamandla Zondi, 'Western Sahara and the UN: A litany of failures and a confluence of possibilities', *Global Insight*, No. 51, June 2005, p.1 (Institute for Global Dialogue, Midrand, South Africa).
22 Tony Hodges, *Western Sahara*, p.308; Tony Hodges, 'Introduction', in Richard Lawless & Laila Monahan (eds), p.4.
23 John Damis, pp.40–2; Jarat Chopra, p.43.
24 Stephen Zunes, 'Indigestible lands?', p.296.
25 Suresh C Saxena, *The Liberation War in Western Sahara*, Vidya Publishers, New Delhi, 1981, pp.81–5; Tony Hodges, *Western Sahara*, p.viii; Karen Thomas, 'A future on hold', *History Today*, Vol. 51(8), August 2001, p.2.
26 Joshua Castellino, p.253.
27 *The Middle East and North Africa 2005*, Europa Publications, London, 2004, p.843.
28 John Damis, pp.82–3; Faten Aggad & Pierre du Toit Botha, p.67; Jacob Mundy, 'Western Sahara between autonomy and intifada', Global Policy Forum, 16 March 2007, p.3, http://www.globalpolicy.org/security/issues/wsahara/2007/0316intifada.htm.
29 Ian Williams & Stephen Zunes, 'Self-determination struggle in the Western Sahara continues to challenge the UN', *Foreign Policy in Focus* (Global Policy Forum), September 2003, p.3.
30 John Damis, pp.45, 86–7; *The Middle East and North Africa 2005*, p.843.
31 Malcolm N Shaw, quoted by Susan Slyomovics, 'Self-determination as self-definition: The case of Morocco', in Hurst Hannum & Eileen F Babbitt (eds), *Negotiating Self-Determination*, Lexington Books, Lanham, 2006, p.146.
32 Susan Slyomovics, pp.147–8.
33 Ian Williams & Stephen Zunes, p.3; Toby Shelley, pp.190–1.
34 Susan Slyomovics, pp.147–8.
35 ICG, *Western Sahara: The Cost of the Conflict*, Report No. 65, 11 June 2007, p.12.
36 *The Middle East and North Africa 2005*, p.856; *The Economist*, 10 March 2007. Also see Akbarali Thobhani, *Western Sahara since 1975 under Moroccan Administration: Social, Economic, and Political Transformation*, Edwin Meilen Press, Lewiston NY, 2002.
37 Ian Williams & Stephen Zunes, p.1.
38 Timothy Othieno & Siphamandla Zondi, p.8; *The Economist*, 10 March 2007; ICG, *Western Sahara: The Cost of Conflict*, pp.1, 5, 12; Toby Shelley, pp.191–4.
39 Tony Hodges, *Western Sahara*, pp.307–10, 315.
40 ICG, *Western Sahara: The Cost of the Conflict*, p.16.
41 Darrell Dela Rosa, 'The UN role in Western Sahara', *UN Chronicle*, No. 3, 2003, p.22; *The Middle East and North Africa 2005*, p.855.
42 Quoted by Tony Hodges, *Western Sahara*, p.319.
43 Quoted by Faten Aggad & Pierre du Toit Botha, p.71.
44 Quoted by Faten Aggad & Pierre du Toit Botha, p.71.
45 ICG, *Western Sahara: The Cost of the Conflict*, p.3.
46 Joshua Castellino, p.185; Faten Aggad & Pierre du Toit Botha, p.71; UN Department of Public Information, 'Western Sahara-MINURSO-mandate',

http://www.un.org/Depts/dpko/missions/minurso/mandate.html; *The Middle East and North Africa 2005*, p.855.

47 Jacob Mundy, 'Western Sahara: Against autonomy', *Foreign Policy in Focus* (International Relations Center), 4 May 2007, p.3, http://www.worldpress.org/Africa/2778.cfm; Jarat Chopra, pp.12–17; Faten Aggad & Pierre du Toit Botha, pp.71–2; Jacob Mundy, 'Western Sahara between autonomy and intifada', pp.3–4.

48 *The Middle East and North Africa 2005*, pp.856–7; Jacob Mundy, 'Western Sahara between autonomy and intifada', p.4.

49 Faten Aggad & Pierre du Toit Botha, p.72; Timothy Othieno & Siphamandla Zondi, p.3.

50 Quoted by Faten Aggad & Pierre du Toit Botha, p.72.

51 Timothy Othieno & Siphamandla Zondi, p.4; UN News Service, 'UN mission in Western Sahara should remain for 6 more months – Annan', 24 April 2006, http://www.un.org/apps/news/printnews.asp?nid=18224; Jacob Mundy, 'Western Sahara between autonomy and intifada', p.5.

52 UN Security Council, *Report of the Secretary-General on the Situation concerning Western Sahara*, Document S/2006/249, 19 April 2006, p.9.

53 Neil Ford, 'Oil potential could provide catalyst for change', *Middle East*, No. 330, January 2003, p.54.

54 U.S. Department of State, *Western Sahara Country Report on Human Rights Practices for 1998*, Bureau for Democracy, Human Rights, and Labor, February 1999, p.2.

55 Mohamed Cherkaoui, *Morocco and the Sahara: Social Bonds and Geopolitical Issues*, Bardwell Press, Oxford, 2007, p.179.

56 Quoted by Neil Ford, p.53.

57 Quoted by *The Middle East and North Africa 2005*, pp.857–8; Timothy Othieno & Siphamandla Zondi, p.7; Neil Ford, pp.52–3.

58 Timothy Othieno & Siphamandla Zondi, pp.5–6; Suresh C Saxena, p.93; Faten Aggad, 'Future prospects for the resolution of the conflict in the Western Sahara', *Africa Insight*, Vol. 36(2), June 2006, pp.40–1. Jacob Mundy, 'Western Sahara between autonomy and intifada', p.5.

59 Timothy Othieno & Siphamandla Zondi, p.8.

60 Faten Aggad, 'Future prospects for the resolution of the conflict in the Western Sahara', p.42; UN Security Council, *Report of the Secretary-General on the Situation concerning Western Sahara*, 19 April 2006, p.1.

61 Jacob Mundy, 'Western Sahara: Against autonomy'; Jacob Mundy, 'Western Sahara between autonomy and intifada', p.6.

62 UN Security Council, *Report of the Secretary-General on the Situation concerning Western Sahara*, 13 April 2007, Document S/2007/202, pp.3, 13; Jacob Mundy, 'Western Sahara between autonomy and intifada', pp.2–3.

63 Quoted in 'Sahrawi independence would be "viable"', *Afrol News*, 2 March 2002.

64 CIA, *The World Factbook*, Western Sahara, 2003.

65 Faten Aggad & Pierre du Toit Botha, p.68.

66 Stephen Zunes, 'UN betrayal of Western Sahara appears imminent', *Foreign Policy in Focus*, 2 June 2001.

67 Quoted by Toby Shelley, p.181.

68 Toby Shelley, pp.181–3.

69 *The Middle East and North Africa 2005*, p.859.

70 Western Sahara News, Résumé February 2008, 27 February 2008, p.2, http://www.arso.org/01-e08-02.htm.
71 Stephen Zunes, 'UN betrayal of Western Sahara appears imminent'; Barry Bartmann, 'Political realities and legal anomalies: Revisiting the politics of international recognition', in Tozun Bahcheli *et al* (eds), *De Facto States: The Quest for Sovereignty*, Routledge, London, 2004, p.28.
72 Joshua Castellino, p.189.
73 See the monthly Western Sahara News Résumé at http://www.arso.org.
74 The monthly Western Sahara News Résumé carries regular reports on NGOs concerning themselves with Western Sahara.
75 Western Sahara News, Résumé January 2008, 14 January 2008, p.4, http://www.arso.org/01-0104.htm.
76 Quoted by Stephen Zunes, 'The future of Western Sahara', *Foreign Policy in Focus* (Washington DC), 20 July 2007, p.3.
77 ICG, *Western Sahara: The Cost of Conflict*, p.2.
78 Stephen Zunes, 'The future of Western Sahara', p.3.
79 UN Security Council, *Report of the Secretary-General on the Situation concerning Western Sahara*, 13 April 2007, p.2; Adil Dekkaki, 'Proposals to resolve the conflict in the Western Sahara', Global Policy Forum, 17 April 2007, p.2, http://www.globalpolicy.org/security/issues/wsahara/2007/0417proposals.htm; Stephen Zunes, 'The future of Western Sahara', p.3.
80 Jacob Mundy, 'Western Sahara: Against autonomy', p.3.
81 Jacob Mundy, 'Western Sahara: Against autonomy', p.3.
82 *The Middle East and North Africa 2005*, p.857.
83 Jacob Mundy, 'Western Sahara: Against autonomy', pp.2–4; Mohamed Cherkaoui, p.61.
84 Moroccan American Center for Policy, 'The Moroccan initiative in the Western Sahara', 11 April 2007, http://www.moroccanamericanpolicy.com/MoroccanCompromiseSolution041107.pdf.
85 Western Sahara News, Résumé November 2007, 6 November 2007, p.1, http://www.arso.org/01-e07-4548.htm.
86 Stephen Zunes, 'Indigestible lands?', p.312.
87 Quoted in ICG, *Western Sahara: The Cost of Conflict*, p.2.
88 Stephen Zunes, 'Indigestible lands?', p.312.
89 Stephen Zunes, 'The future of Western Sahara', pp.1–3.
90 SABCNEWS, 'UN divided on Morocco, Western Sahara dispute', 12 July 2007, http://www.sabcnews.com/world/north_america/0,2172,152402,00...
91 UN Security Council, *Report of the Secretary-General on the Status and Progress of the Negotiations on Western Sahara*, 25 January 2008, document S/2008/45, pp.1–3.
92 allAfrica.com, 'Western Sahara: Security Council extends UN's mission through April 2008'.
93 ICG, *Western Sahara: Out of the Impasse*, Report No. 66, 11 June 2007, from the executive summary, pp.1–3, http://www.crisisgroup.org/home/index.cfm?id=4893&1=1.
94 ICG, *Western Sahara: Out of the Impasse*, from the executive summary, p.1; ICG, *Western Sahara: The Cost of Conflict*, p.i, Jacob Mundy, 'Western Sahara: Against autonomy', p.6.
95 ICG, *Western Sahara: The Cost of Conflict*, pp.i, 8.
96 ICG, *Western Sahara: The Cost of Conflict*, pp.i, 16–19.
97 ICG, *Western Sahara: Out of the Impasse*, from the executive summary, p.2.

Chapter 10: Taiwan

1 Florence Elliott, *A Dictionary of Politics*, Penguin Books, Harmondsworth, 1977, pp.89–90; AW Palmer, *A Dictionary of Modern History*, Penguin Books, Harmondsworth, 1972, pp.78, 180; Guido Acquaviva, 'Subjects of international law: A power-based analysis', *Vanderbilt Journal of Transnational Law*, Vol. 38(2), March 2005, pp.369–70; Jonathan I Charney & JRV Prescott, 'Resolving cross-Strait relations between China and Taiwan', *The American Journal of International Law*, Vol. 94(3), July 2000, pp.454–8; Michael D Swaine, 'Trouble in Taiwan', *Foreign Affairs*, Vol. 83(2), March/April 2004, p.40.

2 Paul Johnson, *Modern Times: A History of the World from the 1920s to the 1990s*, Phoenix, London, 1992, p.388.

3 Quoted by Florence Elliott, p.75.

4 Robert A Madsen, 'The struggle for sovereignty between China and Taiwan', in Stephen D Krasner (ed.), *Problematic Sovereignty: Contested Rules and Political Possibilities*, Columbia University Press, New York, 2001, pp.147–8.

5 The discussion of the ROC's international relations and domestic politics in the period 1945 to 1990 draws on the author's book, *Isolated States: A Comparative Analysis*, Cambridge University Press, Cambridge, 1990, chapters 3–6, 13.

6 A LeRoy Bennett & James K Oliver, *International Organizations: Principles and Issues*, seventh edition, Prentice Hall, Upper Saddle River, 2002, p.89.

7 Robert A Madsen, p.159.

8 A LeRoy Bennett & James K Oliver, p.89.

9 Robert A Madsen, p.176; Thomas D Grant, 'Hallstein revisited: Unilateral enforcement of regimes of nonrecognition since the two Germanies', *Stanford Journal of International Law*, Vol. 36, 2000, p.231.

10 Steven Kuan-tsyh Yu, 'Republic of China's international legal status as exemplified by the Taiwan Relations Act', in Yu San Wang (ed.), *The China Question: Essays on Current Relations between Mainland China and Taiwan*, Praeger, New York, 1985, p.62; Stephen D Krasner, 'Explaining variation: Defaults, coercion, commitments', in Krasner (ed.), *Problematic Sovereignty*, pp.338–9.

11 Quoted by Deon Geldenhuys, *Isolated States*, p.448.

12 Freedom House, 'Freedom in the World – Taiwan (2007)', http://www.freedomhouse.org/inc/content/pubs/fiw/inc, p.1.

13 Deon Geldenhuys, *South Africa and the China Question: A Case for Dual Recognition*, East Asia Project, University of the Witwatersrand, Johannesburg, 1995, pp.9–10.

14 Thomas D Grant, pp.231–2.

15 Deon Geldenhuys, *South Africa and the China Question*, p.19.

16 Eric Ting-Lun Huang, 'Taiwan's status in a changing world: United Nations representation and membership for Taiwan', *Annual Survey of International and Comparative Law*, Vol. 9(1), 2003, p.85; Alan M Wachman, 'A cold war of words', *Orbis*, Vol. 46(4), Fall 2002, p.700.

17 Quoted by Jonathan I Charney & JRV Prescott, p.464.

18 Quoted by Jacques deLisle, 'Law's spectral answers to the cross-Strait sovereignty question', *Orbis*, Vol. 46(4), Fall 2002, p.747; Alan M Wachman, p.698.

19 Alan M Wachman, p.698; Markus G Puder, 'The grass will not be trampled because the tigers need not fight – New thoughts and old paradigms for

détente across the Taiwan Strait', *Vanderbilt Journal of Transnational Law*, Vol. 34(3), May 2001, p.510.
20 Quoted by Jaw-Ling J Chang, 'New dimensions of U.S.-Taiwan relations', *American Foreign Policy Interests*, Vol. 26, 2004, p.309.
21 Editorial, *Taiwan Review*, Vol. 53(11), November 2003, p.1.
22 Anne Hsiu-An Hsiao, 'Some thoughts on Taiwan's "UN referendums" that failed to represent the public will', *Taiwan Perspective* (Institute for National Policy Research), No. 126, 15 May 2008, www.tp.org.tw/eletter/pdf/Taiwan...
23 Sebastian Bersick & Gudrun Wacker, 'Hoffnung auf Stabilität in der Taiwan-strasse', *SWP-Aktuell*, No. 27, April 2008, pp.1–4.
24 See Chapter 1, footnote 120.
25 Markus G Puder, p.517; Stephen Allen, 'Recreating "one China": Internal self-determination, autonomy and the future of Taiwan', *Asia-Pacific Journal on Human Rights and the Law*, Vol. 4(1), 2003, pp.24–5.
26 Steve Allen, 'Statehood, self-determination and the "Taiwan question"', *Asian Yearbook of International Law*, Vol. 9, 2000, p.199.
27 Steve Allen, 'Statehood, self-determination and the "Taiwan question"', pp.191, 207.
28 Richard W Hartzell, 'Questions of sovereignty – the Montevideo Convention and territorial cession', November 2005, http://www.taiwanadvice.com/harintmcexc.htm, p.5.
29 Steve Allen, 'Statehood, self-determination and the "Taiwan question"', p.191.
30 Richard W Hartzell, p.11; Taiwan Association of University Professors, *Peaceful Coexistence: Two Countries, Two Systems*, http://taup.yam.org.tw/1t1c/tp1tce05.html, section V.
31 Jonathan I Charney & JRV Prescott, pp.458–9.
32 Chen Lung-chu, 'Taiwan's statehood is undeniable', *Taipei Times*, 17 August 2007, http://www.taipeitimes.com/News/editorials/archives/2007/08/17/ 2003374626; Jason X Hamilton, 'An overview of the legal and security questions concerning Taiwanese independence', *International Law Review*, Vol. 1(1), 2003–4, p.100.
33 Government Information Office, *Taiwan Yearbook 2007*, Taipei, 2007, pp.99–105; Taipei Representative Office in the U.K., 'Taiwan ranks sixth in BERI investment climate report', 2 September 2007, http://www.taiwan-embassy.org/ UK/fp.asp...; 'Taiwan: Vice President Lu's comments on Council on Foreign Relations Video Conference "Taiwan's future"', US Fed News Service, Washington DC, 17 January 2007, Proquest database: http://O-proquest. umi.com.ujlink.uj.ac.za.
34 Taiwan: World Audit Democracy Profile, 2007, http://www.worldaudit.org/countries/taiwan.htm.
35 Jason X Hamilton, p.97.
36 Steve Allen, 'Statehood, self-determination and the "Taiwan question"', p.199.
37 Ivan Shearer, 'International legal relations between Australia and Taiwan: Behind the façade', *Australian Year Book of International Law*, Vol. 21, 2000, p.121.
38 Jonathan I Charney & JRV Prescott, p.473.
39 Quoted by Jason X Hamilton, p.94.
40 Taiwan Association of University Professors, section V; Chen Lung-chu.
41 Stephen Allen, 'Recreating "one China"', pp.40–1.
42 Taiwan Association of University Professors, section V.

43 Jonathan I Charney & JRV Prescott, pp.471, 476.
44 Stephen D Krasner, 'Explaining variation', p.337.
45 ROC Ministry of Foreign Affairs, 'Taiwan Foreign Policy Report', ca. 2006, http://www.mofa.gov.tw/webapp/ct.asp?..., p.5.
46 *Taiwan Yearbook 2007*, pp.73–4; ROC Ministry of Foreign Affairs, 'Foreign embassies in the ROC (Taiwan)', 2007, http://www.mofa.gov.tw/webapp/1p.asp?...; *Exchange*, No. 81, June 2005, p.34; Editorial, *Taiwan Review*, Vol. 55(6), June 2005, p.1.
47 *The New York Times*, 24 June 2007, http://www.nytimes.com/2007/06/24/world/ asia...
48 Jay Nordlinger, 'Taiwan's two dozen', *National Review*, 13 August 2007, p.26; *Taiwan Journal*, 20 May 2005, p.1.
49 Government Information Office, *Taiwan Yearbook 2006*, Taipei, 2006, pp.110–16; *Taiwan Journal*, 7 October 2005, p.1.
50 *The Banker*, 1 September 2006, p.1.
51 *Taiwan Journal*, 16 June 2005, p.7.
52 *Taiwan Journal*, 30 September 2005, p.1.
53 bilaterals.org, 'ROC, Honduras, El Salvador sign trilateral FTA, 11 May 2007', http://www.bilaterals.org/article-print.php3?id_article=8277.
54 *Taiwan Journal*, 14 October 2005, p.1.
55 *Taiwan Journal*, 20 August 2004, p.1.
56 *Taiwan Journal*, 6 August 2004, p.1.
57 *Taiwan Yearbook 2007*, p.186.
58 Leanne Kao, 'Rallying relief', *Taiwan Review*, Vol. 55(4), April 2005, pp.36–41; Kelly Her, 'Itinerant doctors', *Taiwan Review*, Vol. 55(5), May 2005, pp.12–16.
59 *Taiwan Yearbook 2007*, p.187.
60 *Taiwan Yearbook 2006*, p.117.
61 *Taiwan Yearbook 2006*, pp.117–18.
62 *Taiwan Yearbook 2006*, pp.118–20.
63 *Taiwan Yearbook 2007*, pp.73–4.
64 Scott Pegg, 'The "Taiwan of the Balkans"? The *de facto* state option for Kosovo', *Southeast European Politics*, Vol. 1(2), December 2000, p.95.
65 *Taiwan Yearbook 2007*, pp.73–4.
66 Byron SJ Weng, 'Taiwan's international status today', *The China Quarterly*, No. 99, September 1984, p.463.
67 *Taiwan Yearbook 2007*, p.91; *Taiwan Journal*, 24 June 2005, p.1; *Taiwan Journal*, 1 July 2005, p.2.
68 James C Hsiung, 'The ROC's (Taiwan's) quest for wider international participation', *American Foreign Policy Interests*, Vol. 28, 2006, p.266.
69 Oscar Chung, 'Being seen, being heard', *Taiwan Review*, Vol. 54(11), November 2004, p.40; Oscar Chung, 'Trade secrets on display', *Taiwan Review*, Vol. 55(10), October 2005, pp.34–6.
70 *Taiwan Yearbook 2006*, p.106.
71 *Taiwan Yearbook 2006*, p.111; *Taiwan Yearbook 2007*, pp.70–1.
72 *Taiwan Journal*, 25 June 2005, p.1.
73 James C Hsiung, p.266; Eric Ting-Lun Huang, p.95.
74 Eric Ting-Lun Huang, pp.96–8.
75 Quoted in an editorial, *Taiwan Review*, Vol. 54(10), October 2004, p.1.
76 James C Hsiung, p.258.
77 'UNGA rejects proposal to include Taiwan's UN bid on agenda', 19 September 2007, http://news.xinhuanet.com/english/2007-09/20/content_6762920.htm.

78 James C Hsiung, pp.255, 258–61.
79 Pat Gao, 'In support of health', *Taiwan Review*, Vol. 55(5), May 2005, p.6.
80 James C Hsiung, pp.262–3.
81 *Taiwan Yearbook 2006*, p.114.
82 James C Hsiung, pp.263–4; *Taiwan Yearbook 2006*, p.113; *Taipei Times*, 20 April 2007, http://www.bilaterals.org/article-print.php3?id_article=7966.
83 ROC Ministry of Foreign Affairs, 'Taiwan Foreign Policy Report', p.7.
84 James C Hsiung, p.265.
85 Gary D Rawnsley, 'Selling democracy: Diplomacy, propaganda and democratization in Taiwan', *China Perspectives*, No. 47, May–June 2003, http://chinaperspectives. revues.org/document361.html, p.6.
86 *Taiwan Yearbook 2006*, p.118; ROC Ministry of Foreign Affairs, 'Taiwan Foreign Policy Report', p.2.
87 *Taiwan Journal*, 19 August 2006, p.1; 'Taiwan: Vice President Lu's comments on Council on Foreign Relations Video Conference "Taiwan's future"'.
88 *Taiwan Yearbook 2007*, p.71.
89 Gary D Rawnsley, p.9.
90 Quoted by Gary D Rawnsley, p.6.
91 'Taiwan: President Chen talks with overseas missions chiefs about Taiwan's diplomacy', US Fed News Service, 16 May 2006, http://0-proquest.umi.com...
92 'Taiwan: Vice President Lu's comments on Council on Foreign Relations Video Conference "Taiwan's future"'.
93 Quoted in *The Banker*, 1 September 2006, p.1.
94 ROC Ministry of Foreign Affairs, 'Taiwan Foreign Policy Report', p.6.
95 Robert A Madsen, pp.142, 171.
96 Robert A Madsen, p.169; Steve Allen, 'Statehood, self-determination and the "Taiwan question"', p.218.
97 Quoted by Alan M Wachman, p.708; Gary D Rawnsley, p.8.
98 Quoted in *Taiwan Yearbook 2006*, p.82.
99 Quoted by Dennis van Vranken Hickey, 'America, China and Taiwan: three challenges for Chen Shui-Bian', *Journal of Contemporary China*, Vol. 15(48), August 2006, p.465.
100 *Taiwan Yearbook 2006*, pp.76–7.
101 *Taiwan Yearbook 2006*, p.86.
102 Stephen Allen, 'Recreating "one China"', p.47.
103 Quoted in *Taiwan Yearbook 2006*, p.82.
104 The full text of Ma's inaugural address appeared in *The China Post*, 21 May 2008, http://www.chinapost.com.tw/print/157332.htm; *The Economist*, 29 March 2008.
105 *International Herald Tribune*, 19 June 2008 & 4 July 2008.
106 *International Herald Tribune*, 19 June 2008.
107 Eric Ting-Lun Huang, p.93.
108 James C Hsiung, pp.255, 265.
109 Dennis van Vranken Hickey, p.471.
110 Eric Ting-Lun Huang, p.59.
111 Robert A Madsen, p.164; Eric Ting-Lun Huang, p.94.
112 Jaw-Ling J Chang, p.309.
113 Quoted by Deon Geldenhuys, *South Africa and the China Question*, p.5.
114 Quoted by Dennis van Vranken Hickey, p.465.
115 Freedom House, 'Freedom in the World – Taiwan (2007)', p.3.
116 *Taiwan Yearbook 2006*, p.45.

117 Michael D Swaine, p.41.
118 Quoted by Dennis van Vranken Hickey, p.466.
119 *Taiwan Yearbook 2007*, pp.82, 100.
120 Xinhua News Agency, 18 May 2008, http://www.reliefweb.int/rw/rwb.nsf/db900sid...; ROC Government Information Office, 'ROC offers disaster aid', 19 May 2008, http://www.gio.gov.tw/fp.asp?xItem...
121 Michael D Swaine, pp.40–1; Markus D Puder, p.515; Steve Allen, 'Statehood, self-determination and the "Taiwan question"', p.193.
122 Dennis van Vranken Hickey, p.474.
123 Dennis van Vranken Hickey, p.460.
124 Alan D Wachman, p.707.
125 Byron SJ Weng, '"One country, two systems" from a Taiwan perspective', *Orbis*, Vol. 46(4), Fall 2002, p.731; Alan M Wachman, p.703; *Taiwan Yearbook 2006*, p.86.
126 *International Herald Tribune*, 19 June 2008; Stephen Allen, 'Recreating "one China"', p.48.
127 Jaw-Ling J Chang, p.311.
128 Steve Allen, 'Statehood, self-determination and the "Taiwan question"', p.202.
129 James C Hsiung, p.267; Jacques deLisle, pp.743–4.
130 Robert A Madsen, pp.161–2.
131 Byron SJ Weng, '"One country, two systems" from a Taiwan perspective', pp.714–16; Jaw-Ling J Chang, p.310.
132 Byron SJ Weng, '"One country, two systems" from a Taiwan perspective', pp.713–14; Alan M Wachman, p.697.
133 Alan M Wachman, pp.702, 707; Michael D Swaine, p.41.
134 Quoted by Alan M Wachman, p.708.
135 Quoted by Deon Geldenhuys, *South Africa and the China Question*, p.17.
136 Stephen Allen, 'Recreating "one China"', p.37.
137 Jaw-Ling J Chang, p.311.
138 Stephen Allen, 'Recreating "one China"', p.46.
139 Jaw-Ling J Chang, pp.310, 314.
140 Stephen Allen, 'Recreating "one China"', pp.49–50.
141 Byron SJ Weng, '"One country, two systems" from a Taiwan perspective', pp.730–1; Alan M Wachman, p.698; Stephen Allen, 'Recreating "one China"', pp.36–8.
142 Dennis van Vranken Hickey, pp.471, 473.
143 Stephen Allen, 'Recreating "one China"', pp.34–8.

Index